THE SECRET ORDER OF ASSASSINS

THE SECRET ORDER OF ASSASSINS

THE STRUGGLE OF THE EARLY NIZÂRÎ ISMÂ'ÎLÎS AGAINST THE ISLAMIC WORLD

2-16-11

MARSHALL G. S. HODGSON

PENN

University of Pennsylvania Press
Philadelphia

Originally published 1955 by Mouton & Co., Publishers
Printed in the United States of America on acid-free paper

10 9 8 7 6 5 4 3 2 1

Published 2005 by
University of Pennsylvania Press
Philadelphia, Pennsylvania 19104-4011

A CIP catalog record for this book is available from the Library of Congress.

CONTENTS

APPENDICES

PREFATORY NOTE

A major part of this book was written in 1949-51 as a doctoral dissertation with Professor von Grunebaum and the Committee on Social Thought of the University of Chicago. Much was added in 1953. I have since inserted some further notes, without attempting to alter the body of the work as then conceived.

Transliteration from the Arabic is according to the more popular of the two systems generally accepted for English (except where a form is fully Anglicized).[1] The non-Arabist can pronounce the vowels as in Italian, the consonants in the commonest English way, but unvaryingly — *h* is always pronounced, *aw* is like *ou* in *house; dh* is *th* in *then*. Persian and Turkish names are transliterated mostly according to the rules for Arabic, for there is no sharp line between the languages in this material; Persians pronounce *th* like *s*, *ḍ* and *dh* like *z*, and *w* like *v*.

I want to express my thanks to Dr. von Grunebaum for making my work possible; Professor Nef and the Committee on Social Thought for taking me on and for helping finance the publication; Miss Vindenas of the Chicago Oriental Institute Library for seeing that books were available as needed. I owe gratitude to numerous others for their assistance, some of whom are mentioned at appropriate points in the notes; among them I want to mention Mr. W. Ivanow particularly, who kindly presented me with a number of the volumes he has published.

8 IX 1955

[1] Complete uniformity in details of transliteration is more difficult to achieve for Arabic than for most languages because the Arabic script gives either too little for full identification or too much for clarity. In its usual form that script yields, for one name of God, what can be strictly rendered °*lrz°q;* its fully vocalized form for the same can be rendered °'*al°rrazza°qu* (° indicating a silent letter). Either *al-Razzâq* or *ar-Razzâq* is a compromise, and scholars can differ on which compromise to make.

CHAPTER I

INTRODUCTION: THE ISMÂ'ÎLÎ HERITAGE

The general reader will have heard of the Nizârî Ismâ'îlîs under three guises. He will have heard of the wealthy Indian Muslim leader, the Aga Khan, and of the sect which is supposed to regard him as a divinity. He is likely to have heard, in connection with Fitzgerald's Omar Khayyam, of the three school-fellows in Persia who promised to share equally the success that might come to any one of them; and of Ḥasan-i Ṣabbâḥ, who felt himself cheated of his promised share, and destroyed an empire in his revenge. Finally, he may have heard of the Order of Assassins, itself, "Mohammedan fanatics . . . whose chief object was to assassinate Crusaders"[1] in Syria, at the secret command of the Old Man of the Mountains. India, Persia, Syria, these stories all point to a single sect, whose first two centuries of spectacular development we are to trace; the uncanny Ḥasan-i Ṣabbâḥ of Fitzgerald's tale is known as its founder. The word "assassin", which the West uses for terrorist murderers in general, was originally a nickname of the sect, and had nothing to do with killing. It received this connotation in our languages only by analogy to the famous murders of the "Assassins" – whose "chief object", however, was not murder, and especially not "to assassinate Crusaders".

We will not be concerned here, primarily, with the exotic curiosity of an incredible cult; nor with the romance of legend, or the grim mysteries of a murderous power: though all these elements will enter into our story. Our concern will be with the fate of an aspiring minority group, whose religious and social orientation had been rejected by the bulk of Islamic society; and who were faced with a steadily hardening pattern of orthodox life, hostile to them, and which they could not accept. Such were the Nizârîs in the Twelfth Century in the countries of the Middle East.

[1] *The American College Dictionary*, ed. C. L. Barnhart (New York, 1949).

BUILDING AN ISLAMIC WORLD

The Isma'îlîs (of whom the Nizârîs were a section) formed one of the great branches of the Muslim religion. They had ruled Egypt for two centuries, and numbered adherents throughout the Muslim world. Their heritage was not less rich than those of other Muslim sects in speculative philosophy, in urbane social tradition, in human devotion. In the end the Ismâ'îlîs found themselves in head-on collision with a united Islâm. But this opposition concealed a fundamental unity. With other Muslims, they had shared the cultural background of the Hellenistic Middle East; with other Muslims they had shared the challenge posed by revealed religion to that Hellenistic world. The resulting heritage of life and insight treasured by the Ismâ'îlîs was a particular form of the general heritage of Islâm.

The Caliphate as framework for elaborating earlier traditions on a fresh basis.

At the time of the Muslim conquests in the middle of the first Millennium, the hoary Roman Empire and its Persian Sassanid rival shared between them the vast intellectual and material heritage which had accumulated from earliest times in the Middle East. But the ventures of the classical Hellenistic culture had everywhere spent much of their force. Men had turned to building a new life, which was to be more universally valid, designed for the salvation of their souls. The insistent demands of a Christian, a Jewish, a Zoroastrian world view had turned to their own purposes the varied product of Babylonian experience or Grecian art. It was at this point that Islâm appeared, in the most cultivated nations west of the Indus, offering a more perfect way of salvation.

The Muslim Caliphate was a military government suddenly occupying half the Roman and all the Persian imperial territory. Then for centuries it remained there, with its creed and its language; while within its framework the remaining Classical institutions were preserved till such time as the fresh Islamic genius could mould in their stead one universal religious society, in accordance with the ideals that had now gripped mankind; and dispense at last with the secular frivolity of the Ancients.

The population which this Caliphate held together, and among whom Islâm was built, was enormously varied; even in literary language – Greek, Latin, Armenian, Coptic, Syriac, Pahlavi, Sogdian, Sanscrit; still more so in religion – five or six forms of Christianity bitterly at odds, Judaism, Manichaeism, Zoroastrianism, Buddhism, Hinduism, even a Gnostic Paganism. The various peoples were allowed to carry on their own autonomous communities within the Caliphate; but anyone was free to throw in his lot with the Islamic brotherhood, and to help determine the form which the new society should take. In time the bulk of the population accepted the opportunity. Henceforth in the Middle East it was within the gradually crystallizing Islamic society and faith that the various elements of the general heritage were retained, modified, or eliminated.

Incipient Islâm: Mohammed's demand for civil and religious purity.

Islâm to begin with was hardly even a religion, in the full sense, and far from being the whole system of culture it was eventually to become.[2] Mecca was a commercial town, but situated in the back-country between the Persian and Roman empires, among heathen Arab nomads. Mohammed (d. 632 C.E.) preached there a purified version of the Judeo-Christian monotheism of the more polished nations round about. The unique majesty of God the Creator and Master of all; the inescapable judgment in the end, when God should punish or reward each person according as he had obeyed Him; these towering convictions Mohammed pressed upon his people, together with a recognition of himself as God's messenger to men on a level with the revered figures of Judaism and Christianity. Along with these few principles, he provided a tremendous spiritual impetus. His own spiritual experience was embodied, in all its honesty and grandeur, in the Koran; in which all generations of Muslims have found inexhaustible resources for their own confrontation with their God. All this formed a solid kernel in the midst of the vagaries to which the religious consciousness is subject. But even as set forth in the Koran, these principles did not yet form an integrated fund of interpretation and response to potencies beyond the human, such as we expect of a developed religion.

Yet Mohammed himself had begun such a development. To assure a fitting legal and social expression for his purified faith, he had built himself in Madîna a community set apart from the surrounding tribal life, and reflecting critically the urban society of the Christian empire, as

[2] I. Goldziher, *Vorlesungen über den Islam* (Heidelberg, 1910), p. 36, stresses this.

well as the local bedouin ideals. The old standards of Arab custom and the miscellaneous traditions of Christians and Jews were apparently accepted where there was no divine command against them; but only provisionally. Mohammed both adopted and rejected in a persistent spirit of lucid piety. He introduced a crude fortification (it is said on advice from a Persian), he insisted on more guarded decorum between the sexes than the desert was accustomed to, he established the elements of a written legal code. He acknowledged as learned lore the virgin birth of Christ, and his ascent to heaven. But the claim that Christ was more than God's messenger, was God himself, he rejected as on its face inconsistent with the exalted oneness of God: here the nations had corrupted God's truth, which must be purified. He fought bedouin superstition; but wanted to avoid a like corruption from the older monotheisms; he declared his faith to be that of Abraham, who was before either Jews or Christians; and shifted the direction of prayer from their corrupt Jerusalem to Mecca, sanctuary of Abraham's son Ishmael, ancestor of the Arabs. Thus Mohammed gave to his people an orientation in the religious world of his time which left them open to many influences, yet with a core of independence.

Islamization of the Middle East.

Mohammed had almost consciously attempted to provide for his own Arabia a purified synthesis of the larger urban heritage of faith and practice. When his little community suddenly expanded into the mastery of a large part of the urbanized world, his local attempt offered a fruitful point of departure for a corresponding synthesis for the Middle East as a whole. During many generations, the Muslims formed a very active ruling minority; in each generation their field of interest was more varied, their points of dispute with one another more probing. Quarrels over what Islâm was to become took at first sight a political form: who should have leadership? Those who were excluded quickly expanded the debate into more general religious and social questions, creating a pious opposition of many different hues against the official Islamic regime. A wide range of religious leaders, called *imâms,* arose, each with his eager hearers. Some tried to account philosophically for the nature of man, of the universe, and of the faith; some concentrated on developing a body of half remembered, half improvised tradition aiming at a detailed code of Muslim propriety. Each had his vision of how the total society should be formed, including its political organization.

By the time that Islâm began to encompass the majority of the Middle Eastern population, it was overflowing with the most multifarious vitality. Muslims learned to improve on the science of the Ancients, to develop their own forms of art and literature and history, to transform the law courts and the craft guilds. While the pious hailed an almost monkish asceticism, or fanatically exalted the new traditional code, intellectuals would accept nothing short of the full apparatus of Greek philosophy and Persian lore. A luxurious public concerned itself with a poetry in which the desert Arab genius amplified Hellenistic themes; with a scintillating sophistication able to comment cleverly on Chinese customs, on lunar eclipses, or on the human heart; with a hemisphere-wide commerce to satisfy the curious demands of the vast Caliphate's booming cities. In the midst of this manifold diversity the attempts were never given up to bring into the new society that pious unity which was the ideal of an otherworldly age.

We shall note two problems that confronted attempts at religious synthesis, as of particular importance for understanding the Ismâʿîlîs and their Sunnî opponents. First, the serious-minded sought in Islâm, as they had in the religions its predecessors, a universal validity, an assurance that standards and judgments were right not just for the long-vanished tribal unit, not just for a lone individual stranded in teeming cities, but for any man, anywhere, under any given circumstances. This universal validity could be found in two ways, but the two ways seemed contradictory. One way was through scholastic philosophy, based on the absolute logic and disengaged ideals of Aristotle and Plato. To justify itself, each faith had since Hellenistic times been expected to compel assent to its propositions on the basis of our common human experience abstractly set forth: to pass the test of reason as it was then understood. An alternative way was through accepting the continuity of a community which claimed the allegiance of all men. Increasingly since Hellenistic times men had come to be aligned in religious communities, in conscious groupings devoted to explicit religious tradition, and claiming an ultimate human loyalty. Mohammed had from the first taken for granted the alignment by religious community. An abstract philosophy seemed incapable of directing commitment and loyalty in the bewildering fullness of living, as a community could. Yet it seemed self-defeating for such a community to admit a superior criterion of natural experience open to all men individually. It became therefore a problem, how to accommodate the claims of community tradition and of abstract reason.

A second problem of synthesis facing Islâm was that of reconciling conflicting demands of imaginative piety. On the one hand was the desire for a Deity exalted sternly beyond any defiling touch of humanness; the pure rigor of Mohammed had rejected all sorts of mediation between God and man as infringing on the total devotion due to Allâh, and had restricted prophecy to a very humble role. On the other hand the Middle East, though no longer demanding a pantheon of gods as of old, yet required heroes and saints as palpable bridges to a Divinity so distantly exalted; required imaginative vision, and a personal contact with the divine, which also Mohammed had not entirely rejected. On what level, and with what emphases, should the two orientations of the devotional life be reconciled?

The Sunnî synthesis.

Among the religious leaders, the imâms, and their schools, there was a great deal accepted in common. All accepted the Koran; and the unique authority of Mohammed as it was made clear in the *ḥadîth*, the sacred traditions reporting his words and deeds. All agreed on certain basic rituals; on a minimum body of ethic and law; and on certain basic definitions of belief, such as the formula "There is no god but the God (Allâh), and Mohammed is His prophet" – the *shahâda*, the statement of witness. Sunnism represented a conscious effort to cling to those community symbols which had widest support already, rejecting any conflicting minority emphasis in the name of community solidarity. They supported accordingly the 'Abbâsid Caliphate of Baghdâd, which had been accepted after 750 C.E. by the bulk of the community; they regarded all of the first generation of Muslims with honor, but none with extreme reverence, avoiding any decision on the strife that had divided them. They made their standard the custom of Mohammed and the consensus of his followers.

In delimiting the claims of the community and of reason, they tended accordingly to emphasize strongly the former, and to be suspicious of every independent point of view. They made religion revolve around the basic body of ritual and legal precepts, the *sharî'a*, which all Muslims held in common, and tried to fix it in minute detail. Yet because there was no single codification of the sharî'a which was generally accepted, to preserve community solidarity they admitted the possibility of a number of alternatively acceptable systems of sharî'a, which the faithful might choose among within broad limits. Having thus established a flexible basis for community authority, they allowed themselves (a luxury which many long considered dubious) to defend it in the arena of reason in an elaborately developed scholastic theology, bound in advance to support the favorite formulas of community tradition.

In balancing the demands of piety for an exaltation of God and yet for a personal contact with him, Sunnism emphasized the uncompromising unity of God, his utter remoteness from any human conception. The more personal side of the devotional life was to be cultivated appropriately through a rigorous asceticism – though not indeed to the point of withdrawal from the world, or of celibacy, for Sunnî piety strove to maintain the lucid matter-of-fact attitude that had characterized Mohammed. One's personal response to God could best be expressed through a sober fear of His majesty mixed with a minimum of presumption upon his favor. To this end, the sharî'a, impersonal foundation of all Sunnî piety, served also as foundation for the most personal devotion, which could regard the fulfillment of its most exacting requirements as the first step in personal discipline. Nevertheless, Sunnî personal piety very soon went beyond this negative discipline, and in the form of Ṣûfism cultivated a mystical knowledge and even love of God. Ṣûfism, however, long remained rather suspect among Sunnî traditionists.

The Sunnî approach to Islâm, somewhat one-sided though it may have been at first, had the advantage of undoubted sobriety, and a conservative program to which few could take exception. It arose as a harmonizing interpretation of the official Islâm of the Caliphate at Baghdâd. Giving many of the great teaching imâms and systems of sharî'a a place in its consensus, it was able to create a possibility of common ground for the majority of Muslims; and though these long continued to dispute among themselves, the Sunnî outlook could at least distinguish them from the dissident Muslims that called themselves the *Shî'a*, the party of 'Alî.

ISMÂ'ÎLISM AS OFFERING AN ALTERNATIVE SYNTHESIS

The Shî'a form of Islâm.

Ismâ'îlism was a branch of the Shî'a. The Shî'a had originated as the faction of one of the Muslim leaders of the first generation: they supported the claims to power of 'Alî (d. 661), cousin and a son-in-law of the

Prophet, after the murder of Mohammed's third successor. In the course of a series of risings against the dynasty which had supplanted ʿAlî, they developed, as part of the pious opposition, a variety of religious-political positions. These had in common the notion that ʿAlî and his successors in Mohammed's family were the only legitimate rulers from the start, after Mohammed's death; and moreover the only authoritative religious teachers, *imâms*. Justice on earth could be hoped for only when Mohammed's family received its due; for they alone could and would rule Islâm by the righteous principles of the Prophet. The Shîʿa in its many forms had become so strong by the middle of the Eighth Century, that one branch of it was able to see its candidates, the ʿAbbâsid family, take power as Caliphs. But the ʿAbbâsids at Baghdâd, though members of the family of Mohammed in the broader sense, turned against their Shîʿa supporters and became the stronghold of Sunnism. Accordingly, most of the Shîʿa opposed the ʿAbbâsids quite as much as they had previous Caliphs.

The particular Shîʿa group out of which the Ismâʿîlîs – and indeed most other later Shîʿism – sprang limited the imâmate to one line of ʿAlî's descendants by Mohammed's daughter Fâṭima; they insisted that each imâm from ʿAlî on had pointed out his successor in the office by a particular designation, a *naṣṣ*. This designated imâm alone had the right to determine points of law and ritual; he was not only the rightful ruler, but even when not in power he was the only guarantor of the sharîʿa and guide to the devotion of the pious. This Shîʿa, accordingly, was in a position to develop an interpretation of Islâm very different from that of Sunnism.

One characteristic which is found in all this type of Shîʿism is a rich dramatic piety. Far from a conciliatory (and slightly colorless) acceptance of all the first generation Muslims, the Shîʿa took a violent part in their quarrels, and cursed the great majority of them, and of all later Muslims, as apostates. Strong in its loves and hates, the Shîʿa looked on itself as a saved remnant in a corrupt world.

That such views often had to be kept secret only increased the dramatic tension. The Shîʿa offered its imâms an intense personal loyalty; it invested them with a prestige more than human. The imâm will have inherited something of a divine touch from his Prophetic ancestor. Especially the sufferings of the imâms were dramatized. It was appropriate to the persecuted history of Shîʿa sects that suffering should have religious value. For a legitimate loyalty, men will readily accept scorn and loss: the imâms themselves have been rejected and persecuted, how much more so we? The story of Mohammed's grandson Ḥusayn, who was betrayed and killed in an abortive attempt at the Caliphate, has won oceans of tears through the generations. Mohammed, misunderstood even by the men who hailed him; his weeping daughter, mother of the doomed Ḥusayn; – all the holy family, ranged with a few despised followers against an obsequious but alien world; here was the Shîʿa sense of Passion, cherished tenaciously in the face of the smug sobriety of dominant Sunnism.

Ismâʿîlism as a Shîʿa sect.

Ismâʿîlism seems to have begun to be differentiated from other Shîʿism as early as the time of the great Shîʿite imâm Jaʿfar aṣ-Ṣâdiq (d. 765), imâm at the time of the ʿAbbâsid triumph. It took its name from one of his sons, Ismâʿîl. Among the early Shîʿa there seems to have been much speculation concerning such questions as the nature of the afterlife, the possibility of divine inspiration, the meaning of the ritual prescriptions. There was a tendency, labelled *ghuluww*, exaggeration, by its opponents, to carry these speculations farther than most Muslims felt consistent with religious propriety, giving the imâm and even the ordinary believer too high a spiritual station. It seems that the imâm Jaʿfar was especially zealous to discipline this ghuluww, and keep his Shîʿa within proper bounds. But though he was apparently able to discipline it, he could not and perhaps did not want to ban altogether the questions it raised and the concepts it found of most value. The tendency influenced more or less each of the branches into which his Shîʿa split after his death; especially the Ismâʿîliyya.[3]

We have no clear picture of Ismâʿîlism in its earliest period. Evidently it could include then a great variety of the less orthodox interests of that burgeoning age, certainly not excluding the concerns of the ghuluww. But when after 900 C.E. we first have a clear view of the Ismâʿîliyya, its thinking had been clearly chastened, and ordered in defensible terms.

[3] The early history of the Shîʿa in general and of the Ismâʿîliyya in particular is still very confused. This is not the place to go into the nature of the ghulât "sects", the role of Abû l-Khaṭṭâb, or the original relation of the Ismâʿîlî to the Ithnaʿasharî Shîʿa: such matters are of secondary importance in understanding the total Ismâʿîlî heritage which the Nizârîs carried. The impression of events which is presupposed by this brief exposition is based on a cautious reading of such authors as Nawbakhtî (*Firaq ash-Shîʿa*, ed. H. Ritter, Istanbul, 1931), in the context of the whole of early Islamic development.

The imâm had sometimes been made vaguely divine by the ghuluww teachers; the Ismâʿîlîs tied him to philosophical tradition as the Microcosm par excellence,[4] in whom the metaphysical soul of the universe was personified. He had access to metaphysical reason itself, personified in the inspired Prophet, and could so guarantee a rational interpretation of the Prophet's seemingly arbitrary directives.

The imâm was thus ultimate source of the inward and universal sense underlying the outward, evident sense of Koran or ḥadîth. The outer formulas set forth in these scriptures were called the *ẓâhir;* the hidden meaning of them, which the imâm revealed, was called the *bâṭin.* A practice such as the five daily ritual prayers expected of all Muslims – in itself, apart from its value as a discipline for group worship, only arbitrary movements of the body – could thus be interpreted as symbolizing ulterior matters of religious or philosophical import. In this fashion the Ismâʿîlîs could reconcile the authority of the community – embodied in the outer law – with the demands of absolute reason, given its due in the bâṭin. Moreover, this explanatory teaching by the inspired imâm allowed the faithful to gain considerable knowledge of the workings of a Divinity Whose unknowable transcendance in Himself was never denied, nay was pushed to the extreme. Thus in the same stroke which solved the problem of rational universality, the Ismâʿîlîs opened a whole esoteric world to the pious imagination.

The Ismâʿîlîs accepted the same Koran and developed a like body of ḥadîth as did the Sunnîs; their *sharîʿa,* their body of ritual law, differed little from those which the Sunnîs were developing. Islâm remained a single, if amorphous, community; the overshadowing memory of Mohammed was maintained by all parties in common. But while the Sunnîs tended to confine all piety within the impersonal straightjacket of the legalistic sharîʿa, the Ismâʿîlîs seemed to offer not only the dramatic perspective on life shared by the Shîʿa as a whole, but the possibility of transcending in one's personal spiritual life the limitations of the sharîʿa.

The Ismâʿîlîs linked the community less by rigid symbols than by a living hierarchy of the learned: under the imâm were ranged the supreme *dâʿî* (summoner to the truth) and the subordinate dâʿîs, down to the private believers. Within this hierarchy was cultivated not only a vast body of lore designed to respond to every question the mind might conceive, but a general habit of personal search for "truth" as dominating all of life, and giving at once justification and occasion for the social order.

[4] Cf. on the microcosm tradition, Schaeder, 'Die islamische Lehre vom Vollkommenen Menschen,' *ZDMG*, LXXIX (1925), 192.

It must be noted that here also, as among Sunnîs, there was no question, in principle, of imaginative freedom being granted outright; it was supposed that a closed total of revealed truth was as if already in being, and the search for it was simply a matter of acquiring it as it lay hidden in ancient books, or was expounded by the hierarchy. Yet the great scope prepared for the mind that would accept the discipline of the imâm is revealed not only in occult work of philosophic enlightenment such as that of the *Ikhwân aṣ-Ṣafâ* – a compendium of Medieval science and tolerant spirituality popular also among Sunnîs – but in the sense of urgent, even adventurous personal seeking that is standard in every Ismâʿîlî autobiography.

The Ismâʿîliyya as a conspiratorial revolt.

During the Ninth Century the Baghdâd Caliphate began to lose its political hold on the Islamic world. Early in the Tenth, its power was to disappear altogether. In its place then arose several short-lived local dynasties whose power was often largely military, and which depended for legal justification among the Sunnî population upon a recognition in principle of the overlordship of the Caliphs. When the Caliphate was thus declining, the Shîʿites had an opportunity to realize their hopes. ʿAlid imâms representing one type of Shîʿism, the Zaydî, did establish their power in the mountains south of the Caspian Sea, and in Yaman, at the southern end of Arabia – where the land is still Shîʿite now. Among the Shîʿa groups which traced a line of imâms by naṣṣ to Jaʿfar aṣ-Ṣâdiq, the most important rival of the Ismâʿîlîs was the Ithnaʿasharî or Twelver Shîʿa, so named because they recognized only twelve imâms in all. Some of the military rulers who arose on the ruins of the Caliphal power professed this Shîʿism; but for the sake of their Sunnî subjects they also continued to recognize the ʿAbbâsid Caliphs at Baghdâd, even when they could number Baghdâd among their own possessions. Indeed, if they had wanted to set up an ʿAlid imâm as ruler they could not; for their twelfth and last imâm had disappeared, and was not expected to return till he should come in miraculous triumph at the end of the world. The Twelver Shîʿa has in modern times won many followers, including the majority of ʿIrâq and Îrân; but it has never established the actual rule of an imâm.

In sharp contrast to the Twelvers, the Ismâʿîlîs created an active movement to replace the Caliphal dynasty with the house of ʿAlî. The Ismâʿîliyya challenged the official Islâm, and the Sunnî synthesis developing within it, in the form of a widespread conspiracy apparently involving support from peasant villages and bedouin tribes as well as well-placed officials. The summons to allegiance to the imâms descended from Jaʿfar's son Ismâʿîl was called the Ismâʿîlî *daʿwa.* Representing this daʿwa, travelling *dâʿîs,* summoners, aroused and directed from a concealed central headquarters a general attack against the Baghdâd Caliphate and against other rulers who theoretically recognized its authority. The appeal to the nomads would have been a combination of plunder, Shîʿite loyalism, and tribal independence; to the settled populations it was the usual Shîʿa promise of justice as against the apostate and usurping dynasties of the world.

The hope for a *Mahdî* was widespread: for the promised God-sent ruler to come in due time and fill the earth with justice as it was now filled with wrong. The Twelvers expected their last imâm to return as Mahdî. The Ismâʿîlî dâʿîs assured their hearers that the Mahdî would be an imâm from the house of Ismâʿîl: now in hiding, in the near future he would appear victoriously. For now, the faithful must practice what was called among the Shîʿites *taqiyya,* concealing their true allegiance from the worldly authorities lest persecution wipe out the faith; – meanwhile supporting the imâm with money and arms whenever called upon. But when the Mahdî should come forth, justice would reign, and all believers be free to declare their adherence to the family of the Prophet.

First heard from were desert bands moving between Syria and ʿIrâq, generally called *Qarâmiṭa,* who enthusiastically engaged the Caliphal forces at the end of the Ninth Century. They were defeated bloodily after years of fighting. But meanwhile the movement spread into Baḥrayn in eastern Arabia, where a group also called Qarâmiṭa seized power; into Persia; into the Yaman, where the Zaydî Shîʿa was already active; and west into North Africa. There the Ismâʿîlî imâm himself emerged from hiding (in 909); he founded a great power, and in the course of the century his descendants took Egypt, and built the new garden city of Cairo to show forth their splendor.

The Ismâʿîlî dynasty in Egypt (called *Fâṭimid* after the Prophet's daughter Fâṭima, whom they claimed as ancestress) reigned with prosperity. Benevolent to the trade guilds; tolerant of Sunnîs, of Christians and Jews, and of variety of opinion generally; with a sway ranging from the Atlantic to the borders of ʿIrâq, with such command of the sea that its rule was accepted in Sicily and in Sind, the Ismâʿîlî Caliphate at Cairo consciously rivalled in magnificence the united Caliphate of early Islâm. From Egypt the dâʿîs with continued eagerness spread in the remaining parts of the Muslim territories the hope of a renewal of united Muslim power, with at last a perfect justice and prosperity, under the house of the Prophet; which would then proceed to conquer for Islâm the remaining strongholds of the infidels, in Europe and in the world.[5]

THE FÂṬIMID EMPIRE: PHILOSOPHY OF COSMOS AND OF MAN

The Fâṭimid Empire was a haven for the arts of luxury, and not least for speculative thought. Under Fâṭimid protection flourished at least the Egyptian and Syrian fit proportion of natural scientists both in relatively public fields, as medicine, and in the more occult, as alchemy.[6] By the Eleventh Century the Ismâʿîlî daʿwa, in its organization and its doctrine, was likewise highly sophisticated. The doctrine was being refined and perfected by competent hands. At the beginning of the century the prominent dâʿî al-Kirmânî (d. *ca.* 1019) brought to the review of internal disputes over doctrine both moderation, and a careful delimitation of fine points;[7] suggesting an urbanity like that of the later supreme dâʿî Mu'ayyad Shîrazî (d. 1077) in his sober (though not quite sensitive enough) correspondence with the esthetic moralist al-Maʿarrî.[8] Of the complex structure of Fâṭimid religious philosophy, we can trace here only certain major tendencies.

Rationalism and the bâṭin.

Reason was conscientiously exalted, in the absolute Medieval manner; Divine reason being indeed the Creator of the world. The conception of a universal rational order in nature led on to a conception of ritual, morality, and afterlife which should also be more universal: that is, reconcilable with elements of all men's rational experience, rather than

[5] Cf. L. Massignon, 'Ḳarmaṭians,' *Encyclopedia of Islam*, ed. M. Th. Houtsma, *et al.* (Leiden, 1913-1934), for the early Ismâʿîlî doctrine; he makes his guesses on the basis of a large grasp of the material, whatever may be the validity of any one point. Cf. on early Ismâʿîlîs generally B. Lewis, *Origins of Ismâʿîlism* (Cambridge, 1940), and the materials gathered in W. Ivanow, *Ismâʿîlî Tradition concerning the Rise of the Fâṭimids* (Islamic Research Association Series, X, London, 1942).

[6] P. K. Hitti, *History of the Arabs* (4th ed., London, 1949), chap. xliv.

[7] Cf. W. Ivanow, *Studies in Early Persian Ismâʿîlism* (Leiden, 1948), chap. v; and H. F. Al-Hamdani, 'Some Unknown Ismâʿîlî Authors and Their Works,' *JRAS*, 1933, p. 359.

[8] D. S. Margoliouth, 'Abû l-ʿAlâ al-Maʿarrî's Correspondence on Vegetarianism,' *JRAS*, 1902, pp. 289 ff.

tied to the revealed insight of a particular community. The bâṭin was used not only to provide rituals with more general truths which they should symbolize; every aspect of religion was etherialized. For instance, the afterlife was thought of as a spiritual survival, rather than a bodily resurrection known only by Prophetic prediction.[9]

In "popular" Ismâ'îlism – the Ismâ'îlism of those less well-educated and less responsible nomads or craftsmen whose dream of loyalty and justice provided the fighting strength of the movement – this rationalism of the intellectuals was often understood in a less subtle sense. The notion of the bâṭin was taken to prove the inanity of the formalities of which the stolid, petty orthodox seemed to construct the whole of their unilluminated lives; and led to a persistent tendency to regard all external rules as outgrown and inapplicable once a man understood their meaning, and could act directly in the spirit underlying them. This "popular" tradition came to the surface at many points in Ismâ'îlî history, and eventually had its effects on the learned and official tradition. But in Fâṭimid times such antinomianism was always frowned upon by the scholars and official propagandists of Ismâ'îlism. The symbolical ritual was held to be all the more incumbent on the man of understanding, who could perform it with full consciousness of its implications.

Especially among the intellectuals there went along with this emphasis on Reason, inevitably at the time, a tendency to a rational subtlety, the manipulation of abstract constructions independently of any experiential discipline – to the point where it strikes one as rather a game than a serious inquiry. Sometimes it was simply a matter of frank edification. For instance, in listing the bâṭin of scriptural words or institutions various authors produced a great variety of meanings for any one item, with no sense of contradiction. Thus the institution of legal alms (one fortieth of one's substance per year) was varyingly taken to imply, secondarily: that one should give his whole surplus to the poor; that one should give a fifth of his income to the imâm; that the only true wealth is knowledge, etc. – as the moral or didactic fancy was touched. Sometimes it was a more theoretical matter, as in discussions of the number and character of the principles emanating from the primal One.[10] Here speculation

[9] Cf. H. Éthé, 'Nâsir Chusrau's Rûshanâinâma oder Buch der Erleuchtung,' *ZDMG*, XXXIV (1880), 428, which gives a German translation of Nâṣir-i Khusraw's *Rûshanâ-i Nâma*; and T. J. de Boer, *History of Philosophy in Islam*, trans. E. R. Jones (London, 1903), pp. 81–96, the analysis of the *Ikhwân aṣ-Ṣafâ*.

[10] On the tendency of Philosophy and Ismâ'îlism to be identified: the major Philosopher of Islâm, Ibn Sînâ (d. 1037), came from a family which was both. Ibn abî Uṣaybi'a (d. 1270), '*Uyûn al-Anbâ*', ed. A. Müller (1884, Königsberg).

had almost a free hand, and here especially rationalism needed more guidance than the severe classical logic could afford.[11]

Occultism: the cosmic process of emanation.

There were as yet so few data of public truth, that if one were to order the universe even with probability on the universal deductive principles then thought necessary, one had to depend largely on rather esoteric premises. One must deal with data which, though assuredly rationally convincing once discovered, were not discoverable through generally available channels: that is, one must turn to the *occult*. Accordingly, the rationalism of the Ismâʿîlîs started with its own sort of community tradition, the schematic interpretation of the Koran designed to support the imâm's position – and then beginning quite frankly from the role of the imâm, proceeded to demonstrate a cosmic picture in broad outline inherited from Classical times. In this manner, a doctrine which was couched in such general terms as to be derivable (once known) from general experience nevertheless depended – almost literally – on the imâm and his community tradition.

The system of cosmic order which came to be so derived can perhaps be illuminated by an analogy taken from modern astronomy, where even yet we can witness an attempt to show how present complexities can have arisen from a posited primeval simplicity. We try to trace back the present distribution of planets and stars and galaxies, by an extrapolation of their present tendencies, into an ever more uniform state till we reach a great initial explosion. The Ismâʿîlîs, following earlier leads, tried to trace back the complexity of all existence, via a principle of logical priorities,

[11] A reading of Leo Strauss' *Persecution and the Art of Writing* (Glencoe, Ill., 1952) points up the plausibility, from the Medieval point of view, of the existence of such a bâṭin behind the doctrines transmitted in public. If, in most ages and times, it has been deemed wise by unconventional thinkers to write not frankly, but allusively; if furthermore such a policy can be systematized and justified on the plea that only a few are capable of assimilating truth, and the many must be protected from its dangerous intoxication (and it was so justified in Medieval Islâm); – then it will not be unnatural for men to suppose that not only the prophets, but even the Author of the Universe Himself, will adopt an allusive way of speaking on subtle matters, both in revealed books, and in the very laws of nature. Now if one is thus persuaded that God may speak in cipher, as it were, it is not absurd to seek for the traces of such a cipher; and if a code is suggested which gives consistent results whenever applied in God's works, there will be a high presumption that it is the right one. This is what the Ismâʿîlîs thought they had in their *ta'wîl*, their system of interpretation which they applied so freely both to sacred books, and to all nature.

to a primeval simplicity: if not in temporal, at least in logical sequence. The orders of creatures on the earth – animal, vegetable, mineral – were formed through the combining of the elements – air, water, earth, fire; in turn derived from the principles of hot-cold and wet-dry. These in turn had been set in motion by more ultimate principles, logically prior to them – time and space, perhaps, or (in Fâṭimid times, more sophisticatedly) the various planetary spheres of the Ptolemaic system, revolving with ever greater and more distant uniform perfection about the earth with its vulgar, transient combinations. The eternal motion even of these august bodies had in turn to presuppose, and be moved by, a principle of animation, the *Nafs al-Kull;* which in turn presupposed a final principle of logic, of order, of reason, the *'Aql al-Kull.* But even the primeval simplicity of Rational Order itself must presuppose its cause – the *Command*, the *Amr*, of an ultimate source of being which itself – lest it too require further explanation – must be utterly self-contained, affected by and affecting nothing – and of course quite unknowable. This last is *God:* saved from nullity as the limit of a sequence of abstracting less and less from more and more, only by the implicit assurance of an absolute logic in the transcendent reality of its constructions.

The cosmic return.

But the universe was not merely differentiated into the vulgar complexity of the increasingly disordered earth. There was a contrary motion: the elements, scattered in the various compound beings – minerals, plants – were more and more fully unified, organized; on the level of animals, the elements came to possess a unifying principle of animation, and in man even a more ultimate unifying principle, reason. And among men, said the Ismâ'îlîs, the tendency to return, in this way, to that ultimate single source of being was represented by the hierarchy of worshippers, seeking rational truth on ever higher levels, till their reasons could reach to the ultimate Reason, the 'Aql al-Kull. The members of this community, according as they were closer to complete knowledge, embodied in turn (on the return journey) the positions of the lesser cosmic principles: till in the imâm, or more precisely in his ancestor 'Alî, was attained the principle of universal animation, the Nafs al-Kull; who at the head of the community set all others in motion. 'Alî derived his wisdom directly from the Prophet – ʿAlî being the executor, *waṣî*, of the heritage Mohammed left to his people. The Prophet, representing the ʿAql al-Kull itself, the universal Reason, and so being all-wise, was the ultimate source of a potentially perfect wisdom in the select community.[12]

The apparently positive scientific value of this account was enhanced by the fascinating esthetic value generally possessed by such occult lore – its poetic finesse will even now not be despised by those with the necessary leisure to savor it.[13] This sense of the occult was intimately allied with the sense of personal adventure and of conspiratorial loyalty so prominent in Ismâʿîlî thought and action. Ṣâliḥ, in the didactic tale Ivanow summarized from an early work, begs his questions, weeps tears, and vows vows for the sake of coming upon the hidden truth, and eventually leaves his home secretly upon a blind mission to gain it; and the truth he seeks is mostly in its verbal content a matter of numerical correspondences, letter symbolisms, and the like.[14]

In Ismâʿîlî biographical writing there recurs with great variety the same element of impassioned seeking: a man is seized with a sense of imperative need for the truth, and wanders over the earth through every tribulation till he gets a trace of it; then persists, accepting every condition imposed upon him, till he is accepted by the imâm.[15] As is fitting, this search for the universal truth which is in the imâm's lone keeping becomes itself a cosmic action: it is the seeking of each human soul to escape from the earthly vulgarity of compound and accidental things toward the pure reason which has created all. In its human multiplicity this seeking imperfectly expresses in turn the cosmic desire of the Nafs al-Kull, the

12 Cf. among other places: Strothmann, *Gnosistexte*, p. 57; and Nâṣir-i Khusraw, *Wajh-i Dîn* (Berlin, Kaviani Press, 1343 H.) chap. v.

13 H. Corbin writes suggestively but perhaps romantically of the significance of the ta'wîl in his introduction to Nâṣir-e Khosraw, *Le Livre réunissant les deux sagesses* (Teheran and Paris, 1953), pp. 100-118, 142-3.

14 Ivanow, *Early Persian Ismâʿîlism* (Leiden, 1948), chap. iv.

15 Cf. the search for the imâm by the forsaken dâʿîs in the *Istitâr al-Imâm* (largely translated in Ivanow, *Ismaili Tradition concerning the Rise of the Fâṭimids* (London, 1942)); the Safar Nâma of Nâṣir-i Khusraw (*Relation du Voyage de Nassiri Khosrau*, ed. C. Schefer [Publications de l'école des langues orientales vivantes, ser. II, Vol. I; Paris, 1881]), and incidentally that of the later poet Nizârî; the personal testimonies of the type of the *Kalâm-i Pîr*, ed. trans. W. Ivanow, Islamic Research Association Series nr. 4, Bombay, 1935, chap. i, and of the Ṣaḥîfat al-Nâẓirîn (M. A. Semenov, *Bulletin of the Russian Academy of Science*, ser. 6 : XII part 2 (1918), 2171 : 'Description of Ismâʿîlî Manuscripts No. 7); the very individual story of Hasan-i Ṣabbâh farther on in this book; – all present various versions of this personal adventure. The story of Jaʿfar and the Imâm's flight to North Africa is notable in Islamic literature as a frankly personal description even of a relatively secular adventure (in the *Rise of the Fâṭimids*).

universal soul, to rejoin its author and origin, the principle of reason, the ʿAql.[16]

Position of the imâm: typological conception of history.

The gradation of men in a centralized hierarchism of competence according to their level in the search for truth became a social principle in strong contrast to the egalitarian principle of Sunnism, which rejected so far as possible any sort of ordained clergy, centering on the impersonal sharîʿa instead, demanded of all alike.[17] The authority of the dâʿîs, and of those below and above them, was officially fixed, not dependent upon popular fancy or a warlord's favor. Men were not called upon necessarily to accept a minimum of external symbols as in the Sunnî order; but were allowed, if they persisted in their ignorance, to maintain their fixed cosmic and hierarchical bottom position. The "interconfessionalism" for which the Fâṭimids are noted[18] was probably as much a matter of despising equally all who failed to strive for the imâm's inner truth, as of recognizing the symbols of this bâṭin in the ẓâhir of all the various faiths.[19]

The hierarchism finally depended upon the role of the imâm, ritually effective guarantor of its rational authority. Himself of cosmic conse-

[16] On mankind as channel of cosmic fulfillment, cr. Nâsir-i Khusraw, *Wajh-i Dîn*, p. 52.

[17] It may be noted that there were at least three types of "degrees" of gradation through which Ismâʿîlîs might "pass", and which get indignantly reported, and frequently distorted, in the heresiographers. (The heresiographers suppose an insidious subversive process, imagining that at various "levels" of initiation, quite contrasting, and increasingly impious, doctrines were taught.) There are firstly these hierarchical degrees of authority, called the *ḥudûd*; there are secondly the degrees of "initiation", according to which a convert was educated gradually (how otherwise?) in the principles of the faith – according to Ibn an-Nadîm (d. ca. 995), *Fihrist* (ed. G. Flügel, Leipzig, 1871–2), the whole process took four years; and thirdly there are (commonly mingled wierdly with the others by the heresiographers) the ways which were used in persuading converts to question their previous convictions, and to look to the Ismâʿîlî daʿwa, acting perforce in secret, for enlightenment.

[18] The recognition of the same universal truth behind Christian doctrine as behind Muslim is found frankly in the Druze writings, and Massignon tries to trace to this "interconfessionalism" the structure of Islamic guilds; *Revue Internationale Sociologique*, vol. 28 (1920), p. 473: 'Corporations et métiers.'

[19] Such an approach no doubt needed a centralized strength to keep in line the conflicting interests of various groups that must have been aroused – nomad and settled, peasants and artisans, conservative legitimists and intellectuals. It is suggested that a failure to reconcile peasant and artisan interests was responsible for the weakness in the rural area which made possible the downfall of the still vigorous Qarâmiṭa city al-Aḥsâ in the 11th Century. Cf. M. J. de Goeje, 'Fin de l'empire des Carmathes de Bahrein,' *JA*, ser. IX, Vol. V (1895).

quence, as the point of ultimate appeal he must have a position which the Sunnî impersonalism could yield to no living being. The infallible imâm as such was not too hard for any Medieval to conceive of. Given an approach to knowledge as a finite quantity of fore-ordained facts – rather than a process of inquiry within experience – it could seem not impossible that some person, by inheritance or by nature, should possess all of these facts. It was the imâm's institutional position which made impossible any compromise between the Sunnî pattern and the Ismâʿîlî claims. The imâm was head of an exclusive daʿwa claiming a priority of authority over those external symbols upon which the Sunnîs had agreed to rely for ultimate sanction.

The Sunnî position was based on a lively sense of the decisive importance of certain historical events – the revelation to Mohammed, and the triumph of Islâm; it emphasized the consensus of the community which derived from them by a continuing historical tie. The Ismâʿîlî philosophers required a sense of history and of human nature in direct contrast to this. To support the utter sovereignty of each imâm, historical continuity of development must be replaced by a sense of historical repetition. History became a matter of types: each generation reproduced the recurrent archetypes, so that each moment was complete within itself. It is especially the Old Testament, safely beyond the reach (for Muslims) of any effective historical continuity, which figured in such historical soundings as the Ismâʿîlîs took – even the favorite early Shîʿa heroes were relatively neglected in theology. Even such historical development as was admitted to extend beyond the term of a particular imâm was a matter of recurrent cycles – *dawr*; each began with a prophet and his *waṣî*, executor, and continued to its conclusion with a recurrent number of imâms, each with his own repetitive hierarchy, complete in itself.

Magnificent as the system was, there is an unmistakable frigidity and hardness in it. The exaltation of the imâm's cosmic role, and the associated role of all seekers of his truth, produced a systematic anthropocentrism; nothing possessed meaning except men. But men were considered merely as imperfect images of the perfect microcosm, the prophet or the imâm; their meaning depended on their schematic relation to that microcosm. Accordingly, all other things were similarly schematized: unlike even the loosest of the Ṣûfî interpretations,[20] in the Ismâʿîlî bâṭin

[20] Cf. Tor Andrae, *Die person Muhammeds in lehre und glauben seiner gemeinde* (J. A. Lundell [ed.], Archives d'études orientales, XVI [Stockholm, 1917]), chap. I, p. 79, e.g., especially, for the Ṣûfî deepening to mystical levels of the relatively straight forward accounts of Mohammed.

no effort was made to link the figurative interpretations of Koranic passages with the experience which could be presumed to have underlain them. Accordingly, the anthropocentrism did not seize upon passages so appealing to our imagination as ch. xxx, vs. 72, in which God offers the challenge of faith to the heavens and mountains and they reject it as too great a burden; but man accepts it. Ismâ'îlism made of even this magnificent imagery a schematic paradigm: the "faith" is the oath of allegiance in the da'wa – not necessary to the "heavens", etc. who are prophets and imâms. ... This is in a sense a naturalism: the passage is made to deal with ordinarily experienced human events, rather than mythically animated mountains. Yet it has nothing to do with the sense of a unique cosmic responsibility which underlay the Koranic passage.[21] Such a deeper naturalism would no doubt have been out of place. For only through this schematism was it possible to center all history, like all nature, upon the authority of the imâm of the moment. The only thread of historical continuity which remained, in principle, was the 'Alid ancestry, mediated through the naṣṣ of designation. All else was archetype and analogy.

Such a philosophical structure by no means exhausted the imaginative appeal of Ismâ'îlism. Loyalty to the unhonored or martyred imâms was cultivated despite their metaphysical perfection. The Fâṭimids took a special interest in preserving the head of the fallen Ḥusayn. The vision was not lost of a reunited and rejuvenated Islâm capturing at last Constantinople, and bringing all the world under the sway of the Prophet. But the philosophy played a great part. It served not only to express the high intellectual ideals of Fâṭimid society; but as point of departure for all later attempts to grapple with the meaning of events.

The crisis of Ismâ'îlism and the Nizârî response.

The Fâṭimid empire was blessed with a long succession of able imâms; but in the Eleventh Century this good fortune gave out. The Fâṭimid power ceased to expand; rather, it suffered internal crises which reduced the imâm to beggary and his capital to anarchy. As late as the middle of

[21] But even Ghazzâlî showed a like lack of imagination: in the *Tafriqa* he tried to explain the story of Abraham and the stars on an equally unimaginative basis. (*Tafriqa bayn al-Islâm wa-z-Zandaqa,* trans. H. J. Runge, 'Über Gazâlî's Faiṣal-al-tafriqa baina-l-Islâm wa-l-zandaqa,' Kiel, 1938, p. 38).

this century there was a flare-up of hope, when in a moment of disturbance Fâṭimid armies entered Baghdâd itself; but they were forced to leave almost immediately. The Twelver dynasties which had sprung up in the Caliphal territories were swept away by the fresh power of the Saljûq Turks; the Ismâʿîlîs fared little better than their Twelver cousins; and in the moment of apparent triumph, the Shîʿa cause was overthrown more completely than it had been in centuries.

The Sunnîs had in large measure gained the masses which had turned from older religions to Islâm; masses whose weight eventually began to tell. Perhaps this was due to the neutral, catholic approach of the Sunnîs, able to absorb the systems of so many of the earlier interpreters of the faith. Perhaps it was their greater readiness to compromise with the Ṣûfî movement. The Shîʿa had tended to disapprove of the Ṣûfîs, who gave to other saints the honors due to the heroes of Mohammed's house; but the Ṣûfî ascetics and the Sunnî legists, even when most unfriendly, tended to keep out of each other's way – they were speaking to different human needs. At any rate, the Ṣûfî *shaykh*s – holy men – like other popular preachers, gave their support to the looser structure of the orthodoxy of Baghdâd rather than to the Ismâʿîlî hierarchy; and the Sunnî synthesis captured the popular imagination.

When the Saljûq Turkish tribes gathered up the military power of most of the Middle East in their amateur hands during the Eleventh Century, they found that the popular Ṣûfî shaykhs whose respect they sought to gain urged them to the re-establishment of Islâm on a Sunnî basis. Accordingly they restored the Baghdâd Caliph to the dignity which his Twelver masters had compromised, if not to his power; and allowed such ministers as Niẓâm al-Mulk, long second ruler of the realm, to recognize and give official support to the broadest Sunnî synthesis.

The Sunnî interpretation of Islâm was on the verge of definitive victory; the official Egyptian Ismâʿîlism was on the defensive. Yet the Shîʿite dream of a juster Islâm, renewed to its pristine power, was too recent to perish yet. The alien tribal warlords who now held power added to the sting of Shîʿa defeat a standing insult to all their more polished subjects, by their very presence. In these circumstances, the scattered Ismâʿîlîs in the Saljûq dominions struck out on new policies of their own, and soon split from the Fâṭimids altogether. Called now *Nizârî*s, they sought to storm the Saljûq power, by bits and as a whole, through sheer abundance of hostile devotion. With reckless eagerness they seized precarious fortresses, murdered spectacularly their greatest enemies, and attempted great cities by coups de main. They were killed as individuals and massacred in groups; venture upon daring venture fell short; they tried again. Direct onslaught failed, as the broader, slower-paced Fâṭimid attempt to win Islâm had failed before. Yet for almost two centuries, over areas extending from the Hindu Kush foothills to the Mediterranean, the Nizârî Ismâʿîlîs remained a serious power in the midst of Islamic society; an irreconcilably dissident community holding to an increasingly tenuous ideal, while the Sunnîs steadily consolidated their position. Each generation of the Nizârîs saw new defeats, and tried new ways of adjusting ideals to circumstances, till finally the Nizârî resistance was broken down, and the wave of orthodoxy flowed smoothly over all.

THE TRADITIONAL INTERPRETATION OF ISMÂʿÎLISM

The world has usually heard about the Ismâʿîlîs from their enemies, whose works alone were popular after the Ismâʿîlî cause had gone down to defeat. These developed a damning picture of them which long stood unchallenged; only recently has this picture begun to be replaced by another, sometimes as highly favorable as the first was unfavorable. This reconstruction of Ismâʿîlî history has been inspired partly by new points of view, and partly by the availability of new sources of evidence. It has been conditioned at the same time by the scanty and elusive nature of this evidence. It must be based on scattered chance phrases; or on one-sided types of material, which tempt one to treat the remaining gaps either with unbridled fantasy, or with an indifferent silence. Even where we have positive evidence, its use has been made hazardous by our ignorance of the general circumstances into which it fit, of the whole environment in which the Ismâʿîlîs lived, still far from well-studied. Accordingly, the story of Ismâʿîlî studies is itself not uneventful, and goes far to determine the limitations of any new effort in the field.

The revaluation of Fâṭimid Ismâʿîlism.

The study of Nizârî Ismâʿîlism has of course been closely related to that of Fâṭimid Ismâʿîlism; and one of its great handicaps is that we still possess no adequate general study of the Ismâʿîlism in which we could see what kinds of doctrines, institutions, and expectations the Nizârîs began with. But great strides have been made.

A great variety of Sunnî or Twelver Muslim authors mentioned the Fâṭimid Ismâʿîlîs, each from his own point of view. Accordingly, despite their uniform bias, their variety gives us an opportunity to correct them by each other. The heresiologists are the most important of these, and the most biased: they were generally polemicists, too. Their brief summaries of damning doctrine are suspect; but cannot be disregarded, especially in considering the impression left by Ismâʿîlî doctrines after the subtleties dropped away in the popular mind. The best of the heresiologists touch only a few phases of Ismâʿîlism. Ibn Ḥazm here as throughout his treatment of the Shîʿa seems suspiciously schematized; Shahrastânî covers quite different aspects of the doctrine when dealing with the earlier Ismâʿîlîs than when treating of the Nizârîs; Ashʿarî is concerned only with their stand on the imâmate succession. The heresiologists were sometimes eager merely to show the Ismâʿîlîs as one among innumerable splinter groups of a common depravity: at such times what they say goes back to stock phrases used of any heresy (that they permit incest, for instance). The total result was a very confused picture.

Among the historians emerged a more distinctive picture of Ismâʿîlism, which determined earlier Western impressions. The Qarâmiṭa revolts at the end of the Ninth Century – which culminated in the desecration of Mecca itself – stand out in the historians from any lesser Shîʿa doings. So did the scope of the Fâṭimid Caliphate. For so remarkable and threatening a phenomenon, suitable origins were found. We learn how Ibn Maymûn al-Qaddâḥ, a Persian (or a Jew, or a heretic Christian) determined to subvert Islâm from within, for the sake of dualism (or of atheism), by hoodwinking the extremer Shîʿa into following him and his magic tricks; how he killed the infant imâm at the end of the Eighth Century (or invented him at the end of the Ninth); how he offered to each convert doctrines that would please him, and to the depraved chiefs of the conspiracy his own nihilism; and so elaborately duped all and sundry that his descendants were able as imâms to gain the throne of Egypt – from which religious eminence, presumably, they continued to teach their secret followers the untruth of all religion and the vanity of all authority.[22]

[22] Silvestre de Sacy has the full story in its latest form in his introduction to his volumes on the Druze religion, *Exposé de la Religion des Druzes* (2 vols.; Paris, 1838). Reference to the greater number of pre-Nizârî informants on the Ismâʿîlîs will be found in Louis Massignon, 'Esquisse d'une Bibliographie Qarmaṭe,' *Volume of Oriental Studies Presented to E. G. Browne*, ed. by T. W. Arnold and R. A. Nicholson (Cambridge, 1922), p. 334; and in B. Lewis, *Origins of Ismâʿîlism* (Cambrige, 1940), pp. 101 ff.

Western studies of the earlier Ismâʿîlîs began substantially with de Sacy's study of the Ismâʿîlî background of the Druze sect, which split off from the Fâṭimid daʿwa almost a century before the Nizârîs did. This gave us chiefly the story of Ibn Maymûn; and except for some investigations into the Qarâmiṭa of eastern Arabia by M. J. de Goeje[23] there was no great progress until the Twentieth Century. When Nineteenth Century scholars like C. Defrémery or S. Guyard introduced their studies of Nizârîs they had little to add to de Sacy.

In this century there has been on the contrary a small flood of editions and studies of the Fâṭimid religion. Diverse matters such as Ismâʿîlî influence in Spain,[24] Ismâʿîlî association with popular Arabic philosophy,[25] but above all the persistence of the Ismâʿîlîs of south Arabia and of India[26] – all led almost suddenly to an extreme reappraisal of the movement: from a diabolically masterful scheme to subvert all civilized society, it became the expression of a cultivated school of philosophy; or even a movement of social revolution designed to liberate the artisan classes through an inter-confessional guild organization, while it liberated the intellectuals for philosophic speculation. Louis Massignon, particularly, traced the influence of the Ismâʿîlîs into the Muslim guilds and into Ṣûfism, and into many details of Islamic life generally; and even into some aspects of Western life: suggesting Ismâʿîlism as a major aspect of Islamic history.[27]

A number of scholars, including some modern Indian Ismâʿîlîs, undertook to edit what new Ismâʿîlî texts could be made public, and to reinterpret the older materials. The sources for Ismâʿîlism present special difficulties of their own, added to those general in the ages before printing. The sectarian texts which have survived have done so largely through a jealous secrecy in the face of orthodox bigotries; and in spite of the relative enlightenment of the Nineteenth Century, the Twentieth is giving little incentive to cautious groups to abandon their defenses. Except for a number of items preserved among the Nizârîs – each of which departs

[23] *Mémoire sur les Carmathes du Bahrein* (2nd ed.; Leiden, 1886); and 'Fin de l'empire des Carmathes du Bahrein,' *Journal Asiatique*, ser. 9, V (1895), 5.

[24] Miguel Asin y Palacios, *Abenmasarra y su Escuela* (Madrid, 1914).

[25] P. Casanova, 'Notice sur un manuscrit de la secte des Assassins,' *JA*, ser. 9, XI (1898), 151; and 'Une date astronomique dans les épîtres des Ikhwân aṣ-Ṣafâ,' *JA*, ser. 11, V (1915), p. 5.

[26] E. Griffini, 'Die jüngste ambrosianische Sammlung arabischer Handschriften,' *ZDMG*, LXIX (1915), 63.

[27] L. Massignon, 'Ḳarmaṭians,' *The Encyclopedia of Islam;* also, 'Corporations et métiers,' *Revue Internationale de Sociologie*, XXVIII (1920), 473. Bernard Lewis has followed this lead in his *The Arabs in History* (London, 1950).

one way or another from the usual Ismâʿîlî work of Fâṭimid times – almost our only texts from pre-Nizârî Ismâʿîlism are preserved among the Ṭayyibî sect (called in India Bohras) originally centering in the Yaman, which rejected the Fâṭimid Caliphal line a generation after the Nizârîs did. This Ṭayyibî-preserved literature is kept as secret as the more conservative of the sect can manage; but it seems that even what is potentially available among them – like what has been published – is by and large more illuminating of technical doctrinal points than of general social and spiritual developments. Nevertheless, it is of basic importance for understanding the Ismâʿîlî intellectual tradition, and what has been published is enough to provide a general picture.[28] As a result we now have a tantalizing maze of evidence, on the basis of which little has been yet done, however, to enable us to share in the early Ismâʿîlî life.

The enemies of the Nizârîs.

The Nizârî Ismâʿîlis have suffered almost as drastic changes in appraisal as the Fâṭimids. To begin with, the sources on them were even less favorable. Whereas at least some of the secular writings of Fâṭimid times survived in Sunnî circles, no Nizârî authors were so favored. Their enemies held the field. They give nonetheless valuable information.

Almost every treatment of the time touches to some degree upon the Nizârîs. The chronicles recorded at least their spectacular murders and the terror tales that grew about them, sifted in with other notable events of the day; they cursed the Ismâʿîlîs casually but frankly, and generally tried to report the most reliable gossip exactly as received. (The Ismâʿîlîs themselves would have been unavailable for interviews on most such occasions, presumably, even had the chroniclers been inclined to interview them.) Ibn al-Athîr (d. 1234) is the most comprehensive of these chroniclers. The sketchiness of these historians reflects in part their honesty: they noted of skirmishes or massacres only the bare and ascertainable data; if they reported a more human anecdote, it was clearly set off as such. They give us no insight in depth, but we can be tolerably sure of hearing of it whenever the Nizârîs made a notorious stir.

Not only the chroniclers and historians, but travellers, preachers, almost any writers were likely to mention so inescapable a movement, particularly in its earlier years. Even the Crusaders provide a fresh, but

[28] Cf. W. Ivanow, *Guide to Ismâʿîlî Literature* (London, 1933), and B. Lewis, *Origins of Ismaʿîlism* (Cambridge, 1940), the introduction.

not necessarily more penetrating viewpoint. A Saljûq minister writes of them venomously but cautiously; a wandering noble mentions them casually in his memoirs. It is a tantalizing aspect of Nizârî studies that everywhere they are mentioned; and yet almost nowhere come to grips with. The contemporary Muslim world possessed a stereotype of them as unholy and dangerous fanatics, and little more.

General writers were able to grasp something of the activity of Ḥasan-i Ṣabbâḥ, their leader in the first generation; in later generations, even their political development seems largely unknown. Only the heresiologists and polemicists reflected any contemporary awareness of Ismâ'îlî thought. Ghazzâlî himself, sometimes called the second founder of Islâm, contended in its earliest days with the Nizârî doctrine on a very personal and keen basis. At least two of the later heresiologists made a similar, if not so profound, attempt to enter into the Nizârî ideas; but after the first generation, comment became more perfunctory and second hand. The heresiologists, like the chroniclers, seem quite unaware of the later Nizârî evolution.

After the fall of the Nizârî state, in the Thirteenth Century, a school of Persian historians began on the other hand to trace the story of the Nizârîs as a whole, and with remarkable fidelity. The two earliest are 'Aṭâ Malik-i Juwaynî (wrote 1260) and Rashîd ad-Dîn Ṭabîb (wrote 1310). Juwaynî read records in the Alamût Nizârî library after its capture, before ordering its destruction. He wrote an account based on these sources (and others), but altered in form to suit an anti-Nizârî taste, and decked with curses at appropriate points. Rashîd ad-Dîn, years later, seems to have used Juwaynî, but probably also Juwaynî's sources; for he is a great deal fuller, leaving out little which is found in Juwaynî except the curses. He gives the Nizârî material frankly in the form the Nizârîs wrote it; he also used much Sunnî material. Later Persian writers produced summary accounts, based especially on Rashîd ad-Dîn, but also on other tradition. This school concentrated on the center, Alamût; at the sacrifice of information on more remote territories, we get a reasonably continuous record of internal evolution in this sect, which allows us to make sense of the few items of the time preserved among latter-day Nizârîs.

Von Hammer and the Western legend of the Assassins.

When Western scholars came to study the Nizârîs, they approached them from the point of view of the Crusaders, under the name of

Assassins; unaware at first of the Persian school of historians. Gradually as Crusader accounts were supplemented by late Arab historians, the history and interconnection of the Syrian and Persian groups began to emerge.[29] At the end of the Eighteenth Century de Sacy definitively placed these Assassins in the frame of Islamic history as Ismâʿîlîs – putting an end to many fanciful hypotheses, connecting them with the Kurds, or with yet remoter peoples. But de Sacy was frankly eager to illustrate the depravity of unregenerate mankind;[30] he was led to join together the theme of the diabolically scheming Ibn Maymûn, depicted as founder of all Ismâʿîlism, with a lurid tale of seduction of young men into reckless crime with the ḥashîsh drug, based on Marco Polo. During the Nineteenth Century, this combination set the framework within which historians collected such notices of the Nizârîs as they came across; interpreting them hopefully on the basis of any other chance report that seemed to have something to do with Ismâʿîlism in general. The resultant picture was not edifying.

It was a Viennese literary man, after the French Revolution, who put this story in standard form. The leisured, industrious, but scarcely profound von Hammer-Purgstall made wide use of the Persian tradition on the Nizârîs; but with no trace remaining of Rashîd ad-Dîn's objectivity. He devoted a whole book to their history, but it was conceived more as a polemic against the revolutionary danger of secret societies than as an investigation of the Nizârîs themselves; he stressed all the appalling wickedness of which he found them accused, and implied that one might expect the same of the Jesuits (and of the Freemasons), who were, after all, a secret order like the Assassins. His sanguine watchword as a historian carried romanticism to an extreme: "Das nie gesehene Unglaubliche und dennoch Wahre ist der reichste Stoff der Geschichtsschreibung, wenn nur die Quellen glaubwürdig und zugänglich."[31] His work was translated into English and French, and evidently served as standard interpretation of the unfortunate sect, the numerous imprecations against whom he had indefatigably gathered, resolutely doubting any suggestion that might extenuate their crimes. Even so late as the 1930's it was the chief authority at once for the traveller to the valleys of Alamût, and for the romancer whose historical novel on the Nizârîs held the field alone.[32]

[29] Cf. J. P. L. Withof, *Das meuchelmörderische Reich der Assassinen*, Cleves, 1765.

[30] Cf. his prefatory words in explanation of his *Exposé de la religion des Druzes*.

[31] J. von Hammer, *Geschichte der Assassinen* (Stuttgart und Tübingen, 1818), p. 1.

[32] Freya Stark, *Valleys of the Assassins* (New York, 1934), and B. Bouthoul, *Grand Maître des Assassins* (Paris, 1936); the respective bibliographies.

But a new approach was being prepared. C. Defrémery collected indefatigably the scattered passages touching the Nizârîs, and concerned himself more with dating than with castigating their crimes. Toward the end of the century, texts from the Nizârîs themselves began to appear. This had begun with Salisbury's scanty but exact translations in 1851–2, but these distant American fragments were less noticed than the abundant materials of Guyard in the 1870's, published in Paris itself. By the beginning of the Twentieth Century, a closer knowledge of modern Nizârîs together with a small amount of archaeological data was laying the basis for a new appraisal.

VINDICATION OF THE NIZÂRÎS

In the Twentieth Century the Nizârîs have begun to be treated no longer either as an incident in the Crusade, or as a horrible example with which to frighten radicals; but rather as a people in their own right. The new interest of the latter-day Nizârîs themselves in their history accounts for this in part; much of the recent work has been carried out in India. But the new approach has been beset with many snares.

Problems of dealing with Saljûq and Ayyûbid times.

It must be kept in mind that the sources from which to understand the world where the Nizârîs rose and struggled are far less ample than for the West in the same period. No archives, few letters or documents; few original manuscripts in general. But chronicles and biographical registers we have in some abundance, recording prominent events, political or meteorological, and who's-who data about scholars and other notables; often based upon archives lost to us, and personal interviews. The verse and prose works of authors of the time, of which a wide sampling has been preserved, illustrate other sides of life – and manuscript tradition respected authorship enough to allow us a good view of these. There are notices by Crusaders and other foreigners, and archaeological documents such as coins; altogether we possess potentially enough evidence for a good assessment of the time.

These materials have by no means been adequately exploited by modern Islamists. There is above all no general study of the period in terms of which a study of the Nizârîs could be oriented. But we are not helpless. Many of the historical texts have been edited, or translated into Western languages. Scholars have been interested above all in two features of the time: it is the age of classical Persian poetry, and of the regularization of Ṣûfî mysticism. Some of the great poetical and religious figures have accordingly been studied, and many of their works edited. There is a whole bibliography on a dozen of religious, literary, and even political figures. Nonetheless, for many aspects of Nizârî history the lack of background – especially social and economic – leaves us rather fumbling in the dark.[33]

Nizârî texts.

The attempt to give the Nizârîs their due depend largely on the texts retained among the Nizârîs themselves. These are, however, meager, especially in point of history. Ivanow says that even for modern Nizârî writers – whose rare productions are not generally available – early Nizârî history must be based on the usual Sunnî tradition.[34] The few early texts we have serve to clarify what their enemies can tell, rather than to develop a story on their own. If the Nizârîs are no longer so rigidly secretive as once, it seems they have little to secrete. Even for doctrine, there was evidently no canon of authoritative Nizârî writings which would be preserved with special care.[35] The voluminous writings of the Alamût imâms are mostly lost; what we possess, either in Arabic or Persian, is very miscellaneous, and often of unknown authorship.

[33] Claude Cahen has analyzed in his *Syrie du Nord* the interrelations and relative value for our Saljûq-Ayyûbid period of most of the historians, especially with regard to Syrian affairs. (Cf. the initial chapters: Claude Cahen, *La Syrie du nord à l'époque des Croisades et la principauté franque d'Antioche* (Institut français de Damas: Bibliothèque orientale, I, Paris, 1940). The few other analyses of these materials that have been made are mostly listed in J. Sauvaget, *Introduction à l'histoire de l'orient musulman* (Paris, 1943), chaps. vii and viii. Two or three pieces of work have been written but not published. (Cahen in his *Syrie du Nord* refers to bibliographical work on Ibn Wâṣil; V. Minorsky, review of *The Decline of the Saljûqid Empire* by M. F. Sanaullah, *BSOS*, X (1940–1942), 258–260, mentions others. The Hamdani whose work is there mentioned does not respond to inquiry.)

Materials more directly relevant to social and intellectual development: Brockelmann's *Geschichte der arabischen Literatur*, Vol. I (2nd ed.; Leiden, 1943), and *Supplement* Vol. I (Leiden, 1937), gives a full listing, showing the emphasis on religious subjects.

[34] Ivanow, *Guide*, pages at end; cf. Lewis, *Origins*, p. 16.

[35] The closest approach to a canon seems to have been the writings by or ascribed to Nâṣir-i Khusraw, among the upper Oxus community; these bear only indirectly on the Alamût period.

Yet we can place at least some materials in almost every period.[36] We have a few texts both Arabic and Persian preserved among Nizârî circles from pre-Nizârî times. We have quotations from both Ḥasan-i Ṣabbâḥ and the later imâms, in later sectarian works; some verses and an expository book from the middle period of Qiyâma; and from the final period two treatises ascribed curiously to a man who figures historically as the great betrayer of the sect, Naṣîr ad-Dîn Ṭûsî. To these must be added of course the liberal quotations in Rashîd ad-Dîn from Nizârî historical works and even from an autobiography of Ḥasan-i Ṣabbâḥ; and an interesting summary in the heresiographer Shahrastânî of one of Ḥasan-i Ṣabbâḥ's works. Finally, a good deal of supplementary information and background from which to interpret these isolated texts can come from later Nizârî works. The religious exposition is eclectic, and influenced by later movements; the poetry is of a Ṣûfî type, and written with cautious reference to the eyes of the world; but among these later historical texts is a valuable historical monograph on the Syrian Râshid ad-Dîn Sinân. These materials, so far as they are known, are listed in Ivanow's *Guide*, which he hopes to supplement in the near future.[37]

Ivanow and the modern revaluation of the Nizârîs.

Nihil humani a me alienum puto is a terrifying motto, but in the Twentieth Century scholars – who else? – have been expected to live up to it. The most improbable evil is daily experienced from men; yet even its worst, when fully understood, commonly comes humanly alive, with its element of grandeur and of piteousness. Accordingly, recent scholars have been unready to assume that men would be likely to behave in the infamous manner depicted on the basis of an acceptance and an indiscriminate mingling, as to time and place, of all their opponents had to say about this heresy. Our reversal of judgment on the Ismâ'îlîs generally has involved also the Nizârîs.

Already in the *Encyclopedia of Islâm* the Nizârîs were no longer so mercilessly judged as by von Hammer and his predecessors. However, in contrast to the former curiosity about the Assassins, the new interest

[36] Cf. Appendix III.

[37] Also mentioned therein is a body of later Indian material, mostly in Gujrati, reflecting a new tradition within Ismâ'îlism far removed from the times of the lords of Alamût. To literary evidence should be added archaelogical, such as that gathered by Van Berchem.

has centered on Fâṭimid thought, neglecting the Nizârîs. Perhaps this is in part because of the special difficulties in dealing with the period as a whole, and because of the relatively meager survival of Nizârî materials. At any rate, most scholars have treated of the Nizârîs only peripherally; only W. Ivanow has so far published major work in our field, as editor and as critic of the texts. It is to his work that reference is now commonly made by scholars, in Nizârî matters.

Ivanow presents a viewpoint directly the opposite of von Hammer's tirade, and indeed becomes irate whenever he feels that scholars are still giving the slightest credence to the ancient slanders. Since his first Ismâʿîlî publication in 1922 he has gradually developed an apologetic position, which suggests that Ismâʿîlism developed as a specially pious form of the more conservative and popular wing of Islâm, the Shîʿa. (He has even gone so far – but seems to have retracted this later – as to suggest that there probably were, as the Shîʿa have insisted, passages in the Koran in favor of ʿAlî's rights of succession to Mohammed, which the Caliph ʿUthmân expunged.)[38] He has maintained that those features of Ismâʿîlism which have been most questioned by its enemies are – in doctrine – rather a relatively early and liberal use of Hellenistic thought; and – in practice – purely defensive tactics by a minority against bigoted persecution. Far from admitting any hint of imposture in the Ismâʿîlî leaders, he has even suggested, in his *Encyclopedia of Islam* article on Ismâʿîlîs, that the very dubious claim of the later Nizârî imâms to Fâṭimid descent was probably valid. Together with this apologetic approach, he makes a persistent effort to "decontaminate" Ismâʿîlism from its two most notorious figures – Ibn Maymûn and Ḥasan-i Ṣabbâḥ: the former by making him on the one hand perfectly innocent, and on the other hand no Ismâʿîlî anyway;[39] the latter by reducing him to an inarticulate non-entity.[40]

But unfortunately his sympathy, so keen for the oppressed masses and their religious loyalties, does not extend to what he calls "mysticism" – under which word he lumps together all occult or mythological lore as well as the inner aspects of religious experience more strictly called

[38] Shihâbu'd-dîn Shâh, *Ḥaqîqat-i Dîn*, trans. W. Ivanow, *True Meaning of Religion* (The Ismaili Society. Ismaili Texts and Translations Series B, No. 2 (2nd ed.) Leiden, 1947), p. 51. For his general attitude, cf. on the one hand, 'Ismâʿîlîs and Qarmaṭians,' *JBBRAS*, XVI (1940), 43–85; and for a more moderate view, the first chapter of *Studies in Early Persian Ismâʿîlism* (Ismaili Society Series A, No. 3, Leiden, 1948).

[39] Cf. W. Ivanow, *The Alleged Founder of Ismâʿîlism* (Ismaili Society Series A, no. 1 [Bombay, 1946]), etc.

[40] Cf. W. Ivanow, *Rawḍat at-Taslîm* (Leiden, 1950), p. lxxxv, etc.

mystical. All this he considers as predominantly fantastic and fraudulent, and when he is unable to clear Ismâʿîlism of it altogether, sets down the remainder either to popular ideas or to a superficial intellectual fashion.[41] As a result, his interpretations of Nizârî documents and history, while always alert to find the most considerate view, sometimes seem strained particularly at those points where myth or mysticism are involved.

At various perhaps minor points it is necessary to use his work with care.[42] He has an occasionally whimsical use of words (such as using "obviously" at points where he is playing particularly free, as that the Persian Ḥusayn-plays were "obviously" derived from Medieval Catholic Europe);[43] and a tendency to a freeness in translation, either for the sake of modernizing the spirit of a work, or for the sake of eliminating its "fashionable" mysticism so as to show the rational meaning that may underlie the wording.

We shall have occasion to notice some of the more unfortunate instances later, when particular passages are of importance to us. Nevertheless, he has had a broad and sympathetic acquaintance with Ismâʿîlî groups in India, in Îrân, and in Syria; he has acquired a number of Nizârî texts, and evidently seen yet more; and his various judgments are based on a devoted and untiring labor over the years in preserving, and making available to all so fast as he himself can do the work, the records that are likely to disappear so quickly in that part of the world. He stands unchallengeably as the founder of such modern Nizârî studies as may develop.

The place of a general history of the Nizârîs.

The present work is a general history of the Nizârîs during their career as an independent state. I have no expectation of its being "definitive"; for in any case, much more monographic work is needed on the history of their theology, of their political policy, and (when the economy of the

[41] Cf. W. Ivanow, *The Alleged Founder*, p. 140; *Early Persian Ismâʿîlism*, p. 46 n.; *Rawḍat at-Taslîm*, p. lxvi.

[42] K. Hadank, 'W. Ivanow als Berichtserstatter,' *Acta Orientalia*, X (1932), p. 294. After citing for three pages (with no word of evaluation of Ivanow directly) numerous gross errors made by Ivanow in his overweening attacks on other students of Persian dialects, he ends the article with, "So spricht nur jemand, der sich bloss an sein Gedächtnis hält, statt an zuverlässige Aufzeichnungen."

[43] Ivanow, *Early Persian Ismâʿîlism*, p. 30.

Saljûq period as a whole has been better understood) their economic and social role. But enough spadework has been done by Ivanow and others to necessitate already a general framework, so that we may digest what has been done, and guide our further efforts.[44] Accordingly this is an attempt to trace the course of the Nizârî community as a whole, analyzing military, say, or doctrinal developments only as they bear upon the general development of the community.

This study should throw light not only on the Nizârîs themselves, but through them on the Saljûq period as a whole, in which the Nizârîs played a striking part. This is important, for this period is pivotal in the Middle East, and the Middle East has been pivotal in world developments. One of the most fateful facts of modern history has been the failure, from the times of the Renaissance on, of the Islamic Middle East to continue serving as creative link among the various regions of the Hemisphere. Instead there developed the tremendous gulf between the vibrantly revolutionized West and an unsuspecting mankind, fragmented and overwhelmed, a gulf which has set the tone of present world problems. If this decline of the Middle East is to be traced, as some trace it, as far back as the Mongol conquests, then the Saljûq period which preceded must claim our attention.

But such a study as this should serve above all to acquaint us with the Nizârîs as a human community. Their story has been too long disguised, for such as hear of them, by von Hammer's careless tract. As we are men, the human promise and sin, passion and trials of those Medieval dissenters are also our promise and sin and failure; as we share their experience, we shall know better who we are, and be more capable of judging what is worthy of our endeavors and our tears.

[44] One of the most desirable of these would be a study of the whole development of Nizârî theology – a study which could not stop at the fall of Alamût.

PART ONE

THE ONSLAUGHT AGAINST THE SALJÛQS

CHAPTER TWO

ḤASAN-I ṢABBÂḤ AND THE ISMÂʿÎLÎ CRISIS

THE CONFRONTATION OF FÂṬIMID ISMÂʿÎLISM WITH SALJÛQ SUNNISM

The breakdown of the Fâṭimid power.

In the Tenth Century the Shîʿa and especially the Ismâʿîliyya seemed about to dominate the Islamic world. The Fâṭimid empire was recognized in half the Islamic territories, and its propagandists were making converts, even among rulers, in the remainder. The ʿAbbâsids at Baghdâd were humiliated by Shîʿite upstarts, and in the Eleventh Century the Fâṭimids themselves held Baghdâd for some months.

But this Eleventh Century saw a reversal of fortunes. By 1062 was already beginning the decade of military and economic crisis which put an end forever to the Fâṭimid hopes of universal dominion. The fifth Caliph of Cairo, Mustanṣir, lost control even of his capital, which continued in disorder till a military captain, Badr al-Jamâlî, was able in 1074 to restore the Caliphal dignity – at the price of replacing Mustanṣir's authority, except in name, with his own. In the later decades of the century the imâm Mustanṣir was old and incompetent; Badr joined in a single concern the stability of the state, and his own family fortunes. At last, to be assured of a docile imâm, his son was in a position to set aside the heir designated by naṣṣ in favor of another son, who was at the same time Badr's son-in-law.

Badr was indeed an Ismâʿîlî, but his attitude, and his son's, seems to have been cautious. The solid depth of Ismâʿîlî success had not matched its spectacularly wide extent. With the rise of the Saljûq power, which invaded even Syria, ordinarily an Egyptian preserve, the Egyptian state policy had to become essentially defensive. The Ismâʿîlî system was to be maintained, but scarcely beyond the borders of Egypt and its nearer dependencies – but a small part of the broad Islamic world which the

Ismâ'îlîs had marked out as their heritage.[1] From internal weakness as well as from Sunnî resurgence, the Fâṭimids were losing their prospects of expansion.

Sunnî culture in the Saljûq age.

In sharp contrast to the Fâṭimid decline, by the latter part of the Eleventh Century the Sunnî grandeur was at its height under Saljûq protection. The century had opened with the wide critical investigations of Bîrûnî (d. 1048) and the elegant, unconventionally sensitive poetry of Al-Ma'arrî (d. 1057); it closed with the brilliant mathematician, the type of refined skepticism, Omar Khayyam (d. 1132 or 1123). All the ancient traditions had already been fully Islamicized, yet they had not lost their vigor, or at least their vitality. Islâm as a society was old enough to be wise, yet young enough still to be confident; it was ready for sages such as the mystical theologian Ghazzâlî (d. 1111) and the concerned statesman Niẓâm al-Mulk (d. 1092), to mark out the generous lines of its maturity.

The Saljûq power dominated the Syrian and 'Irâqî centers of Islâm, and the increasingly creative Iranian lands; the main lines of Middle Eastern trade ran through its territories; among eastern Islamic centers, only Egypt and the Afghan centers were free of it. Niẓâm al-Mulk might well gain a magnificent renown: he presided over a power among whose subjects moved the major ferments of religious and mystical experiment, of the developing Persian literature, of the persistent Middle Eastern economic traditions. Nevertheless, the realm was distracted by the rival fractions of the Saljûq tribe of Turks which held power. Foreigners almost as much within their realm as outside it, they had little more connection with the population than that of an armed occupation: the Saljûqid chiefs, despite the efforts at administrative continuity of their Persian ministers, were little more than glorified warlords. Accordingly, a breach between two Saljûq armies divided the political power as much – or as little – as if there were two separate military sovereigns. After the death of the Sulṭân, the supreme Saljûq, Malikshâh (in 1092) such breaches became chronic; with each breach and each reshifting of the fluid personal

[1] Even the connection with the Ismâ'îlîs of Yaman and therefore of 'Umân and Sind seems to have become less close at this time. Among other things, Afḍal is said to have gotten rid of a heretic by sending him to the Yaman. (The reference is obscure: in Ibn Muyassar, d. 1278, *Ta'rîkh Miṣr*, ed. H. Massé, *Annales d'Egypte* (Cairo, 1919), year 515, p. 57, we find that Afḍal banished a certain "Bâṭinî" to the Yaman, since his "madhhab" was openly held there. Some of his followers in Egypt were killed.)

ties involved came new wanton devastations of coveted lands and towns; the uncontrollable military license which had tended to accompany the breakup of the united Caliphate came now to be taken for granted, and made havoc of the proud Saljûq power itself.[2]

Social atomization and religious integration.

In such circumstances, Muslim trade declined,[3] cities tended to lose more often than to gain in prosperity, and the jettisoning of civic institutions continued. The through streets of old Roman cities were cut up into dead-ends and walled town quarters;[4] the attempt at a central government news-gathering agency was abandoned;[5] taxation was given over to a decentralized military system which scattered the troops over the land without attaching them to it. The all-Islamic Caliphate had long since become rather a symbol than a central power. Increasingly, purely local political life tended to become more important than any surviving larger territorial organization.[6]

Sunnî realists had to abandon the Caliphate as an effective power; but their matured outlook gave them a ready substitute: the Caliphal power was no longer necessary. Their stress on the sharîʿa suggested a religious and military egalitarianism in which each individual could rise as high as fortune and his merits permitted, without affecting the universal legal structure. Within the forms ideally held constant across all lines of race or tongue, every adventurer could look for a throne somewhere in the Islamic world at last; every legist, every Ṣûfî holy man, like every general, had the same standing in principle as every other, and depended upon a personal prestige for his authority. Under the Saljûqs this pattern of society was well-established outside of such perpetually centralized lands as Egypt. The Twelver Shîʿa, despite a contrasting theory, accommodated themselves to it; – only the Ismâʿîlîs resisted.

[2] H. A. R. Gibb, 'Considerations on the Sunnî Theory of the Caliphate,' *Archives d'histoire du droit oriental*, III (1948), 401 ff., traces the response of the theorists to this situation.

[3] Cf. Archibald Lewis, *Naval Powers in the Mediterranean, 500-1100* (Princeton, 1951), as an interesting excursion into interregional history, which also touches on this point.

[4] Cf. J. Sauvaget, *Alep* (Paris, 1941).

[5] Cf. W. Barthold, *Turkestan Down to the Mongol Invasion*, trans. W. Barthold and H. A. R. Gibb (2nd ed.; London, 1928), p. 231 and *passim*, for a discussion of the decline of civic institutions, in general administration.

[6] Cf. Claude Cahen, 'Evolution de l'Iqtâʿ du IXe au XIIIe siècle,' *Annales: économies, sociétés, civilisations*, VIII (1953), 25–52.

Sunnî sentiment imposed only such general rules of the game as the great majority had come to honor. It was demanded that all accept the several admitted symbols of unity – the shahâda witnessing to God and his Prophet, the yearly fast of Ramaḍân and the ultimate pilgrimage to Mecca, the common ritual prayer, and the legal alms to the community poor; that all accept the memory and traditional examples of Mohammed and the first generation of Muslims – as codified in varying versions of the sharîʿa. To these ritual and legal matters the mosques, as places of public ritual prayer, were dedicated: which every conforming Muslim was free to use, and none to control. Each version of the sharîʿa, each *madhhab*, was held by its followers still as the true one, properly destined to be universal; yet of necessity they were being forced to recognize one another.[7] Within so broad a framework, each individual could choose his way among those offered by various traditions. But every group must adjust itself to the minimum requirements, or suffer the penalty of isolation.

It was on such a basis that the demand for a logical structure of faith was developed on more popular lines (for the people at large had never accepted the earlier Muʿtazilite efforts in this direction) by the Ashʿarites; who paid a fuller regard to community traditions, such as the special exaltation of the Koran and eventually of Mohammed. Persecuted at the start of the century, the rapidly evolving Ashʿarites were by the end of it widely recognized as authoritative.[8] In the same spirit of compromise on the basis of community symbols, the Ṣûfîs and the Sunnî traditionists proceeded to develop from their generally negligent mutual tolerance an explicit rapprochement. In mid-century Qushayrî (d. 1074), and more especially in the precise years of the Nizârî onslaught, Ghazzâlî (d. 1111) tried with some success to persuade the Sunnî legists (on the one hand) that Ṣûfî mysticism, with its intensive personal piety, was at once the nourisher and the guarantor of the community faith; and to persuade the Ṣûfîs themselves (on the other hand) that conformity to the externals of community discipline was the test of purity in mystic experience. In this way Ṣûfî piety could receive explicit orthodox approval. In the Saljûq institutions was typified a fluid individualization in a society bound together by a universal formalism: illustrated no less in the rulers' loyal

[7] On the gradual overcoming of madhhab rivalries cf. L. Massignon, 'Les Medresehs de Bagdad,' *Bulletin de l'institut français d'archéologie orientale* [*du Caire*], VII (1910), 77. But cf. Asad Ṭalas, *La Madrasa Nizamiyya et son histoire* (Paris, 1939), p. 34 etc., on the still Shâfiʿite character of Niẓâm al-Mulk's madrasa.

[8] For the development of a logical orthodoxy cf. A. J. Wensinck, *The Muslim Creed* (Cambridge, 1932), and L. Gardet and M. M. Anawati, *Introduction à la théologie musulmane* (Paris, 1948).

support of the Caliphal honor and the sanctity of the sharîʿa, than in their arbitrary attitude to their own régimes, to the Ṣûfî shaykhs they patronized, to the poets tied to the adventurous fortunes of a military court.

Tableau of Nizârî Times.

The Ismâʿîlîs refused to accept this solution to the old question, what should Islâm finally be. The Nizârî assault upon the Saljûq power was being prepared in those later decades of the Eleventh Century, while Badr al-Jamâlî consolidated his policy in Egypt, and Niẓâm al-Mulk was left free to cultivate the Sunnî synthesis throughout the realms where the Saljûq power was at its peak. Then within half a decade, in 1090 the Ismâʿîlîs seized the key fortress of Alamût south of the Caspian, dotted their positions of power throughout the Saljûq lands, cut their connections with Fâṭimid Egypt; and laid the basis of a new and unique state, on a very different principle from that of the surrounding Sunnî society, which lasted practically intact for more than 150 years.

Between 1090 and 1256 there were eight lords of Alamût. In a community where the leader was the incarnation of wisdom, they played an important role in demarcating the course of events; it will be useful to divide Nizârî history according to their reigns, and particularly into three groups of reigns. The first three reigns, from 1090 to 1162, serve to establish the community as an independent power: the effort to overthrow the Sunnî pattern is made, and fails; and the more restricted sphere of subsequent Nizârî activity is marked out. In the second period, 1162 to 1210, Nizârism is reconstructed by newly-found imâms, rejecting as hopeless the Islamic society at large, and turning to its own genius for a world within itself: the realm of the *Qiyâma*, the great Resurrection. In the final period, 1210 to 1256, even this effort breaks down, and the Nizârîs attempt to fit into the kaleidoscopic Sunnî society as one state among many – an attempt which came to a violent end almost befitting its narrow ambition.

ḤASAN-I ṢABBÂḤ'S LABORS

The man who gets the credit for launching the new Ismâʿîlî daʿwa of which Alamût was the center is one of the two Nizârî personages upon whom we have anything like satisfactory materials. On Ḥasan-i Ṣabbâḥ we

THE LORDS OF ALAMÛT

Dâʿîs of Daylamân

34 years:	Ḥasan-i Ṣabbâḥ	1090-1124:	the general rising
14 years:	Buzurg'ummîd	1124-1138:	consolidation of positions
24 years:	Muḥammad ibn Buzurg'ummîd	1138-1162:	stalemate

Imâms of the Qiyâma

4 years:	Ḥasan II	1162-1166:	abolition of the outer law
44 years:	Muḥammad II	1166-1210:	self-contained spirituality

Imâms of the Satr

11 years:	Ḥasan III	1210-1221:	alliance with the Caliphate
34 years:	Muḥammad III	1221-1255:	aggressive isolation
1 year :	Khwurshâh*	1255-1256:	fall of Alamût

* The imâms of the Satr each had honorific names – as was increasingly the style then in Muslim dynasties –: Jalâl ad-Dîn, Ḥasan III; ʿAlâ ad-Dîn, Muḥammad III; Rukn ad-Dîn, Khwurshâh. Muḥammad II is also given an honorary title, but it varies: in some manuscripts of the *Kalâm-i Pîr*, according to Ivanow (pp. 44–51), and in the list of the imâms circulated separately, it is *ʿAlâ ad-Dîn*, as also in some historians; in other manuscripts of the *Kalâm-i Pîr* it is *Ḍiyâ ad-Dîn*; and in Rashîd ad-Dîn Ṭabîb it is *Nûr ad-Dîn*. It seems likely that the imâms of the Qiyâma assumed no such mundane styles.

The exact dates of these reigns, according to Qazwînî's edition of Juwaynî, are as follows:

Ḥasan-i Ṣabbâḥ to Alamût,	Weds. 6 Rajab, 483	(p. 194)
d. Ḥasan-i Ṣabbâḥ	(?) Weds. 6 Rabîʿ II, 518	(p. 215)
d. Buzurg'ummîd	26 Jumâdâ I, 532	(p. 221)
d. Md. b. Buzurg'ummîd	3 Rabîʿ I, 557	(p. 222)
d. Ḥasan II	Sun. 6 Rabîʿ I, 561	(p. 239)
d. Muḥammad II	10 Rabîʿ I, 607	(p. 242)
d. Ḥasan III	15 Ramaḍân, 618	(p. 249)
d. Muḥammad III	29 Shawwâl, 653	(p. 255)
Khwurshâh surrenders	29 Shawwâl, 654	(p. 267)

It might be noted that Zambaur worked from inadequate materials; hence in his handbook the section on the Assassins is full of errors. His dates are inconsistent, and should be replaced by the above, pending a future edition of Rashîd ad-Dîn. He does not note that Ḥasan II was murdered, but does not doubt Muḥammad II was; and gives the latter the dubious title of Nûr ad-Dîn. He makes Buzurg'ummîd be a son of Ḥasan-i Ṣabbâḥ, and the Agha Khan therefore Ḥasan-i Ṣabbâḥ's descendant; Ḥasan is listed as a son of "Ṣabbâḥ". He calls the Satr a "return to Islâm" rather than an adoption of Sunnism. He has Khwurshâh *die* already on the date of his surrender.

possess not only the fairly full little biography in Rashîd ad-Dîn's work, and a number of incidental references and quotations elsewhere, but a fairly large excerpt or summary of his writings, preserved by Shahrastânî.[9] It is through Rashîd ad-Dîn's account of him that we have, moreover, almost our only record of the Iranian Ismâʿîlî community just before the uprising and the split from Egypt. Accordingly, Ḥasan stands inevitably in the center of our narrative of his times.

The youthful seeking.

The first part of Rashîd ad-Dîn's account, and of Juwaynî's, is apparently taken from the memoirs of Ḥasan himself: the style is direct; the matter is circumstantial, and accurate where it can be checked.[10] Ḥasan-i Ṣabbâḥ was a seeker, after the Ismâʿîlî fashion, from seven to seventeen. He had been born to a Twelver Shîʿa family, apparently in the traditionally Shîʿa town of Qumm in western Îrân.[11] Ḥasan's quest, however, will have been carried on in the not-distant Sunnî city of Rayy, where he studied to enter the clerical profession, and where he would find represented all approaches.[12]

[9] There seems little doubt that Shahrastânî's claimed translation from Ḥasan-i Ṣabbâḥ is genuine (in his *Milal wa-n-Niḥal*, trans. T. Haarbrucker, *Abû- l-Fatḥ Muḥammad asch-Schahrastani's Religionspartheien und Philosophischen Schulen*, I [2 vols.; Halle, 1850–1], 226–9). Fakhr ad-Dîn Râzî (d. 1209); P. Kraus, in citing him in 'Controversies,' *Islamic Culture* (1938); Massignon (personal letter) and other scholars accept it; and the reference to the same ideas in Juwaynî and Rashîd ad-Dîn seems to support it. Ivanow denies that Ḥasan-i Ṣabbâḥ wrote anything (*Rawḍat at-Taslîm*, pp. lxxxii-lxxxvi), but even the *Kalâm-i Pîr* quotes (p. 74/79) a commentary of his; I suspect that Ivanow has been misled by a sense of revulsion at allowing a figure of ill-repute to have had a large role in Ismâʿîlî development.

[10] Cf. H. Bowen, 'The sar-gudhasht-i sayyidnâ,' *JRAS* (1931), p. 773, on the termination point of the first person account, which is subsequently artificially resumed in Juwaynî in connection with more legendary material. Note that Rashîd ad-Dîn is the fundamental authority on Ḥasan-i Ṣabbâḥ's life, where other sources are not referred to.

[11] In Rashîd ad-Dîn, Ḥasan's father, ʿAlî, was originally from the Arab Shîʿa center, Kûfa, in ʿIrâq; a descendant of the mighty (and legendary) pre-Islamic Ḥimyarite kings of the romantic Yaman at the southern tip of Arabia. Juwaynî has apparently consolidated here, making Ḥasan's father himself move from the Yaman through Kûfa and Qumm to Rayy; this alluring career has no more probability than the account of Ḥasan's origin from a village near Ṭûs in the pseudo-*Wiṣâya*, ascribed to Niẓâm al-Mulk (quoted by Mîrkhwând, ed. A. Jourdain, *Notices et extraits des manuscrits*, IX [1813] 117).

[12] Of Ḥasan's youth, apart from his memoirs, we have only the imaginary story of his rivalry with Niẓâm al-Mulk; and a detail from the unreliable Ibn al-Jawzî ('The Devil's Delusions,' *Islamic Culture*, IX [1935], 556) on his secretaryship to an ʿAbd ar-Razzâq ibn Bahrâm in his youth. I here quote from folio 293 of the British Museum Manuscript: Oriental MSS, add. 7628.

"From the days of my boyhood, from the age of seven years, I had a liking for the various sciences, and wanted to become learned in religion; to the age of seventeen I searched and sought for knowledge. But I held to the Twelver sect of my fathers. In Rayy I met a person by the name of Amîra Dharrâb; from time to time he explained the doctrine ('aqîda) of the Caliphs of Egypt, as before him Nâṣir-i Khusraw, *ḥujja* of Khurâsân and Georgia. It had had no success in the time of the Sulṭân Maḥmûd. Abû 'Alî Sîmjûr and a great number had accepted that way; and Naṣr ibn Aḥmad the Sâmânid and a number of the great men of the court at Bukhârâ had received that doctrine.[13]

"Now, there had never been any doubt or uncertainty in my Islâm; that there is a God, living, constant, omnipotent, powerful, hearing, seeing; and a Prophet, and an imâm to permit and forbid; and Paradise, and Hell, and commands and prohibitions. I supposed that religion and [sound] doctrine were what the people at large possessed, especially the Shî'a, and I never suspected that truth should be sought outside of Islâm, and [I suposed] that the sect of the Ismâ'îlîs was Philosophy, and the ruler of Egypt a Philosopher.[14] Amîra Dharrâb was a man of good morals. When he first conversed with me he said, The Ismâ'îlîs say thus and so. My friend, I said, Don't say what they say, for they are beyond the pale, and it is contrary to [sound] doctrine. In our conversation we had arguments and disputes with each other, and he disproved and demolished my doctrine. I did not yield, but those words had their effect. In the course of our conversation I said, whenever someone dies in that belief it is certainly said: This is the corpse of a heretic [*mulḥid*]; upon such the people at large, as is their custom, pour out a great deal of lies and nonsense. I saw that the Nizârî group[15] was Godfearing, pious, abstinent, and anxious about drink; and I dreaded drink, for it is stated in the tradition [*khabar*]: 'The sum of foulness, and the mother of offenses.' Amîra said to me, At night when you are thinking on your bed [*dar khwâb*] you know that what I say convinces you.

[13] *Ḥujja* was a rank of the Fâṭimid hierarchy, designating one of the great dâ'îs generally associated with a particular territory; this is the Nâṣir-i Khusraw so popular still with the Nizârîs of the upper Oxus. Maḥmûd and Naṣr were rulers: the former was harshly Sunnî, the latter lost his throne for his heresy. Abû 'Alî Sîmjûr was head of Nîshâpûr, under the late Sâmânids.

[14] It must be remembered that Philosophy – the Greek tradition – was in disrepute among Muslims as irreligious.

[15] Assuming that this account is not retouched, it seems to be written in long retrospect—as indeed the whole tenor suggests. Hence the anachronistic use of the word *Nizârî*. Note here, incidentally, the familiar phenomenon of a minority group cultivating special moral rigor.

"Meanwhile I became separated from him; but I found much proof of the imâmate of Ismâʿîl in their books, and then further I came to the hidden imâms [*mastûr*]. I was bewildered, and said, This imâmate depends upon a naṣṣ and upon instructions; and I do not know what these are. In the midst of this a severe and dangerous illness occurred. God desired that my flesh and skin become something different – 'God changed his flesh to better than his flesh, and his blood to better than his blood' applied to me. I thought, Surely this sect is true, and out of my extreme fear I did not admit it; I said, The appointed time has come, I shall perish without having reached the truth.

"Finally I was delivered from that severe illness; I found another of the Ismâʿîlîs, Abû Najm Sarrâj [saddler] by name; I inquired of him about this sect. He so expounded it by explanation and analysis that I was informed of its abstruse points and its final reality. Then I sought [to be given] the oath of allegiance from another person, by the name of Mu'min, to whom the Shaykh ʿAbd al-Malik-i ʿAṭṭâsh had given a license in the daʿwa. He said, You, who are Ḥasan [good], have a greater rank than I, who am Mu'min [believer]; how then shall I take your oath, and receive the allegiance to the imâm from you? After much urging he took my oath.[16] Then in [the month] Ramaḍân of the year 464 [H.], ʿAbd al-Malik-i ʿAṭṭâsh, who was at that time dâʿî of Iṣfahân and Adharbâyjân, came to Rayy. After seeing me he approved of me, and appointed me a deputy in the daʿwa [niyâbat-i daʿwat-i man farmûd]. He said to me, You must go to court."

The visit to Egypt (1078).

At this point the direct quotation of Ḥasan's memoirs in Rashîd ad-Dîn's source evidently ceases, though one may suppose from the continuity of manner that the continuation of the story on till he arrives at the Egyptian court is based on them. ʿAbd al-Malik was evidently charged, at Iṣfahân, with the whole west Iranian daʿwa (for in the course of the story areas as far apart as Adharbâyjân and Kirmân appear to depend upon that center). What sort of position Ḥasan was given is not clear – the term *nâ'ib*, deputy, nowhere appears in a sequence of Ismâʿîlî *ḥudûd*, ranks of the hierarchy; but since the term is twice by Rashîd ad-Dîn associated with the plan to go to Egypt, it may imply that Ḥasan

[16] This hesitancy on Mu'min's part looks like either a later pious insertion, or an early incident reinterpreted.

was ʿAbd al-Malik's representative there.[17] At any rate (at how many years older than seventeen we cannot tell), in about 1077 (469 H.) Ḥasan set off from Iṣfahân for Egypt, going a bit roundabout. First he went north into Adharbâyjân (still within ʿAbd al-Malik's territory); thence to Mayyâfâriqîn; whence he was chased out by the Qâḍî for publicly disputing the right of individuals – that is, other than the imâm – to interpret religion as did the Sunnî legists. At Damascus his way into Egypt was blocked by the activities of a Turkish captain; he went round therefore by sea, finally arriving in the city of the imâm in 1078, where he was greeted by high officials.

Nâṣir-i Khusraw (d. 1074) may have been motivated in his faith in part by the prosperity of the imâm's realms in Egypt and Syria.[18] The items most prominent in Ḥasan-i Ṣabbâḥ's Egyptian trip, on the contrary, have to do with Sunnî and Turkish power, and its disruption of Ismâʿîlî prosperity: Egypt had not long since recovered from the terrible crisis that preceded Badr's regime, and was even now threatened with an invading warlord at its threshold. There was room, accordingly, for the conception of a struggling faith, requiring fighting supporters. Always in Islâm the example of Mohammed, who from Madîna fought the Meccans as corrupters of the truth till he eventually made them yield, suggested readily that a reformer should take up arms. But the tendency to depend upon someone else's arms is also strong. A weak Egypt would not give comfort to such an easy hope, and might be expected to force a mind so inclined to an independent policy of direct assault in any manner possible against the enemy.

As to the question of Ḥasan's relation to Badr al-Jamâlî, from whose faction the whole Iranian daʿwa subsequently split in support of Nizâr, our sources bear evidence rather to the fact that other generations have asked the same question, than to any facts of the time itself. The general historian Ibn al-Athîr has Mustanṣir himself tell Ḥasan-i Ṣabbâḥ that the imâm was to be Nizâr.[19] In Ṭayyibî (anti-Nizârî) sources this story is given a partisan twist: Ḥasan-i Ṣabbâḥ asked the imâm Mustanṣir who should be the next imâm – and was told "Abû Manṣûr", a name of Nizâr; but not given the added explanation that the younger son, Mustaʿlî, was

[17] This injunction to go to the (Egyptian) court need not have been given right away; it was only years later that he actually went.

[18] *Safar Nâma*, trans. C. Schefer, *Relation du Voyage de Nassiri Chosrau* (Paris, 1881), pp. 127 ff. and 155, for the not overwhelming impression.

[19] ʿIzz ad-Dîn Ibn al-Athîr, ed. Carolus Johannes Tornberg, *Ibn-el-Athiri Chronicon quod perfectissimum inscribitur* (Upsala, 1864): referred to as the *Kâmil*: year 487.

to bear the same name.[20] The story Rashîd ad-Dîn has, evidently from later Nizârî sources, is far more detailed, but clearly legendary also. It has Ḥasan well-treated till he incurred Badr's jealousy on account of his support to Badr's enemy, Nizâr, and Mustanṣir's consequent praise of him; thereupon he was imprisoned by Badr, and expelled from the country. The one positive fact it gives us – by an otherwise inexplicable omission – is that Ḥasan-i Ṣabbâḥ apparently did not see Mustanṣir at all. Further, the question of Nizâr's being set aside from the succession had probably, as we shall see, not yet arisen. There remains, then, the fact that Ḥasan remained in Egypt for a year and a half in troubled times: we cannot even be sure that he opposed the ruling clique at the time.

Ḥasan serves in the Ismâʿîlî daʿwa (1081-1090).

Whether already at outs with the Egyptian regime or not, Ḥasan upon returning to Iṣfahân began a series of travels – in Yazd, Kirmân, Khûzistân, ʿIrâq ʿAjamî; these all being in western Îrân, and centers of Saljûq power. During the later 1080's he is represented as looking for a site to set up headquarters. A largescale action is evidently already planned. He had a great number of men at his orders scouting in all directions; but travelled also himself, especially in northwestern Îrân, where he had grown up.

The detailed itinerary of Ḥasan's travels shows how widespread was the daʿwa then.[21] That it was also becoming active is indicated by some notices in Ibn al-Athîr which seem to refer to this period. It was presumably during this time that the Ismâʿîlîs of Sâwa, not far from Rayy and Qumm, came to the notice of the authorities. Eighteen of them were arrested, in the time of the Sulṭân Malikshâh (d. 1092), for joining together in the Muslim festival prayers apart from the Sunnî inhabitants, and presumably praying them according to the Shîʿa rite; they were questioned and released. Subsequently they were reported to have murdered the local muezzin, who voices the call to prayer; allegedly to prevent his revealing their plans, which he had learned as a would-be convert. It seems

[20] This story is noted and refuted by A. A. A. Fyzee, ed., *Hidâyat al-Âmiriyya* (London, 1938), p. 15. Another Ṭayyibî version: from S. M. Stern, 'Epistle of the Fâṭimid Caliph Âmir,' *JRAS*, 1950, p. 20: in ʿAlî ibn Muḥammad ibn al-Walîd, *Majâlis an-Naskh wa-l-bayân*, Ḥasan-i Ṣabbâḥ was told by Mustanṣir he would find out "in due time".

[21] But Ḥasan's itinerary did not reach so far as Ibn al-Athîr's summary would have it – to Anatolia and Turkistân.

that Niẓâm al-Mulk personally insisted on the execution of Ṭâhir an-Najjâr (the carpenter) for the deed – the son of a public preacher.[22] Also before Alamût was taken, if Ibn al-Athîr is right, the Ismâʿîlî head of a fortress near Qâʾin raided a caravan, and the authorities in Qâʾin were defeated in their attempt to punish him. (To be sure, such raids by holders of fortresses were not unusual, and this one need not have been part of any larger activity.)[23]

The taking of Alamût (1090).

Meanwhile, Ḥasan settled upon Alamût as a likely fortress with which to begin. From Shahriyârkûh in Mâzandarân, south of the Caspian Sea, he directed the conversion of the garrison of Alamût in the neighboring province of Daylamân. Ḥusayn Qâʾinî, evidently from the subsequent Nizârî center Qâʾin in Quhistân in eastern Îrân, is credited with the actual conversion; when the garrison was prepared, Ḥasan was asked to go there personally – skirting Rayy, however, where already the agent of Niẓâm al-Mulk, Abû Muslim governor of the town, was set to look for him.[24]

As the story goes, the lord of the fortress, an ʿAlid and probally a Shîʿite anyway,[25] pretended to be converted to the doctrine which his garrison was so taken by, so as to find out and get rid of the Ismâʿîlîs; but he showed his hand too soon, and in the end was outtricked by the patience of Ḥasan and his followers. "He [Ḥasan] sent by small groups some of those who were with him to Alamût; [at last] he also came to Alamût. In those days an ʿAlid by the name of Mahdî held Alamût at the hands of Sulṭân Malikshâh. Ḥusayn Qâʾinî invited the ʿAlid [to accept the daʿwa]. A great many others in Alamût accepted his daʿwa, and the ʿAlid also said, with his tongue, I accept. But his heart did not agree with

[22] Ibn al-Athîr, *Kâmil* under the year 494; the carpenter's father was subsequently murdered, while in a sulṭân's service, by a mob which suspected him too of Ismâʿîlism. Ibn al-Jawzî has the first killing of Bâṭinîs by Jalâl ad-Dîn in the year 474 (*Islamic Culture*, Vol. IX, 1935, p. 555); this may refer to an actual persecution of Ismâʿîlîs, but is probably a misdating typical of Ibn al-Jawzî.

[23] Ibn al-Athîr, *Kâmil*, yr. 494; under the same year at the end (p. 221), he notes that in the time of Muqtadî (d. 1094) some people of ʿÂna on the Euphrates, known to have been Ismâʿîlîs, were arrested and released after questioning.

[24] This we have in Juwaynî, ed. M. Qazwînî, *Taʾrîkh-i Jahân-Gushâ*, III (Leiden, 1937).

[25] Ibn al-Jawzî, *Islamic Culture*, 1935, p. 555–6, says that the man who sold Alamût to Ḥasan-i Ṣabbâḥ had been suspected of Bâṭinism. This probably means he was a (Twelver) Shîʿite, for Ibn al-Jawzî tends to equate the two.

his tongue. He wanted to deceive anyone who had accepted the da'wa. He sent the comrades [who had joined the Ismâ'îlîs] down [from the fortress], and then shut the gate, saying, This is the property of the Sulṭân. Finally after much talk, he gave them admission into the fortress; but after that they did not follow his orders [to descend again].

"Our master [Ḥasan] sent the jurist Abû l-Qâṣim to Shâhkûh;[26] and Dihkhudâ Khusrawshâh also came, from Chinâshak.[27] Then our master came from Qazwîn by way of [two places] to Daylamân; he came from [a place][28] to Andijrûd, which adjoins Alamût, in Rajab of the year 483; and established himself there for a while. Because of his abounding abstinence and piety, a great number became his disciples and accepted his da'wa. Finally on the night of Wednesday the sixth of Rajab of the year 483, he came to the fortress of Alamût; and having given out his name as Dihkhudâ, he lived there secretly. Now in former times that place had been called Aluh Âmût – that is, the eagle's nest[29] – and by a strange and wonderful rare coincidence the letters of Aluh Âmût in the numerical reckoning[30] give the date of his ascent into Alamût, when they brought him into the fortress clandestinely. When the 'Alid Mahdî realized the situation, and had no choice, he was given leave [to go].

"As price of the fortress he [Ḥasan] wrote [a check for] three thousand dînârs in gold on the lord of Girdkûh and chief [ra'îs] of Dâmghân, Muẓaffar the comptroller, who had secretly accepted his da'wa. From extreme abstemiousness and piety, Ḥasan used to write very brief and summary notes; so much so that the following is the check: in a few lines and curves, he wrote: The Ra'îs Muẓaffar, God protect him, will pay the sum of three thousand dînârs as the price of the fortress of Alamût, to the 'Alid Mahdî – peace upon the Chosen Prophet and his family, 'and God

[26] A village in Rûdbâr, according to Qazwînî, Vol. III, p. 393.

[27] Near Astarâbâd, east of the Caspian, according to Qazwînî's footnote, Vol. III, p. 192.

[28] Juwaynî has three quite other names here, and I could not identify Rashîd ad-Dîn's from this mss.

[29] Although Huart, 'La Forteresse d'Alamût,' *Mémoires de la Société de Linguistique de Paris*, XV (1908–9), 130, seems to doubt the local Mâzandarânî origin of the explanation of "Aluh Âmût" as "eagle's teaching", yet since it is based on Mâzandarânî dialect it must be as local in origin as is the rival explanation, "eagle's *nest*". Nevertheless, I am inclined (if I had to bet) to guess that "eagle's nest" was as Huart says, contrary to Browne in the *History of Persian Literature*, the first meaning: for *âmût* as the rare word "nest" would surely be the lectio difficilior as compared with *âmût* as the common "taught", which latter would have been indeed a clever Ismâ'îlî variant for the seat of their da'wa!

[30] Each Arabic letter is given a numerical value – and the value of the sum of the letters in a word is the value of that word.

suffices us, He is an excellent guardian.'[31] The ʿAlid officer took this check, but he thought, The Ra'îs Muẓaffar is a great man, the deputy of Amîr Dâd Ḥabashî ibn Altûnṭâq; how will he give me anything upon the note of this obscure man? After a time, he landed at Dâmghân in straightened circumstances; he tried out that check with the Ra'îs Muẓaffar. Immediately [the Ra'îs] kissed the writing, and gave out the gold."[32]

According to Rashîd ad-Dîn himself, the Ra'îs Muẓaffar was not yet in Dâmghân or Gird Kûh at the time. Unless then his later post is mentioned merely by oversight, this story may be as fictitious as the story of the cowhide: as the Seventeenth Century *Dabistân* puts it, the disguised Ḥasan and the ʿAlid had a dispute in Alamût over the validity of a contract into the making of which deceit had entered, Ḥasan denying it was valid. As if to drive home his point, Ḥasan then persuaded the ʿAlid to sell him, for a large sum, as much land as could be included within a cowhide – and proceeded to cut the cowhide into strips which end to end enclosed the whole fortress. The ʿAlid by his own principle had to yield.[33]

Ḥasan-i Ṣabbâḥ's figure at Alamût (1090-1124).

Once in Alamût, Ḥasan stands out as a figure striking for his intensity and rigor. He is said to have remained continuously within his house, writing and directing operations – as it is always put, during all those years he went only twice out of his house, and twice onto the roof. At the end of his life, Rashîd ad-Dîn tells us, he hid his own fatal illness to the end. His most immediate operations were defensive – channeling water to the fields around Alamût; strengthening the stronghold; and alternately provisioning it, and holding it against the Saljûq power; yet meanwhile he helped to direct an uprising throughout the Saljûq realms, all from within his four walls. During a time of want he sent away his daughters, with their mother, to spin on a common basis with other women in a distant fortress; and did not bring them back. (It is said that this set a precedent: thereafter the Ismâʿîlî chiefs never had their womenfolk with them while executing military command – in consi-

[31] Koran III 173. Such pious phrases were essential to a letter, so neither detract from its brevity nor add to its piety. It is to be noted that some mss. of Juwaynî give an abbreviation for the name *Muẓaffar* – a proceeding which is quite rare, and proceeded more likely from precaution than from brevity.

[32] Rashîd ad-Dîn, mss. above mentioned, folio 294; I have checked with Qazwînî's edition of Juwaynî when this could clarify the mss. text – which was not always.

[33] *Dabistân-i Madhâhib*, written 1645, trans. A. Troyer and D. Shea (Paris 1843), p. 434. This is a motif of folklore.

derable contrast to common Muslim practice.) His sons he had executed one after the other: one on a charge of murder, which later is said to have proved false; the other on suspicion of drinking the forbidden wine.[34] His severity is supposed to have extended to a flute player who was irrevocably expelled – music being linked with dissoluteness in Muslim purism. When his followers wrote up a genealogy for him in the usual elegant style, he is said to have thrown it into the water, remarking that he would rather be the imâm's favored servant than his degenerate son.[35]

One is inclined to suspect that, in regard to his family, he may have leaned over backward to avoid any touch of nepotism; though one will hardly go so far as our good von Hammer: "Human nature is not naturally so diabolical, that the historian must, among several doubtful motives to an action, always decide for the worst; but, in the founder of this society of vice, the establisher of the murderous order of the Assassins, the most horrible is the most likely" – hence von Hammer supposes that Ḥasan's sons were killed less for the sake of a purist strictness, than in a deliberate effort to inculcate in the community a disregard of all natural bonds of affection![36] In any case, an intense and severe logic is undissociable from the figure of Ḥasan-i Ṣabbâḥ; and it characterizes above all his formal doctrine.

ḤASAN-I ṢABBÂḤ AND THE ISMÂʿÎLÎ TAʿLÎM

The leadership of Ibn ʿAṭṭâsh.

The Ismâʿîlîs of this time were not to be despised intellectually; they won the respect even of the Sunnî world. The less obviously Shîʿite works of Nâṣir-i Khusraw were long read by Sunnîs. Niẓâm al-Mulk is able to claim that all Shîʿites are Bâṭinîs (i.e., Ismâʿîlîs), and clever at discovering

[34] The first will have been on the occasion of the murder of Ḥusayn Qâ'inî in 1102, when Ḥusayn b. Ḥasan-i Ṣabbâḥ was made to appear implicated by an ʿAlid who was later killed when his fraud was discovered. The other son, Muḥammad, who drank, may have been punished on the basis of a rigorist ḥadîth which gives death as punishment for a repeated offense – a ḥadîth termed abrogated by the Sunnîs. At any rate, the death of each son seems to have been legal, even though in a very "Roman" sense of legality. (Mustawfî has the two killed for wine and fornication, instead.)

[35] Not necessarily his illegitimate son, as Defrémery, *JA*, ser. 5, XV (1860), 160 (but not Jourdain, from Mîrkhwând), translates it.

[36] Von Hammer, *History of the Assassins*, English translation, p. 72. Apart from the mentioned purist correctness of the penalties, one may note that Ḥasan's nephew, Abû 'l-Fatḥ, was put in charge of Ardahân.

devices to ingratiate themselves as clerks at court. Ibn al-Athîr[37] gives a eulogy of the abilities of Ḥasan-i Ṣabbâḥ in particular, but also of others.

It is therefore possible that Ḥasan-i Ṣabbâḥ did not invent the cogent presentation of taʿlîm here described. Quite apart from the possibility of its appearing among the manifold approaches to be found within earlier Ismâʿîlism (but it was not at any rate prominent there), one wonders whether it was taken over from ʿAbd al-Malik ibn ʿAṭṭâsh, perhaps rendered by Ḥasan from Arabic into the more popular Persian.

This for two reasons: Ḥasan on the one hand records no time, in his own experience, of utter doubt (like Ghazzâlî's) which might generate such an inverted pyrrhonism. On the other hand, Ibn ʿAṭṭâsh must have been a remarkable man on his own account. He was head of the Nizârî community in its germinal period. He converted so stout a man as the Ra'îs Muẓaffar – according to Rashîd ad-Dîn – and gave to Ḥasan-i Ṣabbâḥ his high role in the daʿwa. He won praise from the Sunnîs as a learned man, and so impressed his own community that his son (according to Ibn al-Athîr a much inferior man) succeeded him.[38]

The germinal period, which he dominated, seems to have produced a single attitude politically throughout the Ismâʿîlîs – the seizure of fortresses – which cannot be attributed with assurance to Ḥasan-i Ṣabbâḥ; for he was not alone in coming back from Egypt to such activity. It is likely that there was also a common doctrinal approach then; and Ghazzâlî, indeed, seems to be thinking of a group of expounders of the new doctrine, when he mentions it, though that was just at the time when Ḥasan was becoming known.[39] Nevertheless, Ḥasan certainly adopted the doctrine zealously, and it is with his work that it came to be associated.[40]

The Shîʿite doctrine of taʿlîm.

A fundamental doctrine of the Shîʿa was that Muslims had no right to choose for themselves in matters of religion – *ikhtiyâr* – but must accept

[37] Year 494, *Kâmil*. It is possible that we possess one of Ḥasan-î Ṣabbâḥ's works in Shahrastânî's discussion of the Ṣâbi'a. Cf. Appendix III apud Ḥasan-i Ṣabbâh.

[38] Cf. Ibn al-Athîr, *Kâmil*, year 500.

[39] Goldziher, *Streitschrift*, p. 18; he notes also the several Sunnî authors who had been dealing with the new doctrine, evidently for some time already; but (p. 12) he supposes that the new emphasis did not appear before 1090 C.E.

[40] In addition to its ascription to him by Shahrastânî & Juwaynî-Rashîd ad-Dîn, and the references in the *Rawḍat at-Taslîm* and the *Kalâm-i Pîr*, the doctrine is referred to in the *Dabistân*, in Fakhr ad-Dîn Râzî, and in Abû Muḥammad al-ʿIrâqî (*Firaq* – Istanbul, Sulaymâniyya MS nr. 791; I must thank Prof. Tietze of Istanbul for securing a photostat of it for me).

everything on the basis of the proper authority. This was the doctrine of *taʿlîm*, authoritative teaching; the imâm, of course, was the teacher. The Shîʿites always blamed the Sunnîs for having neglected this principle at the start of Islamic history. The Shîʿites reasoned that men are in no position to judge of the things of God; why else had a Prophet been sent at all? As all agreed, only the authority which the Prophet had from God could suffice to order the foundation of Islâm. But, said the Shîʿites, if the foundation of Islâm required a teacher sent from God, how can Islâm be maintained on a different principle? The same human ignorance which made it necessary that a prophet be sent to found religion in the first place, made it necessary that God should likewise choose and send men to preserve the religion after it was founded, from generation to generation.

But the Sunnîs claimed that the head of the community after Mohammed was not chosen by God, but by the Muslims themselves. They justified the succession of Abû Bakr and ʿUmar to the Caliphate by the doctrine of election by the community. The Shîʿites claimed this was absurd; that it was inconceivable that God should not have been equally explicit about the successor to the Prophet as about the Prophet himself. They could be sure a priori that someone or other was designated – and who but ʿAlî? For the claim was made for no-one else. The Shîʿites felt they had here a very logical proof of the imâmate of ʿAlî, and his family: one had to suppose that God had chosen some imâm or other; but no-one claimed anyone else than ʿAlî to be the divinely chosen imâm. Therefore ʿAlî had undisputed title to the office. In pretending they could select a Caliph by their own choice, the Sunnîs had acted contrary to evident reason, as well as explicit revelation – (for the Shîʿites soon convinced themselves that Mohammed must have explicitly named ʿAlî as his successor in power).

The Shîʿites carried out this doctrine into the whole range of *ʿilm*, religious knowledge: first the person in authority was authoritatively named – Mohammed naming the first imâm and then each imâm naming in turn his own successor. Then all disputed questions were to be settled by the decision of this authoritative person. The early Shîʿites despised the idea of *raʾy* and *qiyâs*, of arguing by analogy, as Sunnîs admitted they were willing to do. The ʿilm came not by raʾy and qiyâs, but by *taʿlîm*, by authoritative teaching. It was this doctrine of taʿlîm which was especially developed by Ḥasan-i Ṣabbâh; he turned it into a sharp intellectual tool in keeping with his whole life and demeanor.

Ḥasan's critique of the doctrine of ta'lîm.

Shahrastânî presents as the main writing of Ḥasan (under the title of the *Fuṣûl Arba'a* – the *Four Chapters*) a series of four propositions in the form of a critique of the doctrine of ta'lîm.[41] We have been warned that Ḥasan was very laconic; even so, Shahrastânî gives us only extracts, which must be understood in the light of other items provided by himself and others. Ḥasan's incisive intellect had no patience for the nuances of unverbalized experience. He gladly accepted the unconditional abstract reasoning of his time, allowing no mere approximations to truth from complementary standpoints in experience. The first proposition is designed to eliminate rationalism – the doctrine of the Philosophers that the individual human reason is the ultimate authority, and adequate to give men the desired absolute truth about God. Either one needs a teacher to know God, or not; but if not, then one cannot prefer one's own speculations to another's – for the denial of another's views is an implicit teaching of him. But in fact men's views on this point are irreconcilably diverse. Accordingly, to maintain any one view means to accept a teacher, an authority – if only oneself. This is a proposition in fact readily acceptable to Muslims, Sunnî or Shî'ite; both admit the need for authority in religion. For Ḥasan-i Ṣabbâḥ, it is merely preliminary.

The next two propositions show that both Sunnî and Shî'ite positions fall to the ground by the same principle they approve as used against the Philosophers. Second, against the egalitarianism of the Sunnî legists; who (in any one generation) must convey their tradition through many men, no one of whom could claim in himself more authority than the most heretical teacher. Either the teacher must be authoritative, he says, or any teacher will do. Clearly, the latter alternative leads us back where we were to start with – it gives no basis for supporting one teacher against another. There must be a single arbiter, the authoritative imâm, as the Shî'ites always claimed. But the crux comes in the third point, where he destroys the traditional Shî'ite version of ta'lîm, likewise. Either the authority of the teacher must be demonstrated, or any teacher must be accepted as authoritative. But in the latter case we are brought back to our starting point; whereas in the former case, how are we to demon-

[41] See the translation in Appendix II. Juwaynî, trans. Defrémery, *JA*, ser. 5, XV (1860), 169, appears to refer to the same as the *Ilzâm*, the *Compeller*: but in Rashîd ad-Dîn compulsion appears only as its purpose, not its name. Though Juwaynî spends some time in refutation, neither of these is as full or as clear as Shahrastânî, though evidently at least in part independent of him.

strate the authority of a teacher without some further authority for our demonstration? Thus the Shîʿites find themselves in as bad a position as the Sunnîs – or the Philosophers.

The fourth proposition then is an attempt to solve this pyrrhonistic dilemma by reformulating the whole question; and to reformulate it in such a way as to show that his own Ismâʿîlî imâm must be the true one. He begins by noting that in spite of its apparent weakness, the Shîʿite position must be the true one – for the knowledge of God, men must have one authoritative imâm. (Provided one assumes that an absolute truth must be available, as men did then, this seems inevitable.) Now this position is possible: but only if one recognizes a dialectical principle in the nature of knowledge. Opposites can only be known through each other. Thus the Aristotelian Necessary is known only by juxtaposition with the Possible; yet on the other hand, the Possible in turn, in its limitations – how merely possible it is – is known only by juxtaposition with the Necessary. Or to take a more telling example for Muslims – the *shahâda*, the formula of witness to the Muslim faith, has the same character. It is in two parts – the *lâ ilâha*, "there is no god"; and the *illâ Allâh* – "except God". Neither, he points out, is intelligible without the other. The *lâ ilâha* by itself is certainly false; the *illâ Allâh* is meaningless. For only when we see the One God as in contrast to the conception of many godlings do we realize the meaning of the conception of *Allâh* itself.[42]

But then not only is the *lâ ilâha* and *illâ Allâh* a dialectical statement. The fuller form of the shahâda, which goes on to add *muḥammad rasûl Allâh*, "Mohammed is the prophet of God", exemplifies the same thing. Here again the two parts are incomprehensible except in juxtaposition. For it makes no sense to speak of the "prophet", unless you have some conception of the God he is prophet of; but on the other hand, our notion of God, Allâh, is but words even at best, until He is revealed through the Prophet. It is (roughly speaking) a case of hen and egg – you can't begin with either one by itself.[43]

Now to come back to the fourth proposition. This dialectic theory of knowledge being accepted, Ḥasan suggests that the dilemma of taʿlîm

[42] L. Massignon has made much of this point in a different connection, in his *Hallaj: La Passion d'al-Hosayn-ibn-Mansour al-Hallaj* (Paris, 1922), p. 789.

[43] To judge by Shahrastânî's generalization, one might fancy that Ḥasan had developed a general epistemology recognizing the dependence of knowledge on the standpoint of the observer, and at the same time allowing for a recognition of the dependence of the observer's knowledge on the thing observed. Shahrastânî says that in all questions Ḥasan returned to the conjunction of the knower and the known. But his point was probably very specialized.

can be solved if one recognizes that also in the case of reason and the imâm a dialectic prevails. Without the imâm, the results of reason are unintelligible; – this we see already in the first two propositions, and the negative results they bring us to. Yet likewise, as we see from the third proposition, without reason the imâm is unintelligible: reason is required to demonstrate who is the imâm. We seem to be deadlocked. But if we put the two together, Ḥasan seems to say, we can see that our reason leads us to recognize our *need* of the imâm, *in toto* – without however by itself leading us to the imâm; while then recognition of the *imâm* makes clear the nature in detail of the need for the imâm, itself, and of all other knowledge. Without the imâm, reason leads to a blank wall. Without reason, the imâm rests unproven, and so unknown. But here is the reasoning, said Ḥasan, and here is the imâm who teaches it: the two together are impregnable. Thus the fourth point shows how the dilemma we are led to in the third point is solved – how ta'lîm is after all possible.

But the fourth point implies something else, which greatly irritated both Ghazzâlî and Shahrastânî. The only true imâm must be that imâm who depends on this dialectical process for his demonstration. Any imâm who seeks a proof in lineage or in miracles or what not is obviously a pseudo-imâm: for any such proofs require recourse to a self-sufficient reason able to judge the imâm himself – as noted in the third proposition. In contrast, Ḥasan had taken up another old Shî'a position, and given it a new seriousness – the imâm is *ḥujja*, is proof of God. That is, the imâm is himself the proof – in his very being. The proof of Ḥasan's imâm is not extrinsic to the imâm, but consists in the logical position of the imâm himself. The very nature of his claims are their own proof. He offers himself as fulfilling and in turn making intelligible the need of men for an imâm, which is up against a blank wall until the imâm presents himself in this particular logical relationship, and by his existence makes everything clear. Therefore, Ḥasan, speaking for his imâm Mustanṣir, could insist that his imâm was the only one claiming to be *his own proof* – and therefore must be accepted, for lack of any other claimant to fulfill the logical necessity. To his critics, Ḥasan seemed to be saying, My imâm is true because he says he is true!

The role of reason in reaching universal validity.

This is the doctrine of ta'lîm as it was disciplined in Ḥasan's hands to a desperately ultimate basis for the whole Ismâ'ìlî da'wa. It is elusive –

only occasionally, and with the aspect of a task that must be gotten through, does it reappear in later Nizârî writings[44] – and almost precious; but the smack of cleverness that one is left with is to a degree removed when the same position is arrived at in other ways, differing from this and yet in harmony with it.

Ḥasan did not restrict himself to one path to his central truth; the dialectical conception of knowledge could be used in several ways to this end. For instance, one could extend the process begun in analyzing the *lâ ilâha illâ Allâh.* One requires the recognition of the Prophet for the intelligibility of the *Tawḥîd*, of the declaration about God. But then similarly the whole declaration *No god but God and Mohammed is his Prophet*, is inadequate by itself. For Mohammed died long ago, we have no direct contact with him – to us this is only transmitted words: unless we have a living imâm to witness to the Prophet.[45] Hence the Sunnîs were both right and wrong in complaining that when Ḥasan's followers limited themselves (in discussing God) to saying, We believe in the God of Mohammed – that actually all they meant was not God at all, but the imâm. The critics were right, in that this seemingly cautious, innocent, and ultra-orthodox way of referring to God actually implied, logically, that the only direct object of knowledge was Mohammed – and therefore in our days the imâm who represents Mohammed. They were wrong in supposing however that the imâm was to be "known" apart from the actual God of Mohammed. The dialectic works both ways, and if the knowledge of God depends on the imâm so does the expectation of an imâm, at the same time, depend on seeking knowledge of God. Both halves of the proposition are equally real and necessary.

On the same basis Ḥasan could maintain that he was supported by the proposition that plurality indicates the false, unity the true. For there are many who claim all external sorts of proofs – whether of an imâm or of a set of learned 'ulamâ'; which external proofs must vary even within each party. But the party of the imâm must in the nature of the case always be one, depending on his unique and unmediated authority. There seems to have been no end to the demonstrations Ḥasan could make of the validity of his conception of ta'lîm – all of them converging

[44] Cf. especially Ṭûsî, *Rawḍat at-Taslîm*, pp. 118/173, perhaps also pp. 104–5/155; also, *Kalâm-i Pîr*, p. 8/13.

[45] Nâṣir-i Khusraw, *Wajh-i Dîn*, p. 68, comments that the shahâda, the phrase of witness, being about unknown things, demands a guarantor: whence the necessity of the imâm. It is a long step from this external sort of guaranteeing an independent truth, to Ḥasan-i Ṣabbâh's insistence that the guarantee is an inseparable aspect of that truth.

to the same point. (As Shahrastânî pointed out, what his case finally amounts to every time, is that he has an imâm, and others don't; a rather unfair way of putting it.) And all of Ḥasan's statements were provocative and to a high degree annoying to a generation which had to assume, with him, that there was one absolute truth about God, which men must above all try to reach.

Accordingly, reason has a genuine role here, but a limited one: our reasons indicate to us only our desperate need: if we are utterly honest with ourselves, we cannot rest until we find that authority which by its very recognition of the desperation of our need itself fulfills it. All the religions that attempt to rely upon extraneous proofs instead are really rationalizations – for if we are truly honest, Ḥasan implies, we would admit that one proof requires another; it is only this negative fact that is given us by our reasons, and even it is rather a need than a knowledge; but it is strictly necessary.

This doctrine of taʿlîm reflects the desperate search for finality which is the theme of all Ismâʿîlî biography. But its attitude to reason, as to all things human, is so radical, and assumes a logical consistency so pitiless, that only an overwhelmingly single-minded earnestness could accept the role it gives to reason at face value and draw its last conclusions. On the one hand, it presupposes an uncompromising scepticism, which seeks out the fallacies in any ultimate construction rising beyond common experience; on the other hand, it presupposes a consuming concentration upon just such ultimate truths, ultimate obligations, which is as unsatisfied with petty conventional justifications for living as it is with fallacious pretensions to knowledge. Ḥasan-i Ṣabbâḥ put the full drive of his soul into that demand for absolute universal validity which had been at the center of the rise of Islâm, and which had received particular expression in the occult rationalism of the Ismâʿîlîs. It was not his fault, but that of truth itself, that the result was paradox.

The dehistoricized, absolute imâmate.

The imâm figure which resulted from this dialectic was quite outside of any developing fabric of history and experience. Already in Ismâʿîlism history had become a matter of recurrent types; like the Ismâʿîlî rationalism, this was pressed to its extreme conclusion by Ḥasan. Juwaynî complains of the cavalier way in which Ḥasan (having reduced all dogmatic history to a dialectical series of assertions dependent upon the current imâm) proceeds to use the traditional conceptions to a hollow purpose. Ḥasan notes that the Sunnî idea of *ijmâʿ* – the doctrine that the community of Mohammed can never be left wholly in error – implies that somewhere in the community the truth must be available; but the others have been proved wrong; therefore the truth must remain with Ḥasan, by the Sunnîs' own doctrine.[46] Such an assertion, of course, presupposes a very different ijmâʿ from what the Sunnîs have in mind. They think in terms of continuity of historical tradition; he uses the notion merely to bolster the assumption, needful for his proofs, that the truth must somewhere exist. Ḥasan's ijmâʿ is, typically, a logical, not a historical concept. Hence Juwaynî's plaintive warning that Ḥasan had best not argue from his opponents' position is futile.[47] Ḥasan manipulates the name of Mohammed in the same cavalier way as the idea of ijmâʿ. Ḥasan can go so far in capturing historical terms for his own purposes, that when asked of God, he can logically say that he means the God of Mohammed – an exasperatingly unimpeachable way of speaking. In the end, as we have seen, this amounts to saying that he means the God of the imâm; Mohammed is merely a link in the logical chain.

It is this logic that gives its special harsh inevitability to Ḥasan's insistence that the ḥadîth tradition of jihâd (imposing on Mohammed the duty to fight men until they admit the unity of God) implies that they must receive this teaching only from Mohammed – or the imâm –; not be allowed to find it themselves. For Ḥasan insists that there can be no true idea of the unity of God apart from Mohammed – and therefore the imâm. It is on the imâm the accent always falls. Despite Ḥasan's dialectic, then, we receive the psychological impression that it is finally not the rational content of the imâm's truth that Ḥasan is interested in, but his sheer authority. The imâm, as Shahrastânî complains, does not guarantee any inherent rationality of doctrine about the world; he guarantees only himself.

It is not surprising, then, that Ḥasan insists that each imâm is absolutely autonomous, not bound by the decisions of any previous imâm on any sort of matter.[48] Truth, itself, seems to be the function of a man's lifetime. Typical of the changed emphasis is the tendency that grows henceforward

46 Perhaps another distinctively Sunnî doctrine is similarly manipulated in Ṭûsî's use of the ḥadîth "disagreement in my community is a blessing". He implies it is a blessing in that it forces men to seek out the authoritative imâm. *Rawḍat at-Taslîm*, p. 102. This kind of dispute, incidentally, underlines the fact that it was against the Sunnîs, rather than merely against other Shîʿites, that Nizârî efforts were directed from the first.

47 Qazwînî ed. p. 197.

48 *Rawḍat at-Taslîm*, ps. 118–119 (174).

to replace the word *da'wa*, with its implications of a fixed body of doctrine, by *ta'lîm*, emphasizing the untramelled will of the authority.

Authoritarian community policy.

Ḥasan states that unity is the test of truth, multiplicity of error. What deeper psychological necessities this emphasis upon a total group devotion may have implied in Ḥasan and his followers I will not profess to discuss. Ismâ'îlism, with its schematized past, had always had its pivot in the future: the coming imâm or the coming victory. In the face of stagnation, the center of meaningfulness must be divorced more than ever from the past, the community resources must be mustered totally for a struggle starting as if from scratch. The watchword is *power*: Ḥasan seems to turn in upon the movement, the community, for its own sake, as indeed often happens in war. All thinking and all hoping must be directed to the community power.

This required no drastic changes. The movement had from the start been secret and conspiratorial, except where victorious as in Egypt; conspiratorial it continued to be. The older Ismâ'îlî sharî'a continued in force, to guide the formal life of the community. The bâṭin, the doctrine of the ḥudûd, was not dropped – though possibly some of the Fâṭimid philosophical speculations associated with the ḥudûd may have been frowned on in the more rigorous mood.[49]

Shahrastânî says that Ḥasan was cautious in permitting even the learned to read Philosophy; and that he denied this to the untutored altogether. This would refer at most to an intensification of the usual Ismâ'îlî care to develop the understanding by degrees; certainly Philosophical pursuits persisted – Ḥasan himself had the reputation of a

[49] Just at what points the various changes which distinguished the later Nizârîs from the Ṭayyibîs entered is debatable. Most of them, doctrinally, seem to date from the Qiyâma and what followed – as we shall see; so far as we know Ḥasan-i Ṣabbâḥ, he accepts the traditional bâṭin. Ghazzâlî (Goldziher, p. 44) says the new Ismâ'îlîs rejected the theory of the sâbiq and tâlî – the first and second cosmic principles; this may mean that they reject the philosophy itself – there is little trace of it later – or that they reject the Sunnî dualistic interpretation thereof. It is also to be noted that Ghazzâlî reports such "popular" notions as reincarnation, which indeed does appear later. But it is doubtful if at this time there was more official sanction for reincarnation among the Nizârîs than there had been with the Fâṭimids, or than there was according to Ghazzâlî's own report for the other "popular" idea that the sharî'a was not obligatory. Perhaps, however, such ideas were already showing the relative strength among the Nizârîs which eventually won them an established position which they did not gain among the Ṭayyibîs.

mathematician and an alchemist. But though the Ismâ'îlî structure as a whole did not outwardly change much, it is appropriate (we cannot say how exact) that Ḥasan is always associated with one new institution in particular: the duty of the *fidâ'î*, the devoted assassin; who replaced, as emissary to kings, the older dâ'î who had so often appeared in court with his fund of esoteric lore.

Ḥasan-i Ṣabbâḥ sought for universal validity in the authority of an imâm whose claims were validated by a devastating scepticism of any more conditional claims – an absolute imâm, with a validity outside of any considerations of experience or history: even the typological history generally admitted by Ismâ'îlism. Nothing was left any independent meaning save the power drive of the one community which dared to accept so ultimate a position. Such is in summary the philosophical position distinctive of the emergent Nizârî community.

This position was distinctive of the community; yet probably not quite typical of it. It was the stated position of Ḥasan-i Ṣabbâḥ, and presumably the ideal of the community to the degree that such leadership was accepted. It is as genuine a development of the Ismâ'îlî tradition, in terms of an intensive personality such as is sketched for Ḥasan, as is the urbane mildness of al-Mu'ayyad fî d-dîn, who corresponded curiously upon the ethics of vegetarianism in the prosperous days of Fâṭimid expansion. But it is a saving grace among us that we balk at an overconsistency, lest we overlook something not yet grasped in words; if such irrational stubbornness irks a reformer, the corresponding hardheaded caution may confound the demagog. Ḥasan-i Ṣabbâḥ, with his purist self-denial, might dread the corruption of drink or the frivolity of music, and exiling his very family shut himself up in single-minded devotion to the negation and the utter reversal of the course of Islamic history. The Nizârî temper at large, we may be sure, remained heavily larded with the zest of personal discovery, or the sense of legitimist or hierarchical good order, which had characterized Ismâ'îlism already.

CHAPTER III

THE NIZÂRÎ REVOLT

THE NIZÂRÎ SCHISM FROM THE FÂṬIMID GOVERNMENT (1094)

The succession dispute between Nizâr and Mustaʿlî.

Alamût was barely taken, the rising against the Saljûqs barely under way, when the Iranian Ismâʿîlîs were forced by events in Egypt to undertake an independent career without the shelter of the Fâṭimid connection – to test, as a separate sect, their newly developed outlook.

Alamût was seized in 1090; two years later the Sulṭân Malikshâh was dead, and the Saljûq power was broken up into quarreling pieces; then in 1094 the imâm Mustanṣir died and his sons disputed the imâmate. The Iranian Ismâʿîlîs were fully in the midst of their farflung uprisings when in 1095 Nizâr, whom one gathers they had supported for the Egyptian throne, was defeated. As it became clear within a few years that the Egyptian daʿwa was to remain in the hands of Nizâr's opponents, these newly militant Ismâʿîlîs of the outlands were faced with the alternatives of reconciliation or schism.

The succession dispute was settled within Egypt, and there is little indication that, taken in itself, it had much religious significance either in its origin or in its development. To be sure the episode is very obscure in its sectarian aspects. The Sunnî historians treated it as a purely secular affair; the Ṭayyibîs, of course, confined themselves to showing the illegitimacy of Nizâr's claims on purely formal grounds; and the Nizârîs are very short on history.[1] Nevertheless, the Nizârîs did not show the succession dispute to be their chief concern.

[1] Nuwayrî, translated in Ibn Khallikân s.v. "Mustaʿlî," and Ibn al-Athîr are the standard Sunnî historians; for a comparison of the similar Ṭayyibî and Sunnî reports see the introduction by Fyzee to the *Hidâyat al-Âmiriyya*; and 'Mustaʿlî,' and 'Nizâr,' *Encyclopedia of Islam*.

Nizâr's right to the Egytian succession by sectarian principles was very strong. The Sunnî historians assume him to have been designated heir-apparent. This "first naṣṣ" would clearly give him claim to Ismâʿîlî allegiance against any later nominee on the analogy of Ismâʿîl himself, whose claim could not be set aside for his brother Mûsâ.[2] The opposing party could at most allege a deathbed designation of another of Mustanṣir's sons, Mustaʿlî; a second naṣṣ of very dubious standing. The Ṭayyibî tradition evidently did not dispute the first naṣṣ of Nizâr, but tried to deny its genuineness as an expression of Mustanṣir's will. The indications assembled in the *Hidâya* of Âmir, however, which is the earliest and clearly the frankest of such attempts which we have, are so minute – the seating order at a certain banquet, a later confession of Nizâr's sister, analogy with a dubious precedent – that they attest as much to the impotence of the defense as to the contemporary character of the document.[3]

Motivation for the schism.

Shortly before Mustanṣir's death, Badr's son Afḍal had succeeded to Badr's ruling position. By marrying Mustaʿlî to his daughter, Badr had planned to make this younger, more pliable son, succeed rather than the mature Nizâr; Mustaʿlî, as imâm, would continue in dependence upon Afḍal, and the realm retain its prosperous stability. Afḍal carried out the plan. Upon learning of the elevation of Mustaʿlî on Mustanṣir's death, Nizâr fled directly. He turned to Alexandria, which had been the center of strength of the military factions which Badr had suppressed; to the Turk Iftigîn, and to Arab supporters.[4] Nizâr was, however, defeated; when he was brought back to Cairo and imprisoned, the revolt was at an

[2] Already Nawbakhtî noted that the Ismâʿîlîs denied that after Ḥasan and Ḥusayn the naṣṣ could pass from brother to brother (that is, from Ismâʿîl to Mûsâ); and so carried it on to Ismâʿîl's son, when Ismâʿîl died before his father. (The Twelvers, who followed Mûsâ, alleged that their father Jaʿfar had withdrawn the naṣṣ from Ismâʿîl to Mûsâ, because of Ismâʿîl's immorality. But it should be noted that such a withdrawal was evidently not historical.) But actually the problem seems to have played no great role in Ismâʿîlî thought.

[3] This was a letter from Mustaʿlî's son designed to defend Mustaʿlî's claims against the Nizârîs. Unpublished letters from Mustaʿlî himself to the daʿwa of Yaman on the subject of Nizâr's rebellion might well yield more details than this diatribe of Mustaʿlî's son Âmir. H. G. Al-Hamdani, 'The Letters of al-Mustanṣir bi'llah,' *BSOS*, VII (1933–5), 307, letter 43. Cf. also: S. M. Stern, 'Epistle of the Fâṭimid Caliph Âmir,' *JRAS*, 1950, p. 20.

[4] Nizâr also got the support of the Alexandrian Qâḍî (Ibn al-Athîr, *Kâmil* yr. 487).

end. No outraged Ismâʿîlî conscience seems to have been aroused to action. Though there were later Nizârid claimants, they are not connected with foreign or local Nizârîs; and none of his known sons or grandsons appeared even as a figurehead for the Nizârî cause.[5]

All this suggests that a personal attachment on the part of the Iranians to Nizâr and his family was not the prime mover of the Nizârî schism. Nor does the Iranian preference for Nizâr seem to have been due to any internal class division. All types of Ismâʿîlîs must have joined together in the new militancy; artisan names turn up repeatedly, while Ḥasan-i Ṣabbâḥ, ʿAbd al-Malik ibn ʿAṭṭâsh, and the Ra'îs Muẓaffar were educated intellectuals. Niẓâm al-Mulk accused all followers of the Shîʿa of being Ismâʿîlîs, in his time, and of occupying high government posts; and his sincerity in noting that it was therefore dangerous to speak ill of them may be attested by his refusal to mention any instances more recent than a century before in his castigation of Ismâʿîlîs in his *Siyâsat Nâma.*[6] Nor is any sense of doctrinal innovation likely to have been enough, at least alone, to account for the schism. Although the new emphasis on taʿlîm must have been prominent for some years before, as we have noted, one can only conjecture whether it was a point of controversy. Âmir goes so far as to accuse the Nizârîs of belief in free personal choice of doctrine, *ikhtiyâr*, rather than of too much emphasis on the reverse. (That is, he accuses them of making their own choice of who should be imâm.)[7]

Nevertheless, there was clearly a sense of independence among the Iranian Ismâʿîlîs. The idea of a new as against an old daʿwa seems to emanate from Nizârî circles – at least Juwaynî claims so, and later Nizârî tradition insists that a new development began with Ḥasan-i Ṣabbâḥ.[8] It is not clear whether this distinction between Ḥasan's emphasis on taʿlîm and the older emphasis on cosmology, a distinction which Shahrastânî and Ghazzâlî reflect, is to be identified with the division which Abû l-Maʿâlî (wrote about 1092) makes between the "two sects" of *Ṣabbâḥiyya* and *Nâṣiriyya*, followers of Ḥasan-i Ṣabbâḥ and of Nâṣir-i Khusraw. For not enough is said about the Nâṣirriyya to show that they were other than a local conservative grouping in the upper Oxus region – as they

[5] This we learn from the *Hidâyat al-Âmiriyya.*

[6] Ed. and trans. C. Schefer, *Siyâsat Nâmeh* (2 vols.; Paris, 1891–7). Ibn Ḥazm was likewise chary of mentioning the heresy of the contemporary Fâṭimid regime except through an attack on its founder. Israel Friedlander, 'The Heterodoxies of the Shiites,' *JAOS*, XXVIII, Part 1 (1907), 69. Râwandi trumps up a like charge against the Shîʿa later, *JRAS*, 1902, ps. 572 ff., 880; ed. p. 395.

[7] Fyzee, *Hidâyat al-Âmiriyya*, p. 8.

[8] I refer to his identification with the *Qiyâma*, as blowing the first trumpet of the new dispensation.

are today – near to which Abû l-Ma'âlî probably lived (in Ghazna).[9] Yet that either distinction should be made indicates a substantial development proceeding outside of Egypt, and without any very urgent reference to Egypt for its authorization. After all, the Egyptian power, as such, had ceased to expand; while quite on their own the Ismâ'îlîs of the Saljûq realms were making great strides; why should they feel a need for Egyptian domination? They could afford to look coldly on Musta'lî's dubious claims. Even the Ismâ'îlîs of the Yaman, who rejected the Nizârî position, were to cut their relations with the Egyptian regime in the next generation.

No doubt, furthermore, there was a resentment at the foreign, military, and conservative domination represented in particular by Badr al-Jamâlî, who was not only military ruler of Egypt, but supreme head of the da'wa.[10] The troops who gave him his power were largely Turkish, like the Saljûqs themselves; and the Ismâ'îlîs may have had a particular dislike of the Turkish soldiery that then dominated the Middle East – we find Ḥasan-i Ṣabbâḥ calling them jinn and not men![11] In any case, a suggestion of the strength of the resentment against Badr is to be found in the story the Nizârîs told later of Ḥasan's relations with him.[12] Badr, as generalissimo, is represented as almost ignoring the will of Mustanṣir. Ḥasan is not permitted to see the imâm, and when Mustanṣir nevertheless speaks highly of Ḥasan, Badr objects; Mustanṣir has to allow Ḥasan's imprisonment. When Mustanṣir's excellence, or Ḥasan's, occasions miraculous intervention (the fall of a tower of the prison), it is determined to send Ḥasan away by ship to the west. But Mustanṣir has foreseen this also, and warned Ḥasan of a storm which then comes and drives the ship back to the east – whence Ḥasan proceeds on his mission in Îrân. A most characteristic note: when Ḥasan is threatened with prison it is precisely

[9] Abû l-Ma'âlî's distinction, apparently reflected by later writers, as Ibn ad-dâ'î ar-Râzî and Fakhr ad-Dîn Râzî, does not necessarily imply a continued general division. Fakhr ad-Dîn explicitly includes the Fâṭimid authors in the Ṣabbâḥiyya. Accordingly, we can suppose that in his mind, at least, the Ṣabbâḥiyya is not a name for the "Nizârîs before Nizâr", but for the Ismâ'îlîs generally.

[10] Ibn aṣ-Ṣayrafî, *al-Ishâra*, in *Bull. de l'Institut français d'archéologie orientale*, vol. 25 (Cairo, 1925), p. 57.

[11] In the *Haft Bâb-i Bâbâ Sayyid-nâ.* (Badr himself, incidentally, was Armenian.) Ivanow in his review of Gordlevski's history of the Saljûqs of Anatolia, *JBBRAS*, XXII (1946), 68–70, emphasizes the great interest in Ismâ'îlism on the part of the Turks there which he believes Gordlevski has shown. Few of the accusations of Ismâ'îlism which are cited there, however, seem at all likely; and in any case Gordlevski seems to give almost no details on the matter. Generally one finds among the Ismâ'îlîs names of Arabs, Persians, and at least one Kurd ('Alî ibn Wafâ, who replaced Bahrâm at Damascus, according to Cahen, *Syrie du Nord*, pp. 347 ff.); but no Turks.

[12] In Rashîd ad-Din, already referred to following the passage we have translated.

men from Daylamân who come to his assistance. A very real original resentment has here taken a legendary form in the minds of the jealously independent mountaineers.[13]

Justification for the schism: the problem of a figurehead.

For some such reasons the Ismâʿîlîs of Îrân, and many others, were loath to accept as imâm the nominee of the generalissimo. For a while, after he was defeated, they could maintain that even in a dungeon Nizâr was the rightful imâm. But sooner or later when Nizâr was dead and no son rose to claim their allegiance in his place, the Nizârîs believing at least as much as all Ismâʿîlîs that a present imâm was essential to the faith, must explain who and where was their imâm.

The commonest idea seems to be that a son of Nizâr – the posthumous son of a concubine, as it is generally said – was carried away to Alamût and kept there secretly. The epistle of Âmir ridicules precisely this idea;[14] the later form of oaths administered to Nizârîs in Egypt presupposes it;[15] the later explanations of the imâmate of Ḥasan II at Alamût make use of it. Abû Muḥammad al-ʿIrâqî, who was surely writing soon after the taking of Alamût, said there was supposed to be an imâm at Alamût – unnamed, as in other cases also.[16]

On the other hand, Ḥasan-i Ṣabbâḥ and his successors do not seem to have claimed access to any such hidden imâm. Rashîd ad-Dîn and Juwaynî make no reference to one. The less reliable Ibn Muyassar has Ḥasan (but only on his death-bed at that) introduce to his successors a child as their lord; where Juwaynî has him commending the community

[13] To be sure, the schism might have resulted from a personal quarrel between Ḥasan and Afḍal, or from an attempt by Afḍal or Badr to dominate the Iranian daʿwa. We have no evidence that is not legendary.

[14] Fyzee, *Hidâyat al-âmiriyya*, p. 23.

[15] B. Lewis, 'Ismâʿîlî Notes,' *BSOS*, XII (1948), 597. Qalqashandi adds to this version the idea that Nizâr himself went out of Egypt in the womb of a slave girl; and supports this idea as being the one the Nizârîs held, by noting that Nizârîs were expected to believe that Nizâr was not publicly killed in Alexandria. But even this version seems to admit that Nizâr at least had a different name when he left the slave-girl's womb!

[16] Ghazzâlî in the *Munqidh* speaks of the imâm as being invisible, and yet in principle accessible to the believers. Transl., *JA*, 1877, ps. 44, 53. Ibn al-Qalânisî – and also Fâriqî – has Nizâr go to Alamût and marry Ḥasan-i Ṣabbâḥ's daughter. Their stories are confused, but witness to the idea of an imâm in Alamût in their time, before the Qiyâma. Ed. Amedroz, *History of Damascus*, p. 127–8. Fâriqî can even name the current imâm (560 or 572) Nizār b. Md. b. Nizār!

to his successors' care until the imâm should come.[17] More conclusive, coins of Muḥammad ibn Buzurg'ummîd, second successor of Ḥasan-i Ṣabbâḥ were issued simply in the name of Nizâr, blessing his descendants as anonymously as his ancestors.[18] The very confusion in the stories that trace the paternity of the new imâm Ḥasan II to the line of Nizâr suggests that at Alamût there had been no official story on a hidden imâm.

Not only did Alamût not claim the imâm who was evidently located there by general understanding; a rather different tradition emanated from Alamût. Ḥasan-i Ṣabbâḥ is said in the *Haft Bâb-i Bâbâ Sayyid-nâ* to have predicted the coming of the *Qâ'im*, the figure who at the end of the world – or rather of this cycle – would cap the series of imâms and complete their work, bringing perfect justice and truth. Though this is an all-Ismâ'îlî prediction, its special ascription to Ḥasan here is noteworthy enough to lend a possibility of foundation to the following, as the Alamût-favored Nizârî position. According to the very late *Bayân-i Shinâkht-i Imâm*, when Nizâr disappeared both of the ordinary indices of the imâm's person were taken away – both the physical descent, and the naṣṣ, the personal designation. In this special test of men's faith, the only remaining link with the imâm was his supreme *ḥujja*, proof, Ḥasan-i Ṣabbâḥ; who in turn was to point out the imâm when he reappeared (by prophesying of Ḥasan II).[19] In any case, a number of sources give Ḥasan the title of *chief* ḥujja as if it were upon him in this special role and not upon an imâm kept secret at Alamût that the community authority depended.[20]

[17] Defrémery translating Juwaynî: *JA*, ser. 5, XV (1860), 188. Zakariyâ Qazwînî, *Âthâr al-Bilâd*, ed. F. Wüstenfeld (Göttingen, 1848), II, 201 has a boy be called imâm; and Ibn Muyassar, *Ta'rikh Miṣr*, ed. H. Massé, *Annales d'Egypte* (Cairo, 1919), p. 68, has the boy be produced from secret at the time of Ḥasan's death.

[18] Casanova, 'Monnaie des Assassins de Perse,' *Revue Numismatique*, ser. 3, XI (1893), 345. The coins are from the years 542, 548, 551, and 555. The insertion of the descendants is not new: cf. Nâṣir-i Khusraw, *Jâmi'al-Ḥikmatayn*, ed. H. Corbin and M. Mu'în (Teheran and Paris, 1953), p. 17, where he blesses Mustanṣir.

[19] *Bayân*, folio 4. Trans. W. Ivanow, *On the Recognition of the Imâm* (Ismaili Texts and Translations Series B, No. 4, Bombay, 1947). *Ḥujja* was used of a certain high rank in the Ismâ'îlî hierarchy – one of the top dâ'îs in Fâṭimid times; but it was also used in general of any hierarchical figure who served as link to a higher one – so that the imâm himself was ḥujja of God, in general. Both in its general sense and as referring to a high-ranking dâ'î in particular, the title could be easily attached to Ḥasan-i Ṣabbâḥ. In occasional passages even in Ṭayyibî literature the ḥujja takes an even more striking place: as in the *Zahr al-Ma'ânî*, Ivanow, *Rise of the Fatimids*, p. 253, where *ḥujja* appears as the rank of Salmân above all ranks (text, not translation, where Ivanow quite deliberately makes this "evolutionary"!); or p. 265, where ḥujja appears as special witness to the person of the imâm.

[20] Both within Nizârî literature – Ivanow, *Kalâm-i Pîr*, p. 44/51; *Rawḍat at-Taslîm*, p. 174; and without – Ijî (d. 1355): *Mawâqif*, ed. Soerensen, Leipzig 1848, p. 352.

If there was indeed no imâm in Alamût, perhaps (one may imagine) there was a highly sophisticated version of the role of Ḥasan as ḥujja of the imâm, which was misunderstood in broader circles. Perhaps – there were after all a number of descendants of Nizâr still in Egypt[21] – Ḥasan could feel that he could know (once having accepted an imâm), a priori that there must always be an imâm: that whether he knew which descendant it was for the moment was irrelevant, for he could now prove his existence and deduce all else needful therefrom – and others could accept the proof from him, who had at least at one time known of the Imâm as a living man. . . . Ḥasan might indeed persuade himself that he was, with his unaccountable keenness of insight, specially elect to represent the imâm as his proof among men in a time of adversity (a role which could be validated by his unique ability to reason himself into assuming it, as the role of the imâm had already been so validated!); he might then be specially elect to show men what would be the inevitable characteristics of the imâm when he should reappear. . . . And such an argument could easily have been misconstrued by outsiders – no doubt even by most Nizârîs themselves – into the supposition that somewhere Ḥasan was concealing (and where but in Alamût?) the imâm himself, till he should be ready to appear.[22]

Or perhaps Ḥasan, finding himself, after a long life, dedicated to a rationally impossible situation, committed a fraud and kept his lonely secret to his death; allowing his successors to trust in a future which to Ḥasan could no longer have any meaning of hope or fear. Or perhaps there was something of both.

In any case, the absolute imâm which Ḥasan had taught and to the authority of which the energies of the whole movement were ideally turned was, in fact if not in feeling a group abstraction. It was the group's acceptance of the imâm's crucial claim which validated his authority in the first place; it was in the group alone that his authority found expression; and what else had so ultimate an imâm save authority? The one permanent teaching of the imâm, theoretically, was the subordination of all things to himself – that is, to the community power. If side by side with the ahistorical theory went in fact a solidly historical community tra-

[21] The *Hidâya* itself admits this, noting that no one of them claimed the imâmate, nor was the claim made for any; p. 23.

[22] The imâm had disappeared, even from the dâ'îs, once before – as reported in the 'Istitâr,' in Ivanow's *Rise of the Fâṭimids*. This would provide precedent for the Nizârîs' being willing to conceive of such a disappearance, despite the technical doctrine that the imâm must be effectively available. The Ṭayyibîs also were shortly after willing to accept the idea of a concealed imâm.

dition of zeal and expectation, this could carry on with an imâm who was a sheer abstraction as well as with one who was only a distant symbol on the Egyptian throne.

The organization of an independent Nizârî daʿwa.

The Nizârî movement seems to have been largely restricted to the Saljûq domains. The Ismâʿîlîs of Egypt and of those areas where the Egyptian government was influential – the Yaman and evidently ʿUmân and part of Sind in India – apparently accepted for the most part the dubious official naṣṣ and the dynasty of Badr, whose virtues had been urged upon them by Mustanṣir.[23] As to the distant Ismâʿîlîs of the mountains north-east of the Saljûq territory, we hear of them no further till after Alamût has fallen. Abû l-Maʿâlî mentions a dâʿî at Ghazna on a level with Ḥasan-i Ṣabbâḥ and Nâṣir-i Khusraw, who appear as founders of sects; this suggests a threefold geographical division in the Iranian-Turkish lands which was probably not transcended for a long time.[24] Ḥasan-i Ṣabbâḥ is listed as working at Iṣfahân and Rayy: major centers of Saljûq power, where indeed we have found him in the account of Rashîd ad-Dîn. Ghazna and Nâṣir-i Khusraw's Oxus valley were outside his range, being outside the Saljûq empire.[25]

Here, already then, is some continuity from pre-Nizârî times carried over into the Nizârî daʿwa at least territorially. It is just possible that this corresponds to an organizational continuity – that the dâʿî of Iṣfahân had been put in charge of the daʿwa in all the Saljûq territory. One has heard of apparently independent dâʿîs in earlier times: Nâṣir-i Khusraw was ḥujja of Khurâsân and Georgia, according to Rashîd ad-Dîn, and the daʿwa of Mu'ayyad in Fârs is well documented by his own writings.[26] But in the time of Mustanṣir there again proceeded, as we know from his letters to the Yaman, a consolidation of the outlying daʿwa: the Sind and ʿUmân were subordinated to the Yamanite dâʿî. Perhaps likewise, as Ḥasan's travels have already suggested, the dâʿî of Iṣfahân had expanded

[23] The letters of Mustanṣir, Al-Hamdani, *BSOS*, VII (1933–5), 307, passim.

[24] Ghazna, of course, never came under Saljûq sway, nor did the principal seat of Nâṣir, Yumghân. Mâzandarân, east of Daylamân, is also given as in Nâṣir's sphere, but it was Saljûq territory when the Nizârîs arose, and the Ismâʿîlîs there joined the movement; e.g., at Ustûnâwand.

[25] Ibn Muyassar, p. 68, connects the Nizârî movement with the Turkish domains.

[26] *Sîrat al-Mu'ayyad fi-d-Dîn*, ed. Kamil Hussein, Cairo, 1930.

his operations to all the Saljûq areas of Transoxania, Îrân, ʿIrâq, etc.; and the resultant central structure for the daʿwa of these areas now continued, but on an independent basis. Without asserting any strong centralization at the first, we may suppose that the Nizârî sect corresponded roughly to the former daʿwa in Saljûq lands.

Nevertheless, in Syria and even in Egypt itself there was a struggle between the Nizârî and the official Fâṭimid daʿwas.[27] In Egypt the majority no doubt supported the government – we cannot be sure – but a number became Nizârîs; Ḥasan-i Ṣabbâḥ is said to have sent them material aid.[28] In Syria the allegiance was in question for a time. Two or three generations before, the Syrian Ismâʿîlîs had been split by the extremist Druze withdrawal of large numbers on the basis of a new dispensation. During the past generation they had been further affected by the withdrawal of Fâṭimid political control and the coming of the Saljûqs. But loyalty to the Fâṭimids was strong in important circles, as Gibb has pointed out – more than one town continued to own their supremacy while rejecting their control.[29] Even the Saljûq ruler of Aleppo, Riḍwân (d. 1113), momentarily accepted the suzerainty of Mustaʿlî, Nizâr's rival, three years after Mustaʿlî's accession. Evidently Mustaʿlî inherited the well-placed, conservative Fâṭimid following.

Nevertheless, after not many years the Ismâʿîlîs of Syria were generally Nizârîs. It seems that under Âmir, Mustaʿlî's son, a scholar coming from the Jazr, a group of towns in northern Syria southwest of Aleppo, was expected to be a Nizârî like his compatriots; and indeed as soon as the people of the Jazr come to be noted by general historians for their activity, it is pro-Nizârî.[30] Âmir's epistle which we have already mentioned was designed to answer questions put by the local Nizârîs to the Fâṭimid dâʿî in Damascus; evidently for a while both groups were to be found there. But within a generation from the death of Mustanṣir

[27] Possibly Iranian missionaries came to Syria in the Nizârî-Iṣfahân cause, but from the fact that subsequently a number of the leaders are either Iranian or ʿIrâqî one cannot be sure of this; the local Nizârî sentiment may have been quite spontaneous. (The Saljûqs had just expanded into Syria.) Iranian as well as Turkish leadership had been evident in Egypt and Syria for a long time, and was to continue so, without being distinctive of the Ismâʿîlîs, or indicating direct control from Îrân. Ibn Baṭṭûṭa (d. 1377) reports that most of the faqîrs, Ṣûfî mendicants, in institutions in Cairo were Persians. *Voyages*, trans. Defrémery and Sanguinetti (Paris, 1853), I, 71.

[28] Ibn Muyassar, *Ta'rîkh Miṣr*, year 518, *passim*; the oaths already cited show that, at least later, there were Nizârîs in Egyptian territory; who might, however, have been Syrians.

[29] H. A. R. Gibb, introduction to *A Damascus Chronicle of the Crusades* (London, 1932), p. 16 ff.

[30] Cahen, *Syrie du Nord*, p. 42.

the word Ismâʿîlî, in Syria, refers simply to Nizârîs; there is no further mention even of clashes between the two groups of Ismâʿîlîs there; certainly after the death of Âmir (1130) neither of the two non-Nizârî Ismâʿîlî groups (Ṭayyibî and Ḥâfiẓî) that succeeded could have had any substantial following in Syria.[31] Already in the time of Âmir, the Syrian Ismâʿîlîs were evidently closely tied with those of Îrân and ʿIrâq.

The success of the Nizârî daʿwa.

The Nizârî daʿwa surely included not only the already existing group of Ismâʿîlîs of the Saljûq realm and of Syria, but also numbers of new converts; for its active propaganda seems to have been effective. We have noted already the conversion of the garrison of Alamût as an example. Cahen suggests that the Nizârîs won Druze support in Syria,[32] at first; this despite the later instance of Druze opposition to the Nizârîs, at the Wâdî Tayyim. As a matter of fact, there seems to have been considerable inter-Shîʿite mobility even up to that time; and no doubt many actively inclined Shîʿites of all varieties would be attracted to the ascendant sect – such as Ḥasan-i Ṣabbâḥ himself. (One wonders if such mass accretions might not have hastened the centralization process which we shall witness, since they had no localized Ismâʿîlî roots.)

That the summons to join in the new daʿwa was not quite indiscriminate is assured us by a passage in Rashîd ad-Dîn, under the reign of Ibn Buzurg-ʾummîd. He tells, from a Nizârî source, of a group of "Mazdakîs" in Adharbâyjân, who refused Ḥasan-i Ṣabbâḥ's invitation. The word *Mazdakî* refers originally to an old Persian heresy, painted in lurid colors. It is used by Muslims to refer to any heretical group considered to advocate license under the cover of religion, particularly in respect to community of wives, when it is felt that a connection with the famous earlier

[31] Possibly we find the distorted names of the Ḥâfiẓiyya and Âmiriyya (= Ṭayyibiyya?) in Dimashqî's list of heretical groups in the vicinity of Damascus around 1300; for among his eight names are two not otherwise identifiable: *Amriyya* and *Ḥafẓiyya. Nukhbat ad-Dahr*, ed. M. Mehren (Leipzig, 1923), p. 200. Cahen seems to believe that the often mentioned Shîʿa group which opposed the Nizârîs in Aleppo in the time of Riḍwân were pro-Mustaʿlî Ismâʿîlîs, *Syrie du Nord*, p. 189. Qalqashandî also says, against the evidence of his oaths, that the Syrian Ismâʿîlîs generally, including Sinân, were Mustaʿlians. This seems clearly in error. Sauvaget seems to have more basis for treating the Alleppines as Twelver Shîʿa, such as are still found in Syria in greater numbers than the Ismâʿîlîs, who are all Nizârîs: he cites Ibn Furât, Vol. II, Folio 159, verso, that in the Shîʿa funerals *twelve* imâms were named. J. Sauvaget, *Alep* (Bibliothèque archéologique et historique, XXXVI [Paris, 1941]), 98 (note 292).

[32] *Syrie du Nord*, p. 189. Zambaur also supposes so.

group might be traced; commonly such groups have some connection also with the Shî'ite movement. The Nizârî writer condemns this particular group with pious horror, saying that they refused to follow Ḥasan because he summoned them to poverty; that they preferred to establish their own easy-going religion; and were accordingly eventually stamped out in blood by the authorities.

It is not clear whether these people were in fact an outside group whom Ḥasan tried in vain to convert, or whether they were an Ismâ'îlî group which refused to follow Ḥasan's lead at the time of the general break with the Fâṭimids over Nizâr, and set up their own rival Nizârî group. (They are given "popular" doctrines which the outside world often ascribed to Ismâ'îlîs, and which indeed as we have noted were probably latent there and came out later among the Nizârîs; perhaps this is a case where such "popular" doctrines came to the surface.) Anyway, their case indicates two significant features of the situation of the time. On the one hand, the Nizârîs, with their power orientation, required too strict an internal conformity for the taste of many who were attracted. But those who conformed had their reward. In the conditions of the time, power was of great importance for sheer survival; and the isolated group was destroyed.

That the Nizârîs succeeded in alienating from the Fâṭimids the bulk of their foreign support seems to be conceded in a curious notice in Ibn aṣ-Ṣayrafî's history of the Fâṭimid viziers.[33] He has it that the second vizier of Âmir (and still vizier at his writing) conceived a pity for a long-deluded group of people, who had been misled from their proper obedience, and seemed impossible to reach. He asked Âmir for a letter of pardon for them, which should include the names of their leaders; for they numbered thousands upon thousands.

THE REVOLT UNDER WAY

The first uprisings: Rûdbâr and Quhistân (1090-1092).

We have traced the Nizârî breach with the Fâṭimid regime before carrying further the story of the Nizârî revolt in Saljûq lands, beyond the

[33] Ibn aṣ-Ṣayrafî (d. 1127), *Ishâra ilâ Man Nâla al-Wizâra*, ed. A. Mukhlis, in *Bulletin de l'Institut français d'Archéologie orientale*, XXV (1925), 112 and preceding. The attitude of the letter would probably be out of the question had there been any large Syrian group still attached to the Fâṭimids; the jealousy of such a group would have had to be taken into account.

taking of Alamût. But we must recall that the alienation from Egypt and the launching of the military campaigns went on simultaneously; indeed, the earlier portion of the risings had gone on for four years before Mustanṣir's death, which formally initiated the schism.

The taking of Alamût near Qazwîn in 1090 would seem to have released a flood of Ismâ'îlî energies, in the direction of which Ḥasan-i Ṣabbâḥ took at least a prominent part from that key spot.[34] Alamût was appropriate to such a role. Alamût itself was in an inaccessible, rough terrain. The geographer Qazwînî in the *Âthâr* says that Rûdbâr is all rocks and trees, and adds (as if part of the same repelling picture) that the inhabitants are Daylamites. (Daylamites had long been famous as hardy soldiers.) But Alamût was also on the shortest route between the important city of Qazwîn and the Caspian Sea.[35] Alamût had been used by a Zaydî imâm in the past as a reliable stronghold; and Yâqût emphasizes its general importance as key to Daylamân.[36]

[34] On the crucial role of the taking of Alamût the general impression is supported by the apparently contemporary evidence of Abû Muḥammad al-'Irâqî. In the narrative of the uprisings generally, the chief authority is Rashîd ad-Dîn with Juwaynî; supported Ibn al-Athîr and Râwandî especially – the three lines appearing largely independent. Rashîd ad-Dîn and Juwaynî must commonly be mentioned together if only because the edited text of Juwaynî is of great help in reading the manuscript of Rashîd ad-Dîn. H. Bowen in 'The *sar-gudhasht-i sayyidnâ*, the "Tale of the Three Schoolfellows" and the *waṣâya* of the Niẓâm al-Mulk,' *JRAS*, 1931, p. 771, has pointed out the close relationship between Juwaynî and Rashîd ad-Dîn. Very often Rashîd ad-Dîn has more facts than Juwaynî, where Juwaynî has more opinions than Rashîd ad-Dîn. Where they coincide, the wording is almost identical – one would suppose, therefore, that Juwaynî was excerpting the originals which Rashîd ad-Dîn copied. Yet in beginning his story Rashîd ad-Dîn seems to quote the introductory phrase of Juwaynî, who had written a generation earlier; so that Bowen suggests that the common original was a first and fuller draft by Juwaynî, which Juwaynî pruned of the more objectionable parts, including the obviously legendary and the less interesting; and of which he redressed the language to make it less offensive to Sunnî ears.

This relationship is persistent: Rashîd ad-Dîn again seems to quote Juwaynî's own words at the opening of the reign of Md. b. Buzurg'ummîd. A passage where Rashîd ad-Dîn appears to be based on Juwaynî's excerpts, not on the originals, is translated here – it deals with the Festival of the Qiyâma. It is rare, however, for Juwaynî to have *more* substance – as against abusive words – than Rashîd ad-Dîn (an example is the occasion of the assassination of Mustarshid, where Juwaynî has some additional matter); on the other hand, in parts Rashîd ad-Dîn has whole pages of material not found in Juwaynî, and gives the Ismâ'îlî authorities for it. In these parts, at least, Rashîd ad-Dîn may well have been adding independently to what he had through Juwaynî. Rashîd ad-Dîn also gives much material independently from Sunnî sources, apparently including Ibn al-Athîr.

[35] Ivanow notes this, with a map, in the *Geographical Journal* for 1931.

[36] *Mu'jam al-Buldân*, trans. Barbier de Meynard, p. 319. Ẓahîr ad-Dîn Mar'ashî, d. ca. 1476, *Ta'rîkh Ṭabaristân*, ed. B. Dorn, *Muhammedanische Quellen* (St. Petersburg, 1850), I, 311.

The operation of fortifying the stronghold, and perhaps of improving the agriculture in its vicinity, must have begun at once; as did the conversion of the rest of Rûdbâr. But very soon the territory was being raided by the nearest military lord, one Altûn Tâsh, and supplies became a problem for the Alamût garrison; when the men suggested abandoning the stronghold except for a task force, Ḥasan persuaded them to hold on by claiming that a special message from Mustanṣir promised them good fortune there – for which reason Alamût was to be called *Baldat al-Iqbâl*, "the place of good fortune". Meanwhile in the year after the taking of Alamût, Sanamkûh, near Abhar to the west of Qazwîn, was taken by the Ismâ'îlîs;[37] and at the same time a number of places in Quhistân, the barren lands in the south of Khurâsân in eastern Îrân, became Ismâ'îlî strongholds.

Probably in both Daylamân and in Quhistân previous Shî'a tradition had prepared the way for a popular support of the Ismâ'îlîs. In Daylamân, within which was Rûdbâr in which was Alamût, Shî'a rulers had been traditional up to the eve of the taking of Alamût. The whole area south of the Caspian had been one of the chief seats of Zaydî Shî'ism; but every branch of Shî'ism had found response there – the great Shî'ite Buwayhid Dynasty had originated from there.[38] That Ḥusayn Qâ'inî who had converted Alamût itself was from Quhistân and was now sent by Ḥasan-i Ṣabbâḥ to his own country as a dâ'î.[39] There the situation was favorable: the Saljûqid agent in Quhistân was making himself unpopular, it seems, desiring the sister of a scion of the local Sîmjûrid family. Accordingly, when the Ismâ'îlîs rose in many parts of Quhistân, taking over Tabas, Qâ'in, Tûn, and other towns, the movement had the air of an expression of local independence.[40]

So soon as it was found that the local lords could not control the situation, on the advice presumably of his minister, Niẓâm al-Mulk, the Sulṭân Malikshâh sent armies in 1092 both to Quhistân and to the Rûdbâr of Alamût. The Quhistân expedition under Qizil Sâriq was supported by extra troops both from Khurâsân to the north and from Sîstân to the south; yet apparently concentrating all its forces on one small place, Dara,

[37] Ibn al-Athîr, *Kâmil*, year 484 (under year 494).

[38] The Zaydî ruler of Daylamân who died in 1083 was particularly popular; his tomb was revered. Strothmann in *E.I.* s.v. Nâṣir.

[39] He is said by Ḥamd Allâh Qazwînî to have been governor of Turshîz when Quhistân was converted.

[40] Ẓahîr ad-Dîn Mar'ashî, d. ca. 1476, *Ta'rîkh Ṭabaristân*, ed. B. Dorn, *Muhammedanische Quellen* (St. Petersburg, 1850), I, p. 200, has the Ismâ'îlîs take over Quhistân from the Banû Washmagîr already in 470 or 471; but this is dubious.

not far from Sîstân,[41] it failed to take it before news of the death of the Sulṭân Malikshâh arrived, upon which it broke up (being dependent upon the person of the ruler and not upon any state mechanism). The Alamût expedition led by the amîr Arslân Tâsh came upon Ḥasan-i Ṣabbâḥ when he had very few men with him, and few supplies; but a dâʿî living in Qazwîn, Abû ʿAlî Ardistânî, gathered a troop of three hundred Ismâʿîlîs from the area about Qazwîn and Rayy who threw themselves into Alamût, bringing also supplies. One autumn night the enlarged garrison made a sally in concord with some Ismâʿîlîs living in Rûdbâr, and routed the Sunnî invaders.

Within a few days of the return of the defeated commander to headquarters, Niẓâm al-Mulk was assassinated at the Sulṭân's camp by a man dressed as a Ṣûfî, offering a petition. The man was thought to be an Ismâʿîlî, and though most historians assumed that the Ismâʿîlîs were here in collusion with Niẓâm al-Mulk's enemies at court, it is said by Ibn al-Athîr that the Ismâʿîlîs claimed it was in revenge for a carpenter – the carpenter whom Niẓâm al-Mulk had caused to be executed at Sâwa.[42] In any case, when the death of the Sulṭân followed in a matter of weeks, any further plans against Alamût, as also against Quhistân, were abandoned. The Saljûq troops were busy disputing among themselves who should be master.

The Ismâʿîlî uprising finds its pattern (1092-1099).

Within three years, the Ismâʿîlîs had by now seized Rûdbâr and many places in Quhistân, and had beaten off the first efforts of the Saljûqs to oust them. During the next seven or eight years, before the seizure of a fortress threatening the Saljûq capital itself, the characteristic features of the early Nizârî movement unfolded themselves in all detail as they took advantage of Saljûq dissension to seize strongholds in widely scattered places.[43] The Sunnîs were baffled and terrified. The Ismâʿîlîs were

[41] *Taʾrîkh-i Sîstân*, ed. Malik ash-Shuʿarâʾ Bamar (Tihrân, 1935), year 485.

[42] Ibn al-Athîr, *Kamil*, year 494 (p. 213). His account on p. 216 differs, mostly by omission, from that of Rashîd ad-Dîn, making in particular the death of Niẓâm responsible for the end of the siege. On Ṭâhir Arrânî's assassination of Niẓâm and the likelihood that it was an Ismâʿîlî deed without collusion, cf. M. Th. Houtsma, 'Death of the Niẓâm al-Mulk' *Journal of Indian History*, ser. 3, II (1924), 147. He further considers the death of Niẓâm to have led directly to the death of the Sulṭân.

[43] I am supposing that for the most part the undated fortresses listed under year 494 by Ibn al-Athîr – and Rashîd ad-Dîn seems merely to abridge the same list – were occupied within these limits; that is, before 494 (for after that date Ibn al-Athîr lists Ismâʿîlî activity year by year) – and after the death of Malikshâh; this latter because:

sanguine; one supposes they expected that every city in the land might soon recognize the authority of their gospel through a combination of suasion and assault. Even the threat of the schism with Egypt apparently did not dampen their enthusiasm.

We hear especially of a third mountainous area – after Daylamân and Quhistân: the borderlands between the southwest Iranian provinces of Khûzistân and Fârs, around the town of Arrajân. A dâʿî Abû Ḥamza, the shoemaker, from Arrajân had like Ḥasan been to Egypt; he seized at least two fortresses near the town, and the resultant fighting brought a thorough devastation to the districts of Arrajân and Zîr.[44] Of one stronghold near there it is noted significantly that it had in former times been a robber hideout. Inaccessibility was an advantage; most of these fortresses were among mountains. Here the insurgents could be relatively secure against armies, yet issue at will to plunder orthodox caravans. Not only in Daylamân, but in the other end, the eastern end of the Elburz mountains they were active, seizing in particular Manṣûrkûh and Ustûnâwand,[45] between Rayy and Âmul; evidently the lord of Ustûnâwand could not be bought off, so he was killed. Sanamkûh, which they took very early, was lost within five years[46] to a task force sent by one of the Saljûq sulṭâns upon a plea from the town Abhar near it; perhaps because it was in a relatively less mountainous area.

Almost the only open stronghold placed in Ismâʿîlî hands was the river town of Takrît, on the Tigris north of Baghdâd. Here, a Saljûq vizier, who was of the Twelver Shîʿa, gave the citadel to an Ismâʿîlî officer, Kaiqubâd (presumably on the supposition that the officer also was of the Twelver, not the Ismâʿîlî Shîʿa); the officer held it twelve years, though

following the fortress of Iṣfahân, which is the occasion of the listing, he notes Alamût, Quhistân, and Sanamkûh, of which last he notes explicitly the dating before Malikshâh's death; then he goes on to note without date the fortresses in question, except to note that one was after Malikshâh; another was Gird Kûh, which we know was taken after Malikshâh's death. Since the whole paragraph is referring to Ismâʿîlî activity as flowing from the quarrels of Malikshâh's sons (as well as since there is no mention of expeditions to points nearer than Quhistân and Alamût in the time of Malikshâh), one may suppose that it was at least Ibn al-Athîr's impression that these undated seizures were after 1092 (485), as well as before 1101 (494) when the fortress of Iṣfahân was seized. The Arrajân fortresses, at least, seem to have been well-established by the time of the capitulation of Shâhdiz.

44 Cf. Ibn al-Balkhî, *Fârs-Nama*, ed. G. Lestrange and R. A. Nicholson (London, 1921), pp. 59, 61.

45 Ibn Isfandiyâr, d. 1216, *Taʾrîkh-i Ṭabaristân*, trans. abr. E. G. Browne, *An Abridged Translation of the History of Ṭabaristân*, E. J. W. Gibb Memorial, II (London, 1905), p. 242.

46 In 489, according to Ibn al-Athîr, *Kâmil*.

being accused of using it to cover robbery and general lawlessness; surrendering it at last to a Twelver Shî'a Arab ruler (the traditional paragon of gallantry, Ṣadaqa), only to avoid its being taken by a new Saljûq sulṭân. Meanwhile, the vizier who had given it to him had been lynched as an Ismâilî by the army chiefs despite the Sulṭân Barkiyâruq's efforts.[47]

Ambiguities of civil war.

Such ambiguous associations of Ismâ'îlîs within relatively more orthodox society as are suggested in such a sequence were baffling and maddening to their contemporaries. The Sulṭân Barkiyâruq lost not only a vizier to his officers, but a preacher to a murderous mob;[48] he was himself accused of being an Ismâ'îlî and of having his enemies among the amîrs killed by them; for several prominent men who had turned against him were assassinated at this time. Yet attempts on his life[49] and the life of his mother's vizier[50] were also laid to them; nor can one be any more certain whether these assassinations are rightly ascribed to them, than whether the vizier and the preacher were justly accused.[51] The confusion caused by conspiratorial secrecy was added to by the multiplicity of the action. The Ismâ'îlîs were at once in one place a warring people, and in another a sect mingled through the population. Accordingly, in the same years in which the Sîstân troops were having *military* engagements in the field with Ismâ'îlî troops established now in Quhistân,[52] the population of Iṣfahân was rising in massacre as against an elusive *party* within their gates - associating with its unknown agents the most depraved and

[47] Ibn al-Athîr, *Kâmil*, year 492, our basic source throughout this, assures us that the vizier, Balâsânî, was no Ismâ'îlî. An analogous case of Sunnî fear of treachery is afforded by the killing of Aḥmad Khân of Samarqand for "Daylamite zandaqa" (heresy) in 488, according to Ibn al-Athîr.

[48] The preacher-father of Ṭâhir an-Najjâr, who had been killed for the murder of the Sâwa muezzin, was long in high favour with Barkiyâruq, but eventually killed by a mob when on a mission to Kirmân. Ibn al-Athîr, *Kāmil*, year 494 (p.213).

[49] According to Râwandî, wr. 1202–7, *Râḥat aṣ-Ṣudûr*, ed. Muḥammad Iqbâl (London, 1921), in 488.

[50] Sumayramî in 1097.

[51] Bundârî, ed. M. Th. Houtsma, *Recueil de Textes* (Leiden, 1889), vol. II, ps. 90–100, gives details of the intrigue in which accusations of contact with Ismâ'îlîs played a part; notably by a certain accuser Khaṭîbî, who was finally exposed.

[52] Rashîd ad-Dîn lists many engagements, whether raids or wars, date by date, in this case 487 and 489; in 495 the Qâḍî Abû Ḥasan was assassinated according to the *Ta'rîkh-i Sîstân*; then the warfare – perhaps growing out of the Sîstânî action in aiding the Saljûqs against Quhistân in 485 – seems to have ceased for some time.

terrifying of activities.[53] There were more than the usual ambiguities of civil war.

We have details of the rumors that terrified Iṣfahân. It seems – according to Râwandî, whose version is the most beautifully worked out – that a beggar woman heard one day groans coming from a house at the end of a narrow lane. She blessed their sick, asking for alms. But rather than giving her anything directly, they invited her to come in. This made her take fright. Innumerable young men had been missing from day to day, and never found; the whole city was in a state of alarm; the woman became suspicious of this house. And in fact the men whom she then summoned found an underground chamber within which were the missing young men in various states of torture and death; and learned that each day at dusk the blind man who lived there had lured the passersby into the lane on pretext of being helped home, whereupon they were seized and sadistically destroyed. The blind man was said to be an Ismâʿîlî and any in the city who were accused of being Ismâʿîlîs were brought and killed with him.[54] Ibn al-Athîr has bonfires built by a Sunnî legist, and the Ismâʿîlîs burned in them.

Meanwhile, in Rûdbâr, where the center of Nizârî power was to be, the Ismâʿîlîs were steadily consolidating their position.[55] They beat off a large raid from the Sunnî people of Rayy (though the military lords had given up, the more pious of the people did not yet);[56] then they persuaded local chiefs to submit to themselves and receive Ismâʿîlî aid. They thus prepared the way for seizing the important fortress of Lammasar, in 1101.[57] Its men had rebelled after submission, and were wiped out when Buzurg-ʾummîd, whom Ḥasan-i Ṣabbâḥ sent there, took it by storm. The local population was thereupon forced to dig channels for watering the fortress, within which were built palaces and gardens, of which the Ismâʿîlîs were evidently rather proud.[58] Buzurgʾummîd stayed in Lammasar without stirring, it is said, as Ḥasan was staying in Alamût, till he was called to succeed his master.

[53] Browne notes a massacre presumably of Ismâʿîlîs at Nîshâpûr in 1096. *Literary History of Persia*, Vol. II (Cambridge, 1928), p. 312.

[54] Râwandî, *Râḥat aṣ-Ṣudûr*, ed. Iqbâl, pp. 157–8; cf. Ibn al-Athîr, *Kâmil*, year 494, p. 214. Perhaps Râwandî's incident was an isolated case of sadism. Ibn al-Athîr and Ibn al-Jawzî scatter the horror over more than one incident, some perhaps not connected with this but with the actual efforts of Nizârîs to preserve secrecy.

[55] Here, again, we must follow chiefly Rashîd ad-Dîn.

[56] Raid on Ṭâliqân, year 486.

[57] The Rashîd ad-Dîn manuscript has year 489, 1096; but Juwaynî and others place it six years later, after Gird Kûh.

[58] It is noted that one of their gardens, rather later, was explicitly laid out on the old cemetery of the kings of Daylamân.

CHAPTER IV

WAR WITH THE SALJÛQS: DECISIVE PHASE

METHODS OF STRUGGLE

The dâr al-hijra ideal and the seizing of fortresses.

The characteristic pattern of the Nizârî warfare was displayed in the first years while the schism with Egypt was still in the making. Though in later years the sect took on a pattern of stability, the Ismâ'îlîs long showed themselves ready to renew their risings on occasion. The Nizârî expectations appear to have been modeled upon the story of Mohammed himself, modified in terms of current circumstances; and in the Nizârî case the pattern of action and reaction followed those expectations at first to a considerable degree. Mohammed, when he failed to convert Mecca, had fled with many of his followers to Madîna, some of whose population were converted to his message while some merely submitted to his rule. Having set up there the community of the true faith, he proceeded by a combination of alliances with surrounding tribes, raids on Meccan commerce, and outright war with Mecca, so to expand his rule as at last to take over Mecca itself; from there, theMuslims proceeded to conquer much of the world.

Madîna was the first *dâr al-hijra* of Islâm, the first *place of refuge* – whence to return in triumph to the unbelieving lands from which one has had to flee persecuted. There had been many since. An early type of purist dissenting group, which had tried to overthrow the official Muslim regime in its first centuries, the Khârijites, had used precisely this idea. Labelling all their adversaries backsliders, they had made adherence to the purist cause and rejection of their enemies the overriding criterion in all things.[1] North Africa had provided a famous dâr al-hijra for the early Fâṭimids,

[1] Quhistân among other places had served as dâr al-hijra for Khârijite groups.

who used it as a base for conquering Egypt and the Arabian holy cities themselves. Accordingly perhaps the most conscious element of the new Ismâ'îlî strategy, as of the Fâṭimids', was a deliberate imitation of that archetype from Mohammed's own career.

The Ismâ'îlîs could congratulate themselves that their opponents reacted with an indignation, a vengefulness, and a clumsiness that suited well the traditional picture of the Meccans' response to Mohammed in Madîna. From their strongholds - so many lesser Madînas - the Ismâ'îlîs made raids on the surrounding Sunnî lands, disrupting commerce; the retaliation of the Sunnîs was at first – except for the single year of Malikshâh's two expeditions - piecemeal and apparently led more by personal rage then by good planning. The Ismâ'îlîs who remained in the towns gave their co-believers secret assistance – as it was supposed Mohammed's uncle 'Abbâs had done in Mecca; while daring Ismâ'îlîs would take the lives of specially influential opponents – a practice also traceable to Mohammed. The outraged Sunnîs reacted with violence and persecution of suspects, even to the point of massacre.

On the other hand there were important differences in the Nizârî pattern from the archetype; both because of the special circumstances of the time, and of the special Ismâ'îlî religious emphasis on authority. There were for the Nizârîs not one dâr al-hijra, but a score of them; but not only Mohammed, also the earlier Khârijite and Ismâ'îlî movements had centered on a single one each. From this one had been sent out regular armies one way or another to an orderly conquest. The Ismâ'îlîs indeed used armies on occasion, as in retaliation against Sîstân, or to take Lammasar by assault; more often they used more piecemeal and personal methods. Takrît will have been taken in the guise of a routine army placement; Alamût was converted; the Sulṭân Barkiyâruq found his authority undermined by the very uncertainty attending their activity. Local chiefs submitted, in Quhistân and in Rûdbâr, for local advantage, and kept their positions and probably their faith; the Ismâ'îlîs from Arrajân tricked themselves into a fortress by playing on old acquaintance of the lord's personal agent there.[2]

Ismâ'îlî revolt in a Sunnî setting.

All this was appropriate to the social atomization of the times. Social power was in the hands of a host of essentially equal and autonomous

[2] Ibn al-Athîr, *Kâmil*, p. 218 under yr. 494.

military and religious leaders, on a personal basis; as we have noted it tended to be among the Sunnîs, with their formal universal legalism. Already the Sunnî society had become accustomed to seeing upstart individuals, robbers or rich rebels, appropriate whole areas and force the paramount power to recognize them as "loyal" but independent vassals. The policy suitable for conquering such a society was to take it over piece by piece, winning or destroying it stronghold by stronghold, leader by leader. The Ismâʿîlî dâr al-hijra need not appear to be on any other footing than that of a "loyal" but free vassaldom if circumstances required caution. The Ismâʿîlî masquerading as a private amîr could if necessary calm men's apprehensions, and await further opportunities untrammeled. The shaykhs and amîrs, a sage here and a ruler there, filling their offices by personal prestige rather than any hierarchical mechanism, were quite irreplaceable in their particular authority; when they were out of the way, the Ismâʿîlîs could be free to establish their own more permanent form of power.[3]

The Ismâʿîlî emphasis on authority, and particularly the intense power-orientation of the new movement, fighting against such great odds as it was, likewise represented a difference from the earlier attempts to renew Islâm starting from a dâr al-hijra. It perhaps complemented the fragmentary character of the uprisings that there should be a tendency to centralize authority within the movement, for the sake of a more ruthless power drive. But this was not extreme, at least in these early years: the official center was still in Egypt, though Ḥasan-i Ṣabbâḥ is represented as at least consulted on occasion;[4] and there is little indication that the Ismâʿîlîs of either Iṣfahân or Alamût exercised any iron control over the other areas. The point at which the emphasis on power at all costs was most distinctively expressed was in the relatively free use of assassination which the Ismâʿîlîs now made.

[3] Joinville supposes that the Templar and Hospitaller orders were immune to attack by assassination, since if the occupant of a post were killed, he was automatically replaced. However that may be, the reverse is even more true of the Muslim order in general at this time than of the secular Christian Crusaders. When the Sulṭân died, his troops were automatically dispersed, and the Ismâʿîlîs saved. When an amîr died, his lands were in disorder, and the Ismâʿîlîs could raid, as Rashîd ad-dîn notes of Bayhaq in 498.

[4] He appears in this role in the story of Aḥmad b. ʿAṭṭâsh, his most obvious rival for leadership. And Aḥmad's father is said to have fled to Ḥasan-i Ṣabbâḥ already at the beginning of the risings – Râwandî, pp. 155 ff.; but this story sounds romanced.

The method of assassination.

A number of Muslim sects had used assassination as a technique. It is recorded of Mohammed himself that on several occasions he exclaimed that one or another inaccessible enemy of his did not deserve to live; and was then gratified by one of his men's finding ways of destroying the enemy in question. The purist Khârijites in early times, who declared all other Muslims apostate and therefore subject to the death penalty, sometimes showed their fervor by killing any individual Muslim in their path. We hear of the word *jihâd* – holy war – being applied to individual killings with a religio-*political* purpose first in connection with early Shî'ite groups. There it is the jihâd *khafî*, the *secret* struggle, as against the public one on the frontiers. One extremist Shî'ite group was called the *khunnâq*, the *stranglers*, for such was said to be their method of killing. None of these groups, however, gave to assassination the major political role which it came to have at the hands of the Nizârîs.

By the end of the Nizârî power at Alamût, the *fidâ'îs* – those prepared to do jobs of assassination at bidding – were possibly a distinct band.[5] How early this was the case is not clear: an office which any might perform could readily have degenerated into the function of a special corps; one gathers that in Syria at least, there was no special corps even later.[6] Even the reference to the name *fidâ'î*, *devotee*, at so early a point as the murder of Niẓâm al-Mulk might be a projection into the past; there is certainly no question of a special corps in Ṭâhir's murder of the muezzin. There seems little reason to suppose that the fidâ'îs in any case formed a bottom rank in the Nizârî hierarchy below the *rafîq*s, or *comrades*, as the bulk of the Nizârîs called themselves; nor that they received special

[5] Khwurshâh was threatened by his "fidâ'îs" if he should try to surrender; and Juwaynî elsewhere seems to use the term to designate a special group (ps. 129, 135); but his usage is suspect. Rashîd ad-Dîn, evidently quoting the Nizârî version of the legend of the three schoolfellows, mentions Ḥasan-i Ṣabbâḥ as calling together his fidâ'îs to ask who could kill Niẓâm al-Mulk.

[6] At the time of the attempt upon Saladin, officers whose lands border upon the Ismâ'îlîs recognized the attempted assassins as, apparently, ordinary members of that people – cf. Abû Shâma, *Rawḍatayn* (Cairo, 1871) yr. 570. Abû Firâs (ed. S. Guyard, 'Un grand maître des Assassins,' *JA* ser. 7, IX [1877]) refers in his anecdotes of Rashîd ad-Dîn Sinân to the *rijâl al-jihâd*, the men of religious struggle, as sent on assasination expeditions, but apparently without designating them as a special group (anecdote nr. 29). The *text* of Ra'îs Ḥasan's poem on fidâ'îs, described by Ivanow, might give indications on the problem. 'An Ismaili Ode in Praise of Fidawis,' *JBBRAS*, new series, XIV (1938), 63–72.

training in languages, or wore special garb, as has been suggested.[7] At the beginning, probably, any able Nizârî might be asked to undertake an assassination, in line of duty.

Assassination as a weapon of desperation.

In any case, the fanatical devotion of the men who offered themselves in such numbers for such suicidal work – for the men whom they attacked were generally armed and surrounded by armed guards – marks an intensity of group sentiment rarily witnessed. No doubt the fidâ'îs were provided with a degree of *personal* as well as social motivation. The case is cited again and again of the mother who thought her son had died on an expedition, for she heard all the assassins were killed; so she rejoiced and adorned herself; but when her son came home safe after all, she put on mourning. (But compare the assassin of Ibn Badî', who jumped into a torrent to escape being tortured.) Sijistânî already had insisted in the older Ismâ'îlî days on the role of the body as purifier of the soul – the *nafs* – that it might rejoin ultimate reason – *'aql*; the doctrine much later reported of the Nizârîs, that by dying in the line of duty they were using their bodies to purify their souls for the realms of light, is surely connected with this, and probably was ready to be called into play from the beginning.[8]

But the *group* purpose in so free a use of assassination was political, and marked its desperate zeal. The ruthlessness of the policy was reflected in the ruthlessness of the Sunnî response – the Nizârîs were feared and detested as few other heretics have been; the policy meant therefore a

[7] E. G. Browne, *Literary History of Persia*, II, p. 209, suggests, in connection with the assassination of Conrad, when one version had the Ismâ'îlîs posing as monks, that the training of the fidâ'îs must have been very excellent indeed for them to be able on call to pose as educated foreigners. Even supposing that version to be correct, the pose as a monk, not necessarily a Frankish one, would in those days require little learning. That the Assassins were trained in all the languages of which the Franks were aware recurs throughout the old Western tradition, and inspires no confidence. As it appears in the pages of Withof, it seems traceable to the report that the forged Assassin letter was written in Latin, Greek, and Hebrew. The rest would be deduction. (This teaching of languages occurs as early as the Rothelin mss. continuator of William of Tyre. *R. H. C. Occid.*, Vol. II, p. 523.) Further: von Hammer's insistence that they were dressed in white seems to rest on an imaginative account by Sanudo of the visit of Henry of Champagne. Browne's idea of the reorganization of the hierarchy seems to rest on an assumption that the heresiologists' reports of degrees of initiation can be taken as they stand.

[8] Sijistânî, *Kashf al-Maḥjûb*, ed. H. Corbin (Ṭihrân, 1949), cf. Introduction, p. 16. For the later Nizârî doctrine, cf. the report of 'Umarî (d. 1349), in the *Masâlik al-Absâr*, trans. E. M. Quatremère, *Fundgruben des Orients*, IV (1814), 368 ff.

frank bid for present power at all costs: regardless of any other human or religious hopes they might entertain. They were not seeking mild conversions, but total devotion or total enmity.[9]

It must be noted that the Nizârîs and their extremist Shîʿite predecessors have by no means been alone in using assassination as a technique. It is a weapon which has appealed particularly to such as have reduced all men to a common level; for as compared with war it is relatively bloodless and merciful, striking the great and guilty rather than the small people, the large numbers who apart from ignorant prejudice are likely as not indifferent to the cause at stake. Now although in matters of the *faith* there was a strict hierarchism, yet for that very reason, in their view of the *natural* man, the Ismâʿîlîs reduced all to a common level; – whereas the very lack of hierarchical status among the Sunnîs went along with a willingness to regard highly natural merit or advantage, and to be shocked – as evidently the Ismâʿîlîs were not – at the loss of a great man (on whom personally they relied for order) more than at the death of many peasants. (We have noticed that the first great Nizârî assassination, that of Niẓâm al-Mulk, was said to have been vaunted by them as being in revenge for a carpenter.)

No doubt from the Ismâʿîlî point of view the method of assassination not only was heroic, but was just and humane. One point lost sight of if such was their judgment was the relative perfidy of an assassination as against even a much bloodier battle; in a perverse way, at least so we like to think, there can be good faith present even in war; but not in an unannounced murder. Though the Muslims at large were commonly not backward in using assassination as an expedient, the adoption of such means as a regular and admitted policy horrified them, and has horrified men ever since.

RISING FORTUNES (1100-1105)

The disruption of the Saljûq power.

The Nizârîs had launched their revolt while the Saljûq power was still relatively intact. But very soon Malikshâh had died; and the Saljûq armies were quarreling aimlessly among themselves during the years when

[9] To be sure this was not the grim mood of every day. Each assassination could be justified in its own particular setting. But the adoption of the policy meant ultimately such consequences; and an ultimate willingness to face them is illustrated in the desperate history of the sect.

these militant Ismâ'îlîs, "thousands upon thousands", were seizing upon widely scattered fortresses, and cutting their ties with the Egyptian regime. The Nizârîs gladly took advantage of the same crisis in Saljûq affairs which the first Crusaders were stumbling upon at the same time. Among the rival heirs of the Saljûq house during the decade after 1092, the most prominent was Malikshâh's son Barkiyâruq, who generally operated around either Rayy or Iṣfahân. While independent Saljûq lords worried Anatolia and Syria in the west and Kirmân and Khurâsân in the east on their own accounts, Barkiyâruq struggled with one or another relative, as well as with more local figures, for the control of western Îrân and 'Irâq.

His chief enemy came to be his half-brother, Muḥammad Tapar, with whom he fought a series of indecisive battles until his death in 1104. Muḥammad then became head of the Saljûq family, and gained a reputation which later made of him one of the mightiest monarchs of Islâm. He did keep more of less peaceful control over the central Saljûq areas, and even over Khurâsân in the northeast through his younger brother Sanjar, till his own death in 1118; till then restoring a diminished coherence to the Saljûq power. Meanwhile, however, both the Nizârîs and the Crusaders had gained solid footholds.

Ismâ'îlîs intervene at the heart of the Saljûq power.

During its first decade, even just after the death of Malikshâh, the Nizârî revolt had confined its actual seizing of fortresses for the most part to relatively inaccessible areas – Rûdbâr and the Elburz mountains south of the Caspian, the wastes of Quhistân, the mountainous borders between Fârs and Khûzistân. As the troubled reign of Barkiyâruq continued, the Nizârîs attempted actions nearer to the center of Saljûq power. Ibn al-Athîr dated their overt activity at Iṣfahân itself, the Saljûq headquarters, from 1093 when Barkiyâruq gave up besieging one of his stepmothers there; it is presumably about that time that the great terror and the massacre of Nizârîs took place there.

But it was only in about 1100 that Aḥmad, son of 'Abd al-Malik ibn 'Aṭṭâsh, seized control of the fortress Shâhdiz, at Iṣfahân, after gradually converting its garrison. Râwandî tells us he became school teacher for the children of the garrison, who were Daylamites – that is, probably already had Shî'ite tendencies; then he built a mission house where he preached every night, till they were all convinced.[10] At first he was evidently not overtly rebellious; for it is said simply that people disliked his ways and predicted a bad outcome. Even at the end he was trying to persuade the Saljûqs to accept him as free vassal, and leave him alone as heretofore. Provided he avoided attacking any lands of the Sulṭân himself, this was by no means an unprecedented arrangement; but in the general circumstances of the Ismâʿîlî revolt it could not last. Shâhdiz in Ismâʿîlî hands was a standing threat to Iṣfahân, and so to the whole Saljûq power and prestige.

At about the same time the Ismâʿîlîs seized Khâlinjân, another fortress near Iṣfahân. (It is said that a carpenter ingratiated himself with the commander, and then got the whole garrison helplessly drunk at a banquet.) Moreover, they were proceeding so well in the conversion of the rank and file of Barkiyâruq's armies that it is said some officers asked permission of Barkiyâruq to appear before him in armor, for fear of their men.

At about the same time, again, a prominent, but of course secret adherent of the Ismâʿîlî cause at Iṣfahân, the Ra'îs Muẓaffar, persuaded one of the Saljûq amîrs, Amîr Dâd Ḥabashî, to acquire and to install him in a prominent fortress on the main way between Khurâsân and western Îrân, Gird Kûh near Dâmghân.[11] As Ismâʿîlîs did elsewhere, the Ra'îs proceeded to make Gird Kûh as self-sufficient as possible, not regarding its occupancy as transient. It seems he had an extremely deep well dug in difficult terrain; but did not himself reach water with it; only years later, after an earthquake, did it produce water.

The Ra'îs, Rashîd ad-Dîn says, was very well connected among high Saljûq personages; it was in this way that he had been able to win the Amîr Dâd's favor, and he did not cease furthering the Ismâʿîlî cause within Saljûq affairs when he had gained his fortress. The Ismâʿîlîs even intervened in a body, five thousand strong, to support the amîr Ḥabashî and Barkiyâruq against the latter's half brother Sanjar in 1100, who was supporting his own full brother Muḥammad Tapar; but the inter-

[10] Ibn al-Athîr, *Kâmil* year 494; Râwandî gives fuller details. Râwandî, followed by Mustawfî (wr. 1330, *Ta'rîkh-i Guzîda*, Gibb Memorial XIV, 1910), gives Aḥmad 30,000 followers, which would provide a very substantial army. But one must practically ignore all such numerical estimates in these cases.

[11] Rashîd ad-Dîn says that the Ra'îs Muẓaffar was seeking a refuge from the gathering storm of repression in Iṣfahân. The acquisition is dated as coming soon after the breach between Barkiyâruq and Muḥammad, 492.

vention failed to win the day.[12] Ḥabashî was killed, and the Ra'îs Muẓaffar kept the amîr's treasure within Gird Kûh. It is said that he there declared himself openly an adherent of Ḥasan-i Ṣabbâḥ; but he was well enough accepted by the population that when Sanjar and Muḥammad were plundering Dâmghân the next year the population took refuge with him at Gird Kûh.[13]

Unorganized anti-Ismâʿîlî violence.

All did not go smoothly for the Ismâʿîlîs, of course; it was a time of enormous turmoil. In some cases, amîrs tiring of their allegiance and setting off on their own tried their hands at attacking the Ismâʿîlîs on the way, and did them much damage. Unar was attacking the Ismâʿîlîs around Iṣfahân at the very time they were acquiring their strongholds there; he was assassinated soon after. Ḥusâmî raided again a couple of years later. Trickier was Jâwalî, who played a large role later in Syrian politics; he was at this time near Arrajân. He had some of his own men pretend to be converted to Ismâʿîlism, and join the Ismâʿîlîs in their fortress. Then according to plan Jâwalî pretended to set out to bring tribute before a stronger neighboring lord; his men within the Ismâʿîlî fortress persuaded their friends to attack him and seize the tribute. They sent out a band of three hundred of their best men, who were of course betrayed; only thirty escaped.

Not only the military lords, but the city populations were glad to attack the Ismâʿîlîs when occasion arose. It seems that a certain secretary had converted the Saljûq lord of Kirmân – a major triumph. But the Kirmânîs objected. A legist who had power among them tried to win the lord, Îrânshâh, back to Sunnism; and leaving the court late one night was killed at the door. An official who accused Îrânshâh of the murder had to flee, but was made welcome by Muḥammad Tapar; meanwhile the army became angry at Îrânshâh, and forced him out. Refused admittance by the people of a not distant town, he finally sought refuge in the fortress of Sumayram with his Ismâʿîlî friend. The Kirmân army followed him here, and when the lord of the fortress found they accused him of Ismâʿîlism, he was driven out again. This time he was caught and killed.

[12] *Akhbâr ad-Dawlat as-Saljûqiyya*, ca. 1264, anon., ed. M. Iqbal (Lahore, 1933), p. 87, has a slight variant. The Ismâʿîlî troops came from Ṭabas under Ismâʿîl al-Kulkulî.

[13] Ibn al-Athîr, *Kâmil*, year 494; the Ra'îs Muẓaffar and the Ismâʿîlîs are not mentioned, but since we know from Rashîd ad-Dîn that it was through Ḥabashi that Gird Kûh was taken, and Ḥabashî had died in 493, this follows.

Saljûqs attempt repression.

Nevertheless, on the whole the Ismâʿîlî prospects were looking up. The Ismâʿîlîs were now not only seizing remote or nearer strongholds, assassinating occasional amîrs; they were intervening directly in Saljûq affairs; and around Iṣfahân and Gird Kûh they were even collecting taxes, on agriculture and trade, such as to cut down the Saljûq revenues. It was clearly time for major action to be taken against them. The opposing armies were even calling Barkiyâruq's men *Bâṭinîs* – that is, Ismâʿîlîs – Ibn al-Athîr tells us. And Barkiyâruq had not only been accused of urging Ismâʿîlî vengeance against those amîrs that opposed him,[14] but had himself been attempted by assassins.[15] Both his reputation and his life were in danger. If it was true, as all seemed to think, that at first he had been tolerant of the Ismâʿîlîs so as to bolster himself politically, they were now far more danger than help. In 1101 he and Sanjar evidently came to an agreement, at last, to try to root out these astonishing Ismâʿîlîs in their respective areas.

Sanjar sent an amîr, Bazghâsh, against Quhistân; who after committing much devastation was according to Ibn al-Athîr bribed to leave the town of Ṭabas alone. Three years later he returned with in addition to his own men a number of volunteers for this Sunnî *jihâd*, holy war; they destroyed Ṭabas and a number of strongholds, perpetrated as much destruction and enslavement as seemed feasible, and then left after exacting from the population a promise not to arm themselves nor to preach their religion. Sanjar was blamed for allowing the Ismâʿîlîs to get off so lightly.[16] And indeed, in the next year it is said that Ismâʿîlîs from around Ṭuraythîth in Quhistân were strong enough to take revenge by plundering a pilgrim caravan as far west as near Rayy.[17]

In 1101, also, Barkiyâruq, pressed by his grandees, tried to rid Iṣfahân of its Ismâʿîlîs by a second and much greater massacre. Accusation without substantiation was apparently enough to destroy a man. The

[14] Such as the shiḥna of Iṣfahân, Sarmaz; and also certain scholars at the Niẓâmiyya seminary.

[15] After taking as vizier Fakhr al-Mulk son of Niẓâm al-Mulk (in place of his brother) – Râwandi, p. 143. Later, in year 500, Fakhr al-Mulk was himself killed at Sanjar's court – and at the same time others of the court were indirectly destroyed by being implicated by the captured assassin. Such was the confusion and terror, that he was believed.

[16] Mîrkhwând, p. 160.

[17] Pilgrim caravans were by no means exempt from attack, especially from the bedouin Arabs. Since they went heavily armed, therefore, there was often much secular merchandise with them.

violence extended as far as Baghdâd, where Barkiyâruq caused his representative to be killed: Asadâbâdî, whose nephew was later active as an Ismâ'îlî in Syria.[18] A professor at the seminary in Baghdâd had to be saved personally by the Caliph. The affair seems primarily to have taken the form of an army purge – numerous officers were accused, some of whom fled. The Kâkwayhid lord of Yazd, of an old Shî'ite family, was one such who fled, but was caught and killed. Nevertheless, no Ismâ'îlî fortresses seem to have been attacked, and the Ismâ'îlîs will have largely held their own.

Ismâ'îlîs in Syria: their patron Riḍwân.

In Syria the Nizârîs were acquiring at this same time a perhaps dubious protector in Riḍwân, the Saljûq lord of Aleppo who had four years before recognized briefly the suzerainty of Musta'lî.[19] Riḍwân's father had been the Saljûq lord of all Syria, and Riḍwân continued to be yielded an intermittent and nominal supremacy among the chiefs who held the various Syrian towns. The advent of the "Frankish" Crusaders in 1097 had first been met like a transient raid from the Byzantines, to be countered or endured as the condition of each amîr's holdings seemed to indicate; when the Crusaders settled down to stay, their presence in several of the coast towns served chiefly to complicate the jealous quarrels of the Turkish amîrs over what remained. By 1101 Riḍwân was faced with the chronic enmity of the other amîrs, who resented his rather impotent claims; as well as the chronic danger from the Franks in Antioch and Edessa, who were glad to encroach on the Aleppine territories. At this point he added to his troubles by allowing himself to be identified to some degree with the Ismâ'îlî movement.

Sauvaget suggests this move by Riḍwân rose from fear, and was designed to conciliate the Nizârîs.[20] It has also been suggested that he wanted a force more dependable than his proud Turks, and was willing

[18] It is said by Ibn al-Athîr that Asadâbâdî offered to procure the death of any man desired, if his own life were spared. He was killed, and there was no praying over his corpse. (Muslims consider it wrong to pray for one whom God has condemned.)
[19] For Syrian matters the most valuable authority here is Ibn al-Qalânisî, though he must be supplemented by the others – Ibn al-'Adîm Kamâl ad-Dîn, Ibn al-Athîr, and the various manuscript writers especially. Defrémery and Cahen, especially, have been helpful in providing access to the material.
[20] *Alep*, p. 98.

to strike a bargain with the heretics. On the other hand, he may have been sincerely convinced of the Nizârî case, though he protected them only when he could do so safely.[21] It is said that he was converted by a learned astrologer, al-Ḥakîm al-Munajjim, who was the chief of the Ismâʿîlîs locally. For a few years evidently the Nizârîs moved openly and perhaps arrogantly in Aleppo. It seems that Riḍwân caused to be erected a *dâr ad-daʿwa*, a building for their preaching.[22] Their enemies accused them of robbing or killing with impunity whom they would, as well as of haughty behavior in the streets; and lay to their door the death of a crucial opponent of Riḍwân among the amîrs,[23] and of the chief religious judge of Aleppo. Nevertheless, it was their enemies who possessed the chief city offices.

The atmosphere of the time may be illustrated by a contemporary report (written in Damascus) of the death of the amîr just mentioned. "And in [that year] arrived the news from Ḥimṣ that its lord, the amîr Janâḥ ad-Dawla Ḥusayn Atâbak, came down from the fortress to the mosque for the Friday prayers, with his picked men around him fully armed; and when he arrived at his place of prayer according to his custom, some three Persian Bâṭinites attacked him. With them was an old man, whom they blessed and listened to in the manner of ascetics [that is, of Ṣûfîs]. He [Janâḥ ad-Dawla?] threatened them, and they stabbed him with their knives, and killed him; and killed with him many of his men. There were in the mosque then Ṣûfîs, both Persians and others; they were suspected and killed unresistingly, unjustly right away, to the last man. The people of Ḥimṣ were much upset by this event, and fled immediately in panic. Most of the Turks living there fled to Damascus, and matters fell into confusion there [in Ḥimṣ]. They sent messages to the malik Shams al-Mulûk in Damascus, requesting him to send someone to take charge of Ḥimṣ on

[21] David Schaffner, 'Relations of the Order of Assassins with the Crusaders during the Twelfth Century,' typed thesis, Department of History, University of Chicago, 1939, p. 14, is sure Riḍwân can have had few religious convictions, because of his vacillating policies in regard to the Ismâʿîlîs. Fortunately, or not, however, it is quite possible for a man to have inner convictions which in practice he fails, and which he may even try to deny to himself.

[22] Ibn Taghrîbirdî, a confused writer, d. 1469, *an-Nujûm az-Zâhira*, *R. H. C. Or.*, III, 481 ff. yr. 507.

[23] Janâḥ ad-Dawla, in yr. 496, whom Riḍwân was tied to by marriage, and had publicly to come to an agreement with. B. Lewis ('Sources for the history of the Syrian Assassins,' *Speculum*, XXVII, nr. 4 [Oct. 1952], p. 495 ff.) notes that the prejudiced Ibn al-Athîr makes Riḍwân explicitly responsible for the murder, and at a moment (yr. 495), when it jeopardized the Muslim resistance against the Franks. Kamâl ad-Dîn has the Ismâʿîlîs stir up troubles between the two; for which reason Janâḥ ad-Dawla tried to capture al-Ḥakîm al-Munajjim at a certain battle.

whom they could depend for its defense [against the Franks]."[24] Soon after this, the Ismâ'îlî chief, al-Ḥakîm al-Munajjim – who had been a special enemy of Janâḥ ad-Dawla's – died; and was succeeded by Abû Ṭâhir the goldsmith.

It seems clear that whatever Riḍwân's motives may have been for his favoring of the Nizârîs, he could be pleased at some of its results. Syria was a medley of religions, and in parts a majority of its population was not even Muslim, but Christian of at least four major sects. Among the Muslims the Sunnîs were closely rivalled by a variety of the Shî'a: Druzes that had separated from the Ismâ'îlîs three generations before; Nuṣayrîs in the mountains west of Aleppo; Twelver Shî'a; as well as both Nizârî and pro-Fâṭimid Ismâ'îlîs. In Aleppo the Shî'a, at least taken together, seem to have outweighed the Sunnîs. It is perhaps a consciousness of contrast to its Shî'ite neighbors, as well as a heritage from early Muslim times, that made the other chief city of Syria, Damascus, maintain a reputation for an unusually zealous Sunnî populace.

Now the Syrians not only kept alive a variety of religious loyalties; they were also, as Gibb has pointed out,[25] one of the more insistent of peoples upon sharing in the determination of their own political destinies. Accordingly, to have the support of one of the popular religious groups could be valuable. If Riḍwân was following a general Ismâ'îlî trend in switching his favor from Musta'lî to the Nizârîs, he may have been reaping his reward when he was able to clear the Franks out of the Jazr lands, southwest of Aleppo, by ordering a rising of the population; for these were, as we know, Ismâ'îlîs; and achieved a feat of which the Turkish occupying armies even when victorious seemed incapable by themselves.[26] We note that at a battle for Artâḥ, in 1105, it was the Aleppine infantry, rather than the presumably Turkish cavalry, that held; Riḍwân was often at outs with

[24] Ibn al-Qalânisî, ed. Amedroz, p. 142 (year 496). For a better translation, cf. H. A. R. Gibb, *The Damascus Chronicle* (London, 1932), p. 57.

[25] Introduction to *A Damascus Chronicle*, p. 26. He compares them especially to the always rather inert population of Egypt; however, some of the Iranian and Anatolian population seem to have yielded nothing to the Syrian in initiative and turbulance.

[26] Ibn al-'Adîm Kamâl ad-Dîn, d. 1262, *Ta'rîkh Ḥalab*, *R.H.C. Or.*, III, 577 ff., year 496. The French translator here allowed his concern for the beauty of his mother tongue to override the repetitiveness of Arabic nouns and the indefiniteness of Arabic pronouns; he has Riḍwân order the *troops* of the Jazr to seize all the *infidels*, while the original has him order an indefinite *them* to seize all the *Franks* – not all the Christians, nor all the enemies of the Ismâ'îlîs or of the Sunnîs. In the next phrase, it is the *people* of the various towns who are credited with the action (*R. H. C. Hist. Or.*, III, 592).

other Turks, and may have preferred to rely upon a virile segment of the local population.[27]

FALLING FORTUNES (1105-1118)

Reversal of the Ismâ'îlî fortunes in Syria (1106-1113).

The relative prosperity of the Nizârîs at Aleppo could not last long, however; the feeling of the Saljûq empire at large was rising against them. Barkiyâruq and Sanjar – operating over larger, but in some ways less diversified territories, among populations more predominantly Sunnî – may not have had Riḍwân's reasons for cultivating the Nizârîs; but Riḍwân soon came to have their reasons for rejecting them. Moreover, after Barkiyâruq's death in 1104 Muḥammad Tapar carried out a more successful campaign against them, which Riḍwân cannot have ignored; being on occasion under direct pressure from him.

In 1106 the Ismâ'îlîs of Sarmîn, a town of the Jazr, managed to seize the citadel of the town Afâmiya, having murdered the unpopular Egyptian appointee, with the aid of local Ismâ'îlîs;[28] this would have given them an independent power in Syria, even though at the time they recognized the suzerainty of Riḍwân; but having not yet put in enough provisions, they lost the place to Tancred by the end of the year. At this time a leading local Ismâ'îlî, Abû l-Fatḥ – probably not the nephew of Ḥasan-i Ṣabbâḥ by that name[29] – was killed, and others were ransomed back to Aleppo including Abû Ṭâhir, the chief leader in Syria.

It was just the next year that Riḍwân was finally led to repudiate the Ismâ'îlîs; having executed a few of them, he expelled a number more from Aleppo. This will have further justified the Nizârî desire for an independent base of operations. It is said that it was from the Ismâ'îlîs that Tancred took, in 1110, Kafar Lâthâ; but the weakness of such lesser places

[27] Ibn al-Qalânisî, *Dhayl Ta'rîkh Dimashq*, year 498, mentions the honorable, but vain, stand of the *aḥdâth* (young bands) of Aleppo when the Armenians in Artâḥ had offered their town to Riḍwân to escape from the Frank Tancred's tyranny.

[28] Ibn al-Qalânisî notes that the population of Afâmiya, being Ismâ'îlîs, had requested a governor from Egypt soon after Mustâ'lî's succession; now at least many of them welcomed the Sarmîn Nizârîs and the proclamation of Riḍwân's rule. Ibn al-'Adîm implies that Abû Ṭâhir, the new Nizârî chief at Aleppo, was not admitted to Afâmiya as ruler there as he had expected; the local Ismâ'îlîs were jealous of outsiders.

[29] He is from Sarmîn, despite what seems a confusion on von Hammer's part.

only emphasized the need for strong ones.[30] It is said to have been just at this time that there arrived from Alamût that Abû Muḥammad, on whose death as head of the Syrian Ismâʿîlîs, by then settled in mountain strongholds, Sinân took over,[31] more than fifty years later.

Nevertheless, Riḍwân's dependence on the Ismâʿîlîs did not cease. Riḍwân decided to hold Aleppo closed to the Saljûq troops sent from Muḥammad Tapar to fight the Crusaders (the Sunnî lord of Damascus, Ṭughtegîn, was also unfriendly to these dangerous interlopers from the east); and in this crisis he was willing to use Ismâʿîlîs as well as other loyal citizens in manning the walls and in protecting his own person from disaffected citizens or soldiers. The next year, 1111, Riḍwân was accused of complicity in an Ismâʿîlî plot to assassinate a wealthy Iranian, Abû Ḥarb, who was travelling through Aleppo, who had been a great enemy of the sect; it was said Riḍwân was to get a share of the goods which would at the same time be plundered. The Iranian fought off his assailants, and the city was aroused into a general massacre of Ismâʿîlîs, which Riḍwân was forced to condone.

Riḍwân has been given a very bad character by most historians, including the Aleppine Ibn al-ʿAdîm, as being devoid of loyalty or honor.[32] Certainly he did not co-operate with other Muslims and particularly with other Saljûqs against the Crusaders; and he antagonized many of the amîrs in other ways. It is said that just before he died he executed two of his brothers – presumably to ensure the lordship to his son, who killed his own brothers in turn. (In a time of repeated wars of brother against brother, this was not unparalleled.) But Ibn al-Qalânisî, one of the earliest writers we have, and neutral (at Damascus) to the Aleppine partisanships, makes him out rather better. Only at the very end did he finally lose the formal acknowledgment of his suzerainty at Damascus, and towns like Ḥamâ and even amîrs were sometimes willing to submit to him voluntarily, in preference to others. At his death there was consternation at Aleppo, and it is said that his officers regretted him. The unsavory reputation of this patron of the Ismâʿîlîs has seemed to reflect upon his protégés; but perhaps the reputation was itself due to his ties with the Ismâʿîlîs.

30 Cahen notes from b. al-Furât a struggle for Maʿarra Miṣrîn between Nizârîs and other Shîʿites.

31 C. Defrémery from Dhahabî, 'Nouvelles recherches sur les Ismaéliens ou Batiniens de Syrie,' *JA*, ser. 5, III (1854–5), p. 400.

32 He and his Ismâʿîlîs have been suspected of more murders than even the latter were probably responsible for. Defrémery lists among his assassinations the case of Mawdûd of Mosul, at Damascus; a case where none could identify the killer's head, and the murder remained unsolved.

Disorganization of the Syrian daʿwa (1113).

Riḍwân died in 1113, two years after the massacre that followed the attempt upon the Iranian traveler. It seems that a good number of Ismâʿîlîs had survived the flurry of popular temper, and till then their organizational order had not been upset. Riḍwân's son was put under contrary pressures in regard to them, but evidently his very precarious position among his envious amîrs counted against the Ismâʿîlîs. Ibn al-ʿAdîm says that the Sulṭân Muḥammad Tapar asked that they all be massacred. At the demand of both Shîʿa (Twelver) and Sunnî leaders they were all arrested or banished; a small number were killed.

Among these, however, were those who had been holding the Syrian movement together, such as a brother of the late Ḥakîm al-Munajjim, and his successor Abû Ṭâhir. At the same time, evidently, the Ismâʿîlîs felt their position insecure in the whole area; one of their chiefs, Ibrâhîm, who had held the citadel of Bâlas, abandoned it; another, Ibn Dimlâj, had already taken refuge in the Mesopotamian town of Raqqa – though Ibn al-ʿAdîm counts him as their chief leader for a while. There he died. A number from various parts of the Jazr now tried to seize control of Shayzar, a fortress both strong and strategically placed in north Syria. There they evidently hoped to establish a renewed center of operations.

The Banû Munqidh, Arab lords of Shayzar, seemed to have a tradition of generous treatment of all. When the Ismâʿîlîs had to flee the Aleppine lands they, like other brands of refugees before them, were treated kindly by the Banû Munqidh. But when on Easter the tolerant family, with most of the population no doubt, went out to view the local Christian celebrations, the Ismâʿîlîs tried to seize their citadel. There ensued a battle from tower to tower, the men of the city entering and holding what they could, the Ismâʿîlîs trying to hold on to the commanding spots, till eventually the Banû Munqidh returned to aid their loyal townsmen. They drove the Ismâʿîlîs within the citadel, and eventually slaughtered them all.[33] Thereupon the Ismâʿîlîs who lived in the town were killed likewise.

Even so, the Ismâʿîlîs were not completely beaten down. Within a couple of years we find them assassinating the amîr Aḥmad Yal.[34] Here-

[33] Gibb's rendering of Ibn al-Qalânisî corrects a common version in older translations which had women pulling their men by cords into the citadels: it seems the reverse was the case, and readers have been confused by an odd grammatical usage of the age (*A Damascus Chronicle*, p. 147).

[34] Ibn al-Qalânisî ed. Amedroz, p. 197–8, year 510. Other years near this are also given.

after their major activity in Syria was no longer at Aleppo, but they continued to have a role in the city and its neighborhood.

Muḥammad Tapar and the Saljûq counteroffensive (1105-1107).

Probably Barkiyâruq and Sanjar had already stopped what might have been an Ismâʿîlî sweep, in ʿIrâq and Îrân, of large portions of the Saljûq realm; yet the Ismâʿîlîs had held their own in spite of them, and had seemed to do almost as well at Iṣfahân as at the more favorably disposed Aleppo. But every reason still existed for destroying the Nizârî power: it was not an ordinary military power, dependent upon a strong individual, which an amîr could share his territories patiently with if its destruction proved too expensive. The Nizârî power aimed to control everyone, everywhere; the scope of its ambition was seen in the variety of its continuing assassinations, not only of amîrs but of civilian scholars.[35] Accordingly, along with the concentration of Saljûq power in the hands of Muḥammad Tapar, had been introduced a time of Ismâʿîlî reverses which was felt even in Syria. Within two years of Barkiyâruq's death, Muḥammad had launched major campaigns against the Ismâʿîlîs which seem to have checked definitively their expanding revolt.

One expedition was to Takrît, with whose capture he charged one of his amîrs; as we have noticed, this expedition failed, strictly speaking, only because the Ismâʿîlî commander of the place preferred to surrender it to the Twelver Arab Ṣadaqa than to the Sunnî Turks; in any case, it was lost to the cause.[36] Ibn Isfandiyâr says that at about this time also, Muḥammad had his brother Sanjar attack Ismâʿîlî Quhistân again, from Khurâsân.

The chief campaign Muḥammad led in person, against Shâhdiz at Iṣfahân. The siege is said to have been delayed even in starting by the maneuvers of the friends of the Ismâʿîlîs within the Saljûq armies; it was

[35] Both Ibn al-Khujandî at Rayy, 497, and his pupil Ibn al-Mashâṭ in 498 were assassinated; and later Ibn al-Khujandî's son, who had been of course an enemy of the Ismâʿîlîs. The killed are often leaders among the orthodox, Ḥanafî or Shâfiʿî equally. But many accusations were as dubious as in the case of al-Aʿazz ad-Dahistânî, one of the instigators of Barkiyâruq's measures against the Ismâʿîlîs. A slave of a man whom he had killed assassinated him in 495; it was said the slave was an Ismâʿîlî, but this would hardly be necessary.

[36] Ibn al-Athîr, *Kâmil*, yr. 500. In this material we are again depending on Rashîd ad-Dîn, Ibn al-Athîr, and Râwandî primarily.

the Sunnî religious authorities who urged it on. Even they, however, were divided by a crucial demand of the Ismâʿîlîs: these maintained that they accepted all the religious prescriptions of the sharîʿa, differing from the Sunnîs only in the matter of the imâmate; that therefore the sulṭân had no grounds for acting against them provided only that they accepted him as military suzerain; which they offered to do. It seems that at first most of the legists were willing to admit the thesis, upon the grounds that Sunnî unity was based on the forms of the sharîʿa – on the utterance of the formula of faith. But one legist is credited with holding out against so general an application of the principle, and with having determined the others to deny that the militant Ismâʿîlîs could be included on the basis of a pure form. Accordingly, the Ismâʿîlî demand was rejected.

The Ismâʿîlîs had enough friends, apparently, that they could delay matters by bargaining for alternative fortresses, or for other privileges. But in the midst of the negotations, an amîr who especially opposed them was attacked. Now the siege was pressed in earnest; the only bargaining that remained was for conditions of capitulation. It was granted that some of the garrison could depart to the Ismâʿîlî strongholds around Arrajân, in Quhistân, and at Alamût; the remainder were to give in when it was heard these had arrived safely. When the news came, however, Aḥmad ibn ʿAṭṭâsh tried to hold one part of the fortifications even while the rest was destroyed; he and his band held out gallantly till finally a traitor pointed out that along the wall they had placed arms, but had not men enough to man them. Aḥmad's wife, at the end, decked herself in jewels and leaped the wall; Aḥmad himself was paraded ignominiously through the streets of Isfahân, and then skinned alive.[37]

The vizier Saʿd al-Mulk was accused of complicity in an Ismâʿîlî plot to poison the Sulṭân Muḥammad at the time, and killed; [33] on the other hand, several of the legists who had shared in the decision against the Ismâʿîlîs were themselves assassinated within the next few years.[39]

[37] Chief guides here are Râwandî and Ibn al-Athîr, yr. 500; Ibn al-Qalânisî, ed. Amedroz, ps. 151 ff. The flowery letter of victory to be read there points up the chief reasons for attacking Shâhdiz (presumably in spite of its offer of allegiance): that Aḥmad attacked and killed Muslims; and that the fortress was dangerously near Iṣfahân, and the center of other Ismâʿîlî activities.

[38] Falsely, according to Bundârî; who also gives the story of Shâhdiz, ed. Houtsma, p. 90 ff.

[39] Including the chief Qâḍî of Iṣfahân, 502; killed by a Persian who managed to get himself between the Qâḍî and his bodyguard; and Ṣadr ad-Dîn ibn al-Khujandî (whose father had already been assassinated), as late as 523. Ibn al-Athîr, *Kâmil.*

The limits of Saljûq reconquest (1107-1118).

It was presumably soon after this that the fortresses around Arrajân, on the Fârs-Khûzistân border, were taken; Ibn al-Balkhî, writing before 1116, speaks of the Ismâʿîlî occupation there as a recent, but past event.[40] After this we hear little of the Ismâʿîlîs who survived there. It is possible that one or more fortresses in this general area continued in Ismâʿîlî hands even later. Benjamin of Tudela, who was in Baghdâd about 1163, heard of Ismâʿîlîs located midway between Susa and Hamadân, in the mountains. There were four Jewish congregations living among them, who joined them in their warfare.[41]

Alamût seems to have claimed more attention from the first, for the next year[42] the new vizier, Aḥmad, a son of Niẓâm al-Mulk, was sent against it, with that Jâwalî who had attacked the Ismâʿîlîs near Arrajân. He accomplished a good deal of destruction, but was defeated. (It is evidently at this time that the Bâwandid neighbor of the Nizârîs, offended at Sulṭân Muḥammad's arrogance, refused to give help against the Ismâʿîlîs.)[43] Later, Aḥmad was attacked by the Ismâʿîlîs, but survived.

Muḥammad then commissioned the amîr of Sâwa (where one of the first of the Ismâʿîlî incidents had occurred, not too far from Alamût), Anûshtagîn Shîrgîr, to handle Alamût. Evidently deciding that an assault would be of little use, he tried attrition: each year, according to Juwaynî, his troops destroyed all the crops or other supplies in Rûdbâr that they could; it was during this period that Ḥasan-i Ṣabbâḥ as well as many others temporarily sent their womenfolk to happier places, such as Gird Kûh. A number of strongholds were taken, whose garrisons were allowed to go to Alamût itself.[44] At length in 1118 Shîrgîr determined on a settled siege with the aid of various other amîrs and their troops, sent by Muḥammad to be at his orders. These came, it seems, unwillingly, evidently from jealousy of Shîrgîr. Shîrgîr was noted for his piety, and was probably not a winning man.[45] When the garrison of Alamût was near

40 S.v. Arrajân and Jîlûya.

41 A. Asher, tr., *The Itinerary of Rabbi Benjamin of Tudela* (London, 1840–1), p. 120. The accuracy of this (though Benjamin's distances, at least, are seldom accurate) may possibly be confirmed by a reference to Ismâʿîlîs from ʿIrâq, along with Khurâsân and Daylamân, at the Qiyâma of Ḥasan II.

42 Ibn al-Qalânisî, yr. 501; Ibn al-Athîr has Muḥammad himself go with his vizier in 503; perhaps there were two expeditions.

43 Ibn Isfandiyâr, p. 241.

44 Particularly, yr. 505, ʿAlî b. Mûsâ, from Kîlâm; and a stronghold Bîrâ about twenty miles from Qazwîn. Ibn al-Athîr, *Kâmil*, under yr. 511.

45 Sibṭ ibn al-Jawzî, quoted in Amedroz' Ibn al-Qalânisî, p. 151.

exhaustion, and everyone (as Bundârî reiterates)[46] was joyful with the prospective victory, news arrived of Muḥammad Tapar's death. Shîrgîr's pleading was to no avail; even after promising to stay just three days more, the other amîrs broke camp and left him in the night.[47] Fighting a rear-guard action against the triumphant Nizârîs, he lost many men, but far more supplies; and the Ismâʿîlîs ate.

[46] Bundârî, *Ta'rîkh*, ed. Houtsma, 1889, p. 117, 123, 147.

[47] Perhaps their defection was encouraged by Shîrgîr's bad standing with the next sulṭân, who indeed summoned and killed him. *Akhbâr ad-Dawlat as-Saljûqiyya*, p. 82. Bundârî says a certain Dargazînî incited the sulṭân against him, and was afterwards rewarded with numerous murders by the Nizârîs. Ed. Houtsma, p. 146. It is probably going too far, however, to ascribe the whole failure to Dargazînî's pro-Ismâʿîlî intrigue (D'Ohsson, *Histoire des Mongols* (Amsterdam, 1852), III, 161).

CHAPTER V

THE NIZÂRÎ STATE

BUZURG'UMMÎD AND TERRITORIAL SETTLEMENT (1118-1138)

The great Saljûq counter-offensive had come to its limits now; in the closing years of Ḥasan-i Ṣabbâḥ's life and in the time of his successor, Buzurg'ummîd, though the struggle continued briskly, little change occurred in the fortunes of either side.[1] The pattern of Nizârî revolt eased almost imperceptibly into one of a permanent Nizârî state with a fixed, though scattered, territory.

The Ismâ'îlîs among the amîrs (1118-1126).

The Saljûq chieftains, after the death of Muḥammad Tapar, were not very glamorous as guardians of the Sunnî dominance, and yet perhaps effective enough. Sanjar, allowed the precarious position of supreme Sulṭân among the Saljûqs and their amîrs since his brother's death, held Khurâsân and dominated with increasing difficulty Transoxania on the one hand and the sulṭâns at Iṣfahân on the other. These latter struggled with an increasingly independent Caliphal power at Baghdâd and allowed the more distant amîrs to operate on their own.

The Nizârî chiefs now took their place among these amîrs, from the point of view of the outer world. Gradually the Nizârîs ceased to be a revolutionary faction within each city, and became a territorial people instead, their various dâr al-hijra forming rather a permanent homeland than a mere base for aggressive action. Such Ismâ'îlîs as remained in Sunnî territory made little stir, and gradually the relations of the independent Ismâ'îlîs with the Sunnî lords ceased to be based upon an all-out campaign one against the other, and came to be a matter of particular

[1] Rashîd ad-Dîn notes how the Ismâ'îlîs were relieved at Muḥammad's death, and expanded; but such expansion seems to have been local – no doubt the regaining of the fortresses Shîrgîr had taken.

cases – even of involvement in local political squabbles. To be sure there was still unrelenting war between the Nizârîs and whatever Sunnî chiefs made pretensions to representing Islâm. Even a Nizârî homeland was still above all an instrument in the holy struggle. But already in the time of Buzurg'ummîd the chief active phase of that war looks as if it had been introduced by a purely local incident.

The Bâwandid ruler of Mâzandarân had refused when Muḥammad Tapar had summoned him to join in the campaign against Alamût. The Mâzandarânî folk were maintaining their independence of the arrogant Saljûqs; and when a vassal town aided the Saljûq army that was sent to punish the Bâwandid ruler for his indiscretion, the Saljûq army was routed and the vassal town found its men's faces marked with the names of Muḥammad and ʿAlî to shame them.[2] However, sometime after Muḥammad Tapar's death the Ismâʿîlîs assassinated one of the Bâwandid ruling family;[3] and the new ruler of Mâzandarân became their enemy. Along about this time (Ẓahîr ad-Dîn gives no dates, only reigns) another vassal lord asked (in vain) aid of the Ismâʿîlîs for his revolt against the Bâwandids; who were themselves being aided at this point by Sanjar's nephew Maḥmûd, the sulṭân at Iṣfahân.[4] When next dates appear – through Rashîd ad-Dîn and Ibn al-Athîr – Maḥmûd is instituting his part of a general campaign against the new-found Ismâʿîlî enemies of his equally new-found Bâwandid ally.

Defeat of the renewed Saljûq offensive (1126-1131).

In 1126 began an attack both on Quhistân and on Rûdbâr. For two decades we have had no notices of any activity by Sanjar against the Ismâʿîlîs; it may be that this peace was an actual truce, and that it is to be connected with a repeated tradition that Sanjar did not fight the Ismâʿîlîs. This tradition takes the form, in Rashîd ad-Dîn, of a long undatable story of the great respect paid by Sanjar to the Ra'îs Muẓaffar at Gird Kûh, who offered his military submission to Sanjar even while maintaining his allegiance to Alamût.[5] It is also noted that "since it was the

[2] Ibn Isfandiyâr, ed. Browne, *History of Ṭabaristân*, pp. 241–2. Whether the Shîʿa tendency of such a trick indicates that the Mâzandarânî complaisance toward their Ismâʿîlî neighbors sprang from a common Shîʿa feeling is not clear, but doubtful.

[3] Abû Jaʿfar, according to Ibn Isfandiyâr, between 511–534.

[4] Ẓahîr ad-Dîn, ed. B. Dorn, *Muhammedanische Quellen zur Geschichte der Südlichen Küstenländer des Kaspischen Meeres* (St. Petersburg, 1850), I, 224.

[5] In this story Muẓaffar, very aged, is received with honor by Sanjar on one of his

time of Sanjar, none made any attempt to destroy the Ismâʿîlî fortresses";[6] and Juwaynî records finding kindly letters from Sanjar in the Alamût library. Sanjar's inaction is explained by a story with several variations, which is told also of Nûr ad-Dîn and of Saladin: that a dagger is thrust in the floor by his bed, and subsequently he is informed that it will be thrust in his heart if he does not give up his plans to attack.[7] It is made the explanation, in Rashîd ad-Dîn, of Sanjar's and Bazghâsh's "leniency" to the Quhistânîs.

Although the story that Ḥasan-i Ṣabbâḥ had scared Sanjar off may be apocryphal, since what we have noted of Sanjar's relations with the Quhistânîs does not bear it out; yet a general attack on the Ismâʿîlîs in 1126 just two years after Ḥasan's death does suggest an attempt to find whether Ḥasan's successor will prove as strong, in the role of warlord, as did Ḥasan himself.[8] Rashîd ad-Dîn's Ismâʿîlî sources stress the troubles Buzurg'ummîd had to face from his enemies upon his accession. The major battle of Askûd appears to have happened right after his accession, but before the Saljûq attack. Also in the year of Ḥasan's death occurred a major massacre of Ismâʿîlîs in Mesopotamian Âmid: seven hundred killed.[9]

If so, they misread the character of the Ismâʿîlîs. Neither Ḥasan nor Buzurg'ummîd were amîrs on the order of the Saljûqs. The people of Ṭuraythîth and Tarz in Quhistân beat back Sanjar's vizier, Muʿîn al-Mulk, and his troops from Khurâsân;[10] and Shîrgîr's nephew, sent

trips into the western provinces from Khurâsân, in spite of the complaints of courtiers that Muẓaffar had taken all of Ḥabashî's funds for sectarian use. Muẓaffar answers them by citing the great dignities he gave up in the Sunnî world to be addressed in a very simple manner by the Ismâʿîlîs, because he believed them to have the truth; whereat Sanjar and his court marvel. This is probably an Ismâʿîlî romance, like the story of the three schoolfellows. Certainly it is undatable, for Sanjar went into the western provinces several times; and while Rashîd ad-Dîn has Muẓaffar die in 498 (the year of Barkiyâruq's death, when Sanjar was about 20), he is also made to die forty years after occupying Gird Kûh in about 493. It is a rather typical point in this story that the Nizârîs seem to take delight in approval and honor from outsiders; it is also typical of the Nizârî state that the Ra'îs was succeeded by his son – the Ra'îs Sharaf ad-Dîn Munshî. Rashîd ad-Dîn fol. 297b, l. 22. Ibn al-Athîr has Sanjar besieging Gird Kûh about 35 years after 493.

6 Juwaynî, trans. Defrémery, *JA*, ser. 5, XV (1860), 189.

7 The *Dabistân* adds an apologetic note to the story, explaining that the dagger was not put in Sanjar's heart only because the servant who was at Ḥasan-i Ṣabbâḥ's command had eaten Sanjar's salt, and murder would be ungrateful!

8 Ibn al-Athîr records the assassination of Maḥmûd's vizier Sumayramî even before Ḥasan's death – in 516 – indicating some kind of hostility already then, if the ascription of the assassination was right (Ibn al-Athîr is glad to assume their guilt), and the dating.

9 Ibn al-Athîr, *Kâmil*, yr. 518.

10 Ibn al-Athîr, *Kâmil*, yr. 520.

against Rûdbâr, was beaten soundly. The Nizârîs captured one Tamûr-ṭughân, but released him at Sanjar's request; they had worse luck against one Sâlâr. At Rûdbâr they proceeded, meanwhile, to erect and seize more fortresses; most notable was the building of a new major fortress, Maymûn Diz, in this same year.[11]

The next year we find (the historians through whom we receive these scraps are very occasional and anecdotal, supplying no continuous Nizârî thread among them) the Ismâ'îlîs sending an envoy, a Khwâja Muḥammad Nâṣiḥî Shahrastânî, to Maḥmûd to treat of peace. On leaving Maḥmûd at Iṣfahân, he was lynched, and though Maḥmûd apologized, he refused (prudently enough) to punish the culprits; accordingly two years later the Nizârîs raided Qazwîn (nearer than Iṣfahân to their base) in revenge and slaughtered four hundred persons. The Qazwînîs counterattacked; but fled, say the Ismâ'îlîs, as soon as a single Turk of theirs was killed.[12]

Meanwhile the Nizârîs had assassinated Sanjar's vizier, who had led the attack on Quhistân;[13] Sanjar now destroyed all Nizârîs he could find about him, and went to Rûdbâr also, where he is credited with an enormous slaughter. But the Quhistânîs had their hands free enough to invade Sîstân about this time.[14] A few years later – after their raid on Qazwîn – Maḥmûd returned for an ignominious attempt against an outlying fortress of Alamût in Qazwîn's direction;[15] and the next year was attacking Lammasar itself, without success.

Magnificent gestures from Alamût (1131–1138).

At this point, in 1131, Maḥmûd died; for a number of years there was turmoil over his succession, and this was a sign for a general reshuffling

[11] Even before the building of Maymûndiz, the Nizârîs had taken Ṭâliqân; also in 520 they built Sa'âdat Kûh; and in 524 installed Kiyâ Bû Sâr in Manṣûra. It is worthy notice that many of the individuals referred to by Rashîd ad-Dîn among these Ismâ'îlîs bear the titles *Kiyâ* (a local form), *Khwâja*, and *Dihkhudâ*; and thus we find here also Dihkhudâ 'Abd al-Malik Fashandî as a leader at this time.

[12] It is also recorded by the Ismâ'îlîs – as showing the terror they inspired – that Maḥmûd's army asked for peace without even a battle.

[13] Ibn al-Athîr, *Kâmil*, yr. 521. Rashîd ad-Dîn's manuscript – often wrong – places it in 528.

[14] *Ta'rîkh-i Sîstân*, yr. 523.

[15] Ibn al-Athîr has Maḥmûd take Alamût in 524. Mîrkhwând puts the Qazwîn raid in 523. Râwandî, without a date, cites Maḥmûd's ignominy before the Qal'a Qâhira, and denies circumstantially any success generally. Assuming that Ibn al-Athîr read hastily an overly glamorous report, I have put the two together; Maḥmûd's reign was short in any case, and the result is surely not badly misleading.

of military roles. The Ismâ'îlîs, for instance, got in another raid on Qazwîn. The lord of Khwârazm in Transoxania, it seems, seized for his own deputy one of the strong places near the Nizârî Rûdbâr territory, on a secret plea to Maḥmûd's brother that he would get rid of the Ismâ'îlîs. Thereupon the previous holder of the place, Bartaqash, took refuge with the Ismâ'îlîs. The lord of Khwârazm (Khwârazmshâh) asked that the rebel be given up, on the grounds that while Bartaqash held the place in question he had fought the Ismâ'îlîs, but he, Khwârazmshâh, had been friendly to them. Indeed, Bartaqash had been both a dangerous and a treacherous enemy; having first led a Qazwînî force to rare victory over them; and later betrayed their confidence in him, killing numbers at Lammasar. Buzurg'ummîd refused to deliver him up, though he admitted these facts, maintaining that he would not betray a man who had taken asylum with him; Bartaqash was given a minor fortress for his refuge. We hear no more, however, of Khwârazmshâh's actions against Alamût.

The remainder of the reign of Buzurg'ummîd is marked with similarly large-minded events, though not all quite so noble to our taste. One must allow, to be sure however, for the prejudices of the unknown Ismâ'îlî author of the Book of Buzurg'ummîd, which Rashîd ad-Dîn follows. In any case there was an unedifying run of assassinations and warrings, also.[16] They are said to have raided so far as Georgia. The fright which the Nizârîs still inspired in the Muslim world is shown in the ascription to them of the burning of the cathedral mosque of Iṣfahân.[17]

About the time of Maḥmûd's death, a Zaydî imâm, Abû Hâshim, set himself up in Daylamân, his mission reaching as far as Khurâsân. "Kiyâ Buzurg'ummîd wrote a letter of advice to him, calling his attention to the divine proof [ḥujja] ... [Abû Hâshim] said, What you say is all unbelief and heresy; if you come and discuss it, your unbelief will become clear. They gathered an army ... they gave him battle, and Abû Hâshim was defeated ... The Ismâ'îlîs caught him, proved matters to him abundantly, and burned him."[18] We hear no more of Abû Hâshim's party.

[16] Abû Sa'd al-Harawî at Hamadhân, 519; the Ra'îs of Tabrîz, 528; a muftî of Qazwîn, 529 – to follow Ibn al-Athîr rather than the Rashid ad-Dîn manuscrîpt which here as elsewhere seems to follow him. It is said that in 528 Sanjar attacked Gird Kûh. For 531, the Ismâ'îlî author gives a detailed picture of how the Ismâ'îlîs destroyed utterly the place called Qaṣr al-Bardîn, killing or enslaving its population. (Yâqût has Ṭuraythîth fall to the Ismâ'îlîs only in 530, yet it has been repeatedly mentioned before that date as an Ismâ'îlî center.)

[17] Ibn al-Athîr, *Kâmil*, yr. 515. About the same time, they assassinated Aqsunqur Bursuqî, ruler of Baghdâd. Kamâl ad-Dîn ibn al-'Adîm, *Ta'rîkh Ḥalab*, year 520.

[18] Rashîd ad-Dîn, fol. 300 v.

The Ismâʿîlîs were equally glad to destroy another rival claimant to the imâmate, who was in a far more powerful position: the Caliph himself. In the course of the war between Maḥmûd's successor Masʿûd and the Caliph Mustarshid, the latter was captured; and the Ismâʿîlîs – a large band of them – found opportunity to kill him while he was neglected in Masʿûd's camp. One cannot avoid a suspicion that Masʿûd was deliberately negligent in this case; for at the time Sanjar was insisting that Masʿûd give up the fruits of his victory and allow the Caliph to go home. Yet the Ismâʿîlîs probably needed no urging if the opportunity was presented.

To lesser men, the Ismâʿîlîs liked to think themselves generous. First to their own – one of the last events in the reign of Buzurg'ummîd is the resettlement in a place called Manṣûrâbâd of some Ismâʿîlî refugees from the vicinity of Rayy, who were persecuted there. But also to others. The Ismâʿîlî historian records a lucky capture of a band which included several of the chief men of Qazwîn. Certain enemies of theirs they put to death, but the others they let go – presumably for ransom. The historian does not mention the ransom, but does mention that in return for their freedom the Qazwînîs were asked not to carry on enmity against the Ismâʿîlîs, whether the government did or not. They swore to this, it is recorded, and broke their oaths.

DEFINITION OF THE ISMÂʿÎLÎ POSITION IN THE WEST

Career of Bahrâm at Damascus: the Syrian daʿwa revived (1125–28).

The Nizârî adventures in Syria, meanwhile, seem to have had little immediate connection with those in Rûdbâr and Quhistân; yet they carried the Ismâʿîlîs in much the same direction. To begin with, after the death of Riḍwân they repeated more briefly at Damascus, a decade or so later, their experience with him at Aleppo. But Damascus was Sunnî; they looked to protection from its ruler, but did not long make the city their headquarters. In 1125 Damascus was threatened by the Franks. Muslims from the surrounding territory as well as the untrained citizenry were rallied for its defense; there came also from Ḥimṣ and elsewhere bands of Ismâʿîlîs "famous for their courage", as Ibn al-Qalânisî notes The next year Ṭughtagîn, the amîr of Damascus, gave to the Ismâʿîlîs' chief the frontier fortress of Bâniyâs to hold against the Franks of Jerusalem.[19]

This Ismâ'îlî, Bahrâm, seems to have had his own sum of adventures. His uncle al-Asadâbâdî had been among those court figures killed by Barkiyâruq in the great purge; Bahrâm is said to have fled to Syria, and gone about secretly as an Ismâ'îlî dâ'î until he was able to persuade the then amîr of Aleppo, Îlghâzî, to recommend him to Ṭughtagîn. At Damascus he preached openly, under his own name. He found a following among both craftsmen and the peasantry; and Ṭughtagîn's vizier, Mazdaqânî (though he was no Ismâ'îlî, it is said), was his special protector. There are reports that the Nizârîs now terrorized the Sunnî population, as at first at Aleppo; especially after receiving the stronghold of Bâniyâs. Presumably that means none dared speak against Bahrâm, as in the case of other grandees also. From Bâniyâs evidently Bahrâm tried to bring much of the countryside into obedience; he is accused not only of slandering men of good repute, but of petty highway murder – undoubtedly the first accusation would have grounds, for he surely would not spare his opponents' reputations. He is said to have lured a respected chief in the Valley of Tayyim into his hands, and killed him. The chief's brother swore revenge, and Bahrâm found it necessary to march to the Valley to crush a combination of the inhabitants: Druzes, Nuṣayriyya, etc. He was surprised, beaten, and killed.

Defeat and withdrawal to the mountains in Syria (1129–40).

The next year his successors in both Damascus itself and in Bâniyâs were also overwhelmed. In Damascus Ṭughtagîn's son Bûrî, soon after his accession, did away with his vizier, and set off a general massacre of the Ismâ'îlîs in town: the rumor was that they had planned to betray Damascus to the Franks in return for being given Tyre. So soon as it was known that the vizier had been killed, the militia and the mob began to seize known Ismâ'îlîs, killing them and their families; they dragged them even from their refuges in the homes of powerful citizens (which were usually well-protected by armed servants). They were especially enraged

[19] Nizârî activity did not completely die out in Aleppo meanwhile, of course. In 512 they had assassinated the leading Shî'ite, Ibn Badî', who had helped engineer their suppression there at Riḍwân's death, in 507. Six years later, according to Cahen, they assassinated a similar enemy there, Ibn Khashshâb, militia head. In 514, according to Quatremère, they were not only assassinating a man whom they claimed was a spy from Afḍal in Egypt, but asking the amîr for a fortress at Aleppo. This is ascribed to Abû Muḥammad, now the local Ismâ'îlî chief at Aleppo, and ultimately the chief in all Syria.

against one Shâdhî, a freedman who had been taught by Abû Ṭâhir at Aleppo, whom they considered the root of the mischief – him they crucified on the city wall. The chief instigators of the massacres then proceeded to take precautions against possible retaliatory assassination.[20]

At the same time Ismâ'îlîs of Bâniyâs had had to trade that fortress to the Franks who were again advancing on Damascus, and themselves go into exile among those same Franks.[21] Ismâ'îl, their leader, soon died there. The continuing movement under 'Alî b. Wafâ in Damascus was very weak; nor was it evidently helped when Bûrî was attacked by assassins (allegedly sent direct from Alamût), and died of the festering wound a year later.[22]

It was about 1133, shortly following the Sunnî outbreak at Damascus, as well as Maḥmûd's offensive against Rûdbâr, that the Nizârîs finally acquired Qadamûs in the Jabal Bahrâ, north of the Lebanon. Only a few years before taken by the Franks, it had just been retaken by the mountaineers, presumably Nuṣayrîs, and given to a member of a local ruling house, the Banû 'Amrûn; who sold it to Abû l-Fatḥ the dâ'î.[23] This was a strategy whose need had been evident since the days of Riḍwân; now the need was more pressing than ever. The modern Ismâ'îlîs of Qadamûs had a tradition that their ancestors had migrated there en masse from Damascus in the Eleventh Century.[24] The date is surely wrong, and the picture is oversimplified; but the idea of the transferance of the scene of their activity definitively out of the cities was apparently sound.

[20] The story of Bahrâm and the Damascus Ismâ'îlîs comes of course from Ibn al-Qalânisî, under the year 520.

[21] As Schaffner points out at length, the rumor was surely not true, or it would have been mentioned by the Frankish chroniclers. Exactly why the debacle occurred in each case is not clear. It would seem that Ṭughtagîn's son killed the vizier personally; he may have held a grudge primarily against the vizier, only incidentally against a group which might avenge him. Ibn al-'Ibrî appears to consider the loss of Bâniyâs as a military victory for the Franks over the Ismâ'îlîs, and it may have been as much due to the untenability of the position as to Sunnî-Ismâ'îlî squabbles (The *Chronography*, transl. E. A. T. W. Budge, Oxford, 1932, p. 254). It is said that Ṭughtagîn gave the place to Bahrâm in the first place because he could not hope to hold it himself (A. S. Tritton and H. A. R. Gibb, 'The First and Second Crusades from an Anonymous Syriac Chronicle,' *JRAS* (1933), p. 98). (It is from William of Tyre that we learn that Bâniyâs was given to the Franks in exchange for other lands within Frankish territory: ed. Paulin (Paris, 1880), Vol. II, p. 25.)

[22] Ibn al-Qalânisî, yrs. 525 and 526.

[23] Dussaud believes that the Ismâ'îlîs bought these fortresses in *Nuṣayrî* territory from *Muslim* castellans (p. 27). Presumably this is not the Abû l-Fatḥ Sarmînî who was killed by Tancred. Kamâl ad-Dîn, via Defrémery, *JA*, 1854, p. 417.

[24] F. Walpole, *The Ansayrii and the Assassins, with travels in the further East in 1850-1* (London, 1850–1), III, 299.

Thereafter they acquired a number of strongholds in the same area, often similarly lately regained from the Franks.[25] Another one of the Banû 'Amrûn sold Kahf to the Ismâ'îlîs, to avoid its falling into his cousins' hands; Maṣyâf was sold by the local holder to the Munqidhites of Shayzar, whose agent there was then tricked and killed by the Ismâ'îlîs, who took over. Kharîba they took from the Franks, and held it despite a temporary occupation by Zangî's troops from Ḥamâ – whom they ousted again by trickery. Between the taking of Qadamûs and 1140, the taking of Maṣyâf, they managed to get eight or ten fortresses in this small area, most of which they held then persistently against both Franks and Muslims.[26] In the time of Sinân there were still Ismâ'îlîs in the north Syrian towns of Aleppo, Bâb, and Raqqa, as well as in the Jazr. At the start of the Thirteenth Century the Jazr was still considered Ismâ'îlî.[27] Nevertheless, the move to the Jabal Bahrâ fortresses had shifted the weight of the community. Henceforth, almost as much as elsewhere, in Syria also the Ismâ'îlîs came to be primarily the inhabitants of a small mountainous area, engaged in a special sort of war with the rest of the world, but increasingly lacking any great faction within the towns held by the enemy.

The end of the contest with Fâṭimid Ismâ'îlism.

Through the reign of Muḥammad Tapar in Iṣfahân and Baghdâd, and for a few years afterwards, Musta'lî and his son Âmir continued to reign over a strong Ismâ'îlî movement in Egypt, in rivalry to that of the Nizârîs. But in the later years the contest between the two movements produced no new results; and before the end of Buzurg'ummîd's reign, it had ceased to be significant for either party. For each had retired into the own limited territory, one way or another.

We have noted that the Ismâ'îlîs of Syria fairly soon threw in their lot with those of Îrân and the rest of the Saljûq territory. Such a move

[25] But it is not clear that the Nizârîs were able to establish themselves there due to their friendship with the Franks after the Bâniyâs deal, as Cahen says, p. 347 ff.
[26] Cahen, ps. 352 ff., gives more details on the taking of these fortresses, as well as exact references in each case. Earlier, ps. 170 ff., he gives a detailed description of the southern Jabal Bahrâ area and its fortresses generally, where the Ismâ'îlîs were.
[27] Yâqût has both Kafar Lâthâ and Sarmîn be populated by Ismâ'îlîs in his day; and in speaking of the Ismâ'îlîs (under article *Jabal as-Summâq*) says that most of them are under the rule of Aleppo – a phrase which probably has in mind more the Jazr than the mountain fortresses.

was not made without a great deal of passion. As long as Afḍal lived he was their enemy – in Aleppo they killed an agent they believed he had sent to spy among them.[28] Some accused them of Afḍal's murder, but there seem to be higher agents to blame.[29] It is rather more possible that they did kill Âmir himself.[30]

When Mustaʿlî's son Âmir became effective head of the Egyptian state, he inherited the dispute. Perhaps it was felt that the Nizârî objection had been to the generalissimo Afḍal personally, and that on his death, and the resumption of personal rule by Âmir as the imâm, the Nizârîs might be won back.[31] It is about this time that the letter of pardon was written which we have mentioned, inviting the Nizârî leaders by name to return to their allegiance without penalty. (That the Nizârî matter was then a touchy one is indicated by Ibn aṣ-Ṣayrafî's reticent way of mentioning it in his history, written very soon after: – at Mustanṣir's death he does not mention Nizâr at all, only the "Alexandria trouble"; although he must have been well informed, as Ibn Muyassar names him as the actual writer of Âmir's epistle on the schism.) This letter of pardon may have been identical with the known epistle of Âmir, occasion for which was given in the year following Afḍal's death by a "confession" of Nizâr's sister that Nizâr had known he was not the true heir. This confession was made the center of a proclamation to be read throughout Egypt. Then it was mentioned in a polemic epistle, in which Âmir tried to prove Mustaʿlî's legitimacy to the Nizârîs, and then to refute the Nizârîs' prompt answer.

The Nizârîs did not respond to the appeal; in fact, even while the epistle setting forth Nizâr's sister's confession was being composed, Âmir and his vizier, Ma'mûn, professed to uncover a threat to assassinate themselves on the part of Ḥasan-i Ṣabbâḥ.[32] It seems that both money and

[28] Quatremère, *Fundgruben des Orients*, IV, under yr. 514.

[29] Ibn al-Athîr, *Kâmil*, year 515; but Ibn al-Qalânisî denied it was they. It was undoubtedly Âmir's work; though Âmir professed to blame the Nizârîs, according to Ibn Muyassar.

[30] Ibn al-Athîr, *Kâmil*, p. 467, yr. 524, notes that he was killed by some sort of Ismâʿîlîs, who alleged his misrule as reason.

[31] Ibn Muyassar notes as central to Nizâr's revolt and the Nizârîs' loyalty to him, the fact that Afḍal was lord of Egypt at Mustanṣir's death.

[32] Stern (*JRAS*, 1950) suggests that this discovery caused the tone of the Egyptian government to be changed; that they had been planning to send the letter of pardon mentioned by Ibn aṣ-Ṣayrafî, and now decided to send instead the far less honeyed epistle which we possess; accordingly, that the attempt to conciliate Ḥasan-i Ṣabbâḥ was now given up. This is possible, but not clearly indicated; if the news of the assassination scheme be taken to interrupt any letter, Ibn Muyassar says that the letter in any case was to center on Nizâr's sister's confession.

men were being sent in to Egypt from Alamût; Ma'mûn tried to keep track of all knife-sellers, all visitors in Cairo, even (says the historian) of all agents who started from Alamût. More seriously, Ma'mûn arrested several men in the army, one of whom was found to have money upon him. He could congratulate himself on escaping assassination – until at length he himself was involved in a disloyal plot, and done away with.[33] The Fâṭimid government rejoiced to receive the head of Bahrâm, the leader among the Syrian Nizârîs who was killed in a battle near Damascus; and paid a proper reward for it. Meanwhile, both in Âmir's reign and afterwards, we hear of revolts by Nizârids; however, apparently they had no connection with our Nizâriyya; the last such was a rising among the western bedouins. Yet they must have added to the Fâṭimid anxiety.

The Ḥâfiẓî-Ṭayyibî schism in the Fâṭimid daʿwa (1130).

But on the death of Âmir in 1130, the ruling Fâṭimids came to have heresies even closer home than the Nizârîs to think about. Âmir died without sons. Loyal Ismâʿîlî forces, therefore, were faced with a predicament which by the principles of their faith was impossible: for the world can never be without an imâm, and each imâm was the designated son of the preceding. For a couple of years a Twelver vizier took over, and ruled in the name of the hidden imâm of the Twelvers. Then a cousin of Âmir's, al-Ḥâfiẓ, who had meanwhile been regent (a concubine of Âmir's had for a time been pregnant with a girl), proclaimed himself the imâm, and took power.

His followers (the Ḥâfiẓiyya) were opposed by most of the Ismâʿîlîs of the Yaman;[34] who maintained that an unknown baby son of Âmir's was the true imâm, but had gone into hiding. The dâʿîs of the Yaman now set themselves up with an autonomous religious authority in the name

[33] M. b. Muyassar, *Ta'rîkh Miṣr*, ed. Henri Massé, *Annales d'Egypte*, Cairo, 1919, pp. 65–69. Corresponding passage in Ibn aṣ-Ṣayrafî is p. 49 (*BIFAO*, XXV, 1925).

[34] Ḥâfiẓ' claim to the imâmate is shown among other things by his coins; for the Ṭayyibî polemic, see Strothmann, 'Kleinere Ismailitische Schriften,' *I. R. A. Miscellany*, I (Calcutta, 1948), 143. Ḥâfiẓ might have maintained that his own father, and neither Mustaʿlî nor Nizâr, had been Mustanṣir's designated heir; and that Mustaʿlî and Âmir had been merely protective "fronts". But at least publicly he seems to have limited himself to showing that the imâmate can pass between cousins. See S. M. Stern, 'The Succession to the Fâṭimid Imâm al-Âmir,' *Oriens*, Vol. 4 (1951), nr. 5, pp. 193 ff. Cf. the ambiguities, however, reflected in Fâriqî, that Ḥâfiẓ was said to be son of Mustaʿlî or of Mustanṣir. Amedroz, ed. *History of Damascus*, p. 127–8.

of the baby imâm, Ṭayyib. This *Ṭayyibî* da'wa was now as independent within its area as were the Nizârîs within theirs (but far less dynamic). The Ḥâfiẓi branch of Ismâ'îlism was restricted almost to Egypt itself.

Fâṭimid Ismâ'îlism persisted in Egypt officially only for another generation. When in 1171 Saladin liquidated the Fâṭimid dynasty he had to close a *dâr ad-da'wa*, and to institute a greater rigor against the guilds which, Massignon believes, had formed a part of the Ismâ'îlî fraternal structure; as well as to change the formulas of prayer to those sanctioned by the Sunnîs.[35] But there seems to have been little sectarian impulse left among the supporters of the dynasty. The most notable opponent of Saladin in the name of the fallen dynasty was a Sunnî poet, Umâra, who praised the last imâms not as Ismâ'îlîs, but simply as descendants of the Prophet.[36] To judge by Qalqashandî's oaths, the Ḥâfiẓiyya and Nizâriyya continued to hate each other; but when the former were restricted almost to Egypt, and then lost power even there, while the latter retired to their mountains, there was little occasion for them to trouble one another. Finally, even from the death of Âmir, one may say, it was the Nizârîs alone among Ismâ'îlîs who were maintaining any effective struggle, even from their relatively retired dâr al-hijra, against the enveloping Sunnî synthesis.

ISMÂ'ÎLÎ POLICIES: ASSASSINATION

The taking of Maṣyâf and the death of Buzurg'ummîd, the last of Ḥasan-i Ṣabbâḥ's chief companions, provide a suitable moment for surveying the political and social policy and structure which had been gradually crystallizing in the course of the Ismâ'îlî struggles, retreats, and strategical consolidations. There seems to have been no deliberate attempt to construct a state. The state was formed under the pressure of Saljûq strength, and was as unintentional as the relative slackening of the military struggle at the same time. Such origins were reflected in its unique forms of polity, both internally, and of course in its relations with the world.

[35] Cf. Massignon, 'Ṣinf,' *Encyclopedia of Islam.*

[36] Ibn al-Athîr, *Kâmil*, year 569; but cf. Ibn Khallikan, *Biographical Dictionary*, II, 369. Kamil Hussein comments on this Sunnî's use of exaggerated language, 'Ismaili Ideas in the Egyptian Poetry of the Fatimid Period,' *Actes du XXI (1948) Congrès Internationale des Orientalistes* (Paris, 1949). However, not all of the Ḥâfiẓiyya died with the dynasty. The Musta'lian Ismâ'îlîs whom Qalqashandî mentions were Ḥâfiẓîs, according to his list of their imâms. Did they, too, have a hidden imâm for a time?

Patterns of assassinations and massacre.

At least as striking a phase of the Nizârî struggle was formed by the assassinations – and their complementary massacres – as by the more conventionally military activities. We have seen how assassination arose as a Nizârî institution at the time of the all-out assault against the Saljûq power. Unfortunately, our means of interpreting these more irregular events as a phase of the continuing policy are understandably inadequate. By and large, news of only the more prominent assassinations will have filtered through to us. This makes it impossible to be sure how representative were the cases singled out – victims of humbler classes would hardly be mentioned. At least as important, we cannot know how full the coverage of any one age or place is in our record; an apparent epidemic of assassinations in connection with one or another event may reflect simply one man's industry in collecting the names and another man's curiosity in passing them on. Finally, there is no way to be sure (except in rare special cases) that any particular assassination was actually the work of Ismâʿîlîs, for assassination and murder were common enough among their opponents, and even those cases owned to by the Nizârîs might have been falsely claimed for political purposes. Accordingly, a discussion of their place in the whole state policy can be at best tentative.

Ḥamd Allâh Mustawfî, looking back on the whole episode, was sure that the Ismâʿîlîs thought it their duty to do all possible harm to any and all Muslims: thus the more Muslims killed, and the more cruelly, the better; and if leaders could be killed, that was best of all.[37] Though the Ismâʿîlîs came to have little reason to love the Sunnî populace, they apparently did not in fact attempt the destruction even of all the Sunnî leadership. Much of the time most of the Sunnîs were on passably good terms with the Ismâʿîlîs about them; and even important enemies of the sect often seem to have escaped assassination or even attempts at it, perhaps not solely by their vigilance. Similarly, although at times a mob or a ruler would set the goal of destroying all Ismâʿîlîs at once, the resultant massacres were seldom persistent (though they were bloody enough – all accusees being popularly presumed guilty). The townsmen would shortly after be living at peace with the Ismâʿîlîs who survived. Neither the Ismâʿîlîs nor their opponents seem to have maintained a consistent policy of doing away with each other.

Where it is clear what the motive for assassination is, it is usually

[37] Mustawfî, *Ta'rîkh-i Guzîda*, trans. Defrémery, *JA*, ser. 4, XII (1848), 270, etc.

very specific defense or retaliation.[38] We find two types generally selected for assassination. On the one hand military chiefs: often they attacked amîrs who had led attacks against their strongholds, or viziers who did the like; occasionally they attacked sulṭâns who had acted against them. The two Caliphs of Baghdâd whom they killed had not apparently been their particular enemies, but were both outside of Baghdâd and physically exposed at the time; their murder was presumably symbolical. Even so, we find Juwaynî giving as (apparently) their defense for killing Râshid, that the latter was on his way to attack them in revenge for his father – rather improbable under the circumstances.[39] On the other hand they attacked local civil personages who opposed their teachings or their privileges, or who incited against them: legists and city chiefs; several times we hear that they assassinated the Qâḍî, the religious judge, of a town. It is perhaps an accident only that we hear of very few of the Twelver Shîʿa being assassinated – there are exceptions at Aleppo – although a number of that Shîʿa were prominent in this period; but all the Shîʿa, after all, were commonly themselves on the defensive (and those who listed the Ismâʿîlî outrages were mostly Sunnîs).

One suspects that a third type of victim also occurred, but was not usually listed: the ordinary person who had learned something of the Ismâʿîlî secret doctrines, and then proposed to turn informer, or just talked loosely. This was apparently the case with the first victim listed by Ibn al-Athîr, the muezzin of Sâwa; and such a practice is almost unavoidable for a party in revolt which expects to keep its activities and its beliefs secret.

Assassination at the request of non-Ismâʿîlîs.

A different sort of victim was the enemy of one who was friendly to the Ismâʿîlîs. We have noted several occasions when the Ismâʿîlîs intervened militarily in non-Ismâʿîlî disputes; for instance, in favor of Barkiyâruq and Ḥabashî against Sanjar. It seems that from a very early time they intervened likewise with assassination. There were general suspicions on this score in regard to Barkiyâruq already, for it was said that many of their victims were his enemies. As noted, it was reported that

[38] Thus when Aḥmad Yal of Marâgha was assassinated in a public session with Ṭughtagîn, it was at first thought the assassin was sent by the Sulṭân against the latter; till it was found it was the Ismâʿîlîs, against whom Aḥmad Yal had been particularly active; whereupon the case became understandable. Kamâl ad-Dîn, yr. 509.

[39] Juwaynî, ed. Qazwînî, p. 221.

Barkiyâruq's envoy to Baghdâd, when about to be killed in the great purge, offered to turn the Ismâ'îlî daggers against anyone required if he should be spared. It is said that the vizier of Ṭughril (who succeeded Maḥmûd as Sulṭân as Sanjar's candidate) bragged to his master that he had sent Ismâ'îlîs against Ṭughril's enemies, and therefore was executed forthwith.[40] (A slave of Shîrgîr is said to have finished him off: for the sake of his late master, he would have a special hatred for the Ismâ'îlîs.)

Later in Syria, at least, such politic assassination was probably practiced: a vizier of Aleppo forged a letter, in about 1177, from his lord asking that certain rivals be done away with; the Ismâ'îlîs who did the deed were caught and carried before the same lord and reviled bitterly; whereat they complained that after all he had, as they supposed, ordered it.[41] The much later Syrian Ismâ'îlî writer Abû Firâs freely avows an assassination on behalf of Saladin; but his testimony is not sure, for it may be influenced by later practice under the Mamlûk Sulṭâns of Egypt.

It seems improbable that the Ismâ'îlîs will have accepted money for such favors in the earlier years, when it was a matter of strategy to strengthen those the least dangerous to them; perhaps they did indeed destroy Barkiyâruq's enemies even without his knowledge, in justified fear of a victory by Muḥammad Tapar. But later it is generally assumed that the Ismâ'îlîs were paid. Still later, in the Fourteenth Century, Abû Firâs speaks of a gift in gratitude from Saladin in such a case (but again this is not a sure witness of Saladin's time); it seems that the Nizârîs of Abû Firâs' time, no longer independent, under the Mamlûk sulṭân's, were paid at a fixed rate per murder.[42]

There are several occasions when the murder of Franks or of other Christian rulers is referred to the Ismâ'îlîs, but only in the later period, following the reign of Buzurg'ummîd. In connection with almost all of these there is dispute whether the Ismâ'îlî ascription is correct, and especially in whose interest the deed was done. It seems that any assassin-

[40] Aḥmad Yalî Aqsunqur, of Marâgha, was so killed according to *Akhbâr ad-dawlat as-Saljûqiyya*, pp. 103–4. Ibn al-Athîr, *Kâmil*, yr. 527, has Mas'ûd accused of the deed. We have also noticed the accusations Bundârî brings against Dargazînî, year 518.

[41] Lewis, in *Speculum*, Oct. 1952, suggests that such an alibi might be merely a "cover story", furnished the assassin in case he were caught; but in this case the alibi appears to have been confirmed later from some Sunnî source, whoever it was that revealed the vizier's intrigue. Nor would it be impossible for a simple assassin to be aware of the reason for his deed, if it were done out of group policy, and not for money paid privately to the Ismâ'îlî chief.

[42] Ibn Batouta, *Voyages*, trans. C. Defrémery and B. R. Sanguinetti (Paris, 1853), I, 167.

ations of Franks that did occur are to be connected with non-Ismâʿîlî quarrels; they will be considered in the course of the later developments.

Assassinations and the local struggles for power.

In any case the assassinations for the benefit of non-Ismâʿîlîs, whether done for money or not, apparently formed a small portion of the total. The assassinations which were associated with the military campaigns against the Ismâʿîlî dâr al-hijra were at least in the earlier period probably more numerous. These include a large proportion if not most of the assassinations of military personages. But where assassination played a major role seems to have been in that almost unknown aspect of the Nizârî venture, the struggle to prepare the various local scenes for the rule of the imâm. The majority of assassinations appear to have been directed against men, military or civilian, who stood in the way of the local daʿwa.

We can imagine the effort to recruit an able corps of men for the cause, an effort increasingly difficult as the initial hopes of success were checked, and then in the time of Muḥammad Tapar were indefinitely postponed; an effort which would be countered with increasing ease by the Sunnî leaders, with both arguments and threats. We can imagine the desire to force dramatically upon men's attention the demand for a yes-or-no choice between the cause of the imâm and the cause of the world. The Ismâʿîlî assassinations differed from the many murders that took place in the general political life not only by being less personal, less a matter of individual rivalry; but by being more often public, frequently dramatically staged in the mosque, in the court. There is nothing covert about them. The Ismâʿîlîs seem almost never to have been suspected of using poison.[43]

To judge by the assassinations, this local activity persisted for some time in a more widespread area than that to which the fortresses themselves were restricted after Muḥammad Tapar's time. We find mentioned Khurâsân in the east; Mâzandarân, ʿIrâq ʿAjamî, Âdharbâyjân, and the northern Mesopotamian Basin in the center; Syria in the west; but no

[43] An exception would seem to be the accusation against the vizier of Muḥammad Tapar, at the taking of Shâh Diz, who was accused of suborning a barber to poison Muḥammad with his knife, in the Ismâʿîlî cause. Oddly enough, in the unaccountable tradition among reference works which selects the misinformation to be offered the general reader on such matters, *secret* murders are sometimes made a chief characteristic of the "Assassins", as *Lincoln Library*, 1946; *Webster's Collegiate*, 1946; *Winston's*, 1937.

longer the more southerly lands such as Kirmân, Fârs, Khûzistân, ʿIrâq; to say nothing of the Arabian peninsula, or Egypt. These local murders appear to cease almost abruptly a few years after the death of Buzurgʾummîd, when the Nizârîs had come to be no longer a great faction within the all-Islamic towns. At the same time there ceases the line of massacres in such towns. No doubt there was no sudden transition; in the five years following Buzurgʾummîd's death there are recorded an unusual spate of assassinations; but this apparent increase may merely be due to an unusually rich source for those years, lying at Rashîd ad-Dîn's disposition. Nevertheless, it seems clear that both the local massacres, and the local assassinations of anti-Ismâʿîlî personages characterize the first decades of the Nizârî struggle within the towns; both are infrequently recounted thereafter.

SOCIAL AND POLITICAL STRUCTURE

Nizârî solidarity and vigor.

The Nizârî territory was broken into at least four parts: a section of Quhistân, in eastern Îrân, a large tract with many towns; Gird Kûh, in Qumis, evidently a single fortress; Rûdbâr, with Alamût, a small tract with many fortresses and villages; and the southern Jabal Bahrâ, in Syria, similar to Rûdbâr.[44] In Syria and possibly in Quhistân there were in addition some areas (notably the Jazr) largely or in part Ismâʿîlî, but not regularly incorporated in the Ismâʿîlî state. Within each of the four parts there seems to have been a continuity of territory – the Sunnîs had no bases, at any rate, within the area outlined by the Nizârî strongholds in the Jabal Bahrâ and in Rûdbâr; Juwaynî noted a stream near Maymûndiz as boundary of the Ismâʿîlî territory in the latter case.[45] Much later, when Ḥasan III was introducing the Sunnî forms, he had to send out to the ʿIrâq ʿAjamî (and to Khurâsân, for Quhistân) for his instructors, there being none available, one must suppose, locally.[46] Nevertheless,

[44] Minhâj-i Sirâj, *Ṭabaqât-i Nâṣirî*, tr. H. G. Raverty (London, 1881), p. 1205–6, says there were seventy strongholds in Quhistân at the end, and thirty-five in ʿIrâq – that would mean Rûdbâr. Gird Kûh had one or two hundred men in it. Juwaynî, p. 268, has forty-odd strongholds in Rûdbâr.

[45] P. 266, ed. Qazwînî.

[46] Juwaynî, trans. C. Defrémery, *JA*, ser. 5, XV (1860), 243. There is some question as to how continuous the Nizârî territory was in Quhistân. In any case, it did not cover the whole province. Around the year 1160, Ibn al-Athîr tells of an Ibn Anaz who as lord of Quhistân raids the Ismâʿîlîs there; and tells of an Ismâʿîlî raid on Ṭabas,

within these Ismâʿîlî territories we find that numbers of Sunnîs were allowed to live – for many emigrated under Ḥasan II.

The Nizârî lands were marginal territories (and yet as near the great centers of Islamic life from Khurâsân to Syria as they could be and remain marginal). Within their territories they were independent now not only of the Fâṭimid regime, but of the surrounding Saljûq powers. A sense of solidarity in maintaining that independence seems to be now as evident as any sense of solidarity in a general campaign against the Saljûqs. After the debacle at Damascus, they evidently ceased to form, even in Syria, private armed bands that could support their friends, or offer to take over a citadel within the Sunnî world; but their troops were still feared; more than once Sunnî forces are said to have fled without a blow.[47] Qâʾin was described by Yâqût as a dirty little town with a barbarous dialect; but the Quhistânîs were jealous of any outside invasion of their barbarous corners.

Unlike the bands of the warlords, the Ismâʿîlî strength could survive even serious defeats; for it was based on a free patriotism rather than on pay. Throughout the Middle East, such a spirit tended to survive in more out of the way spots, in contrast to the situation in most places, where responsibility for rule was left to an alien soldiery. The Ismâʿîlî appeal, as we have noted, came in places as much from such local spirit as from the ideal of the cause; now that spirit was enhanced. It was a vigorous local community that forced the lord of Ṭuraythîth to adopt Ismâʿîlism, and to keep it. It seems that that lord had even imported a Turkish soldiery to keep down the Ismâʿîlî sentiment; but found the remedy worse than the disease. Later his son succeeded him, and tried to restore openly the secret Sunnî faith of his father, beginning with the father's funeral. But the son only forfeited his position.[48]

which must be regarded as the Ṭabas in the western part of Quhistân. The Ismâʿîlî Ṭabas must have been the one farther east. The eastern part of Quhistân is more mountainous than the western, and is the area where the Ismâʿîlîs are mostly listed. Perhaps some Ismâʿîlîs were to be found, as in Syria, outside the fortified areas: around 1200, a Ghûrid lord was visiting Quhistân and was evidently surprised to find that one of the places nearby was held by the Ismâʿîlîs (he immediately set about destroying it); and a few years later an amîr's course through southeastern Quhistân was unexpectedly checked by the Ismâʿîlîs (*Taʾrîkh-i Sîstân*, p. 395). Probably there were also some changes in the extent of area held from time to time, which are not recorded. We have to go by incidental scraps. But cf. Le Strange, *Eastern Caliphate*, p. 360.

[47] Cf. a lengthy and amusing description of this fear in Ibn al-Athîr, *Kâmil*, year 560 *à propos* of Qazwîn.

[48] Yâqût, *Muʿjam al-Buldân*, ed. C. Barbier de Meynard, *Dictionnaire géographique, historique, et littéraire de la Perse et des contrées adjacentes* (Paris, 1861), p. 390. Cf. also Ibn al-Athîr.

Raiders' life in Alamût.

From the pages of Rashîd ad-Dîn on the reigns of Buzurg'ummîd and his son, we gain something of a picture of the life of the Ismâ'îlî raiders in Rûdbâr. One gets the impression of an almost petty scale of affairs. They counted just how many sheep were taken as booty, as well as how many men were killed. The horsemen got two shares to the footmen's one – which indicates that even here the wealthier (able to afford a horse) had as elsewhere an advantage, though not an overwhelming one. Differences in wealth cannot have been great in such circumstances. Sometimes they held a man for ransom.

It is seldom mentioned what the particular occasion of a raid was. Once a woman was captured by the Qazwînîs, who refused to allow her to be ransomed back. Sometimes other inimical deeds are cited. But usually it seems to be assumed that the "enemies", who are mentioned as disappointed as each new reign gets successfully under way, offer a reason for raiding just by being there. For despite the counting of sheep, the Ismâ'îlîs were still consciously waging a major war. Those who killed the 'Abbâsid Caliph Mustarshid are labelled among their fellows "'Abbâsî" – on the model of *Scipio Africanus* and the like.

Accordingly, we cannot think of these men as rustics. Pretension to culture is not lacking among these mountaineers. Sometimes the names reveal at least a reputation of one or another in this line, as with the man referred to as the *Adîb* – the *polished.* Buzurg'ummîd himself seems to have been of good family. His sister is recorded as being the wife of Hazârâsf of Rustamdâr, a local dynast; while his wife was the daughter of Shâh Ghâzî Rustam.[49] We are also not allowed to forget that the main concern of the community is still supposed to be spreading the faith. The dâ'îs are involved in several events; and we find recorded the death, among other enemies, of one Jamshîd, who seems to have been formerly a dâ'î, but to have gone back on his calling, and to have suffered the penalty of apostasy.

[49] Perhaps both connections were acquired while Buzurg'ummîd was still a young man. Hazârâsf reigned contemporarily with Ḥasan-i Ṣabbâḥ; but this seems less likely with Shâh Ghâzî, who reigned till as late as seventy-five years after the taking of Alamût! This would be an alliance before that king became so violent against the Ismâ'îlîs, unless there is some confusion which Justi has not traced down. For instance, there is a Kiyâ Buzurg noted in Ibn Isfandiyâr, p. 252, as reigning in Daylamân; also p. 57 in Ẓahîr ad-Dîn. But in general, F. Justi seems to have found all the dynastic marriages recorded of the Ismâ'îlî lords, from Ẓahîr ad-Dîn and others. *Iranisches Namenbuch* (Marburg, 1895), p. 457.

Alamût as the center of the Nizârî power.

Each group worked largely on its own; but outsiders never made them work against each other (the only case that smacks of disunity was that at Afâmiya, where the local Ismâʿîlî chief did not let the dâʿî from Aleppo intervene; but this was to no outsiders' advantage). There had never ceased to be some successor to the central leadership the dâʿî at Iṣfahân seems to have exercised. We have noted the leading part Ḥasan-i Ṣabbâḥ at Alamût tended to take among the dâr al-hijra at the time of the revolt. The dâʿî at Alamût came to be, apparently, the unquestioned head of all. Abû Muḥammad, considered the Syrian chief at about this time, is said to have been sent originally from Alamût; and the Syrian amîrs at the time of the Damascus massacre are said to fear reprisals from Alamût. The wars of the Quhistânîs are associated with those of Alamût, and it was Ḥasan-i Ṣabbâḥ who is said to have threatened Sanjar in this connection, from Alamût. On Ḥasan's death we hear of Abû ʿAlî going about to all the fortresses, gathering declarations of allegiance to Buzurgʾummîd. By the time of Ḥasan II, Buzurgʾummîd's grandson, even the most drastic orders from Alamût were obeyed everywhere among the Nizârîs.

The lead of Alamût may have resulted from its relative success in withstanding the Saljûq counterattack, as compared with the Ismâʿîlîs of Iṣfahân; or it may have resulted from the ability of Ḥasan-i Ṣabbâḥ to shoulder responsibility for the vacant imâmate. Some centralization, in the light of the Ismâʿîlî hierarchical principles, was almost inevitable; the Nizârî state maintained the apparatus of a Muslim state – the Sharîʿa was (until the Qiyâma) enforced strictly, and Qâḍîs were sent out (Ḥusayn Qâʾinî is so denominated in Rashîd ad-Dîn) – and in the Ismâʿîlî view this required a central source of authority. Eventually, we find the chiefs of both the Quhistânî and Syrian communities being sent out by Alamût.[50] Nevertheless, it is doubtful whether Alamût was much more than a center of ultimate recourse; the local life remains very vigorous. Sometimes at least the Syrian chiefs were locally elected.

When Ḥasan was on his deathbed, he summoned Buzurgʾummîd from Lammasar, and appointed him heir to his own post; with three of the experienced leaders to assist him. Abû ʿAlî Ardistânî, who had saved Alamût at the time of the first attacks, was apparently put in charge of

[50] The chief in Quhistân, and in Gird Kûh, was at least sometimes called the *muḥtashim;* that in Syria, the *muqaddam* or *nâʾib*. The Quhistânî Ismâʿîlîs evidently had a common treasury, called the *daʿwat khâna,* we learn from Minhâj-i Sirâj.

finance;[51] Ḥasan Âdam Qaṣrânî, and Kiyâ Abû Ja'far, who was in charge of the army, were also made advisers. The four were told to rule in harmony till the imâm should come to head his realm.

Stability of the Nizârî dynasty.

As striking as the diversity of its policies is the overall stability of the Nizârî state. Von Hammer, zealous in support of the Sunnî Muslim law as if he had never read St. Paul, improved on his authorities to make the lords of Alamût a whole series of parricides, and their reigns a tale of depraved disorder; every whisper of foul play is enlarged to a certain fact. "Their guards, the devoted to death, were common murderers. Hell reserved for the grand masters themselves the privilege of parricide."[52] Such a view still influenced the scholar Dermenghem, in 1947, to write of the Nizârîs as the lone and bloodcurdling example in Islâm of the doctrine that might makes right.[53] Indeed, the lords of Alamût were not free in the least from strife and violence; in three cases out of six the relations of father and son were sorely strained. Two lords, possibly three, were murdered; in a fourth case there was accusation of murder.

Yet the record compares well with that of other Muslim ruling houses where the sovereign ruled as well as reigned, as in Alamût. There seem to have been no succession disputes, and none of the fratricide elsewhere so common at times in Islâm; as to parricide, there are two accusations, but only one seems even worth considering. Reigns of thirty-four, thirty-five, forty-four years are longer than any attained in the all-Islamic Caliphate before al-Qâdir, twenty-fifth Caliph and militarily impotent under the Buwayhid regime. For a century and a half the Nizârî state kept its hold on a remotely scattered territory with few losses or humiliations, and with little internal disruption: this should be a sign of moral strength.

In harmony with his picture of internal chaos, Von Hammer portrayed the external policy of the state as a diabolically consistent hostility to all social good: assassination of the pillars of society and asylum for its renegades. Yet even Von Hammer had to note, and try to discount, the more startling variations in policy – which set off Alamût (even more

[51] Though the passage in question is in Juwaynî, unfortunately Qazwînî has not been able to clear up the text, p. 215, so as to make it exactly clear what his job was.
[52] Von Hammer, *History of the Assassins* , tr. O.C. Wood (London, 1835), p. 164.
[53] E. Dermenghem, 'Notes sur les valeurs permanentes et actuelles de la civilisation musulmane,' *L'Islâm et L'Occident*, ed. by J. Ballard (Paris, 1947), p. 377.

than does its relative stability) from the monotonous aggressiveness of the usual Muslim dynasties of the time. Four or five contrasting policies toward the outside world can be traced in the eight reigns. In the first two was continued the all-out attack against the established regime by any means available, including terrorism; though the policy of retiring to the mountains in fact soon shifted the emphasis. By the time of the third reign, perhaps unconsciously, this had become almost a policy of defensiveness. Under Ḥasan II, there was a conscious about-face: the spiritual resurrection excited a new sort of zeal among the freshly liberated Ismâʿîlîs; and under his son the new spiritual life seems to have absorbed that zeal in itself, as if the nothingness of unbelievers called rather for their ignoring than for their destruction. His grandson Ḥasan III reversed position dramatically, declaring himself an orthodox Muslim, and tried to establish a dynastic power allied firmly with the best families of the lands about. His son, retaining a forward political policy, played once again religiously and militarily a lone hand; but when this policy seemed to be failing aginst the Mongols, the last lord, in turn, sought the safety of his garrisons in an abject submission, and, it would seem, an acceptance of the role of a sect rather than a state. There was nevertheless a persistent orientation throughout these variations of policy – a strong sense of unity as against the outside world, and a strong sense of dignity and initiative among the local Nizârî groups. Despite all variations, the community retained its solidarity and much of its vigor to the end.

CHAPTER VI

REACTION OF THE ISLAMIC WORLD

SOCIAL AND LEGAL REACTION: PROSCRIPTION

The reaction of the Muslim community at large to the Nizârî threat was violent and unanimous. All who did not share in the Nizârî revolt – Twelver Shîʿa as well as Sunnî – united to resist it. At times there seem to have been closer ties between the Ismâʿîlîs and the Twelver Shîʿa, as in the case of Takrît where a Twelver allegedly gave the citadel to a Nizârî in the first place, and the Nizârî ultimately gave it up to another Twelver rather than let it fall in Sunnî hands. However, in such cases we are led to believe that the Twelver was unaware that the person was an Ismâʿîlî, not a Twelver, Shîʿite. In Aleppo the other Shîʿites and the Sunnîs frankly joined hands to petition the destruction of the Nizârîs. The violence of the reaction was correspondingly on the level of the lowest common denominator. It is expressed at its fullest in the recurrent massacres; which, being motivated by animal fear more than by anything more refined, could extend to obvious innocents – such as the Ṣûfîs we have mentioned as being slaughtered in one case, where the assassins happened to wear Ṣûfî garb.

The popular terror and scorn.

An illustration of the popular feeling – at least as reflected in an educated person – is given in a poem by Khâqânî, in which he is attacking not the Ismâʿîlîs, but his own teacher. He attacks this teacher as an atheist, a dog, a bastard, a sodomite, a brother of the devil; he makes him elaborately more evil than the Pope; and spends almost half the poem making him an Ismâʿîlî, to the same general purpose. He has his teacher, as an Ismâʿîlî, believe that Ḥasan-i Ṣabbâḥ was a prophet, and Buzurg'ummîd a prince; and at the same time that Mohammed was an alchemist, who married Zayd's wife (a well-known case of near-scandal) by trickery. He represents Qazwîn as being deserted because of their wickedness.[1]

The threat was felt, in a general sense, as one of nonconformity to the accepted order; this nonconformity was interpreted, in the popular fears of the unknown, as expressing an unlimited enmity to ordinary Muslims – as has been noted in Mustawfî's reaction to the rumors of Nizârî horrors.[2] Lewis suggests that more in particular it was a subversion of existing vested interests that was feared – that it was in economic matters that the Sunnî and conforming Shî'a leaders "felt themselves to be threatened."[3] Such a danger, of course, will trouble almost all classes of society, if they have any stake at all in existing obligations; nevertheless, it will trouble the lowest classes least. It was noted by Ghazzâlî, Lewis reminds us, that it was accordingly to the least prosperous that the Ismâ'îlîs appealed especially. At any rate, it is clear that the heresiologists and historians like to condemn them, like some other sects, as appealing to the discontented and the stupid. Niẓâm al-Mulk and others attack them by linking them with the tradition of Mazdak, who was supposed to have ordered a communism of property and of women in Sassanid Persia; and treat them as primarily interested in the expropriation of wealth, and in general license.[4] If the leaders are diabolically clever, their followers are represented as infinitely gullible. Qazwînî says of the Alamûtîs whom Ḥasan-i Ṣabbâḥ converted, that they were so dumb they sawed off the limbs they were sitting on.[5] Of such men, supposedly, anything mad might be expected.

From the rather vague insecurity aroused by such expectations, as well as from the insistent secrecy with which the Ismâ'îlîs themselves acted, arose naturally the horror tales, such as that noted above in regard to the blind sadist of Iṣfahân. Also related of the Iṣfahân affair was the variant story of the woman who was found lying on a matting which was spread over forty corpses. She was killed, and the whole

[1] N. de Khanikov, 'Mémoire sur Khacani,' *JA*, Aug.–Sept., 1864, p. 137.

[2] There was certainly a tendency at first for wide popular sympathy with the anti-Turkish cause – and perhaps some class sentiment also; hence the wide recruitment of followers and sympathizers in the time of Barkiyâruq. But this sympathy soon died out.

[3] Goldziher, *Streitschrift des Ghazâlî gegen die Bâṭinîyasekte* (Leiden, 1916), p. 24, etc.; and Lewis, *Origins*, p. 93.

[4] *Siyâsat Nâma*, ed. C. Schefer (Paris, 1891), p. 168. As Marx pointed out, the communism of women should follow naturally that of property in the minds of a society where women are to be possessed! It has been suggested, however, that the Ismâ'îlîs put fewer restrictions on the life of women than the Sunnîs had come to do, and that this may have been taken for license.

[5] Zakariyyâ Qazwînî, *Âthâr*, s.v. Alamût.

area burned.[6] The assassinations in particular were given an eerie flavor. One man dreamed of dogs attacking him, and was duly warned by friends not to go out in public for some time – but he refused to forego the Friday public prayers at the mosque, and was killed there.[7] Another dreamt that the Prophet's martyred grandson, Ḥusayn, was summoning him; he stayed in the house on the anniversary of Ḥusayn's death, but even there he was killed by a man seeming to offer a petition.[8]

But the most usual condemnation by sober Muslims was the old accusation that the Ismâ'îlî purpose was indeed to destroy Islâm but not necessarily any and all Muslims. The old stories were revived of the conspiracy of adherents of the old Persian faith and of the Philosophers, plotting how they could best harm Islâm and introduce atheism and other evils. Ibn Maymûn was still the chief villain; surprisingly little was deemed necessary to be added. Even such rather casual efforts as were made to prove the accusations of a Zoroastrian *dualist* origin – the Ismâ'îlî 'Aql and Nafs are *two* principles, for instance – were repetitions of older efforts.[9]

The legal problem of conformity by lip-service.

Legists expressed the fear of Nizârî subversion in more precise form. They debated whether or not the Ismâ'îlîs were to be considered admissible as fellow-Muslims on the basis of the broad Sunnî principle of accepting any who uttered the formula of faith. Individuals had denied this before, but now in the face of the Nizârî challenge it came to be denied officially.

Z. Qazwînî maintains that the first legist formally to denounce the Ismâ'îlîs as beyond the pale was Abû l-Maḥâsin Rûyânî, soon after the Ismâ'îlîs were established at Alamût. A prominent and widely travelled man, when he came to Qazwîn he persuaded the Qazwînîs to decree death for anyone coming from the direction of Alamût, lest mingling with the Ismâ'îlîs should give rise to disaffection within Qazwîn. To his political argument he added a judicial one: that the Ismâ'îlîs' exclusive exaltation of ta'lîm threatened the religious law, which they made to

[6] Ibn al-Jawzî, *Islamic Culture*, 1935, p. 555.

[7] Kamâl ad-Dîn ibn al-'Adîm, *Ta'rîkh Ḥalab*, year 520.

[8] Ibn al-Athîr, *Kâmil*, year 500.

[9] Minorsky, *E.I.* on Khayyâm, notes that 'Umar Khayyâm mentions the Ismâ'îlîs dispassionately among other seekers of truth, in a treatise whose authorship, however, is suspect. Not everyone will have been dazed by the Ismâ'îlî attack. On the other hand, later Ismâ'îlîs have claimed 'Umar Khayyâm as a secret adherent.

depend upon the imâm's word alone. (He was killed by the Ismâʿîlîs in Âmul in 1108.)[10] In the wider world beyond Qazwîn, a similar attitude soon triumphed. The decision at Iṣfahân that the offers of military obedience of the garrison of Shâh Diz should be rejected is the most obvious turning point: there it was held that the Ismâʿîlî claim was to be rejected, that – since they held to all the formal law – their only difference with the Sunnîs was on the point of the imâmate.[11]

Such a decision was forced and enforced by the popular panic, no doubt. But probably the work of Ghazzâlî (d. 1111), who was the greatest theologian and legist of the time, helped to mould this decision to a critical precision which gave it not only a definitive place in the Ismâʿîlî struggle, but perhaps in the whole self-definition of Islâm. He had worked out a careful analysis of what it must in fact mean to profess the formula of Muslim faith, and so be permitted the privileges of acceptance in the Sunnî society; in this analysis, which we shall examine more closely shortly, he drew a line between the milder Shîʿa – in error, but still genuinely professing the faith – and the Ismâʿîlîs, who did not mean by the formula the minimum amount that it had to mean. By rejecting the plain meaning of the Prophet's teachings, the Ismâʿîlîs rejected in fact Muḥammad's prophethood; and were therefore beyond the pale.[12]

Granted now that Nizârîs were not to be admitted even as erring members of the Muslim community; certain problems arose in regard to the Ismâʿîlî principle of secrecy in the case of the Ismâʿîlî who repented and accepted Sunnî authority. One problem in this respect had already before Nizârî times been considered by the theologian Baghdâdî (d. 1037): must the repentant Ismâʿîlî respect the oath of secrecy he had made when being admitted into the Ismâʿîlî community? Baghdâdî thought not, at least if it had been made with the mental reservation that one was taking it only so as to be able to do the Ismâʿîlîs harm precisely by revealing their secrets.[13] The greater theologian Ghazzâlî

[10] I am combining here data from Zakariyâ Qazwînî, *Âthâr al-Bilâd*, ed. Wüsttenfeld (Göttingen, 1848), p. 250; with Ibn Khallikân, transl. MacGuckin de Slane, vol. II, p. 146; evidently the same individual is in question.

[11] The same question came up again, it is said, in a negotiation between Sanjar and Muḥammad ibn Buzurg'ummîd, and was decided temporarily in favor of the Ismâʿîlîs; but before many years even Sanjar was again at war with them. If this negotiation, noted by Rashîd ad-Dîn probably from an Ismâʿîlî source, was real, it was soon overruled.

[12] Goldziher, *Streitschrift*, p. 73.

[13] Baghdâdî, *Farq bayn al-Firaq*, trans. A. S. Halkin, *Moslem Schisms and Sects*, Part II (Tel Aviv, 1935), p. 291/148.

now went into this problem in more detail. The Ismâ'îlî oath included within itself its own special penalties for transgression – for instance, divorce of all wives, present or future; Ghazzâlî pointed out that since Muslim law already provided considerably smaller penalties for breaking an oath, any disregard of larger penalties (themselves merely part of the broken oath) would be atoned for in the same mild manner as the rest of the oath. But the oath itself he considered binding, if it had not been made with suitable reservations, as, *God willing*.

This case in conscience for the repentant individual was, however, not to be the most important problem for the Sunnî legist. Ghazzâlî already recognized the question whether a claim to repentance by an Ismâ'îlî was to be accepted by Sunnî society as genuine. Ghazzâlî advised the standard Sunnî approach, that God alone can judge the hearts, and in absence of further incrimination the lips must be believed. Ghazzâlî's most serious concession to the panic of the time seems to be his decision that all Ismâ'îlîs are to be regarded as personally apostate, and hence subject to the death penalty if they do not repent – including here even the children brought up to the faith by their parents.[14]

Later legists were more harsh in their formulations for the most part. During the following century we know of two rather formal collections of judicial sentiment on the point. In about 1181 the legists of Samarqand were asked how to treat the Ismâ'îlî who claimed to be repentant. The mildest answer was that he must be required to try to bring back all whom he had led astray (that he must inform on others?); but generally no repentance was admitted, and the death penalty was required, on the grounds that the most explicit declaration could be construed in the Ismâ'îlî's mind to mean its opposite. A similar decision by the legists of Balkh, evidently recent, was cited at Samarqand.[15]

It is only after the Nizârî political power was at an end that we hear of rules accepting the remaining Nizârîs as a part of Islamic soicety, and prescribing their role: whether their foods could be eaten, or their army service accepted.[16] But even so the convention of their absolute rejection was retained, having been established when their power was so greatly feared; and the theologian, in laying down these rules, retains a suitable disgust and horror.

[14] Goldziher, *Streitschrift*, p. 71.

[15] Îjî-Jurjânî, trans. E. Salisbury, *JAOS*, II (1851), 286. Perhaps repentance only *after* a man has been caught is implied; in their time the Ismâ'îlîs were more a community apart, and the case of the morally stricken repentant convert would be rarer.

[16] Ibn Taymiyya, trans. E. Salisbury, *JAOS*, II (1851), 288 ff.; by Ibn Taymiyya's own standards, this decision applies not only to Nuṣayrîs but to Ismâ'îlîs in general.

In the case of the Nizârîs the Sunnîs had to face directly the problem of drawing the outer limits of the Muslim community's catholicity. They had made it in principle a formal matter; but here was a group which accepted the forms, and claimed the privileges of membership, while working for the total overthrow of the Sunnî interpretation of Islâm. It is possible that here the Sunnî ideal of finding a lowest common denominator among all believers as the basis for community found an important test case, as a result of which the ideal had to be limited – preparing the way for the relative intolerance of later Islâm against deviation.[17]

THE INTELLECTUAL RESPONSE: GHAZZÂLÎ AND THE CHALLENGE OF THE TAʿLÎM TO REASON

Ghazzâlî's defence of a Sunnî alternative to taʿlîm.

More personally interesting, though perhaps less significant for the development of the Islamic community, was the serious attempt on the part of some Sunnîs to wrestle with the intellectual problems raised by the Nizârî position. The first and most monumental of these attempts was that of Ghazzâlî himself, who wrote many treatises against it, and admitted in the *Munqidh*, his spiritual "autobiography", the great role it played in his thinking. It was surely only in the very years of the Nizârî uprisings, just when Ghazzâlî was undergoing his spiritual search, that the Ismâʿîlî doctrine could have played fourth in a game where the other hands were scholastic theology, Philosophy (the Greek tradition), and mysticism. Ghazzâlî so honored no one other teaching. The schools of theology, like the schools of Philosophy or of the Ṣûfî mysticism, he merged under generic heads; other religions than Islâm, and other Muslim sects, such as the Twelver Shîʿa, he refused the character of seekers for truth, and quite ignored in that crucial treatise; though he was acquainted with Christianity, for instance, as were few if any other

[17] Cf. generally, Goldziher, 'Katholische Tendenz,' *Beitrag zur Religionswissenschaft*, I. Jahrgang, 2. Heft. In Huart, 'Les Zindiqs en droit musulman,' *Onzième Congrès Internationale des Orientalistes, Actes* (Paris, 1897), Sect. III, pp. 69–80, one finds that much later, in Ottoman times, the principle holds that certain groups of a reputation for insincerity (including the "Stranglers" from early Shîʿa times apparently, but not, interestingly enough, the Ismâʿîlîs), and then generally those who propagandize against religion, are to be permitted repentance as alternative to death only if they repent before they are caught.

Muslims. The circle of Ḥasan-i Ṣabbâḥ (for he shows less interest in the older Ismâʿîlîs) is given the status of Kindî, Fârâbî and Ibn Sînâ combined; of Ashʿarî, Mâturîdî, and Juwaynî combined; or of Makkî, Bisṭâmî, and Junayd.[18]

Goldziher suggests that Ghazzâlî's interest in the Ismâʿîlîs results from two considerations: the great prominence of the sect at the time; and its insistence upon accepting doctrine blindly from others, a principle which Ghazzâlî combatted, as *taqlîd*, within Sunnî circles. This points up Ghazzâlî's special interest in taʿlîm, which would correspond on this view to the Sunnî taqlîd; but it seems an inadequate explanation. The Ismâʿîlîs themselves attacked taqlîd, in the form at least of unquestioning acceptance of doctrine from the first Sunnî master at hand: they encouraged a great deal of questioning on the part of the unsaved. Had taqlîd been the center of interest for Ghazzâlî in this case, he would have concentrated on showing that submission to the imâm involved a variety of that taqlîd which the Ismâʿîlîs themselves condemned, and let it go at that. His many writings on the Ismâʿîlîs do not reduce to this.

It was indeed, however, the doctrine of taʿlîm and not the apparatus of emanationist philosophy (though he attacked that also), which engaged Ghazzâlî's attention. The first reference Ghazzâlî seems to have made to the taʿlîmî tenets was a brusque denial of them, and a statement that they were not worth even a refutation.[19] Ghazzâlî seems to have been trying to prove this to himself the rest of his life. The argument which he maintained in the *Mustaẓhirî* must be used against the Ismâʿîlîs was that of the *reductio ad absurdum*, which he granted could be so effectively used only against them;[20] (and in fact it is at best a superficial argument, all human speculation being reducible to absurdity if pushed too far within fixed terminology). This is consistent with his estimate of the small worth of the doctrine; yet he was not really satisfied, despite his ridicule of those who dealt with it more at length and more historically, to give its doctrine a ridiculous twist, and then leave it without noting the life and principles at its basis. It was a persistent and deep challenge to him, and at crucial points he permitted himself profundity in meeting it.

In the *Mustaẓhirî* he included a number of arguments against the taʿlîmî principle, adapted to the various degrees to which one might have accepted it. Thus he suggests that the Prophet had evidence (evidentiary miracles) to prove his authority, which Mustanṣir, the imâm

18 *Munqidh*, tr. Barbier de Meynard, *JA* 1877, ps. 19, 41–2. Cf. L. Massignon, *REI*, 1932, on Ghazzâlî's acceptance of certain Ismâʿîlî methods.

19 Goldziher, *Streitschrift*, p. 10.

20 *Ibid.*, p. 21.

of the time, did not; but this is no refutation of Ḥasan-i Ṣabbâḥ's claim, in effect, of a logical miracle. He suggests that there are a number of persons claiming infallibility – but the uniqueness of Ḥasan's imâm lies in the particular rational basis for the claim. He suggests that Mustanṣir himself did not in fact claim this infallibility: but even if this could be proven, Ḥasan might have maintained that if the claim is made for the imâm, and not denied, this is enough to establish a logically valid source of authority.[21]

The most radical argument, of course, as well as that most clearly attempting a *reductio ad absurdum*, was that by their own critique any reason by which they can arrive at the inadequacy of reason must be itself inadequate. The Nizârî answer to this would be that reason is able to give a negative, but not a positive, answer in these matters: it could be adequate to show its own lack of authoritativeness without being adequate to lead to any positive conclusions. The Nizârî position would have been at least as tenable as its contradictory; we seem to be involved here in the theory of logical classes. But a greater difficulty was that Ghazzâlî himself recognized the justice of the argument that reason must be supplemented by an imâm, only differing in the qualifications of the imâm and the relative positions of imâm and reason.

Problem of authority solved in terms of history.

For Ghazzâlî, whether as a result of the Ismâʿîlî ferment or not, was greatly impressed by the weaknesses of reasoning as a means to religious truth. In contrast to the Ismâʿîlîs, however, he was concerned to retain as far as possible the validity of the rich positive experience of the life about him. Accordingly, when he lost his primal innocence and began to doubt, his spiritual-intellectual search was not, like that of the Ismâʿîlîs, for a single definitive truth which once found was to be exclusively embraced. He sought rather the re-establishment on sound foundations of those beauties and truths (for so the religious experience which he told of in the *Munqidh* made him account them) which he had apparently lost.

Ghazzâlî like Ḥasan posited a thorough intellectual doubt on religious matters; but rather than piercing through it with a dialectic of authority,

[21] "If I assert the taʿlîm, and there is none but me who takes the taʿlîm position, then the designation of the imâm rests with me."

he set it aside by an act of faith, as a trap. Assured explicitly that God could not mislead his worshippers – an assumption which must also implicitly underlie Ḥasan's dialectic – he preferred to base his faith upon sincere and general experience. The undoubtable "balance" which he opposed to Ḥasan's "balance" was not one of internal logic, but of criticism of given doctrines.[22] The inadequacies of reason applied only to its use for initial discovery, which was the proper sphere of revelation instead;[23] the role of reason in ultimate matters was a critical one, to judge among alternative proposals as to which were incorrect. It was only through examining a large number of details that the one true position would then be found satisfactory. If one believed the Prophet for his miracles, this was not enough; magicians did wonders, too;[24] if one believed him for his moral advice, here also there have been other wise men; but taken in all aspects together, the Prophet was impregnable to criticism.[25]

The authority of recognized prophets must be supposed valid, therefore, until shown point by point impossible. Ghazzâlî was not content to leave it at that entirely – eventually the ever-present witness of the inward experience of Ṣûfî mystics must back up the outer testimony of history. Yet the witness of history was valid in itself; and it was its validity, rather than the more far-reaching but more equivocal witness of the mystics, that was appropriate to refute the a-historical Ismâʿîlîs. Ghazzâlî was quite frank to admit the way in which prophets became recognized – not by demonstration, but by the sword – or more generally, by the threshing of history; yet if God does not mislead, history too is in His providence. Simple folk believed unquestioningly what was established, and that was good (so far as it went); the task of reason was

[22] *Munqidh*, tr. Barbier de Meynard, *JA*, 1877, ps. 50–52.

[23] By assigning a prophetic origin even to medicine, astronomy, etc., Ghazzâlî was not only accepting a popular notion (cf. Mirkhwând's early history), but accepting a doctrine which was particularly espoused by the Ismâʿîlîs, who traced secular knowledge of all sorts to the imâm. *Munqidh* tr. p. 68. Cf. Goldziher, *Streitschrift*, p. 20.

[24] Ghazzâlî's attitude on miracles is multiple. Here in the *Munqidh* he seems to reject them; yet at one time in the Mustaẓhirî he urges the evidence of Mohammed's miracles over against Mustanṣir. His position – consistently with his idea that reason in matters of faith was of value only to counter criticism – varied with the level of the argument he was opposing. At a low level, he could contrast Mustanṣir and Mohammed, among other things, for their miracles; at a higher level, he could rise above even the conventional ways of distinguishing evidentiary miracles from other sorts of wonders, and base his case on experience which surpassed in breadth that of the technical survey of wonders in the same degree that this latter surpassed the crude acceptance of miracle.

[25] *Munqidh*, transl. p. 90.

to disprove the alternative fancies which less simple folk invented for themselves.

Ghazzâlî's "Balance" as answer to Ḥasan-i Ṣabbâḥ's four propositions.

Ghazzâlî thus substituted his own equally radical solution for the Nizârî dialectic. There remained only the necessity of showing that on fundamental points reason could in fact clearly cut away the false, granted the fundamental authority of the Prophet and the Koran. It must be shown that the "many teachers" of the Sunnîs could come to agreement. This was the function of his *balance*, expounded in the *Qisṭâs*, which he directed precisely against the Ismâʿîlîs. He was assured that honest men must agree to the principles of this balance if once they understood it, and that therefore it could serve to quiet the fundamental disputes that remained among the followers of the Prophet. Substantially, it was a matter of showing to what degree a statement in scripture must be taken literally, and to what extent figuratively. If a statement could not in logic be taken literally, it could then be taken figuratively to a fixed mild degree; only if this were also inappropriate could one resort to the next more general type of interpretation; and so on till very few statements could be interpreted with such freedom as Ismâʿîlîs commonly used.[26] In the end he had a standard which not only gave coherence to the Sunnî approach, but gave a basis for logical rejection of the Ismâʿîlî doctrines in detail. Thus it took care both of the overall principle of taʿlîm, and of the particular teachings which taʿlîm claimed to validate.[27]

Such a method allowed him to insist that an infallible imâm can provide no substitute for the general experience of the community. He could then press with zeal the contrast between the fullness of wisdom which Sunnî tradition brought, and the artificiality of Ismâʿîlî doctrine. Even with an imâm there could be no daily recourse to agreed authority, nor did the Nizârîs have answers ready, as a result of finding their imâm, to various intellectual questions submitted them. To the Nizârîs, of course, such questions were probably unreal, having to do with difficulties not

[26] In the *Tafriqa* he used the principle to show that the Ismâʿîlî bâṭin went beyond the Muslim pale at crucial points; for it substituted less literal interpretations for legitimate more literal ones at points such as the physical resurrection, belief in which was essential to Islâm.

[27] Perhaps he did not always have these correctly. For instance, the *Wajh-i Dîn*, p. 99, rejects (what Ghazzâlî accuses Ismâʿîlîs of), that "God is wise in that he causes to be wise". Cf. Nâṣir's precisions, *Jâmiʿal-Ḥikmatayn* (Teheran and Paris, 1953), p. 249.

arising within their authoritative system; to Ghazzâlî their system was itself thin and unreal, rejecting as it did so much of the vital experience which he valued. The true imâm representing the authority of Mohammed was that personification of the community tradition, the Caliph at Baghdâd.

Finally, then, Ghazzâlî was able to meet the Nizârî challenge through a robust appreciation of the historical basis of the Sunnî approach to Islâm. He contrasted to the tenuous and hidden role of the Ismâ'îlî imâm the universally known miracles of Mohammed and the vast impact which his advent and especially the development of his community made upon the face of the world. If God truly did provide guidance for his worshippers (and this was guaranteed by the universal experience of Ṣûfîs), and granted that naked reason was not the channel of that guidance, the channel would be the continuity of public experience, developed through large social and historical means – even the sword – and critically defensible point by point over the whole range of life.

Variations upon Ghazzâlî's response later.

No other Sunnî thinkers seem to have met the Nizârî challenge so profoundly, nor to have allowed it so large a place in the development of their thinking. The writers of the first generation or so wrestled with it valiantly, but without becoming too involved; later generations, after the Nizârî movement had gone on within its own circle to such very different developments as the Qiyâma, continued to discuss the original Nizârî challenge; but at a calmer distance.

Abû Muḥammad al-'Irâqî, writing presumably soon after Ghazzâlî, attacked the Ismâ'îlîs frantically; labelling them as far more dangerous to Islâm than were Christians and Jews. His chief serious condemnation of their doctrine was that it made the Prophet superfluous, by giving all authority to the imâm. Since the imâm is made to depend historically upon the Prophet, such a Nizârî depreciation of the Prophet would be (one supposes) self-defeating; but Abû Muḥammad was too severely shocked to spell out his objection, which must ultimately spring from a sense of history similar to that of Ghazzâlî's.

The prominent theologian and heresiologist, Shahrastânî (d. 1157), treated the Nizârîs more soberly but with equal seriousness in the following generation. He gave them a section to themselves rather than range them incidentally among dozens of lesser sects, as had been done by heresiologists before. At the end of his description of the Nizârîs, we find a record of his personal attempt at evaluation – not a common thing with him (and indicating that in 1127, under Buzurg'ummîd, the da'wa could still be an active challenge to the individual Muslim).

But he was not seeking in it an answer, evidently, to any searching question of authority. Rather he expected it to make sense of the questions dealt with in Sunnî dogmatics. Inevitably he could find nothing in it to satisfy him; his final complaint was of an imâm, a "teacher", who has nothing but his own being to teach.[28] This was to miss the point: the purpose of the da'wa was not to bring additional tidbits to the Sunnî table of doctrine. Yet it touched after all on the same historical point to which Ghazzâlî had pointed Sunnî thinkers. The cumulative experience of the community was given no significance by the doctrine; the community must therefore reject the doctrine.[29]

Jamâl ad-Dîn Qazwînî (*ca.* 1156) was apparently inclined to deny even the inequalities in human reason, so as to attack an Ismâ'îlî contention that reason cannot be the ground of salvation, for that would make an inequality among men.[30] But later authors not only took no account of the Qiyâma and subsequent Nizârî development; they tended to merge even Ḥasan's ta'lîm doctrine with the rest of Ismâ'îlî tradition, refuting it all as something out of the past. Ibn al-Jawzî (d. 1200) ridiculed the idea both of ta'lîm and of the bâṭin (in no fresh ways); and wanted to say to the chief of the Ismâ'îlîs, in effect, if he chanced to meet him: look, our Islâm has swept the world; how can you hope to win with your few fortresses and your occasional secret convert? Why not give up?[31] This was in one sense a return to the historical argument!

Fakhr ad-Dîn Râzî (d. 1209) was the next really great Sunnî writer within the Alamût period after Ghazzâlî; he was evidently the last writer to take the Nizârî case seriously. He criticized Ghazzâlî warmly as supposing that merely by giving reason a role in addition to the imâm he had upset the Nizârî position; whereas actually Ḥasan-i Ṣabbâḥ did accept a certain role for reason. However, he shows no signs of having considered Ḥasan any more closely than he evidently considered Ghazzâlî; his own defense of the positive supremacy of reason is summary – any denial of

[28] Ghazzâlî makes a similar complaint. Perhaps it is not quite fair, since neither scholar was willing to undergo initiation.

[29] If it should prove true that Shahrastânî made use of Nizârî writings in his treatment of the Ṣâbi'a, this would serve to underline the interest he had in what the Nizârîs had to say, even though he took quite a different sort of harvest from them than did Ghazzâlî.

[30] Goldziher, *Streitschrift*, p. 111.

[31] Ibn al-Jawzî, *Islamic Culture*, IX (1935), 554. Cf. his *Muntaẓam* (Somogyi, *RSO*, 1932). By his time, the supposed degrees of initiation had mounted to twelve!

reason will itself involve reason. In any case, the Nizârî question even with Râzî had become a purely theoretical one; no longer compelling a searching inquiry, but a means of polemic against a fellow Sunnî.[32] Ismâʿîlism had dwindled to a secluded sect, no longer appealing to all Muslims personally.

When Juwaynî, after the fall of Alamût, set about refuting the claims of Ḥasan-i Ṣabbâḥ, he could not feel the force of them. Ḥasan had said that imâm and reason were both necessary; and Juwaynî did not feel his own position threatened by so obvious a thesis. He saw no difference between the Prophetic tradition among the Sunnî teachers as supplement to reason, and Ḥasan's imâm; and could therefore see no point in Ḥasan's affirmation.[33] Sunnî Islâm, in large part through the efforts of Ghazzâlî, had worked out its own balance between reason and revelation. Ismâʿîlism was outmanoeuvered – it was defeated not only militarily.

IMAGINATIVE FRUIT

The violent hostility which the Nizârîs aroused merged in time with the general bigotry which Islâm displayed toward all dissenting groups after the orthodox synthesis came to be taken as a matter of course. The legal expression thereof probably helped to clarify the Sunnî attitude toward marginal groups. The intellectual reaction to the Nizârî impact was not very fruitful except in the case of Ghazzâlî; though since it entered into the whole fabric of his thought, through him it entered into all Islâm. Perhaps the most generally lasting fruit of the Nizârî movement in Islâm was in the realm of the imagination.

The legend of the garden.

The very name by which we commonly call the Nizârîs, *Assassins*, has been the occasion for one of the most remarkable of the tales about the sect being given great currency even in the West. The name had been traced to every sort of origin, suggesting correspondingly varied histories

[32] Kraus, *Islamic Culture*, IX (1938); cf. also Râzî's *Iʿtiqâdât, Firaq al-Muslimîn wa-l-Mushriqîn* (Cairo, 1938), which adds little. Râzî is the theologian said to have been threatened by a fidâ'î sent by Muḥammad II, and to have moderated his statements thereafter. (He is also noted, incidentally, for having insisted, within Sunnism, on the probably Shîʿite idea of the sinlessness of prophets.)
[33] Juwaynî, ed. pp. 195 ff.

for the sect. It was therefore a great advance when de Sacy determined, a century and a half ago, that the Arabic form of the name "Assassin" was *ḥashîshiyya* or possibly *ḥashîshiyyûn* – that is, presumably, the users of the drug *ḥashîsh*, intoxicating hemp. He showed that not only Christian and Jewish, but some Muslim writers used this term of them. The question then arose, why was this term applied to the Nizârîs?[34]

William of Tyre, the Crusader writer, explicitly noted his ignorance of the name's origin.[35] When de Sacy found the meaning of the word, he admitted that the origin of its application was still conjectural; but he did venture to offer a theory. De Sacy disposed in advance of one possibility which has nevertheless been suggested repeatedly since, that the ḥashîsh was used to drive the fidâ'îs to that frenzy of recklessness necessary for their public murders. Although when mixed with other drugs the ḥashîsh can drive men to frenzy, yet the necessity of long, patient stalking, and of carefully seizing the exposed moment, would eliminate use of any drug as a momentary stimulant. The same considerations would eliminate any habitual use of the drug – it is debilitating – as occasion for the name. De Sacy turned instead to the aura of legend surrounding the sect, extracting therefrom one item which might have a historical foundation.

It had apparently early occurred to the Muslims that the murderous fidâ'îs must somehow have been artificially prepared for their deeds; no man in his senses would have risked his life so. We find Ibn al-Jawzî giving an explanation already a bit more complex than that of Qazwînî (who had the Alamûtîs be so dumb as to saw off the limbs they sat on). He has Ḥasan-i Ṣabbâḥ invite a simpleton, and feed him on walnuts, coriander, and honey to expand his brain. Then Ḥasan expounds the woes of the Prophet's family; recounts how the Khârijites sacrificed their lives in fighting against their own enemies; and tells the man he should be at least as willing to sacrifice his life for the true imâm.[36]

In a historical novel, which Von Hammer discovered for us and was inclined to take seriously despite its admittedly fictional character, we find a far more elaborate conception. In the *Sîra Ḥâkim* we read of an Ismâ'îl in the time of the pre-Nizârî Fâṭimid ruler Ẓâhir, who lands at Tripoli laden with plundered jewels and surrounded by his fidâ'îs. He then went to Maṣyâf and had built a vast garden, with a four-story

[34] Cf. S. de Sacy, 'Mémoire sur la dynastie des Assassins,' *Mémoires de l'académie des inscriptions et belles lettres*, IV, Part 2 (Paris, 1818), 55–59, etc.

[35] William of Tyre, *Guillaume de Tyr et ses Continuateurs*, ed. P. Paris (Paris, 1879), II, 357.

[36] *Islamic Culture* (1935), IX, 556.

pleasure-building in the midst; the windows were painted with stars, and the rooms fiilled with luxuries. He brought finely dressed and perfumed slaves of both sexes to the house; he filled the garden with all sorts of tasty or beautiful plants, and with graceful animals, like gazelles. He then dug a tunnel between the pleasure-building and his own residence, where he entertained all day men attracted by his munificence. In the evening he chose some to sit by his side, and told them of the excellence of ʿAlî; then drugged them, and carried them to the garden. When they awoke, they were assured that they were now dreaming and seeing their places in paradise in the dream; but when on being drugged again they returned to Ismâʿîl's house, Ismâʿîl assured them it was no dream, but a miracle of ʿAlî; that if they kept it secret and served Ismâʿîl they would receive that place in paradise permanently; but if they divulged the secret they would suffer terribly.[37]

This novel happens to be in Arabic, but a like story must have been current in Îrân also; for it was apparently there that Marco Polo picked up a very similar tale of a wondrous garden to which the Old Man of the Mountain took sleeping youths that they might suppose they had been in paradise, and so be willing to serve his whims.[38] Relying on Marco Polo's tale, De Sacy suggested that the ḥashîsh, though not mentioned in these stories as such, was at that time the secret property of the Nizârî chiefs; and was used (without the superfluous aid of a garden!) to stimulate dreams of paradise in their fidâ'îs. These would then be willing to do their lethal duties, supposing that their chiefs could send them to Paradise at will.

The word "Assassin".

The garden could not successfully be excluded once the root idea was admitted, and Polo's story came to be given all the more credit, since De Sacy's scholarship seemed to confirm it. But unfortunately, we shall have to look elsewhere for an explanation of the term "Assassin". Reliable historians did not mention such a scheme – Juwaynî, when investigating the history of Alamût on the spot after its fall did not look for such a garden as Polo heard tell of. Even apart from the garden, that the ḥashîsh was no secret monopoly of the Nizârî chiefs at that time is clear not only from positive evidence, but from the very use of the name:

[37] J. von Hammer, 'Min al-juz' ath-thânî min sîrati amîr al-mu'minîn al-Ḥâkim bi-amr Allâh,' *Fundgruben des Orients*, III (1813), 201–206.
[38] Ed. Moule, 1938, pp. 40 ff.

already in the *Hidâyat al-Âmiriyya*, written in the first generation of the schism, the term *Ḥashîshiyya* is used, without explanation, of the Nizârîs.[39] If indeed it referred to their secret use of ḥashîsh, that use must already have been public knowledge! That the drug was later sometimes associated with the Nizârîs may be ascribed in part to expectations aroused by the name itself, but more to the fact that, already despised as a minority, they had special opportunities to become associated with the prevailing vices.[40]

The ascetic morality of Ḥasan-i Ṣabbâḥ will already have suggested an alternative explanation of the fidâ'î fanaticism: a strong sense of in-group purity and devotion. More than once we hear of a first assassin failing and falling, and immediately a second, and then a third rising to complete the job; we have cited the famous story of a mother who received the news that all the fidâ'îs on a mission in which her son took part had perished: she dressed herself as at a time of rejoicing, and when her son proved to have escaped after all, she put on mourning.[41]

Recently more than one student has suggested also an alternative explanation of the name.[42] To the Nizârîs such behavior was heroic; to their opponents it was both mad and base. Nothing prevents us from supposing, therefore, that a popular name for them would be less likely to describe a secret practice of theirs, than to express the loathing and the fear felt for them. The name *Ḥashîshiyya* would suggest not only a loathesome habit, but a comparison with men made berserk by drugs. The comparison might be strengthened by an uncritical tendency to suppose the fidâ'îs were actually drugged. The term was used specially in Syria, we are informed.[43] Even there it seems to have been avoided by

[39] Fyzee, *Hidâyat al-Âmiriyya*, p. 27. D. Schaffner, *Relations of the Order of Assassins with the Crusaders Nuring the Twelfth Century* (typed thesis, Dept. of History, University of Chicago, 1939), p. 18 ff., cites the evidence for earlier use of the drug than de Sacy was aware of.

[40] Langlois reports a pair of Ismâ'îlî exiles who, idle in an alien atmosphere, were ḥashîsh users; but ascribes ḥashîsh also to one of two groups into which Syrian Ismâ'îlîs of his time were divided. *Athénaeum français*, III (November, 1854), 1044–6. That an Ismâ'îlî introduced to Egypt, according to de Sacy's citation of Maqrîzî, a special form of ḥashîsh might be guardedly compared to the selling of liquor by Christians, while even those Muslims who drank had to keep up appearances by not dealing in the stuff.

[41] Ibn al-'Adîm, *Zubdat al-Ḥalab fî Ta'rîkh Ḥalab*, *R. H. C. Hist. Or.*, III, 577–694: year, 520.

[42] Cf. Schaffner, *Relations of the Order of Assasins*, p. 18 ff., who notes some of the inadequacies of de Sacy's interpretation. Margoliouth, 'Assassins,' *Encyclopedia of Religion and Ethics*, also suggests that the term *Ḥashîshî* was scornful rather than descriptive.

[43] Ibn Muyassar, p. 68.

the more careful writers, though it is found in Abû Shâma's sources. It is only in the violently polemical second half of the epistle of Âmir that it occurs. Probably it was a local popular term, and hence was especially picked up by Christians and Jews, who got their information orally.[44]

Legend of the three school-fellows.

It seems to have been the Nizârîs themselves who created the tale of the three schoolfellows, which became – after Rashîd ad-Dîn published it – an inseparable part of the glamorous story of Niẓâm al-Mulk, and has entered into Western lore via Fitzgerald's preface to his Omar Khayyam. Omar Khayyam, Ḥasan-i Ṣabbâḥ, and Niẓâm al-Mulk, talented students of the same master, agreed that surely one of them would rise to high fortune; and that whichever did so would share equally with the other two. In due time Niẓâm al-Mulk rose to command as vizier the mighty Saljûq empire. Omar, scholar and lover of ease, chose not a province to rule but a pension for his leisure; but the ambitious Ḥasan insisted on a high post at court, where he and Niẓâm al-Mulk entered into a mortal rivalry. With clever subtlety, Ḥasan ecipsed his rival in the Sulṭân's eyes. When marble was brought from afar for the Sulṭân's building, the vizier was called upon to divide between the merchants the total payment agreed upon, and did so in direct proportion to the weight carried – whereupon Ḥasan insisted that in justice the division should have been adjusted according to the excess of weight over the proper load in each case. The Sulṭân was charmed with his acuteness.

When a general accounting of the revenues of the realm was demanded of him, the vizier asked two years for the task – whereupon Ḥasan insisted that it need take no more than a number of weeks. The Sulṭân assigned him the task, and put at his disposal all the scribes of the capital; and when in the prescribed time he was ready to present the grand accounting in full audience before the Sulṭân, Niẓâm al-Mulk despaired of his own place. Getting hold of the readied papers at the last minute, he so jumbled their order that the unsuspecting Ḥasan, beginning to read

[44] S. Pines, *Rev. Hist. Juive en Egypte*, 1947, p. 22, notes a Jewish writer of the year 1148 CE who discussed a religion of al-ḥashîsh, born in his times: that life is as the perishing herbs (ḥashîsh), God not caring for it; that souls transmigrate into grass [again ḥashîsh] to be purified. This probably refers to the Nizârîs; and seems to include two different attempts at explaining their popular name, on the basis of a misunderstanding of their doctrine.

from them, was covered with confusion. A judicious remark from the old vizier completed his rout, and he fled disgraced from the empire.

But Ḥasan would have his revenge. Learning in his Egyptian exile the secrets of the Ismâʿîlî faith, he returned in secret to Îrân, organizing the daʿwa. Residing with one of his followers, he exclaimed that with just two men as determined as himself, he could overthrow the mighty Saljûq edifice of empire. His follower thought him mad, and began to serve him medicines for the brain; whereat Ḥasan departed upon his mission. When Ḥasan was established in Alamût, Niẓâm al-Mulk assassinated, the Sulṭân dead, and the empire shattered among quarreling amîrs and a prey to Ismâʿîlî risings, his follower came to him there. Said Ḥasan, Which of the two of us was mad when you gave me medicines?[45]

In the presumably original Nizârî version Ḥasan-i Ṣabbâḥ represents in a very personal way that injured justice which it was the role of the imâm to avenge; but it is the sheer scale of the conception of contest which in giving the tale its thrill most faithfully reflects, surely, the sanguine Nizârî imagination. Later Sunnî writers often attempted to whitewash Niẓâm al-Mulk, and to depict Ḥasan's revenge as the move of a bitter man mad for power.[46] Yet, however distorted, the story continued to bring to Islâm at large some part of that spirit of personal adventure which the Ismâʿîlîs had always cultivated.

Horrified awe.

Apart from such special legends, the Nizârîs seem to have grasped men's imaginations by their very being. The Western reverberations of their reputation were striking – it went so far that Richard Lion-Heart was accused of imitating the Old Man of the Mountain in training murderers; and found it necessary to have a group of men in England plead guilty to such operations against himself. The descriptions by Westerners of the Nizârî life are at least as lurid as those by Muslims.[47] Indeed, the Muslim historians seem to have taken special pains, generally, to keep within sober limits.[48]

45 For speculation on the possible origins of this apocryphal tale in less dramatic relations between certain other figures, cf. Harold Bowen, *JRAS* (1931), pp. 771–82.

46 E. G. Browne, *Literary History of Persia* (Cambridge, 1928), II, 191, discusses these versions.

47 Cf. the lists in C. Nowell, 'The Old Man of the Mountain,' *Speculum*, XXII, No. 4 (October, 1947), 497; and Schaffner.

48 Strangely, Arabic writers do not seem to have made anything of the fact that "Alamût", as written in Arabic characters without short vowels, is identical with "al-mawt" – "death".

Nevertheless, it was among the Muslims that the imaginative picture of the Nizârîs was created, a picture that has lasted to our own times. The thrill of ḥashîsh and dagger offered to the sober and proper world a terrified gaze into fantastic possibility. All those things farthest beyond the daring of the ordinary man, yet most appealing in their perversity, could be believed of the astounding Nizârîs. In horrified awe men told of the garden of the lord of Alamût, where were all the delights – flowers, scents, wines, sensuous women – of the roaming imagination. In the sleep produced by a magic potion handsome youths were taken thither and given their full of dallying – to be sent out in the following days to kill at the price of their own lives the mighty of the earth. The delights of heaven were theirs, and an irresponsible freedom where ties of past and future disappeared; and theirs was the exquisite horror of a dread deed and a devoted death.

In the power of Alamût was thought to be all the wild malice and destruction a soul could dream of: at a word the dagger was ready, at a word were kings and lords laid low. No fear of earthly punishment or divine displeasure: only a total immersion in the power of death, as in the delight of sense. Of this atheistic devotion the ordinary citizen must hardly think: yet he was permitted a glimpse in the stories of the secret master of such men. A god to all about him, he owned no god beyond. At his command, the company would assemble at night in forbidden orgies, celebrating the rites and the rights of sex with any to hand in the covering darkness, to the nearest and most forbidden;[49] or at his glance, fifty men would leap from the turrets about him to a far death below.[50] So splendid a luxuriance had as arresting a fascination as it had impossibility in real life; and it became a favored possession of the Muslim, and thence too of the Western, imagination.

[49] Ibn Jubayr on the Ṣufât seems to be the earliest to report this.

[50] Cf. especially Abû l-Faraj, *Chronography*, trans. E. A. T. W. Budge (Oxford, 1932), p. 387; the pseudo-Brocardus, *Directorium ad Passagium Faciendum*, 1332 - *R. H. C. Doc. Arm.*, II (Paris, 1906), 368; Ibn al-Jawzî, *Islamic Cullure*, IX (1935), pp. 555–6.

PART TWO

THE GOSPEL OF THE QIYÂMA

CHAPTER VII

STALEMATE AND A NEW START: ḤASAN 'ALÂ DHIKRI-HI S-SALÂM

MUḤAMMAD IBN BUZURG'UMMÎD: MOUNTAIN LORD (1138–1162)

When Buzurg'ummîd died, in 1138, the Nizârî state had found its territorial limits, and had begun to live its own life apart from Islamic society at large; though it was still in active conflict with that society, seeking over large areas to overthrow it. It is perhaps symbolic of the development of the Nizârîs into an autonomous community with their own line of development, parallel to more than rebelling against that of Islâm at large, that it was not this time an independently prominent leader as twice before, but Buzurg'ummîd's own son who succeeded to the headship. Hereditary leadership was found elsewhere among the Ismâ'îlîs, where local chiefs kept their positions, as in the case of Ṭuraythîth; or, as in the case of the Ra'îs Muẓaffar at Gird Kûh, son followed father even in power freshly founded under the Ismâ'îlî aegis. Possibly if Ibn 'Aṭṭâsh's son had had more success at Iṣfahân, he would have succeeded to his father's position. But it was only now that hereditary rule was permanently attached to the central direction of the movement.

Persistent expectancy despite a local outlook.

One of the earliest events of the new reign was the assassination of the Caliph Râshid, successor of Mustarshid who had been assassinated toward the end of Buzurg'ummîd's reign. Râshid, like Mustarshid, was at the moment out of favor with the Saljûq rulers, and had been forced to resign, and go to Iṣfahân. There some Ismâ'îlîs were able to do away with him. It was evidently thought at Alamût that he was on his way at the time to avenge Mustarshid's death (though this seems unlikely); but the simple fact that he was a Sunnî Caliph would account for the great celebrations held there upon the news of his death: the tymbals were beaten for seven days.[1] At Iṣfahân, on the contrary, the populace felt themselves aggrieved and endangered, and massacred all they thought they could identify as Ismâʿîlîs.[2]

In the early years of the reign, and even occasionally thereafter, we find a large number of assassinations listed: three Qâḍîs, and a number of military men, scattered through the sub-Caucasus area and the northern parts of Îrân. These seem to indicate some continuance, in a secondary manner at least, of the struggle in the midst of the Sunnîs. There seems to have been at least one major effort to expand beyond the mountains in this reign. Minhâj-i Sirâj (writing 1259) – who loved to be seeing wicked heretics everywhere, but who knew the Nizârîs first hand – reports that toward the end of his life the famous ruler of the Afghan lands, Jahân-Sûz Ghûrî, invited dâʿîs from Alamût. They spread their propaganda secretly throughout his territories with his protection. He died in 1161, and his son had the dâʿîs all killed, as well as any converts they had made.[3]

But what claimed the attention of the Ismâʿîlî chronicler even in the earlier years was the taking of certain local fortresses in the Alamût area, in Daylamân and Gîlân. The chief expedition, at the very start of the reign and soon after the death of Râshid, was that which resulted in the taking of two such. The Alamûtîs sent Muḥammad ibn ʿAlî ibn Khusraw Fîrûz to Saʿâdat Kûh (Mount of Happiness), whence he set about the siege of Gurjiyân, which had been attacked already in the last reign. The garrison appealed to the (apparently Shîʿite)[4] lord of Daylamân and the hereditary ruler of Ṭabaristân, and were accorded refuge; they retired and Muḥammad ibn ʿAlî was given that stronghold also, under the name of Mubârak Kûh (Mount of Blessing); the Ismâʿîlîs restored the place. The next year they were able to raid still further into Gîlân, and settle their men there. The very names they chose for their outposts reflect their enthusiasm – what great hope they were putting into such local victories.

It is at this time that we find one of the few cases which appear to

[1] This item is from Mîrkhwând; but otherwise, most of this material on the reign of Muḥammad ibn Buzurg'ummîd is from the relevant pages of Rashîd ad-Dîn.

[2] Ibn al-Athîr, *Kâmil*, year 532.

[3] *Ṭabaqât-i Nâṣirî*, trans. H. G. Raverty (London, 1881), p. 263.

[4] He is called *dâʿî*, and one supposes he is Zaydî like the last imâm mentioned in the area.

involve internal discord. But this also reflects the local outlook of the mountaineers. Some members of the Khalîl family are said to have conspired with the citizens of the nearby town of Ṣârim; but they were betrayed, and caught; though they denied all, witnesses were brought against them, and they were kept in prison.

Revolt in stalemate: campaigns degenerate to quarrels.

Under Buzurg'ummîd it was still clear that the campaigns – though hope were deferred of accomplishing the whole task at once – nevertheless formed part of a general war with the Saljûq power. Though this is still in principle the case under his son, the particular fighting that went on seems chiefly determined by petty quarrels, localized in their effect. There was a continuing series of raids and counterraids exchanged with neighboring Qazwîn.[5] The exalted hopes involved shine through only in the name of one of the forts which they erected near Qazwîn: Jahân-Gushây, "world conqueror".[6]

More dramatic were the relations with Mâzandarân, evidently beginning with an assassination recorded by Rashîd ad-Dîn in the year 1142. This would seem to have been the son of Shâh Ghâzî Rustam; whose assassination caused that ruler's lifelong enmity to the Ismâ'îlîs. Shâh Ghâzî is said to have built several towers of Ismâ'îlî heads; after serious victories in Rûdbâr.[7] He devoted the whole income of the Daylamite portion of his territories to fighting them, and his chronicler insists that he made them lie low, in his days. From the Nizârî chronicles reported by Rashîd ad-Dîn later historians got the idea, quite reasonably, that Muḥammad ibn Buzurg'ummîd's reign was constantly victorious; but a relative quieting down in its later years may indeed reflect the results of Shâh Ghâzî's hostility.

Meanwhile, however, the Ismâ'îlîs were carrying on a series of quarrels involving the Saljûq powers one way or another. In 1141 they had assassinated Jawhar, an amîr in Sanjar's camp; and Jawhar's delegate in Rayy, 'Abbâs, conceived the same kind of vindictiveness against them as Shâh Ghâzî. There was a massacre at Rayy; and 'Abbâs set about building a tower of Ismâ'îlî heads. A few years later, 'Abbâs was assassinated on a

[5] We find activities listed for the years 535, 537, 538, 539; 548; 552, 553, 555 (Rashîd ad-Dîn).
[6] Râwandî: Browne, in *JRAS*, 1902, p. 874.
[7] Ẓahîr ad-Dîn, p. 57. Munajjim Bâshî seems, as often, to be no help here in dating.

visit to the Saljûq Sulṭân of ʿIrâq; Rashîd ad-Dîn implies that the Ismâʿîlîs claimed credit for the deed, but it was probably arranged by the Sulṭân for his own purposes – perhaps not without Ismâʿîlî help.[8]

An agreement with Sanjar during these years is implied in Rashîd ad-Dîn's narrative at a number of points.[9] About the time of ʿAbbâs' death we find the Ismâʿîlîs sending an envoy to Sanjar; and in the next few years we find war and negotiations between them. It is in the following years, at the end of Muḥammad's reign, that Ibn al-Athîr dates the attempt by the lord of Ṭuraythîth in Quhistân to restore his father's Sunnî faith. He had to go to Sanjar's court for help, and Sanjar sent an amîr, Qajaq, to attempt to restore him. Two years later began the struggles of the Quhistânî Ismâʿîlîs with Ibn Anaz, presumably acting for Sanjar, lasting for at least six years.[10] At points, they paid him tribute. Each of these sets of raids and troubles seems limited in time and space to the personal quarrel with which it originates. Perhaps in the same category were the raids the Quhistânî Ismâʿîlîs twice made upon the Ghuzz Turks, who were devastating Îrân at that time. The public must have regarded this as one scourge scourging another.[11]

Nizârî rigorism and the young heir.

Despite the setback administered by Shâh Ghâzî of Mâzandarân; despite the incidental character of the fighting that still went on; the Ismâʿîlîs did not feel themselves defeated. The changes between the time of Muḥammad ibn Buzurg'ummîd and that of his father were not so striking that they are likely to have been noticed as they proceeded. The fundamental defiance of the Sunnî world, the claim to be preparing the way for the general rule of the true imâm, continued.

But the pettiness of the raids and of the quarrelsome fighting – almost feuding – must have been increasingly obvious, in contrast to the initial ideal. As they lost the promise of freshness, the limitations of their efforts in space and in scope became chronic rather than initial. There must have been comparisons drawn between the inglorious present, and

[8] Ibn al-Athîr, *Kâmil*, year 541.

[9] Though two men in Sanjar's camp are assassinated, yet it is implied that ʿAbbâs of Rayy had to rebel against Sanjar in order to massacre the Ismâʿîlîs, and it is noted that a rebel against Sanjar is assassinated. The assassination of the Saljûq lord of Tabrîz (which is connected by Mustawfî with a massacre of Ismâʿîlîs there) would also enter here.

[10] Ibn al-Athîr, *Kâmil*, years 545, 546, 549, 551, 554.

[11] Ibn al-Athîr, *Kâmil*, years 549, 553.

the early successes. No doubt men hoped increasingly that the time was near when the imâm himself would return from his hiding, and bring his blessing among them again, as it had been among them in the days of Egyptian glory; and indeed in the first years of their own revolt against the Saljûqs, when he promised that Alamût would be a place of good fortune – Baldat al-Iqbâl.

Clearly, the old sense of great expectancy was maintained into the second and third generation among the children of those determined insurrectionaries. When the second Ḥasan (d. 1166), the son and heir-apparent of Muḥammad, became restless within the old sober but limited militancy, large numbers seem to have sympathized with him. In contrast to his father's undeviating purism, he sought a restoration of the more personal and occult aspects of Ismâʿîlism. The sense of personal adventure which had been associated with the search for the true imâm must have been forced into relatively narrow channels for those who inherited the extreme power orientation of Ḥasan-i Ṣabbâḥ; an orientation dynamic for initiating a movement, but perhaps thin as a tradition. The second Ḥasan seems to have been interested in somewhat different strains of the older tradition of the sect; according to Rashîd ad-Dîn he studied the older Ismâʿîlî writings; the Philosophers – Ibn Sînâ; and the Ṣûfîs. Soon he began to preach a spiritual interpretation of Ismâʿîlism which strikes us as far removed from the rigorism of his father and grandfather, but to which the people of Alamût now responded warmly.

As designated heir, Ḥasan commanded much of the respect due to the lord of the sect himself; but he seems to have been a lovable young man in addition, and to have won most hearts.[12] He was eloquent, and seemed learned in comparison with his father, as Rashîd ad-Dîn and Juwaynî put it; the Ismâʿîlîs liked his teaching, in which he recurred to earlier Ismâʿîlî doctrines, but also introduced Ṣûfî ideas. But his generosity and ability to please is stressed equally with the penetration of his mind and his intellectual achievements. Already in his father's time the Ismâʿîlîs were obeying him.

It seems that many of them went further, and assured themselves he was the awaited imâm. It is said that he drank wine in secret, and was able to conceal the fact from his father, and even quiet his suspicions on the point. But his followers took this as a sign of the imâmate – that he was above the law. His father at length had to refute this idea at a public meeting, showing that an imâm must be son of an imâm, which Ḥasan

[12] Cf. Juwaynî, trans. C. Defrémery, *JA*, ser. 5, XV (1860), 194.

was not. We are told that Muḥammad even killed 250 of Ḥasan's followers, who refused to recant, and exiled 250 more. Ḥasan also took pains, in epistles, to refute the notion. For the time being, we gather, Ḥasan curbed his eloquence, waiting till he should succeed his father.

THE PROCLAMATION OF QIYÂMA: ḤASAN II AS DÂʿÎ AND IMÂM

When Muḥammad died, Ḥasan was about thirty-five years old; evidently his enthusiasm was young enough and his experience mature enough, to allow him to prepare a fundamental alteration of the sect's position and introduce it throughout the scattered lands of the community. There seems to have been little question whether he should inherit the headship of the Nizârî community, though he could claim at most it seems the title of dâʿî. Despite the authority of the three previous heads of Alamût, religiously speaking the primacy of the dâʿî of Alamût cannot have been self-evident in Syria and Quhistân. Therefore that Ḥasan was able to maintain his authority through what followed sets him off as a man of unusual ability and astuteness.

Festival of the Qiyâma: the resurrection from the dead (1164).

Ḥasan introduced his reign by letting a number of captives from Rayy, Qazwîn, and elsewhere go freely home. Then he is said to have relaxed the rigorist atmosphere at Alamût, refusing to chastise breaches of the ritual law. But only after two and a half years as dâʿî was he ready to introduce his great religious reforms.

On one of the days listed as anniversary of the death of ʿAlî, in the month of fasting (Ramaḍân), he gathered the people together for what came to be called the *Festival of the Resurrection*, of the *Qiyâma*. We shall quote Rashîd ad-Dîn. "On the 17th of Ramaḍân of the year 559 he ordered the people of his territories, whom he had caused to be present in Alamût at that time, to gather together in those public prayer grounds [at the foot of Alamût]. They set up four large banners of four colors, white, red, yellow,[13] and green, which had been arranged for the affair,

[13] This was the Fâṭimid color. Qalqashandî, *Subḥ al-Aʿshâ* (Cairo, 1337), XIII, 244.

at the four corners of the pulpit [minbar]." (We shall insert into Rashîd's narrative here an excerpt from a report of the event preserved in the *Haft Bâb-i Abî Isḥâq*, an Ismâ'îlî book of the Fifteenth Century, which except at this point is less revealing than Rashîd ad-Dîn, though it confirms his account.)[14] "The lord 'Alâ Dhikri-hi s-Salâm, wearing a white garment and a white turban, came down from the fortress about noon, and came to the pulpit from the right side; and in a most perfect manner mounted the pulpit. He said greetings three times: first to the Daylamites [in the center], then to the right hand [those from Khurâsân, i.e., Quhistân], then to the left hand [those from 'Irâq].[15] He sat down for a moment; then rose up again and baring [?] his sword said in a loud voice: O inhabitants of the worlds, jinn, men, and angels!" (And now Rashîd ad-Dîn again.) "He mounted the pulpit, which faced toward the Qibla [the direction of prayer – Mecca; usually the pulpit faces away from the Qibla], and declared to the comrades: someone had come to him in secret from the leader, that is the supposed imâm, who was missing and nonexistent, and had brought an address, for their enlightenment, setting forth the doctrines of their faith. Then from the top of the pulpit he presented a clear and eloquent epistle, and at the end of the address he said,[16] The imâm of our time sends you blessings and compassion, calling you his specially selected servants.[17] He has lifted from you

[14] W. Ivanow, *Kalâm-i Pîr* (Islamic Research Association Nr. 4), Bombay, 1935, p. 115. Ivanow gives a translation of the whole passage on ps. 60–61 and 116–117. (At this point, where reference to Ivanow will become more frequent, the reader should be referred to the note on his translations in Appendix III.)

[15] 'Irâq here is presumably 'Irâq 'Ajamî, western Îrân. This might (in a Quhistânî writer) be a vague enough expression to include Gird Kûh, in Qumis; but only with difficulty Syria. Perhaps it applies to remains of the Ismâ'îlî strength in the Arrajân area, in the Zagros mountains, which may have survived; as we have suggested on the basis of Benjamin of Tudela's account. On the other hand, it may refer merely to such Isma'îlîs as were not yet gathered into the mountains.

[16] In order to feel the reaction of orthodox Muslims to these proceedings, we may quote here the version of Juwaynî, who is less restrained than Rashîd ad-Dîn: "When the 17th of Ramaḍân arrived, he ordered the people of his territories, whom he had caused to be present in Alamût at that time, to gather together in those public grounds. They set up four large banners . . . and he declared to those bewildered, unfortunate folk, who through his seduction and misleading were turned toward misery and loss: someone had come to him in secret from the despicable leader, I mean the supposed imâm, who was missing and nonexistent, and had brought an address and a declaration, for their enlightenment, setting forth the doctrines of their wicked faith. Then from the top of the displaced pulpit he delivered an epistle on the propositions of his false and unreasonable creed, saying".

[17] Juwaynî has here an additional sentence, that the imâm has opened the door of mercy to their ancestors, and now also to them. (The better attested reading, according to Qazwînî, is "to the Muslims", but "to their ancestors" seems to offer better sense.)

the burden of the obligation of the sharî'a [ritual law], and has brought you to the Resurrection [qiyâma]. Then he delivered an address in Arabic, such that those present became bashful; alleging that it was the word of the imâm. He had posted someone [the legist Muḥammad Bustî][18] who knew Arabic at the foot of the pulpit, to give orally the translation of those words in Persian to those present. The sense of the address was along this line: Ḥasan ibn Muḥammad ibn Buzurg'ummîd is our representative [Caliph], our dâ'î, our ḥujja; our shî'a must be obedient and submissive to him in the affairs of this world and the next; considering his command incontrovertible and knowing his word to be our word. They must know that our Lord [mawlâ-nâ] has interceded for them, and has brought you to God. He read an epistle packed full of such words; after its recitation he came down from the pulpit and performed the two prostrations of the Festival ['îd] prayer. Then he set up a table and seated the people to break the fast; they made merry and exulted in the manner of the ritual festivals. He said, Today is the Festival [of the end of the fast – usually held only at the end of the month].[19] Ever after that the Malâḥida [Heretics] called the 17th of Ramaḍân the Festival of Resurrection [Qiyâm]; on that day they used to show their joy with wine and repose, and used to play and make entertainment openly."[20]

Ten weeks later a second proclamation was made, in Mu'minâbâd in Quhistân. The pulpit was similarly rearranged, and a formal message from Ḥasan was read. He declared that just as formerly Mustanṣir was God's representative (caliph) on earth and Ḥasan-i Ṣabbâḥ was Mustanṣir's representative (caliph); so now Ḥasan II himself was the representative of God on earth, and the Ra'îs Muẓaffar (not, of course, the man of Gird Kûh) was Ḥasan's representative in Quhistân, and was to be obeyed in all things.

In these ceremonies Ḥasan was undertaking three revolutionary innovations; all three of which were accepted thereafter to one degree or another by the Nizârîs everywhere. He proclaimed himself no longer just dâ'î, but Caliph and divinely appointed ruler; he ended the sway of the sharî'a, the ritual law; he proclaimed the resurrection of the dead, the end of the world having finally come. Each of these moves seems more daring than the last. To get himself accepted as Caliph in a community where the Caliph, as imâm, must be the direct descendant of a particular

18 From the *Kâlam-i Pîr* account excerpted above.

19 I here correct the Rashîd ad-Dîn mss. on the basis of Qazwînî's edition of Juwaynî. Some mss. (as mine of Rashîd ad-Dîn) insert "Qiyâma" after "'îd", but this is likely to be a scribal error.

20 Folio 304.

ʿAlid line was already an achievement. To proclaim the end of the law – to use Pauline terms – and the dispensation of grace instead was a far-reaching reversal not only in regard to Islâm at large, where the sharîʿa was the basis of morality; but among the Ismâʿîlîs themselves, where a strict purism had been the dominant rule. Finally he asserted that the end of the world not only was about to come, but had now in fact happened; that those who in spirit had responded to his call were now risen to life immortal, and those who had been deaf to him were now judged and banished into nonexistence. Ḥasan had either to be laughed at or adored. He was in fact adored; and the commonest *name* for him came at last to be simply a blessing: ʿAlâ Dhikri-hi s-Salâm" – "upon his mention peace".

Return of the imâm: Ḥasan's claims.

None of the three moves was entirely unprepared for, to be sure; in particular, the reappearance of a divinely appointed ruler in Alamût can appear almost a logical necessity. It is not clear in fact just what were Ḥasan's actual claims in this respect, and what were the claims only made for him by his son, Muḥammad, who succeeded within a year and a half after the Festival of Qiyâma. The community itself may not have had time to become fully acquainted with Ḥasan's claims. But Muḥammad certainly maintained that Ḥasan was not only Caliph, but the imâm himself. And it seems likely that Ḥasan himself finally claimed to be imâm in the spiritual sense, in the bâṭin, though without claiming to be a descendant of Nizâr in the outward sense, the ẓâhir.

At first, at least, Ḥasan claimed only to be the deputy of the imâm.[21] In the declaration at Alamût he is dâʿî (like Buzurgʾummîd and his son), ḥujja (like Ḥasan-i Ṣabbâḥ), and Caliph, or representative, of the imâm who is sending him the message. This appears by implication also in the *Haft Bâb-i Abî Isḥâq*, where not only does Ḥasan speak of the imâm in the third person; he continues to stand respectfully while the translation of the message is being read.[22] This use of the term *Caliph* for a special position in the religious hierarchy is unusual; but although its use here

[21] Cf. Nâṣir-i Khusraw, *Wajh-i Dîn*, p. 166, where it is said that the Qâʾim, upon his coming, will first uphold the ritual law, the sharîʿa, and only after a time make his rank known. A gradual revelation of one's position is thus already provided for.
[22] The two later versions of this book published by Ivanow in the *Kalâm-i Pîr* both manage to obscure this: the "*pseudo-HBAI*" even substituting an entirely different speech for the one given in its original, and omitting the details that follow.

is justified in appearance as meaning merely *representatieve*, it is clearly coupled with *dâʿî* and *ḥujja*, and used in fact to designate a technical position which Ḥasan was claiming. Even in the second declaration, when he is presented as the Caliph of God, in the same position as Mustanṣir himself, the term is clearly not simply a synonym for *imâm* – though in Egypt in fact only the imâms were entitled to the secular title of *Caliph*. For the term *imâm* is itself consistently avoided. Rashîd ad-Dîn explains that Ḥasan means he is the "unique deputy" ("nâ'ib munfarid") of the imâm; and as such he might well occupy the imâm's own position in the earth, without being himself the imâm.

But Rashîd ad-Dîn tells us that after the public proclamations Ḥasan sent about epistles, sometimes secretly, in which he laid claim to being the imâm in *ḥaqîqa*, in inward actuality, even though not after the flesh. Spiritually he was the descendant of Nizâr. It is presumably to these letters that we are to trace the various quotations in later Nizârî literature ascribed to Ḥasan, in which he makes his higher claims, such as that he was the author of the realms of spiritual existence. Even these epistles did not satisfy his son Muḥammad, for we learn from the *Haft Bâb-i Bâbâ Sayyid-nâ*,[23] written in his reign, that Ḥasan had revealed his own status only in part. We may therefore suppose that Ḥasan claimed merely a spiritual imamâte.[24]

There is nothing improbable in the notion of an imâmate separated from the lineage of ʿAlî. The imâm of Ḥasan-i Ṣabbâḥ's taʿlîm was

[23] This is translated in Appendix I; it will be referred to as the *Haft Bâb*, and should not be confused with the *Haft Bâb-i Abî Isḥâq*.

[24] *The Rawḍat at-Taslîm* (ed. W. Ivanow [Ismaili Society Series A nr. 4], Leiden, 1950), p. 89, has an ambiguous passage: "As to the imâm and his offspring: from the holy words of ʿAlâ Dhikri-hi s-Salâm: Know that this imâmate is ḥaqîqî (in inner reality), it will never turn, it will not change or alter; it will always be transmitted in the line of our Lord [mawlâ-nâ], and will not turn from them in [outer] form, in [inner] meaning, or in ḥaqîqa." (One is inclined to trust the ascription of a sentence to an old imâm, since each new imâm taught in his own name, not requiring authority from the past; even Rashîd ad-Dîn seems to have kept the imâms' testimony apart.) The passage starts out quite consistent with Rashîd ad-Dîn's statement that Ḥasan claimed the imâmate only in ḥaqîqa, but then goes on to imply that the imâmate must remain in the family outwardly as well as inwardly. To be sure, in the Persian there are no quotation marks to show where the saying from Ḥasan ends! But it is in any case not clear what it may have meant in its own context: does it refer only to the lineage of the future? Later on in the passage the ambiguity becomes even more interesting. It is said that persons can be members of the imâm's family on several levels – in maʿnî (bâṭin) only; in ẓâhir (outwardly) only; in both maʿnî and ẓâhir; and finally in all three levels including ḥaqîqa. It implies that the reason one must have imâms who are offspring in ẓâhir is for the ẓâhir public (which is annihilated at Qiyâma!); but the only possible combination of levels it says nothing about is just that which Ḥasan seems to have claimed – in ḥaqîqa, or in maʿnî and ḥaqîqa, without ẓâhir.

certainly already potentially independent of any such extraneous authority as could come from ancestry. Ḥasan II is said in the *Haft Bâb* to have written on the limitations of reason – like Ḥasan-i Ṣabbâḥ. He studied philosophers like Ibn Sînâ, and the Ṣûfîs, for whom all religious authority is by rights spiritual. After so many years without an evident imâm, he may very well have felt that his predecessors at Alamût had as good a title to the position as any, and that he (with his rational knowledge, along the lines of Ḥasan-i Ṣabbâḥ) had a very sure title to it in all that the imâmate truly and inwardly stood for. Accordingly he need feel no need, even while claiming imâmate, to deny his descent from Buzurg'-ummîd – which Juwaynî reported still stood engraved, unaltered, on a gate inscription in Alamût.[25] His imâmate could seem to be not a radical breach with the past, but simply a natural consequence of what he knew had gone before.

The Resurrection: Ḥasan as Qâ'im.

There was another position which went along with Ḥasan's claim of the imâmate. As the imâm who brought the Resurrection, he was also the Judge of the Resurrection, the *Qâ'im of the Qiyâma.* This figure had always received great honor among the Ismâ'îlîs. In the *Wajh-i Dîn* of Nâṣir-i Khusraw, for instance, where mention of the mere titles of the Ismâ'îlî hierarchy calls for no special blessing (not even *nâṭiq*, the Prophet's title), the Qâ'im is blessed as an individual, and at least as elaborately as the Prophet himself. He is generally thought of as one of the line of imâms who, however, has the special role of consummating the dispensation of Muḥammad at the end of time – or of the current cycle, in Ismâ'îlî thought. He holds, accordingly, not only the ranks of imâmate and of prophecy, which the Prophet held, but that of qiyâmate in addition.[26] This makes him distinctly a greater personage than Mohammad, who is merely one of six prophets who foretell the Qâ'im's advent. The imâm whom Ḥasan proclaimed was this Qâ'im,[27] of whom accordingly

[25] Defrémery's Tr., p. 200.

[26] *Wajh-i Dîn*, p. 153. It is of course futile to try to decide which of the cosmic ḥudûd of the Ismâ'îlî cosmology – 'aql, nafs, etc. – a particular hierarchical ranking may correspond to; many answers may be available, all likely to be contradicted. But in the case of the Qâ'im, it makes no trouble for him to be both imâm and nâṭiq, both nafs and 'aql perhaps; for in the grand consummation all ranks are merged in one anyway.

[27] It is as Qâ'im of the Qiyâma that he is praised in the *Haft Bâb-i Abî Isḥâq*.

he was Caliph; and here, in fact, we find some precedent for the term: Nâṣir-i Khusraw tells us that the Caliph of the Qâ'im will save men from intellectual drought.[28] When Ḥasan turned out to be the imâm himself, he was at the same time the Qâ'im himself, and as such he was chiefly celebrated among the Ismâʿîlîs.

The function of the Qâ'im is to introduce Paradise on earth: in one text, we find that the ritual laws will be abolished; there will be neither work nor illness; generation will take place only in the Spring; and so forth.[29] According to the Wajh-i Dîn, the ḥujja of the Qâ'im will come first, preparing the way. By the time the Qâ'im himself comes, all men must have accepted the imâm; for at the Qâ'im's coming it will be too late to repent, and all unbelievers will be annihilated. Thereupon the Nafs al-Kull will finally return to unity with the ʿAql al-Kull; the striving of nature and of man – those men who have accepted the imâm – will be fulfilled; and all will be peace: all motion will cease – in Medieval times the great metaphysical ideal. Then will come the true cosmic Sabbath when work will cease, and reward and enjoyment will take its place.[30]

The Ḥujja had no doubt been Ḥasan-i Ṣabbâḥ. He had blown the first of the two blasts of the trumpet that proclaimed the resurrection; playing the role of Jesus, whose return was to herald the end. This warning of the end of all things was surely adequately given in the universal terror inspired by the vast scale of the Nizârî efforts, unprecedented as they were! Now was surely time, therefore, for a new wonder that should not be an anti-climax. The Resurrection, the Qiyâma, was called for; the second blast of that fateful trumpet. It did come, roughly forty years after Ḥasan-i Ṣabbâḥ (an appropriate interval of time, in that Jesus' reign was commonly expected to last forty years before the last day); Ḥasan II fulfilling the announcements ascribed to Ḥasan-i Ṣabbâḥ that the time was at hand.[31]

But they were not fulfilled in the physical guise expected by the orthodox Sunnîs – like the trumpet blasts themselves, the resurrection was spiritual. Already earlier Ismâʿîlîs had called the rising of the soul, of the

[28] *Wajh-i Dîn*, p. 131.

[29] Strothmann, *Gnosistexte*, 1941–3, A, 1.

[30] Nâṣir-i Khusraw, *Wajh-i Dîn*, pp. 153, 131, 48.

[31] Ṭûsî, *Rawḍat at-Taslîm*, p. 118/173. There seems to be no clear evidence that Ḥasan II himself made Ḥasan-i Ṣabbâḥ ḥujja not just of the imâm, but in particular of the Qâ'im, as here presented. But in the lack of adequate evidence, we may go on the next generation's interpretation, as reflected for instance in the *Haft Bâb*. (That Ḥasan II called himself ḥujja – and also dâʿî – of course, merely fits in with his being imâm: for each higher rank includes in itself the lesser ones.)

mind, from one realm of apprehension to a higher one in this life a minor qiyâma; and said that the final qiyâma for any individual was his release into a purely spiritual existence at death.[32] (This presupposed, of course, the Ismâʿîlî doctrine of spiritual afterlife; in contrast to the tenet of the stricter among the Sunnîs that the qiyâma was only a bodily resurrection, at the end of time.) Paradise being the life of the spirit, moreover, it was even claimed that Paradise itself could be attained already before death; at least, in a potential sense, which our death will merely actualize. (And likewise, ignorance is already Hell potentially, and when actualized – when escape from it is no longer possible – it is Hell in fact).[33]

Ḥasan apparently proclaimed that through the truth he was bringing (and for which Ḥasan-i Ṣabbâḥ had prepared the way), all men could come to know God directly, immediately (as the Ṣûfîs did); he proclaimed "a day when one does not know by signs, and doctrines, and indications", but "he who particularizes the self of the Essence with his own self, particularizes all signs and indications";[34] and therefore "deeds and words and indices come to an end"; for whoever would "reach it through names and through its distorted and twisted attributes is veiled [from the truth]". By bringing knowledge of the truth into its fullness, evidently, Ḥasan had actualized the Paradise that some individual Ismâʿîlîs had been able to approach in potentiality; and opened it to all men. Now men could see God directly, with their spiritual eyes, as was appropriate to Paradise; and at the same time those who still refused to accept the truth were condemned in their wilful ignorance for ever. This was the great Resurrection toward which all lesser searchings, all partial truths, all former prophecies had been tending. This was the culmination of the ages.

Qiyâma as ending taqiyya, fulfilling Ismâʿîlism.

Whatever glamor may attach to the idea of proclaiming the end of the world, the most consequential departure for the Ismâʿîlî community lay in one of the corollaries to be drawn from that idea: that the sharîʿa was now done away with. This proposition was presented to the community under the form of the lifting of the taqiyya, the Shîʿite precautionary

[32] H. Corbin, ed. Sijistânî, *Kashf al-Maḥjûb* (Ṭehrân, 1949), pp. 83 ff. The same idea lies back of the qiyâma as a rising in the hierarchy, *Zahr al-Maʿânî*, p. 55; in which incidentally the imâm is given a position within his generation corresponding to the Qâ'im of Qiyâma.

[33] Nâṣir-i Khusraw, *Wajh-i Dîn*, pp. 32, 40.

[34] *Haft Bâb-i Abî Isḥâq*, pp. 65–66. This second of these four phrases is "fa-man ʿayyana ʿayna dh-dhâti bi-ʿayni-hi fa-huwa ʿayyana jamîʿa l-âyâti wa-l-ʿalâmât."

dissimulation of the true faith. The most important symbolism of the Festival of Qiyâma was concerned with this. It was perhaps suitable to pick the day of ʿAlî's death to proclaim a resurrection of the dead, as well as to proclaim the advent of an imâm in whom the authority of ʿAlî was restored to men. But the crucial thing was that the festival was in Ramaḍân, the month of fasting; and moreover explicitly broke that ritual fast with a feast. For one of the most constant of the ta'wîl explanations is that the fast of the Ramaḍân symbolizes the taqiyya; the Festival at its end will therefore signify its suspension.

The end of the rule of taqiyya followed naturally from the coming of the Qâ'im, whose manifest and universal power would make taqiyya unnecessary for the protection of the faithful.[35] But its meaning here was no longer simply the guarding of the inner religious truth of the mission of ʿAlî from prying Sunnî eyes. All those outer forms which the Shîʿa shared more or less with the Sunnîs had come to be lumped together in popular Ismâʿîlî consciousness as being enforced by taqiyya. In the Qiyâma now the learned Ismâʿîlî tradition, in the person of Ḥasan II, was indirectly admitting the validity of their notion. The lifting of taqiyya was made to involve the rejection of all the outer ritual law. The imâm was now of his mercy granting permission to live without cult, in the spirit alone, which he had formerly forbidden. The end of the sharîʿa could conceivably have been presented as itself a natural consequence of the Resurrection – and no doubt it was so taken in part: there will be no laws in Paradise. But it is the breach of taqiyya that is emphasized; just as in the Festival, Ḥasan invited men to eat during Ramaḍân (a weighty breach of the sharîʿa) on the grounds that now was the Festival of breaking the fast, the taqiyya.

But the popular notion was not irrelevant to the actual situation. If Ismâʿîlî philosophers had not taken the step of deprecating the sharîʿa, as sometimes their principles designating the outer form as a mere husk concealing seeds of truth seemed to suggest, it was probably in part for fear of the opinion of Sunnî society: it was in fact, if not in law, taqiyya. For it was in abrogating the sharîʿa that came the great break with Sunnî Islâm. The Muslims might not much care whether this spiritual awareness was called the Resurrection, or whether the Shîʿite imâm was called the Qâ'im; such things they were not wholly unused to among fairly respectable Ṣûfîs. But they would care that now the Ismâʿîlîs had in fact done

[35] The Twelver Shîʿa had the same expectation: Ibn Bâbûya says that taqiyya is compulsory on the believers only till the coming of the Qâ'im. *Risâlat al-Iʿtiqâdât*, trans. A. A. A. Fyzee, *A Shiite Creed* (London, 1942), p. 111.

that villainous deed they had been long accused of doing, thrown off the shackles of the law. Rashîd ad-Dîn indeed notes that at this point the Nizârîs had set up a rival Caliphate to that of Baghdâd, which they had not done before (ever since their rejection of that at Cairo). But this is a lesser matter; the point that makes him say that it is from now that the Ismâʿîlîs are to be called *Mulḥid*, "heretic", is that they have now rejected those universal forms of law which held the Islamic community together. Hereafter there can be no question, as there was at Iṣfahân and still later with Sanjar, of the Ismâʿîlîs trying to get themselves accepted as legitimately deviant members of Sunnî society.

The day meant, therefore, for the Nizârîs, a declaration of independence and of sovereign authority; they refused to guide themselves by what Islamic society might think of them. But at the same time it was an admission of defeat in the attempt to take over Islâm at large. What this meant to the remaining Ismâʿîlîs scattered out in the Sunnî cities we cannot tell.[36] Perhaps, as in a town in Syria to which we shall come again, a few quiet massacres wiped them out; perhaps any who could emigrated to Paradise, filling the place of the recusants who left there. At any rate, apart from an occasional personal conversion, no longer is there an attempt to rival Sunnism from within the Islamic society.

At the same time that the merciful imâm returns to his people, bringing forgiveness, therefore, the harshness of the Nizârî tradition is turned to a final judgment against its opponents – whoever is not now saved, never will be. Not only Ḥasan's amiability, but the community self-reliance shines through an anecdote told of Ḥasan at the end of the *Haft Bâb*. He was asked if now that the time of love and forgiveness had come he would not revive even the arch-enemy of the Shîʿa, ʿUmar, and give him too a chance for repentance and for Life. Forgiveness of the very type of the Sunnî persecutor is here expected of him; and in his answer there is indeed no sense of revenge or condemnation, only a trace of the Nizârî rigor; ʿUmar, having failed to choose Life when he had the opportunity, does not now exist to be revived.

The resistance to the Qiyâma:
Ḥasan is murdered.

Ḥasan seems to have been rather militant in enforcing his new dis-

[36] Although there probably were such, their numbers will not have been so large as suggested by Râwandî (wr. yr. 1202/3), who lists towns like Qumm as Bâṭinî. Râwandî, a good Ḥanafî, is bitter even at the Shâfiʿites; and seems, like Ibn al-Jawzî (d. 1200) to see an Ismâʿîlî in every Twelver Shîʿite (Ed. Iqbâl, 1921, p. 395).

pensation. Though spiritually all who did not accept his gospel were by that fact dead, yet physically they remained; and Rashîd ad-Dîn tells us that Ḥasan at least suggested the death penalty for those in his territories who continued to cling to the sharî'a. Just as in the days of sharî'a it was a capital crime to behave on a free spiritual basis – the imâm had required one to impose taqiyya on oneself – so now in the days of the spiritual Qiyâma it should be capital to follow the old law.[37] Juwaynî says that many chose exile under the circumstances, and that all who remained conformed to the new dispensation at least outwardly.[38]

Perhaps such exiles helped to stir up war anew against the Ismâ'îlîs, or perhaps Ḥasan hoped to put down what must have been in his mind resistance to his proclamation even in the Sunnî world outside. At any rate evidently precisely in the years when Qiyâma was being proclaimed there was a local intensification of effort against Qazwîn. After several years with no raiding listed, in 1165 we are told that the Ismâ'îlîs had built a fortress just outside the city, and were carrying on something of a siege.[39] (Mustawfî of Qazwîn says that Ḥasan II was called *Kûra Kiyâ*, "village lord", in Qazwîn: a fact which suggests they were especially acquainted with him.)[40] At the same time, but perhaps fortuitously, the Quhistânî Ismâ'îlîs were raided by Ibn Anaz.[41]

Ḥasan's militancy was well supported. He seems to have had most of the people with him from the start; indeed, according to Rashîd ad-Dîn's account, it was initially not he but the people who had decided he must be the imâm. It is not clear on the other hand what the learned leadership thought of him – the remains of that Ismâ'îlî hierarchy which had loomed so large in Ismâ'îlî history. As we have noticed, they continued to exist; but one gathers from the lack of any practical notice of the hierarchical rankings except the dâ'î, that in the fortress society they were ceasing to be ordered in the old formal way, or else that such rankings were ceasing to play a great role. Under the new dispensation, as we shall see, with the whole population at least potentially on a common level in the presence of the imâm-qâ'im, there was no further room for such rankings at all.[42]

37 Cf. Juwaynî, tr. Defrémery, *JA*, 1860, p. 210.
38 Juwaynî, ed. Qazwînî, p. 239.
39 Ibn al-Athîr, *Kâmil*, year 560. (Cf. Râwandî.) Ibn al-Athîr is not free from errors in Ismâ'îlî affairs, so this date may be a confusion.
40 *Ta'rîkh-i Guzîda*, facsimile by Nicholson (Leiden, 1910), p. 523.
41 Ibn al-Athîr, *Kâmil*, yr. 559.
42 Ivanow speaks of the democratization of Ismâ'îlism by the Nizârîs, in getting rid of the old hierarchical rankings. *Kalâm-i Pîr*, p. XXX.

Ḥasan II was murdered a year and a half after the day of Qiyâma. His murderer, Ḥusayn-i Nâmâwar his brother-in-law, was of a local branch of the Buwayhid line, which had ruled in western Îrân as a Twelver Shîʿa dynasty at the same time as the height of Fâṭimid power in Egypt. Ḥasan's son Muḥammad may have believed that the whole family was implicated, for he had them all executed. Rashîd ad-Dîn saw in the plot by this prominent family an attempt to restore a pure Islâm, against the Qiyâma; but in any case it would have been a Shîʿa Islâm – probably an Ismâʿîlî Islâm, only faithful to the sharîʿa.[43] Ḥusayn-i Nâmâwar represents the only serious effort we find recorded to renew the sharîʿa upon Ḥasan II's abolition of it; but there is no indication as to how they proposed to choose a new dâʿî, or whether perhaps they even had in mind a Twelver Shîʿa regime on the model of the older Buwayhids. Ḥasan's son Muḥammad, whom he had designated heir, gave them no chance to show their hand. Although only nineteen years old, he was strong enough to take the reigns of power, and confirm the new dispensation. He got himself recognized in his turn as imâm, and seems to have devoted his long reign to a systematic elaboration of his father's doctrines.

[43] Cf. ʿAtâ Malik-i Juwaynî, *Ta'rîkh-i Jahân Gushâ*, ed. M. Qazwînî (E. J. W. Gibb Memorial, XVI [Leyden, 1937]), Vol. III, 239.

CHAPTER VIII

THE PREACHING OF THE QIYÂMA

MUḤAMMAD II: DEVOTION ORIENTED TOWARD THE IMÂM

(1166-1210)

Rashîd ad-Dîn tells us that Muḥammad wrote a great deal, and was more extreme than even his father; but he does not report what his teachings were, except that they were couched in the terms of the Philosophers. We are left to assume that those doctrines associated with the Qiyâma, but which go beyond what is reported of Ḥasan II, are to be attributed to his son. If so, he is apparently responsible for sharpening the cleavage between the period before and that after the Qiyâma; and for systematizing and adapting its doctrines to an ongoing life, equally exalted in its spiritual sentiments, but perhaps less militant toward the world. He seems to have altered, or precised, Ḥasan's teachings at at least two points. He established Ḥasan as imâm in the fullest sense, and not merely the representative of the imâm; thus changing the very genealogy of the family. Then he associated the believers' seeing God, in Paradise, with the imâm: God was to be seen in the figure of the imâm. It is in his time that the gospel of the Qiyâma, in its main lines, became the definitive spiritual ideal for the Ismâ ʿîlîs which it afterward remained.

Muḥammad's interpretation of his father's claims.

It is at no point clear how much of the doctrine which we finally find in such Qiyâma texts as the *Haft Bâb* is from Muḥammad; and how much stems already from his father, or was developed by other initiative within the community. But the three elements can be sorted out most clearly in the discussion of who Ḥasan was. Ḥasan himself probably said he was imâm only in ḥaqîqa, at most. But Muḥammad claimed imâmate for himself as Ḥasan's *son*, and so had to prove Ḥasan's *'Alid* imamâte. That it is *Muḥammad's* imâmate that was really at issue is suggested by the fact that the argument was made to rest in the *Haft Bâb* on Ḥasan's own words largely. For instance, that he denied that he was of this or that rank on one occasion – but never denied he was the Qâ'im. Even Muḥammad seems not to have been too explicit about the matter, but he clearly countenanced and presupposed the idea of the ẓâhir imâmate.

From Muḥammad, Rashîd ad-Dîn reports an analogy between Ḥasan's case and that of Abraham and Ishmael.[1] This case must have been close to Ismâ'îlî minds, because Ishmael was an imâm – had to be, as the ancestor of 'Alî – yet Abraham was a major prophet. Now prophets possessed also the degree of imâmate, in the old teaching, and so could father an imâm; but with the popular tendency to exaltation of the imâmate it became evidently desirable that there be a single line of imâms throughout history, free of the added role of prophethood – as was indeed already the case with Mohammed and 'Alî, with Jesus and Peter, with Moses and Aaron. The case of Abraham and Ishmael was a glaring exception.[2] How could Ishmael be a full imâm while his father (imâm before him) was still alive? If Abraham was in fact his father, there could have been no effective imâm complementary to Abraham as prophet within his lifetime. Already there may have been attempts to get around this situation; certainly a new twist in this regard would not be quite unexpected. Muḥammad II (thus again indirectly acknowledging the validity of the popular feeling) asserted that Ishmael was only apparently a son of Abraham, but actually a son of the imâm, Malik as-Salâm, substituted with Abraham's knowledge; and likewise, Ḥasan II was apparently the son of Muḥammad ibn Buzurg'ummîd, but actually a son of the imâm; but this time without Muḥammad's knowing it.[3]

It would seem that if Muḥammad II was the one who suggested the lines of the 'Alid birth, the popular imagination had a share in its further elaboration. For it is to the people, rather than to Muḥammad, that Rashid ad-Dîn ascribes a story which the above statement of Muḥammad is to authenticate. Two babies were born at once, one to the imâm living in

[1] Cf. Juwaynî, trans. C. Defremery, *JA*, ser. 5, XV (1860), 207.

[2] So might be the cases of Adam and Seth, and of Noah and Shem; but they were historically more distant from Muslim consciousness.

[3] Later, Ṭûsî in the *Rawḍat at-Taslîm* confirms Rashîd ad-Dîn on the point of the parentage of the imâm apparently son of Abraham.

a village at the foot of the hill, unknown; one to the dâʿî living in the fortress as lord. An old woman exchanged them three days later without anyone seeing her. To this standard theme of folklore is added an alternative story, which Juwaynî says was more widely believed, the story of the exchange being limited to the Buzurg'ummîd family and the people at Alamût proper. The imâm who lived at the foot of the hill committed adultery with Muḥammad ibn Buzurg'ummîd's wife. In this version, Muḥammad found it out, and killed the imâm; and the people therefore hated him, and dishonored his tomb where it stood next to Ḥasan-i Ṣabbâḥ's.[4]

At some point Ḥasan received a good Fâṭimid genealogy: Nizâr, Mustanṣir's son, had held the regnal title of Muṣṭafâ; his son was now given the title of Hâdî, and his grandson, allegedly brought as a baby to Ḥasan-i Ṣabbâḥ, in whose care he grew up in the village at the foot of Alamût, the title of Muhtadî. Ḥasan II, as his son, bore the title of Qâhir, the Victorious. Presumably he actually adopted this style when claiming the Caliphate; and when the idea of Caliphate as a special rank was dropped, the use of such titles fell into disuse also. None of the later imâms at Alamût had Fâṭimid-type regnal names,[5] and it was soon forgotten that Ḥasan was the same as Qâhir, who became for some still another link in the chain of imâms.[6] Once Ḥasan, and therefore his son Muḥammad, was endowed with an ʿAlid genealogy, the breach with the time when there were only dâʿîs in Alamût was complete, and the new dispensation inaugurated with all propriety.

The imâm as revelation of God.

In spite of the metaphysical impersonality of its conception of the Ultimate, Ismâʿîlism had always cultivated with special zest a sense of perso-

[4] This latter story is omitted in my manuscript of Rashîd ad-Dîn; perhaps by accident – a second story seems to be implied; but Rashîd ad-Dîn seems to be unwilling to repeat the most damning reports of this reign. The author of the *Dabistân* says that adultery would have been legal for the imâm, but was not necessary; and suggests that a pregnant wife of the imâm was given into Muḥammad's care. This will be later Ismâʿîlî explanation.

[5] The continuator of Ibn Isfandiyâr gives Muḥammad III the title of Qâ'im in the Fâṭimid form, but this is likely to be a confusion based on the fact that the imâm also held the position of Qâ'im. Gibb, transl., p. 259.

[6] One gathers that Rashîd ad-Dîn and Juwaynî are reporting the genealogy on the basis of tradition at the fall of Alamût – it is only then that a confusion about the *Qâhir* is likely. But they do not, as they do of Ḥasan, report Muḥammad as using the Buzurg'ummîd genealogy.

nal seeking for God. God was always in some sense available to those in the world; his very ineffable character, which made equally impossible any conceivable modes of imagining Him, will have helped to make it seem less unlikely that – if He were to be found at all – He should be found in the most arbitrary circumstances. Practical piety had found no difficulty in centering on the person of the imâm.

Muḥammad accepted such an approach and articulated its implications. The purpose of the world is to know and see God – this had been said before – and the exclusive means of this fulfillment is a spiritually complete knowledge of the imâm. For the imâm is himself the full revelation of God. A characteristic of the Qiyâma texts is largely to ignore the Prophet, and even the earlier imâms. It is the current imâm who is all-absorbing. Here the Islamic search for universal validity is brought to a simple solution; perhaps too simple, in spite of the elaboration given the theory, for the varied perceptivity of men. It seems to carry Ḥasan-i Ṣabbâḥ's rejection of any historical grounding to a logical conclusion.

This conception of the imâm was justified, evidently, in terms of the traditional Ismâ'îlî cosmic order. The older Ismâ'îlism had allowed for a great deal of variation in the ḥudûd and their relation to the cosmic emanations from the One. Particularly it was not rare that 'Alî was elevated in fact above Mohammed, in spite of his more usual subordination.[7] Yet when in the Qiyâma the imâm took on the role of the Qâ'im, a major reshuffling was called for if the doctrine were to be fully systematized. Technically, to be sure, each higher rank can be said to include the lower ones, and the Qâ'im is said to possess also the rank of imâmate; but in fact, at Alamût the emphasis seems to have come to rest not on the position of Qâ'im, but on that of imâm, who was incidentally also in this case the Qâ'im. Consequently, it became normal now for the imâm to take a rank notably higher than Mohammed's, which was considerably depreciated. 'Ali was made to appear always as simple imâm: a special role for him as asâs – implying subordination to the Prophet – was henceforth almost an insult. Even among the Nizârîs the ranks varied; but the imâm was regularly identified with the *Kalima*,[8] the "word", or the *Amr*, "command" of God: his Word of Command by which the 'Aql itself, the Reason, is brought forth. That is, so soon as God becomes intelligible

[7] For instance, in Nâṣir-i Khusraw, *Wajh-i Dîn*, p. 132, the *nâṭiq*, the Prophet, is linked with the Nafs-i Kull; the *asâs*, 'Ali, with the 'Aql: the reverse of the usual order. The *Zahr al-Ma'ânî* is especially fond of exalting 'Alî. Nor does this occur only among Ismâ'îlîs.

[8] Typical in Ṭûsî is *Rawḍat at-Taslîm*, p. 82.

at all, it is in the cosmic point which is reflected in the imâm. No higher rank than imâm was henceforth conceivable.

Ivanow cites as the distinctive innovation of the Nizârîs one which illustrates the overly simple character of this conclusion.[9] The classical Ismâʿîlî statement that God *neither* has nor has not attributes is turned, at least by some uneducated authors, into an assertion that God *both* has and has not attributes.[10] A guardedly negative impersonalism of the old metaphysics has become in this popular approach a positive, paradoxical assertion, which enables the sectarians at once to maintain, in appearance, an extreme *tanzîh* (keeping the conception of God clear of human limitations), and yet also to claim a complete revelation of God in their imâm, whose attributes are held to be the attributes of God.

In such a formulation, logically irresponsible as it is, the community is at once removed from the concourse of the world; it is as if Ismâʿîlî thought no longer had to maintain an intellectual respectability now that it was no longer competing with the general public. The habit of avoiding *taʿṭîl* and *tashbîh* – exhausting God of all meaning on the one hand, and anthropomorphizing Him on the other – remained, in the words: but in fact such a formulation involved both *taʿṭîl* and *tashbîh*.[11]

Presumably there was a more adequate formulation of the thesis, which Muḥammad with his philosophic terminology will have used. It may have run something as follows. God in His essence has no attributes; but for the sake of revelation he can adopt any attributes he may choose – appearing (as the *Haft Bâb* reiterates) one time as an infant, another time as an aged man, another time as the embryo in a womb. It is in this sense that must be understood the phrase that God made Adam in His own form (*bi-ṣûrati-hi*), which the *Haft Bâb* takes to be a Koranic passage, but is evidently an echo of Genesis.[12] But such a formulation by Muḥammad seems to have been lost.

[9] W. Ivanow, *Kalâm-i Pîr*, p. xxxii

[10] Nâṣir-i Khusraw, *Wajh-i Dîn*, p. 68, for instance notes that God is neither known nor not-known. *Kalâm-i Pîr*, pp. 59–60, has the reverse approach.

[11] From the Medieval point of view, where every sort of experiential contingency must be expressed within a set of fixed and absolute concepts or else left out of account altogether, a recognition of aspects of a situation leading beyond the confines of the received concepts could be legitimately expressed in such a formulation as the neither-nor one. This was of course rather an unsatisfactory channel for the expression of the more paradoxical religious insights, particularly that of the inapplicability of logical rules to God; but so long as the Medieval intellectual inflexibility was maintained, any attempt to transcend such limits was properly looked on as opening the way to an indefinite intellectual license. Perhaps we are not free of the danger even now!

[12] *HBBS*, beginning of chap. ii. Throughout this discussion on Qiyâma doctrine this *Haft Bâb* is to be kept in mind; as found in the appendix.

The beatific vision.

The imâm is in his very form ḥujja, proof of God: more than ḥujja, he is all the form God has. Therefore one sees God by him as one sees the sun by the light of the sun – that is, by the sun itself.[13] To know him is to know God, to see him is to see God, so far as God can be known or seen. Perhaps more fundamental to the message of the Qiyâma than the tag which Ivanow called to our attention is the insistence that in the Qiyâma we no longer have the indirect approaches to God that were to be had in the earthly life – we have, as is suitable to Paradise, the presence of God Himself. Ḥasan claimed that he did not just summon to the worship of God – he summoned to God immediately.[14] This was not to lose its force when the imâm was considered the vehicle of such immediate revelation.

Rather, it was through the imâm that a feat impossible for ordinary mortals was made possible. The imâm did for the believer what the Ṣûfî shaykh, religious guide, did for his disciples; by focussing their attention on him, they could be made to forget themselves, and be led to the divine hidden within him. For the vision of God in the imâm did not consist merely in knowing who the imâm was – in the sense of the general Shîʿite notion that the knowledge of the imâms is the knowledge of God:[15] that he who accepts the right imâm possesses all the saving knowledge of God that he needs. Any individual in the ẓâhir world could do that. To truly see the imâm meant penetrating and appropriating the metaphysical and mystical signfiicance of his person.[16]

But in contrast to the varied personal devotion of the Ṣûfîs, this Shîʿite devotion of the Nizârî Qiyâma is centered upon a single cosmic individual[17] In the old Shîʿite phrase, "if for a moment there should not be an imâm, the world would cease to exist." Or to put it more pertinently, without a particular imâm there could be no knowledge and fulfillment of divine

[13] Cf. Shihâb ad-Dîn Shâh, *Risâlat dar Ḥaqîqat-i Dîn*, ed. W. Ivanow, *True Meaning of Religion* (The Ismaili Society, Series B, No. 2 [2d ed.; Leiden, 1947]), p. 20/34.

[14] This phrase in the *HBBS* is re-echoed in the *Rawḍat at-Taslîm*, p. 148/100, which is however rather closer to what Rashîd ad-Dîn reports. Cf. also p. 154/104: "in the other world, they know the Truth by the Truth," rather than by the teller of truth.

[15] Majlisî, for instance, accepts this – D. Donaldson, *The Shîʿite Religion* (London, 1933), p. 353. Nâṣir-i Khusraw among Ismâʿîlîs had said that the imâm, and also his name, is a name of God. *Wajh-i Dîn*, p. 111. Among the Twelvers we find accepted many of these terms: the imâms are manifestations of God, and ḥujja. Donaldson, p. 310. To be sure, something at least of the same extreme doctrines here developed among the Ismâʿîlîs has affected the Twelvers.

[16] *Rawḍat at-Taslîm*, p. 96/66.

[17] Cf. *Rawḍat at-Taslîm*, p. 112, where he deprecates the false vision of the Ṣûfîs.

purpose for the world or for any individual in it – that is, the world could not exist spiritually; upon which existence, as "final cause", its existence in any other sense depends.[18] The role of the imâm not only as uniquely visible revelation of the Divine but as objective focal point of existence, allowed him to provide what no shaykh could provide, bound as he was supposed to be within the Sunnî framework: a concrete cosmic center for a man's whole religious life. As such, devotion to him was not, of course, limited to a personal attendance as in the case of the menial service of the Ṣûfî disciples; for indeed back of all devotion anywhere, even the blindest, was still the imâm, however remotely a man might approach him.

To be sure, the Ismâʿîlîs never forgot that without knowing the imâm no man could be saved. For the true seeker will recognize the falsehood of the other seventy-two sects, and be led by God to an Ismâʿîlî dâʿî. The unbelievers have not truly sought – God has not driven them to do so.[19]

True viewpoint as salvation.

It is as reflection of (or form taken on by) the Kalima, the word of God, that the imâm-qâ'im sustained the world, and presented God directly to the faithful. But naturally this spiritual function of the human form called the imâm was not readily perceivable. From those who went in for the doctrine in full, at least, an adequate spiritual viewpoint was called for so that they might see the imâm as he truly was. This viewpoint is what was made possible by the Resurrection, in which men died, and were created anew, in a new universe. Every detail in life was now to be seen as part of a spiritual whole – as a feature of Paradise.

Accordingly, the manner of devotion developed in the *Haft Bâb* is not just that of disciples of a Ṣûfî shaykh: self-cultivation guided by the leader's insight, whom each of his followers may expect to emulate though at present they might worship him. Rather it is the cultivation of a very systematic viewpoint toward the universe as a whole and toward the imâm in particular. From a viewpoint which is merely partial, and relative to the ability of the creature, all things are matter – and so meaningless,

[18] Cf. Ṭûsî, *Rawḍat at-Taslîm*, pp. 88, 91.

[19] *Kalâm-i Pîr*, p. 93. Ivanow, in this connection, thinks of the Nizârî discipline as a gradual ascent by teaching, and thence absorption; the soul is a matter of amr (divine command), not of fiʿl (deed). Hence the disobedient are as dead, without souls. *Kalâm-i Pîr*, p. xlviii.

transient (the ideas were equated in the Middle Ages); but from a total point of view, which goes beyond the partiality and contingency of the creature, and so sees reality – ḥaqîqa – all things are spirit, and nothing is to be distinguished from the Divine. In particular – and through this insight alone is the broader insight possible – from the relative, partial viewpoint the imâm is a mere human organism in a natural environment; but from the ultimate, total viewpoint, in ḥaqîqa, he is the revelation of God; and his environment, of the Court of God.

THE UNIVERSE OF THE QIYÂMA

The doctrine of Qiyâma was more complex than the simplicity of its central ideal might suggest. While Muḥammad II philosophized, he or someone else was at work giving a colorful content to his categories. Into the imaginative fabric, in which men were supposed to live as resurrected beings, went many an obscure religious idea that the Middle East was treasuring. In the comments on the *Haft Bâb* in the appendix much of this is brought out; here we must be content with the main lines by which the universe of ḥaqîqa was held together.

Identification of Qiyâma and Ḥaqîqa.

The doctrine rests on an identification of the ḥaqîqa of the Ṣûfî inner experience with the spiritual afterlife of the Ismâʿîlî Philosophical tradition. As we have seen, the Ismâʿîlî bâṭin explained religious externals in terms of symbolical references not only to the hierarchy, but also to cosmological and spiritual realities shared largely with the Philosophers. This was so in particular of the afterlife. To the Philosophers, the physical world was eternal; there was no end of the world when the *body* would be restored, and enter Paradise or Hell; rather, the *soul* at death entered Paradise or Hell according to its spiritual condition – according as it was or was not purified of need to depend upon a material body. If it was able to contemplate pure intellectual and spiritual Reality – that is, God – then by being freed from the veiling interference of the body, it was immediately before God in Paradise.[20]

[20] Taṣawwur 15 of the *Rawḍat at-Taslîm* expounds the spiritual resurrection from the standard Ismâʿîlî philosophical viewpoint very clearly, though with some elements distinctive of the Qiyâma interpretation in particular. His ability to introduce the bâṭin serves him in good stead, in an auxiliary way, when proving the (contingent) eternity of the world as a whole, as against the limited duration of particular religious "worlds".

Meanwhile the Ṣûfîs, with a not too dissimilar point of view, were developing their analyses of the spiritual states of the soul in its search for mystical closeness to God in its worship. They divided men into various levels of being, according to their freedom in this life from the bonds of this world, which interfered with the divine vision. The highest degree commonly expected is a lasting presence with God – amounting in fact to Paradise on earth.

Now the Ismâʿîlî imâm was always received as representative of cosmic reality; and turning to him was never merely, in the all-Shîʿite sense, to give him military service; it was a turning from appearance to truth. Accordingly, the imâm is in a position to accomplish for the believers all things at once. When the imâm appears as Qâ'im, his summons to himself is at the same time a summons to the Resurrection – Philosophically interpreted, to abandon the realm of bodily impediments to seeing the truth. Here the all-Islamic expectation of a return at the end of life to face the Author of life is combined with the Shîʿa demand for turning in obedience to the imâm. Moreover, this resurrection to which the imâm-Qâ'im brings his followers is an entering in this life into the realm of reality, into the presence of God. Accordingly, qiyâma, originally an event, is identified with ḥaqîqa, originally a metaphysical or mystical apprehension, as a level of being or of consciousness.

Existence as personal: tashakhkhuṣ.

At the level of Reality, of the Resurrection, all meaning in the cosmos lies in relations among personalities. The world is destroyed: only men are summoned to the accounting. (By personality we mean here, of course, not the *individually* expressive growth often implied by the term now, but only a metaphysically conceived unit of responsible consciousness.) There was an attempt to make of life a continuous holy awareness of such a personal figure, the imâm; one can suppose that physical, objective things ought to lose meaning then except as symbols of this universalized personal attitude. The outside world ought no longer be the theater of devotion. But when in consequence persons' attitudes to metaphysical persons become the only significant thing (any individual variability being disregarded as merely outward), it will not be surprising if persons should be confused with the spiritual offices they hold, and the principles they represent.

A sense of the personal significance of all things is very strong in the

Haft Bâb, and only less so in the later work of Abû Isḥâq; but still later tends to disappear again as the doctrine of the Qiyâma wears away. Thus, in Chapter Four of the *Kalâm-i Pîr*, Abû Isḥâq in speaking of the purpose of creation does not say simply that it is the knowledge of God on the part of his worshippers; nor even only that it is God's self-knowledge through the cosmic emanational process. He goes beyond, to say that men are unique in that all existence proceeds through mankind. For not only do men, as microcosm, represent all realms of being; they absorb all other life, and in the end no life in all these realms is fully real except insofar as, in the spiritual world, it has become human.[21] The very clods of earth, it is pointed out, are to speak as men in the Resurrection. Yet more, therefore, items of religious import, such as the Black Stone at Mecca, or the bridge over Hell. The whole sharî'a is meaningless, not truly existent, except insofar as, in the spiritual resurrection, a changed perspective upon the things it speaks of shows them as foreshadowing the personal office of holy figures.

This can justify the insistence, almost crude, in the *Haft Bâb* on personification, personal embodiment: *tashakhkhuṣ*. This idea was by no means absent from the earlier learned tradition, having been used to express the relation of the human ḥudûd to the cosmic emanative principles. But it is insistently extended to cover all eschatological notions. It recalls here some of the earliest symbolic doctrines of the popular Shî'ite ghuluww, which said that the warnings against Hell, for instance, were directed against certain evil men – one should avoid them. The idea is not just that here. Here Hell is not the *name* for a historical person; it is apparently the outer, false *appearance* of a metaphysical person, Mâlik. Nevertheless, it is curious to find, happily side-by-side with the doctrine that Daylamân (the realm of the imâm) is Paradise, the statements, Paradise is a man, Hell is a man.[22]

The deathless sage; Melchizedec as imâm and Qâ'im.

It is the figure of the imâm himself which exemplifies most thoroughly the merging of the person into the office which he represents in the world

[21] Abû Isḥâq, *Kalâm-i Pîr*, pp. 53, 56.

[22] *Haft Bâb*, p. 20/20 and 31/30. Cf. *Kalâm-i Pîr*, p. 92; Hell and Paradise as "shakhṣ mardî". In *Rawḍat at-Taslîm*, p. 119, such ideas are used to uphold the imâm's unconditional authority. It must be noted that it is not clear just what the various aspects of tashakhkhuṣ meant to each writer.

of ḥaqîqa. The imâm becomes merged with the most exalted personages of the past, and loses any effective moorings in time and space. This feeling for him is reflected in a new cosmic figure who now appears in the Ismâʿîlî lore.

There had always been a tendency, entering even the learned tradition, to identify ʿAlî and the current imâm as one single light-substance. Typical is the passage in the Ṭayyibî-preserved *Zahr al-Maʿânî* where the identity of ʿAlî and the Prophet as a single light is stated, and the superiority of ʿAlî forever renewed in his descendants, the imâms, is implied.[23] This feeling is to be found more graphically portrayed in the *Umm al-Kitâb*, preserved among the upper Oxus Ismâʿîlîs even though it has originally little to do with Ismâʿîlism proper: it seems to be typical of the less cautious Shîʿa generally. ʿAbd Allâh is visiting the young imâm Muḥammad Bâqir at one point, to find him transfigured before him into the forms of ʿAlî, his wife Fâṭima, and his sons.[24]

With the doctrine of the Qiyâma this feeling crystallized into a romantic new figure, a perennial imâm-Qâ'im, placed high above even the prophets. This figure combined many traditions, and its original diversity is still visible when it takes the form of a new series of contemporaries to the Prophets, replacing the usual series of *waṣîs*, "executors" at points where these would be given, otherwise. Since ʿAlî's post was now higher than that of Mohammed, so that he was hardly a mere waṣî any more, the corresponding personages in other generations also could no longer be the traditional subordinates, agents or even sons of the Prophets. We have seen the difficulty already, in the case of Abraham and Ishmael; now the role of the personage who acts there as imâm, father of Ishmael, seems to have been generalized.[25] The result is a series of names quite new, as a series, to the Ismâʿîlî tradition; to whose bearers the prophets turn as to their lords, not as to their heirs.

The personages, as given in the *Haft Bâb*, are these. ʿAlî, to be sure, has enough glory to be retained in his own place correlated to Mohammed. But the imâm-Qâ'im in Jesus' time is Maʿadd (an Arabian patriarch), not Peter; in Moses' time, not Aaron or Joshua but Dhû l-Qarnayn (a prophetic royal figure in the Koran, identified with Alexander); in Abraham's time, Malik as-Salâm (whom we have already met with); in Noah's time, not Shem but Malik Yazdâq, who ordered the flood; in Adam's time,

[23] W. Ivanow, *Rise of the Fâṭimids*, p. 62/253 and p. 74/268.

[24] *Umm al-Kitab*, ed. W. Ivanow, *Der Islam*, XXIII (1936), p. 100/39.

[25] To be sure, it may not have been from this Malik as-Salâm that the idea was generalized; but he is the most vital of the figures. Abû Isḥâq, in *Kalâm-i Pîr*, tr. p. 59, says the Ismâʿîlîs still mentioned Malik as-Salâm in their prayers.

Malik Shûlîm. But the new figures turn out in fact to be only three; ʿAlî, like Ḥasan II himself, being a beneficiary of the dignity of the series, and not a new figure. There is the Biblical Melchizedec, thrice over (the last three names); Dhû l-Qarnayn *Khiḍr* (for in fact, Dhû l-Qarnayn here is identified with the Koranic figure which has been called Khiḍr); and Maʿadd. In each case we have, it would seem, the mysterious superhuman personage that does not die.

This is the role of Melchizedec in Middle Eastern Christian thought, Vajda points out. He shows that the names of Malik as-Salâm and of his two predecessors all derive from the name or title of Melchizedec, that royal priest to whom Abraham submitted, and whose timelessness Paul stressed in making him a type of Christ.[26] Dhû l-Qarnayn Khiḍr, of course, is the old Babylonian Utnapishtim, the man who drank the water of life – the unpredictable master of Ṣûfîs in all ages; he now became the Ismâʿîlî Qâ'im, refound in Ḥasan II. The case of Maʿadd is not so clear; his name is presumably included here only as the most prominent in the line of descent between Ishmael and ʿAlî. But in this case the deathless hero is nevertheless present – this time in Jesus himself. For while in the other cases the return of the imâm-Qâ'im himself is predicted, here the *Haft Bâb* lingers instead over the promised return of Jesus himself, who in the Koran never died.[27] (All these had returned, of course, in the Qiyâma – the imâms in Ḥasan II, Jesus in Ḥasan-i Ṣabbâḥ.)

Quite early, possibly even from the Qiyâma itself, this series of imâm-Qâ'ims was, however, confused with the older series of waṣîs, "executors" to the prophets. That they must have been quite distinct to begin with is suggested not only by the strictly different names, but by an utterly different function – and in fact Ṭûsî retains this function as superiors to the Prophets even when he is identifying the new series of names with the old. Ṭûsî is careful to point out for instance that even though Malik as-Salâm is more often called the son of Abraham (that is, Ishmael, as the *Kalâm-i Pîr* says directly), he is not his son really; rather, all these imâm-Qâ'ims

[26] G. Vajda, 'Melchisédec dans la mythologie ismaélienne,' *JA*, CCXXXIV (1943–5), 173–183.

[27] As to Maʿadd, it may be worth noting that the article in the *Encyclopedia of Islam* points out that unlike most legendary tribal founders, Maʿadd's offspring – this includes the whole north-Arab nation – are not the "Banû Maʿadd" (children of Maʿadd), but simply "Maʿadd". Could this be a lingering trace of an earlier recognition that Maʿadd was no genealogical link, but the nation itself *numbered* throughout its generations (the word may be derived from numbering) – and if so, would there linger just enough mystery about the name to make it interesting?

[28] The relevant passages in Ṭûsî, *Rawḍat at-Taslîm*, are at p. 101/149; those in the *Kalâm-i Pîr*, at p. 59/64 and also 69/74 and 98/102; those in the *HBBS* at p. 10/8.

form their own line distinct from the Prophets.[28] The confusion with the waṣîs produces rather untoward results in Ṭûsî. Particularly, to make Ishmael be identical with, rather than the son of, Malik as-Salâm seems to have bothered even Ṭûsî, who quietly omitted Ishmael's name. To equate Aaron with the world-conquering Dhû l-Qarnayn is a bit preposterous; but no more so than to identify the founder of the Arab nation with that of the Roman church: at which point Ṭûsî (no Arab) calmly proceeds to call the name "Simon-Peter" the commoner of the two! But more commonly the two lists are kept separated at least, as in the *Kalâm-i Pîr*, even when they are identified; and the members of the new series are never referred to as waṣîs, but as Qâ'ims.

The individual in the Qiyâma:
three levels of being.

There remains to be seen the way this works out for the individual: the mass of men who, in contrast to the deathless and timeless figure of the imâm-Qâ'im, are all frail mortals, the distinctions among ḥudûd having faded away. In this resurrection of all life, where only the human position has any meaning and all else is essentially nonexistent, the level of being depends upon the relation to the imâm.

All mankind, in regard to the imâm-Qâ'im, are on one of three levels in the Resurrection. There are the mass of "opponents" of the imâm – those who depend upon the sharî'a (and this would include not only orthodox Muslims, but all who, not being of the imâm's elect, *ought* to be following the Muslim law!): the *ahl at-taḍâdd.* They have always been like brutes, feeding on the husks of truth, ignorant and careless of what grain the husks were meant to protect. In the Qiyâma, these have been startled already by the first blast of the trumpet into the fear that they may have made a false choice;[29] now such of them as have remained unrepentant have been destroyed and are – on the level of reality, in the realm of ḥaqîqa – nonexistent.[30] They have existed only on the realm of appearance, and when they die, and the appearance of them in the environment of the imâm is gone, they too are gone, like 'Umar in the anecdote about Ḥasan II. Now with the coming of the Qâ'im their existence has become in general superfluous, irrelevant to the cosmic purpose; they are no longer even persons; they can be ignored.

Then there are the ordinary Ismâ'îlîs, who have gone beyond the ẓâhir of the sharî'a to the inner meaning, the bâṭin. These have always been

[29] Ṭûsî, *Rawḍat at-Taslîm*, p. 66/96.
[30] *Kalâm-i Pîr*, p. 111.

the loyal servants of the imâm. They have found a *juz'î*, "partial" truth; it is they who have been distributed in ranks, in ḥudûd, in the earthly worship of God. They are the *ahl at-tarattub*, the "people of order", of ranks. But such people are not yet in the realm of ḥaqîqa, for they are still in the realm of plurality. Whereas the ahl at-taḍâdd, the people of opposition, see only the appearance of things, having no truth at all, and cannot recognize the imâm; the ahl at-tarattub, having some truth, can see both the appearance of things, and the imâm. But the *ahl al-waḥda*, the people of union, have the *whole* truth, *kullî*; they discard the appearances, and see only the imâm; it is they who are truly existent, having arrived in the realm of ḥaqîqa. It is these last who have truly been resurrected, for it is their level of being which has been made possible only through the resurrection.

There is a vast amount written – considering the small total quantity of Nizârî literature which we possess – about these several levels of being. The imâm, of course, is on a fourth level: beyond either partial or total truth, neither juz'î nor kullî. But it is the other three levels which have chiefly engaged the attention. I shall abstract from Ṭûsî a list of a number of such sequences, which will illustrate compactly what is involved.

ʿâmm (common people)	khâṣṣ (the elite)	akhaṣṣ-i khâṣṣ (the super-elite)
taḍâdd (opponents)	tarattub (order)	waḥda (union)
ẓâhir (externals)	bâṭin (inner meaning)	ḥaqîqa (reality)
sharîʿa (ritual law)	ṭarîqa (the way)	qiyâma (resurrection)
shakl (form)	maʿnî (meaning)	ḥaqîqa (reality)
ʿadm (nonexistence)	juz'î (partial)	kullî (total)
naẓar (reasoning)	taʿlîm (imâm's teaching)	ta'yîd (direct inspiration)
mushâbaha (similarity in appearance)	mubâyana (distinction)	waḥdâniyya (unity)
jismânî (bodily)	ruḥânî (spiritual)	ʿaqlânî (rational – i.e. in Reason)
intikâsh (bent over, like beasts)	istiqâma (standing erect)	waḥda (union)
quwwa (potentiality)	juz'î (partial)	fiʿl (actuality)
tanzîl (outer revelation)	ta'wîl (explanation of it)	ḥaqîqa (reality)
muslim (submitter to Islâm)	mu'min (faithful)	
dunyâ (this world)		âkhira (the last world)

These sets are derived from every sort of religious and philosophical origin, but all applied alike. Ṭûsî uses some of them in a way befitting his own time, that of the Satr, rather than the Qiyâma itself; nor is he entirely consistent in his use of these terms even so. Nevertheless, the fundamental contrasts among the three realms seems clearly that of the Qiyâma itself as expounded in the *Haft Bâb-i Bâbâ Sayyid-nâ.* The old Ismâʿîlî bâṭin is here split in two – the inner meanings on a relatively simple level, and particularly those involving the religious hierarchy, being treated as the bâṭin proper, while the further flights of aspiration, and particularly those reflecting doctrines of mystical union, are given a distinct status, a new inward within the inward.[31]

Here, it would seem, the philosophical and mystical insights which Ismâʿîlism expressed, even exaggerated to a degree, no longer need to be bolstered by a complex religious system, either of rankings or of argumentations. There is no need felt to prove their Muslim orthodoxy by being able to interpret the awkward texts in the Koran. Such a bâṭin, which meant much to the travelling dâʿîs of Fâṭimid times, is felt to be almost as external as the text itself. In the Qiyâma, the multiple classified degrees in the hierarchy have been replaced by a relatively simple sequence of subjective growth (always within a logical categorical framework). This is inward enough that the living and the dead (assuming a spiritual afterlife) are on a par within the sequence, and death as a demarcation line is irrelevant, as it ought to be after the resurrection!

Resolution of the emanational system.

In the Paradise already before death, where the whole meaning of existence is to regard the revelation of God in the imâm, the role of various persons in the Divine Court is the sole proper realm of concern. Where the Creator is present, only such persons as are involved in this Divine self-revelation have any valid reality. Even when he set about expounding

[31] This truth beyond even the bâṭin may reflect a heterodox tendency in earlier Ismâʿîlism. It reminds one of a corresponding claim on the part of the founders of the Druze faith; but among the Druzes the inner truth seems to have been little more than a reshuffling of the ḥudûd, and a making of them more visible and more august. Unlike the Nizârî Qiyâma there does not seem to have been so clearly, despite the deliberate appeal to the Pauline view of Christianity, a total spiritualizing, which did away with external ḥudûd altogether, and made the degree of spiritual growth a matter of attainment of a pure viewpoint. But cf. S. de Sacy, *Exposé de la Religion des Druzes* (2 vols.; Paris, 1838), I, 52, where each man sees our Lord according to his capacity.

philosophy, Ṭûsî sould not say that the specific nature of man is to be rational; he must say that it is to have supernatural knowledge – via the Perfect Man, the imâm, to be sure.[32]

This is a variant of the all-Islamic doctrine which gradually came to see in Mohammed the Perfect Man; the Ismâʿîlîs see in the imâm the microcosm in whom all the essences of the scattered world are bound into one whole, wherein is the essence of the whole world. But the Ismâʿîlîs proceeded from this, in the ever-present character of their Resurrection, to bring every believer into the circle. Each man fulfilled his role in the perpetually redenominated circle of Paradise. Just as the imâm was forever again ʿAlî, in all respects that were relevant, in ḥaqîqa, so the full believer was ever again Salmân, the demiurge, creating through the imâm's reflected light the earth about him;[33] and at last every unbeliever was ʿUmar, forever annihilated.

As always among the Ismâʿîlîs, history was but of the moment, the recurrence of ever repeated archetypes in cycles. But now even the cycles seem to have disappeared; Paradise itself closes in perpetual Divine unity even the history of types. The historical moment contains within it the whole of history, the microcosm consummated already. A great wealth, to be all within the mind! In the Resurrection, the Ismâʿîlîs tried indeed to depart this world.

THE QIYÂMA AS DECLARATION OF SPIRITUAL MATURITY

The Christian analogy to the Qiyâma.

Despite the more bizarre aspects of the faith, fundamentally it was an attempt to express the same sort of spiritual adulthood as that of the Christianity that also threw off the yoke of the Law. That is, the time had come when artificial rules meant to curb the ignorant for his own good were no longer necessary, for the child had learned to manipulate his environ-

[32] *Rawḍat at-Taslîm*, Taṣawwur Thirteen.

[33] Ra'îs Ḥasan, in *Faṣl dar Bayân-i Shinâkht-i Imâm*, trans. W. Ivanow, *On the Recognition of the Imâm* (The Ismaili Society Series B, No. 4, [2d ed.; Bombay, 1947]), folio 9 v. (One wonders whether there might be one of the believers set up as perfect type of the believer, as Salmân par excellence – perhaps for instance the Ra'îs Muẓaffar of Mu'minâbâd. For by the time of Ṭûsî such a "ḥujja" has taken on a very important place.)

ment himself in full awareness of what was involved; he could allow his decisions to arise not from a contrived code or an imposed ritual of reminder, but from the spirit of the situation. The sense of the divine presence should of itself govern his life.[34] The Ismâ'îlîs themselves noted the similarity of many of their positions to the Christian in this respect.

A comparison of the system of the Qiyâma with that of the Gospel according to John will bring out considerable similarities, as well as overwhelming differences. Indeed, the Nizârîs seem to have been partly aware of this. Knowledge of the Christian scriptures was a tradition with Ismâ'îlîs, dating back at least to Kirmânî.[35] The Druze rebels from Ismâ'îlism also were aware of the tenets of Christianity; and Muqtana' blamed the Christians for not being faithful to the dispensation of grace entrusted to them, and for returning to a legalistic approach.[36] The Nizârîs in turn took advantage of the material, but with less sophistication; evidently they merely adapted to their needs passages formerly used to illustrate the old Ismâ'îlî bâṭin.[37]

It is to prove that Deity can be manifested in man that the *Haft Bâb* refers to Jesus' heavenly father.[38] (The old Ismâ'îlî interpretation had been that his virgin birth was his coming to religious maturity without the instruction of a teacher, a spiritual father.) The *Kalâm-i Pîr* cites a statement that Jesus came from Above, in connection with the doctrines of tashakhkhuṣ, and of union with God.[39] Jesus is presumably a good example of both. Ivanow lists a text which he says is substantially a translation of the Sermon on the Mount.[40]

But the correspondence is more extensive than is indicated by such quotations. When John defined the life eternal as knowing God – and

34 Not that this was as central an element in the Christian dispensation as it was in the Ismâ'îlî Qiyâma, where indeed it was not the only element.

35 P. Kraus, 'Syrische und Hebräische Zitate in den Ismailitischen Schriften,' *Der Islam*, XIX (1931), 243.

36 De Sacy, *Religion des Druzes*, II, 502, 538, etc.

37 Some passages which seem very relevant to the Qiyâma doctrine, and are quoted in Qiyâma texts, appear nevertheless only in connection with points which may have been taken over blindly from the older work. Thus that one must be born again to enter the Kingdom (which was used already by Kirmânî) is used in the *Kalâm-i Pîr* in connection with the teaching of the ta'wîl (inner explanation) as against the tanzîl (words of revelation) – and may refer simply to the dâ'î becoming spiritual father to the initiate. It is in a similar connection that Jesus is quoted, that he came not to destroy but to fulfill the law. *Kalâm-i Pîr*, p. 114.

38 *HBBS*, p. 11/12.

39 *Kalâm-i Pîr*, p. 111. If one could read *khabar* rather than *khayr*, the passage would suggest a parallelism with the imâm as ḥujja of God. But in any case, the passage is at best a paraphrase of Johannine concepts.

40 Ivanow, *Guide*, No. 654.

when he added that he that has seen the man Jesus has seen the Father – he was teaching what must have seemed to the Nizârîs undiluted Qiyâma doctrine. It is the knowledge of God through the imâm that was always the Ismâʿîlî aim, and now in the Qiyâma the further twists given this idea are precisely those found in John: the visibility of God himself in the imâm ("I am in the Father, and the Father in me"); and (but pushed still farther) the presence of eternal life already in such knowledge. The directness of Ḥasan II's method, in which he claimed to teach not about God, or the worship of God, but God himself,[41] is found again in "I am the way". The exhortation to turn to God so that one's very being, one's existence, will be through the imâm, can be rendered with the parable of the vine. The rejection of the sharîʿa at the Qiyâma is inevitably paralleled by the Christian rejection of the Law ("Neither in this mountain, but in spirit and in truth"), a rejection which also has come only in the fullness of time ("the time is coming and now is"). Though in John the Resurrection has not yet arrived as such, yet some elements to be associated with it are there already: "If I had not spoken to them, they had not sinned; but now they have sin." Already at Jesus' word, his disciples are clean, and are to abide in him; and following his personal resurrection, they shall know the truth, and the truth shall make them free – the great message of any gospel of the presence of the Spirit.

The most remarkable difference between the two gospels is the lack in that of Alamût of Passion and Love.[42] Even in that minished corner, the sense of material power as essential attribute of the Divine revelation persists, and though he is generous, and amiable, Ḥasan II is still the ruler: he washes no feet. Though the sheer military power which even at the time of the Qiyâma maintained the war against Qazwîn is not stressed, yet there is no suggestion on the other hand that suffering may be a divine role.[43]

41 Ṭûsî, *Rawḍat at-Taslîm*, p. 100/148.

42 Perhaps a Christian can be forgiven for adding that he fails to find the biographical "life and power" in the hereditarily selected Ḥasan which he finds in Jesus, or in Francis, who was given a similar role by the Spirituals; Ḥasan seems to be more nearly an arbitrary symbol of a community experience.

43 It is a striking fact that though Ḥasan II was persecuted by his father and early murdered after his proclamation, and though the Shîʿa as a whole has made much of the sufferings of the murdered Ḥusayn, Ḥasan's sufferings have nothing to do with the fulfillment of the law: here is no Ismâʿîlî Passion. In a Syrian piece, indeed, perhaps from the same time, the all-Islamic tendency to deny suffering to the favored of God is extended to the point of assurance that Mohammad and ʿAlî had false substitutes to suffer for them the indignities they received – an idea not unknown elsewhere in Islâm. In Ismâʿîlism, the substitutes seem even to have entered the emanational scheme. Salisbury, *JAOS*, III, part 1 (1852), 177.

However, perhaps the clearest differences between the Johannine and the Alamûtî gospels in human and historical vitality spring from the contrasting historical circumstances of the two communities. Christianity in the First Century was in the turmoil of a new growth still forming itself. John's was one interpretation among others of a common experience, a common surge of life moving among all, and before which the world lay receptive. But for Ḥasan II the community was already formed; he was already its master; the proclamation of spiritual liberty was a directive from above. And the Middle East had already found its own way to universality and unity.

Nizârî ambivalence toward Sunnism.

The Ismâʿîlîs seemed not to care what the Sunnîs did. Giving up their all-Islamic program, they directed their old sense of adventure to the direct seeking of God. They were not to be cumbered even with the old hierarchy, which was perhaps in any case a bit out of place in the smaller community, where the imâm would be relatively available to all.[44] In these later writings the presumably less formal *muʿallim*, the transmitter of taʿlîm teaching, takes the place of the *dâʿî* and his daʿwa summoning the wide world to the Truth.[45]

When we speak of this quest for a spiritual maturity and independence, to be sure, we must probably think of its happening primarily in the persons only of the more active members of the group. It is doubtful whether (as appears to have been demanded by Ḥasan II) the whole group actually achieved the level of ḥaqîqa, of union, even though all were invited to. When the Qiyâma doctrine makes provision for an intermediate status, not opponents but not fully saved, this reflects no doubt not only theory, but practice. Yet it is doubtful that there was too sharp a line drawn between the new rankings, such as there had been in the hierarchy. Probably, for instance, the ahl-i tarattub, the half-saved "people of order", dropped the sharîʿa in any case, even though in principle not ready for such a step. The Ismâʿîlîs were at one in their rejection of the world.[46]

[44] Yet compare the considerable hierarchism of *khalîfa* and of *pîr* below the imâm, distant in India, which is to be found in modern Shughnân. Cf. R. Majerczek, 'Les Ismaéliens de Choughnan,' *RMM*, XXIV (1913), 202–18.

[45] Ivanow notes this, *Rawḍat at-Taslîm*, p. xlv.

[46] Perhaps the difference between the two levels within Ismâʿîlism was comparable to that between the saved, in an American Fundamentalist group, and those who have not yet gotten around to taking the step.

Nevertheless, that world diffused itself subtly in their midst as never before. Ṣûfî mystical thinking appears for instance unmistakably – even in terminology. In the story of Ḥasan-i Ṣabbâḥ, that saint is ascribed *karâmât* by Rashîd ad-Dîn, presumably following his Nizârî sources; while the imâm Mustanṣir is given muʿjizât: a differentiation used by Sunnî Ṣûfîs. In the time of the *Haft Bâb*, likewise (about 1200), Ṣûfism was taken as the Sunnî norm, and Ismâʿîlism was analyzed in its terms – the imâm being the true *Quṭb* (pivotal spiritual personage upon whom the spiritual world depends) of whom the Ṣûfîs talked.[47] The Ṣûfî character of the Qiyâma as a whole was noticed by Rashîd ad-Dîn and Juwaynî, and we have already discussed it.

On the other hand, there is an independence born of the Ismâʿîlî heritage in the new development. Overtones of the old interconfessional tendency help to make the new faith independent of all-Islamic elements. This Qâ'im of the Qiyâma is the One prophesied by all religions alike. Not only Islâm and the recognized scriptural faiths, but even the Manichaens and the Hindus (followers supposedly of an ancient imâm) are put on a level.[48] The very adoption of antinomianism, while common to many mystics, is of a distinct Shîʿite character: almost in the Christian manner, it is made possible (not through a purely individual enlightenment but) through the appearance of a God-participating man, who fulfills in his coming the requirements of the outer law, and can therefore bring those faithful to him into a plane of life higher than the law.

It might be said that the very willingness of the Ismâʿîlîs to make so free a use of Ṣûfî elements is a measure of their abandonment of their all-out assault upon Islâm. On the one hand, it demonstrates their inevitable implication in a now dominant Sunnî-Ṣûfî society; against whose life they no longer have a point-by-point counteroffensive, and which has swept beyond them. On the other hand, it suggests a lack of responsible opposition to Sunnî life: Sunnism appears as something alien, to be imitated or turned at will. Where Ḥasan-i Ṣabbâḥ had lately led an all-out attack in an attempt to conquer, Ḥasan II was rejecting even any further attempt at recognition within an Islâm which had been consigned already to the outer darkness of the past.

The independent use of the Ṣûfî materials is itself a measure of the creative energy still available among Ismâʿîlîs even after they had supported so vigorous a final offensive. Nor had they at all lost their sense of honor. Ḥasan II is said to have declared, "I have plucked out the eye

[47] *Haft Bâb-i Bâbâ Sayyid-nâ*, p. 13.

[48] Mânî is cited in *Kalâm-i Pîr*, p. 51; Hindus in *HBBS*, end of chapter II.

of discord; and who but I could have done it?" Interpreted in the light of Ḥasan-i Ṣabbâḥ's doctrine, this would mean that the imâm had put an end to ignorant controversy by providing the truth in his very person.[49] But it was a different spirit from Ḥasan-i Ṣabbâḥ's which was content to regard this as the end of the matter, rather than its beginning.

THE QIYÂMA IN THE WORLD: ITS LACKLUSTER (1166-1192)

Sunnism and the mystics: stolen thunder.

Meanwhile the consolidation of Sunnî orthodoxy was continuing. It was now in the latter part of the Twelfth Century that the Ashʿarite compromise between the men of traditions and those who tried to establish faith by reason was accepted definitively among the Shâfiʿite Sunnî school.[50] Sunnism was rapidly finding the basis on which to conserve its forces institutionally and theoretically. By now the variations of canon law and scholastic theology were no longer the great points at issue; it became increasingly understood to what degree there could be variation – and to what degree not. The Sunnî world view expanded exultantly: this was the time of the triumphal sweep of the poets and mystics, profiting by the *entrée* given the imagination into the good graces of the Law to veer covertly toward pantheism and toward hero-worship and the many things which the compromise synthesis originally was intended to shut out: provided only that in symbol they conformed, and made no hint of disrupting the universal legal forms of the community.[51]

In this atmosphere, challenges from beyond could be largely ignored. Every sort of Shîʿism was at a low ebb. There is a rather startling contrast between the effect on Islâm at large of the revolt led by Ḥasan-i Ṣabbâḥ, and of the great Qiyâma of Ḥasan ʿAla Dhikri-hi s-Salâm. Ḥasan-i

[49] *Rawḍat at-Taslîm*, ps. 55–6.

[50] H. Laoust, *Contribution à l'étude de la méthodologie canonique de Taqî-d-dîn Aḥmad ibn Taymiyya* (Cairo, 1939), p. 4; contrast Halkin's assertion that already in the time of Baghdâdî Ashʿarism was orthodox and taken for granted: A. S. Halkin, *Moslem Schisms and Sects* (Tel-Aviv, 1935), pp. i-iii.

[51] Cf. L. Gardet et M.-M. Anawati, *Introduction à la théologie musulmane* (Paris, 1948) p. 75 ff., on the theologians themselves.

Ṣabbâḥ is prominent in every historical survey of his time, and a number of thinkers then and even later devoted considerable time to the refutation of his ideas: every Muslim was aware of the Nizârî revolt of 1090 C.E. On the contrary, Ḥasan II's Qiyâma was quite unknown to his contemporaries.[52] Not a writer mentions it till after the fall of Alamût, when it was learned of from the internal sources; even so comprehensive a writer as Ibn al-Athîr obscured the matter completely, having the wrong man succeed to the throne at the time, with not a word of the Qiyâma.[53] Even the later writers who were concerned with the Ismâʿîlîs were still refuting Ḥasan-i Ṣabbâḥ two generations after the light of the Qiyâma had flooded his heralding torch into insignificance. The trumpet of Qiyâma blasted the "people of opposition" into an eternal nonexistence so profound that they were quite unaware even of the trumpet blast itself.

Yet the Ismâʿîlî theme which took so grandiose a form in the Qiyâma was at that same time being developed by a controversial figure within Sunnî Islâm itself. It was the time of the expansive melodies of the Persian mystic poets Ṣanâ'î, ʿAṭṭâr, and Rûmî, reweaving the stuff of the older ascetic disciplines into a fervent overflowing paean of the love of God. In the same way, more elaborate theoretical outpourings could find place – all within the forms of the most rigid traditional Sunnism. Eighteen years younger than Muḥammad II, Muḥyî d-Dîn ibn al-ʿArabî was becoming the exponent *par excellence* of the doctrine of Mohammed the Prophet as Perfect Man, supreme microcosm; and was becoming famous throughout Islâm, coming east to win general acclaim a decade before the death of our imâm of the Qiyâma. If the Qiyâma reflected the recent fashions in Sunnî Ṣûfism in general, that Ṣûfism, in adopting the vision of the Perfect Man, was developing what was anciently an Ismâʿîlî theme. Asìn Palacios, following the example of Muslim scholars also, has traced the inspiration of Ibn al-ʿArabi in particular to sources in Spain associated with the Ismâʿîlî speculations.[54] Ibn al-ʿArabî himself may have been aware of the connection; as if defending himself against its implications, he cited Ghazzâlî's *Mustaẓhirî* to show that knowledge of the bâṭin could not dispense with the obligation of the ẓâhir, tacitly admitting that his own esoteric explanations of the religious life had

[52] No doubt the Qazwînîs were aware of it, for instance, but had discounted in advance anything the Ismâʿîlîs might do, and so were not surprised.

[53] Ibn al-Athîr, *Kâmil*, yr. 559.

[54] M. Asìn Palacios, *Abenmasarra y su escuela* (Madrid, 1914), p. 111. It does not seem to me clear that he has shown, however, that it is the distinctively Ismâʿîlî side of Ismâʿîlî doctrine that has been involved. The association, however – in view of our fragmentary explicit information – is very suggestive.

much in common with the Ismâ'îlî bâṭin.[55] We have no sign that the Ismâ'îlîs regarded this as a case of stolen thunder; yet it might well take much of the edge off of a purely local Qiyâma, to be confronted with the *Meccan Revelations*, Ibn al-'Arabî's chief work. As in Caliphal Egypt; as in Ḥasan-i Ṣabbâḥ's incisiveness confronted with the leadership of Ghazzâlî; so now even on its home ground, whither it had withdrawn in a magnificent gesture of final discovery, Ismâ'îlism was outbid.

Sunnî powers after Sanjar: dissension and the Syrian ghâzîs.

Politically, Sunnî Islâm was divided and to all appearance weak. After the death of Sanjar, shortly before the accession of Ḥasan II, the remains of any Saljûq hegemony over the military lords disappeared. Various lines of generals maintained themselves out of habit in the provinces. The most aggressive of rulers, and also probably the nearest to making their warlord position into one of effective civil rule, were the great *ghâzîs* in Syria, the leaders of the holy war now at last undertaken seriously against the Crusaders. Nûr ad-Dîn and Saladin began by taking Egypt from the remaining Fâṭimids (thus saving it from the Franks); and proceeded to vindicate the claim of Islâm to the Holy Land.

These rulers and their people were all still anti-Ismâ'îlî;[56] it is in this period that the anti-Ismâ'îlî judicial decisions already mentioned were handed down at Samarqand and Balkh. But no ruler was clear enough of struggles with rivals, to say nothing of the Franks, to attempt any general campaign against the Nizârîs. There was no great empire to charge itself with the concerns of Islâm as a whole. The Nizârîs in their mountains could do as they pleased.

Muḥammad's defensive peace in the Iranian territories.

For their part, the Ismâ'îlîs of the Qiyâma seem to have been fairly willing to let the nonexistent pursue their nonexistence as they might. After the death of Ḥasan II there seems to have been no major aggressive activity. We are told that the Alamûtîs continued to make their raids,

[55] Goldziher, *Streitschrift*, p. 32. The idea of a "bâṭin" was, however, very widespread.
[56] Cf. Râwandî's tale of Saladin's plans to attack Alamût – yr. 581.

and caused much trouble. Unfortunately, for this reign Rashîd ad-Dîn does not seem to have found a detailed history, as for Buzurg'ummîd and his son; perhaps events did not seem worth recording. Even from outside sources, the first part of Muḥammad's reign seems strikingly uneventful. Outside of Syria, in the first twenty-six years we come across one assassination, that of a Caliphal vizier; and one case of an outsider taking refuge at Alamût from rebels in his own lands – Hazâr Asf of Rûyân.[57]

The latter seems to have been a strong ruler, and so displeased his nobles; they accused him of softness to the Ismâ'îlîs, and of sharing their disregard of the law. He had to flee to Rûdbâr at length, and with Ismâ'îlî help was able to raid his former territories; but eventually being worsted, he fled to the Caliph this time. The Caliph, however, decided against him on the grounds of his sympathy to the Ismâ'îlîs; and after further adventures not connected with Ismâ'îlism, he was put to death by his Mâzandarânî suzerain. A subsequent ruler of Rûyân, Bîstûn, had like him, in the latter part of Muḥammad's reign, to flee to Alamût, but evidently did not attempt to raid from there.

There is one good yarn from the period, about a brush with the great theologian, Fakhr ad-Dîn ar-Râzî (d. 1209). Rashîd ad-Dîn narrates that Râzî used to speak very harshly against the Ismâ'îlîs, so that Muḥammad II decided to have it stopped. He sent a fidâ'î to become one of Râzî's pupils, and seek out an opportunity of dissuading him. One day Râzî was quite by himself in his room. The fidâ'î found a chance to accost him. Throwing the theologian to the floor, he brandished a dagger, and complained of the way Râzî cursed the Ismâ'îlîs at each mention. Râzî promised that he would not do so again; whereupon the fidâ'î gave him, instead a thrust, a bag of gold; saying that it would be regularly renewed if he kept his promise. Thereafter upon mentioning the Ismâ'îlîs, Râzî omitted all cursing or unnecessary ill-use. When asked why, he replied that he had been persuaded by arguments both pointed and weighty.[58]

Nor were the Ismâ'îlîs evidently much occupied with internal dissensions. Any suggestion of resistance to Muḥammad's claims as imâm would have to be inferred from the *Haft Bâb*'s argumentation in support of them, which gives no clear indications. There was at all events a certain amount of literary activity. Ivanow considers that the poems of the Ra'îs Ḥasan will date from this reign, as does the *Haft Bâb* itself.[59] We have

[57] Ẓahîr ad-Dîn, pp. 74 ff.

[58] It is Dawlatshâh who adds the point about the "pointed" arguments. It can be added, in explanation, that it was very common for Muslims to curse their religious enemies, or anyone who they felt was under the curse of God.

[59] 'An Ismaili Ode in Praise of Fidawis,' *JBBRAS*, 1938.

noted that Muḥammad II himself was a very productive writer, and no doubt such of the "blessed epistles" later cited as do not go back to Ḥasan II are his.[60] Even so, we do not find many books of this time being later quoted. Iranian Ismâʿîlism was quiet. Even the remarkable Ismâʿîlî activity in Syria seems remote from it.

[60] Ivanow supposes these *fuṣûl-i mubârak* are the work of imâms, at any rate, and this is also my impression; for they are always cited as authorities, and never with ordinary persons cited as authors. *Kalâm-i Pîr*, p. xxviii, n. Muḥammad III, according to descriptions, is not likely to have written much, Khwurshâh will not have had time, and Ḥasan III would not write in the role of imâm; this leaves Muḥammad II as most likely author in the Alamût period.

CHAPTER IX

QIYÂMA TIMES IN SYRIA: RÂSHID AD-DÎN SINÂN

With the taking of their fortresses in the Jabal Bahrâ, the Syrian Ismâʿîlîs had carved out their own niche far from the eastern, Persian-speaking centers of the sect. Now, during the larger part of the reign of Muḥammad II, Syrian Ismâʿîlism received a permanent impress from one of the most prominent figures of Nizârî history. Râshid ad-Dîn Sinân stands out for his personal qualities – he earned himself the repute of being the founder and head of his sect before he died; and he also seems to have been the man who did most to organize that isolated community in its definitive form, leaving it in a strong position from which it has not yet been totally dislodged.

SINÂN IN SYRIA: CONSOLIDATION WITHIN AND WITHOUT (1140—1192)

Sinân received unusual attention both within and outside the sect, and is therefore better known to us than most of the other names in this story, especially those in Syria. We have a eulogy on him by a later Ismâʿîlî, Abû Firâs, which is made up of brief but revealing anecdotes; we have what is probably the complete biography of him by Kamâl ad-Dîn, of Aleppo;[1] and we have a variety of references to him and his people both in Syrian Ismâʿîlî and in Sunnî and Crusader writings. Even so, his career is by no means fully illuminated; at key points we are left guessing.

Military problems.

To follow primarily Kamâl ad-Din: we can suppose Sinân as brought up in

[1] Bernard Lewis, 'Sources for the History of the Syrian Assassins,' *Speculum*, XXVII (October, 1952), p. 486. As I have mentioned, for Syrian matters I have sometimes had to rely on others' use of manuscript materials. For Kamâl ad-Din on Sinân see now B. Lewis, 'Three Biographies', *Fuad Köprülü Armağanı* (Istanbul, 1953), p. 336 ff.

lower ʿIrâq, probably as some sort of Shîʿite,[2] and fleeing when young, perhaps because of a family quarrel, to Alamût (as did others at outs with the world). There he studied, and became a companion of the young Ḥasan II before his accession. When Ḥasan's father was dead Ḥasan sent him to take charge of Syria. He travelled cautiously, staying with Ismâʿîlîs when possible, in Raqqa and Aleppo; and remained finally in Kahf making himself personally popular, until the aged Abû Muḥammad was dead. Thereupon he settled a succession dispute with authority from Alamût, reconciling two parties, and took power on that basis.[3]

Sinân in Syria was faced with the general problems of the Ismâʿîlîs in the generation of Hasan ʿAlâ Dhikri-hi s-Salâm, problems of imaginative frustration to which the Qiyâma was the answer in the Iranian territories. He was faced even more pressingly, however, with the military and political problems of a small community set right in the midst of an active and complex political life. While in Îrân the Sunnî powers were split hopelessly into fragments, Syria, challenged by the Crusaders, was developing a strong Sunnî consciousness. Sinân's time coincided with the height of power of the great Syrian Ghâzîs, Nûr ad-Dîn of Aleppo and Saladin; both of whom fought against the Crusaders as heads of a moral resurgence within Islâm. Nûr ad-Dîn is remembered not only as having united Syrian Islâm into a single powerful state, but as having cultivated the new methods of fostering the Sunnî faith through *madrasa* schools, which had first been used in the east. Saladin seems to have been even more devoted to a vision of a united and purified Islâm, and went even further than Nûr ad-Dîn in trying to rule his domain on the purest Muslim principles. While the Franks were the chief enemies against whom the new enthusiasm was directed, the Ismâʿîlîs were an obvious target also.

Sinân's first role, then, was to order his diplomacy, his intervention in Muslim affairs or his conciliation of their rulers, cleverly enough to hold off the threatening Muslim powers; and meanwhile to consolidate the most defensible area held by the Ismâʿîlîs into a firmly controlled block of territory, buttressed by strategic strongholds. For he had to face not only

[2] According to Yâqût, *Muʿjam*, ed. Wüstenfeld, III, 275, Sinân was born in a village between Wâsiṭ and Baṣra, which was inhabited mostly by Nuṣayrîs and Isḥâqîs.

[3] Abû Firâs has Sinân remain seven years in Kahf before taking power, which seems too long. Al-Jarîrî also has Sinân arrive early, in 555. It is possible that Sinân had to flee a few years before Ḥasan's accession, in fear perhaps of Muḥammad, and took power from the successors of Abû Muḥammad only when Ḥasan came to power. (In this case the dâʿî of Alamût who is said to have tried to kill him might have been Muḥammad b. Buzurg'ummîd.) The interview with Sinân of one ultimate authority of Kamâl ad-Din is dated in 552, which is impossible.

the rulers and their armies, but the vigilante action of the aroused Sunnî enthusiasts; and even a vigorous set of neighbors in his own mountains, the Nuṣayrîs – the Syrian mountains being crowded then, as now, with the relics of every sort of religious movement that has stirred the Middle East.

Perhaps the first thing Sinân had to do when he took power in Syria was to put an end to some fighting with the Crusaders. Benjamin of Tudela, who travelled there about 1163, about the time Sinân arrived, reported that the Ismâʿîlîs had been at war with the Franks, especially Tripoli.[4] Already in 1142, two years after the Ismâʿîlîs took Maṣyâf, the lord of Tripoli gave the Hospitaller Order the fortress of Krak, at the southern end of the Jabal Bahrâ.[5] Thus the military orders enter the scene, with which the Ismâʿîlîs thereafter had much to do; and probably already with the Ismâʿîlîs in mind, who had occupied strongholds not long before in Frankish hands.

In the next few years, the Franks and Ismâʿîlîs seem to have fought over strongholds in the area; there appears to have been fighting over Manîqa in1151,[6] and the Ismâʿîlîs may have lost Ḥisn ash-Sharqî before 1163.[7] In 1152 the Ismâʿîlîs are said to have assassinated the count of Tripoli; and Defrémery suggests that it was at this time that the Ismâʿîlîs were forced to begin paying that tribute to the Templar military order which they long continued to pay.[8] At any rate it will have begun during the fighting of this period – perhaps it was the price Sinân paid for bringing it to an end. In 1157 the Ismâʿîlîs were not yet at peace with the Crusaders: they are recorded to have saved Shayzar from the Franks, though without holding it themselves.[9]

In Sinân's time, the relations with Nûr ad-Dîn, lord of Aleppo, and then with Saladin were more prominent. When the Aleppo mosque burned, the Ismâʿîlîs were suspected of arson.[10] Shortly before his death, Nûr

[4] Tr. Asher, p. 50.

[5] Cahen, *Syrie du Nord*, p. 511. Elsewhere this date appears as 1145.

[6] Cahen, *Syrie du Nord*, p. 353.

[7] Cahen, *Syrie du Nord* p. 179.

[8] Defrémery, *JA*, 1854, p. 421.

[9] Ibn al-Qalânisî, yr. 552, who has the Franks defeated by them, seems preferable to William, who has the Franks withdraw simply as a result of internal squabbles. Another curious item from this year is a note in Matthew of Edessa that a "Karmoud" helped the Armenian Stephen in his warfare; that is, the Qarmaṭ? It seems unlikely that this would be our Ismâʿîlîs at such a time.

[10] Yr. 564. About this same time, according to a report in Ibn Furât relayed by Quatremère, the Ismâʿîlîs are said to have demanded a certain fortress of Nûr ad-Dîn; who out of policy pretended to accede, but amused the Ismâʿîlî envoy till the local population, on his orders, had destroyed the fortress in question. The same story comes up elsewhere. *Mines de l'Orient*, IV, 1814, p. 346.

ad-Dîn was planning an expedition, which some have said was against the Ismâ'îlîs; Grousset suggests that it was in fear of Nûr ad-Dîn that the Ismâ'îlîs applied – just before his death – to the Franks of Jerusalem for an alliance, in the form of their accepting Christianity.[11] Sinân evidently carried on an unfriendly correspondence with Nûr ad-Dîn also.[12]

Sinân and his friend Saladin.

But when Nûr ad-Dîn died, his son had nowhere near his strength, and was threatened with losing his power to Saladin, who was coming north to join Nûr ad-Dîn's heritage with Egypt in a strong single force against the Franks. Saladin was a greater threat to any smaller power in Syria than Nûr ad-Dîn had been, and when Nûr ad-Dîn's son asked Sinân for protection, Sinân had reason to try to accord it. He sent assassins on two occasions against Saladin, but on both occasions failed to harm him. Once they were recognized as Ismâ'îlîs by a local ruler, and the attempt aborted; the second time Saladin's personal adroitness saved him. Saladin's letters to the Caliph, justifying his attack on Sunnî Aleppo, are full of denunciation of the Bâṭinite connections of the Aleppine regime.[13] When he had taken Aleppo, Saladin undertook an expedition against the Ismâ'îlîs, ravaging their lands, and besieging Maṣyâf; after some time he withdrew, without having taken it.

His withdrawal had probably a combination of motives. His uncle is said to have interfered, out of fear for himself and his lands – in northern Syria – which might suffer Ismâ'îlî vengeance later.[14] On the other hand, it is said that he could not longer keep gorged troops tied up on so relatively unprofitable an expedition, when the Franks were still threatening anyway. Abû Firâs has him frightened away by a knife at his bedside, placed there by Sinân himself. Ibn Khallikân records hostile letters of

[11] R. Grousset, *Histoire des Croisades*, II, 598. One might add that possibly the death of Nûr ad-Dîn brought the negotiations to an end, and not simply the violence of the Templars.

[12] Ibn Khallikân, *Biographical Dictionary*, III, 340–41. Clearly both Nûr ad-Dîn and Saladin are considered Sinân's correspondents here, though a particular quotation is referred only to Saladin. Zakariyâ Qazwînî records a rather fancifully described hostility between Sinân and Nûr ad-Dîn. In the course of it, Sinân is credited with having stopped an attack by Nûr ad-Dîn by the method of having a knife planted by his bed. Ed. Wüstenfeld (Göttingen, 1848), p. 138.

[13] Abû Shâma, *Rawḍatayn*, in *RHC Or.* ps. 570, 572. The Qâḍî al-Fâḍil's letters appear in vol. IV, ps. 181, 214. Cf. B. Lewis, 'Saladin and the Assassins', *BSOAS* XV, 1953.

[14] Yr. 572, Abû Shâma, and Ibn al-Athîr, *Kâmil.*

Sinân's to Saladin along with those to Nûr ad-Dîn. But evidently Saladin was not directly defeated by the Ismâʿîlîs; the reverse would rather be the case.

Thereafter we find the Ismâʿîlîs acting – if anything – in concert with Saladin. Abû Firâs refers to Saladin as Sinân's dear friend; and he, like Nûr ad-Dîn, is blessed when mentioned. (In fact, Nûr ad-Dîn is even given the title of shahîd, matryr.) One suspects that such extravagances from an Ismâʿîlî author date from a later time, when the Ismâʿîlîs were under Mamlûk tutelage.

It was with the local Aleppine government that the Ismâʿîlîs had closer relations – good and bad – even under Saladin. In the year following Saladin's withdrawal, the Aleppine vizier – forging a request from his master Nûr ad-Dîn's son – provoked an attack by the Ismâʿîlîs upon his rivals within the government.[15] It was at this same period that Sinân was able to intervene at Aleppo, when an attack on an extremist Ismâʿîlî group was planned, asserting his right to handle them himself. But when Aleppo later presumed to seize an Ismâʿîlî village, and refused redress, some Ismâʿîlîs came to Aleppo and managed to fire the bazaar in revenge.[16] Thereafter we see no further suggestions of an Aleppine alliance.

The most prominent occasion upon which Sinân's action seemed to serve Saladin's purpose also involved the Crusaders. This was the murder of Conrad of Montferrat in 1192. It has been lengthily disputed, and has not yet been settled, who was to blame for the murder. Abû Firâs, in a rather thoroughly distorted tale, ascribes it to Ismâʿîlîs who were sent by Sinân because he perceived that his friend Saladin was in difficulties. Ibn al-Athîr,[17] Saladin's enemy on behalf of Nûr ad-Dîn, agrees in laying the incident at Saladin's door; but many prefer for good reasons to suppose that Richard, Conrad's enemy within the Frankish ranks, was back of it, or someone else again – or that the Ismâʿîlîs chose to do it on their own.[18]

There are indications indeed that the Ismâʿîlîs were not on good terms with the Franks in these latter years. In 1186 we find the Hospitallers making their military headquarters in Marqab in their vicinity; and Cahen

15 Yr. 573, Ibn al-Athîr, *Kâmil.*

16 Defrémery, *JA*, 1855, p. 22, yr. 575.

17 Yr. 588, *Kâmil*; but in the history of *Mawṣil* this accusation is not made.

18 Cf. the lengthy discussion in Schaffner. That Saladin allowed the Ismâʿîlîs at this time to erect a *dâr ad-daʿwa* in various cities as Abû Firâs says seems very doubtful in spite of what Guyard calls contemporary evidence: the statement of Abû Firâs that they were still so called in his time: *wa-hiya tuʿrafu bi-d-daʿwa ilâ zamâni-nâ hâdhâ.* This shows neither that they were established when Abû Firâs supposes, nor that at any time since the Fâṭimid regime they were used for Ismâʿîlî – and especially for Nizârî – purposes, and not just remembered for their previous connections.

suggests that the Nizârîs had just before that been making some advance and were now turned back.[19] In any case, the assassination of Conrad eliminated one of the Frankish chiefs; and when, soon thereafter, Saladin was able to make peace with the Franks, the Ismâʿîlîs were included in it at Saladin's request.[20] In the next year after Saladin's death, the Ismâʿîlîs were said to have assassinated a prince who was threatening the lands of Saladin's brother.[21] Cahen suggests that the visit of Henry of Champagne to the Nizârî fortress a few years later, in 1194, at their suggestion during his voyage, was designed to restore friendly relations.[22]

The internal administration.

It was within the Ismâʿîlî territory that Sinân did his great work. He was much concerned with constructing or reconstructing fortresses.[23] Sinân evidently did not have any personal troops, nor even a bodyguard. Rather, he ruled by his strength of personality; thus at the taking of ʿUllayqa he was able to prevent any plundering.[24] He is represented in Abû Firâs as travelling from one village – or fortress – to another, escorted by the men of each village in turn. His headquarters at Kahf or Maṣyâf or Qadmûs (all are mentioned) cannot have been more than sites of preference; there was no bureaucracy to make him immobile, apparently. Yet the several fortresses were closely knit together; in spite of rivalries among them, they could emulate one another in repelling invaders, in building new strongholds, in overcoming Nuṣayrî resistance.

Probably a more dangerous enemy than Saladin were the more local bands of the *Nubuwwiyya* whom we read of in Abû Firâs and in Ibn Jubayr. From the latter we learn that they formed a lay order of Sunnî fanatics designed to harrass the great number of the Shîʿa of all sorts in Syria, drawing their inspiration, as Salinger points out, from the general *futuwwa*

[19] Cahen, *Syrie du Nord*, p. 514 ff.

[20] Abû Shâma, in *RHC Orientales*, V, 77, yr. 588 – on the basis of al-Qâḍî l-Fâḍil; such a source would not lightly suggest an alliance with Ismâʿîlîs.

[21] Abû Shâma, *RHC Or.*, V, 107, yr. 589, from ʿImâd ad-Dîn; that they assassinated Sayf ad-Dîn Bektimûr of Khilâṭ in Armenia just as he was about to try to seize Mosul. But others assign this murder to quite different auspices. Cf. Defrémery, *JA*, 1855, p. 44.

[22] *Syrie du Nord*, p. 585.

[23] Abû Firâs shows us incidentally Sinân reconstructing the fortresses of Khawâbî, Ruṣâfa, and ʿUllayqa; anedcotes XV, XIV, XI.

[24] Abû Firâs anecdote V.

movement (itself often of a Shî'a coloring), which was designed to express manliness and group solidarity among the townsfolk. Damascus, that Sunnî stronghold, could naturally produce a pro-Sunnî vigilante band on this basis; what is a little more odd is Abû Firâs' description of their defeat at the hands of Sinân. They are allowed to gorge themselves upon lush fruits, and then are beaten easily: as if they had been a band of bedouin.[25] But probably the most usual answer to such vigilantes may have been the assassination of their leaders. Abû Firâs speaks of the sending out of such "men of jihâd" as very usual.

In addition to the vigilantes, Sinân had to face the Nuṣayrîs, who had probably held the land before the Ismâ'îlîs entered it. They are now, and probably were then, more numerous than the Ismâ'îlîs, and must naturally have been jealous of alien intrusion in their fastnesses. Sinân seems not only to have fought them, but sometimes to have won them over.

Seven of Abû Firâs' thirty-one anecdotes involve the relatively unusual subject of transmigration. It is to be noted that elsewhere in Ismâ'îlism, reincarnation, when it appears in the popular lore (being excluded from the learned), tends to be restricted to return in human bodies only.[26] In the Umm al-Kitâb, for instance, the type of religion, etc., of the family into which a person is reborn will depend upon his age at death and the like. Reincarnation also appears in some of the Guyard fragments. Men are reborn till they recognize the imâm of their time.[27] But transmigration is less frequent even in popular tracts.

Since transmigration appears especially among the Nuṣayrîs, Guyard supposed that Sinân must have been originally a Nuṣayrî; especially since the district from which he came is said to have been one frequented by such heretical groups as the Nuṣayrîs.[28] Dussaud came forth with a contrary theory, that Sinân was deliberately appealing to the Nuṣayrî potential converts to his own faith. Abû Firâs tells of certain chiefs who

[25] Ibn Jubayr (fl. 1187), *Travels*, ed. Wright and de Goeje (E. J. W. Gibb Memorial, V [Leiden, 1907]), 280; G. Salinger, 'Was Futûwa an Oriental Form of Chivalry,' *Proceedings of the American Philosophical Society*, XCIV, No. 5 (October, 1950), 481. Guyard, in his translation, supposes the Nubuwwiyya to be a sect, and so adds the word "secte" in his translation, though it is not in the original; as was commonly the practice in French translations at that time. S. Guyard, 'Un grand maître des Assassins au temps de Saladin,' *JA*, ser. 7, IX (1877), 418 and 470.

[26] That reincarnation was a live issue at one point or another in Ismâ'îlism is shown by its being used as an accusation against rival philosophers – e.g., by Nâṣir-i Khusraw against Sijistânî, on the grounds that any bodily resurrection whatever is already reincarnation. Corbin, introduction to Sijistânî's *Kashf al-Maḥjûb*, p. 17.

[27] This is stressed particularly in Fragment XVI.

[28] Yâqût, in Wüstenfeld, *Mu'jam al-buldân*, III, 275: Sinân is from the Wâsiṭ area. Kamâl ad-Dîn had him from Baṣra. No doubt he lived in both places.

came to pay homage to Sinân; one of them saluted the sun behind Sinân's shoulder rather than Sinân, and Sinân accordingly, without commenting upon this invisible fact, omitted the chief's portion of reward. Whereupon the chief repented.[29] Dussaud suggested that the unidentified word used to refer to these chiefs be read Shamâlî, and that they be identified with those among the Nuṣayrî, called that, who worshipped ʿAlî as being in the sun. Thus far he seems to have made a probable case.

He went on to say that Sinân must have been substituting himself for ʿAlî as God, and supported it by showing that in one of the Guyard fragments ascribed to Sinân the divinity is made each time to be the asâs, ʿAlî, who contrary to standard Ismâʿîlî practice (but in accord with Nuṣayrî practice) is there elevated above the nâṭiq, Mohammed.[30] This last is unlikely: in the fragment in question, which we shall take up shortly in detail, there is great ambiguity about who is elevated above whom; and in any case, the exaltation of ʿAlî would appeal on a popular basis to Ismâʿîlîs as well as to Nuṣayrîs. The Nuṣayrîs are said to have called him "lord of the mountain".[31] One suspects that as a part of his campaign to consolidate the Ismâʿîlî territories, Sinân subjected to his rule, though not to his creed, some Nuṣayrî enclaves; in the process, a stress on transmigration might have been both natural and convenient. Indeed until modern times there apparently continued to be a Nuṣayrî village or so dependent upon the few Ismâʿîlî fortresses remaining.[32]

In addition to his fortresses in the Jabal Bahrâ, Sinân's religious authority, at least, probably extended over the Ismâʿîlîs of the Jazr, and other Syrian areas where Ismâʿîlîs were mingled with the Sunnî population. There were numerous Ismâʿîlîs still reported in the Jazr by Yâqût in the 13th and Dimashqî in the 14th Centuries.[33] Sinân was able to intervene for their protection when Aleppo wanted to attack them; and then was able to discipline them himself, as we shall see. He was presumably as much in charge of them as of the fortresses in the Jabal Bahrâ. But perhaps the key to the durability of his work is that he concentrated on the mountain strongholds. Of these he made sure, and turned only his excess energies to the more exposed Ismâʿîlîs scattered amongst their enemies. And his work in the mountains endured.

29 Abû Firâs, *JA*, ser. 7, IX (1877), 486, Fragment XXVII.

30 Dussaud, *Histoire et religion des Nosairis* (Paris, 1900), pp. 54, 79. Cf. his article on the influence of Nuṣayrîs on Sinân, *JA*, 1900.

31 Abû Firâs, anecdote XVII.

32 Walpole, *Ansayrii* III, p. 303.

33 Dimashqî, *Nukhbat ad-Dahr*, p. 203.

ABÛ FIRÂS' PORTRAIT OF SINÂN: THE HERO

Sinân as a one-man show.

In the Syrian Ismâ'îlî tradition, Sinân has a hero's role. His religious personality was clearly outstanding. Honor for him went so far that there was a later expectation, among some, that he would eventually return from a cave in Kahf into which he was said to have retired.[34] Certainly he was loved, and anecdotes of his tenderness still touch us. He sends villagers home early one day from laboring on some fortifications, because a child has hurt itself unperceived by any, and needs help.[35]

Another time, "Some of the comrades tell that the lord (his peace be with us) was heading toward Maṣyâf, and entered a village called al-Majdal. Its people came to him offering hospitality, and the village head came bringing some food covered with something which hid it. The lord (his peace be with us) ordered that that food be put in a place apart, and that no-one uncover it. When the lord rose to mount his horse, the village head said to him, Lord, why did you not eat of my food and comfort my heart? He said to him privately, Her haste made your wife forget to take out the insides of the chicken; I did not want anyone to know that, it being a matter of shame. The village head looked, and it was as the lord (his peace be with us) had stated."[36]

Sinân is more than once shown as concerned with kindness to animals. "One of the comrades has told me that once when the lord Râshid ad-Dîn (his peace be with us) was in Maṣyâf, the butcher wanted to slaughter a bull which was still a calf, but it broke the ropes, and took the knife in its mouth from the butcher's hand; and then fled, and no-one could catch it. The lord Râshid ad-Dîn said, Don't slaughter it, for it has already been slaughtered seven times in this place. And he had its master swear it."[37]

Even more than love, Sinân inspired awe. Abû Firâs delights above all to tell how Sinân was so signally favored by God that the great and learned of all countries had to admit the fact even against their wills.[38] (We must note that the preoccupation here displayed with acceptance by outsiders as Muslims probably does not reflect the mood of Sinân's

34 Dimashqî, *Nukhbat ad-Dahr*, p. 208.

35 Anecdote XI, p. 472.

36 Anecdote VI (p. 457–8).

37 Anecdote XXIII (p. 483).

38 He is particularly eager to show that Sinân's wonders were not mere magic, but genuine signs from God. Anecdote VII, p. 463.

own time.) "A trustworthy comrade has told us, The lord Râshid ad-Dîn (his peace be with us) went down from al-Kahf to Maṣyâf and stayed there for a short time; and one day said to his companions, Know that a group of legists is on their way to us from Damascus, forty in number, and the eldest of them is So-and-so; their purpose is to dispute and argue with me. Tonight they are staying in Ḥimṣ; tomorrow at the end of the day they will reach Maṣyâf. When they arrive, have them stay in the garden of al-Jirsiq, and send there live cattle and fowl, and pots and dishes and new spoons, and coins, so that they may buy with them whatever they want, and may cook for themselves whatever they wish. That is because they believe you are not Muslims, and [therefore, as legally required] they do not permit themselves to eat your food.

"[All this happened as stated, and Râshid ad-Dîn eventually received them at Kahf, where they were accorded similar treatment.] When he had them brought before him he said, We will set a special day for each of you, and the disputation and argument on that special day will be with him, in such wise that no other will take part at all either with a question or an answer, till he is stopped and finds no answer and his proofs are vain, or he overcomes [me].[39] Then he did not cease to argue with each of them on his special day, stopping him with eloquent proofs and decisive and elegant demonstrations; then his companions bore witness against him, and he [Sinân] took their signatures to that effect. Finally there was left of the forty one man, the eldest; he set about compelling him [to silence], and he [the legist] became unable to answer before the time of afternoon prayer. The lord said to them, Legists – if you [sing.] want a respite, we will accord it to you. He said, I find no way to escape and free myself from this impass. There upon he [Sinân] had his friends witness against him that he had been stopped and unable to answer, as he had had them witness against those before him, and took their signatures to that effect.

"Then he said to them, Legists, you know that since your arrival here you have not eaten any of our food, nor drunk with us water or anything else, and we only sent you sums, that you might spend them on what you would arrange for yourselves of food of your own choice; for you dislike our food, and claim that we are not Muslims. They said, that was before that test and justification and assurance; but now we do not distrust nor doubt you, but say that you are the unitarian Muslims. He said, God knows your consciences, and your secrets are not concealed

[39] This particular rhetorical notion of discussion seems to have been widely prevalent at the time.

[from Him]. Then he took their signatures, that they had not eaten any food with them, and said to them, You have declared the reverse of what you have in your hearts. Such and such of you will die when you have travelled to such a place – till he had numbered a group of them by name and patronymics; and in such and such a place a group of you will die – then he named them as he had named the previous ones; and did not cease to name group after group, mentioning that they would die in place after place, till he had named thirty-nine men. Then he said, This eldest of you will reach Damascus, visit the chief Qâḍî, and tell him what passed between you and us from the beginning to the end; then he will go home and die that same night. [And all happened exactly as predicted.]"[40]

Sinân was not unlearned. He is reported as having read the Ikhwân aṣ-Ṣafâ, at any rate; and doubtless had some notions on the subject of his own position. If Sinân did, as reported, know Ḥasan II as a youth and exchange ideas with him, Sinân might well have developed a conception of divine *ta'yîd* (inspiration of the imâm and ḥujja) which would hold for all the heads of the holy sect; while Ḥasan was developing through the same sequence of ideas – but being better-placed – the conviction of his own unique inspiration. Such a position was claimed for Sinân by his followers; a position so high that the latter-day Ismâ'îlîs, to justify Sinân's independent reception of ta'yîd, have insisted he was an imâm – was Muḥammad II himself.[41]

At any rate, Sinân acquired a reputation for the spectacular. It is said that he cultivated statuesque poses, which impressed people with his superhuman dignity – speaking little, and not letting himself be seen eating. Sinân was at one time lamed (evidently in an earthquake, as noted by Abû Firâs), and his people had such confidence in him, they are supposed to have demanded that he be killed, so as to return to them perfect.[42] With such prestige, Sinân proceeded to impose a one-man show upon the Syrian esoteric tendencies, permitting some to develop freely when they could support a loyalty to himself, but keeping anything within bounds that threatened ultimate dissolution of the group.

[40] Anecdote XII (p. 472–4). The still longer anecdote XIII is evidently a doublet of this. There he silences a select delegation from Baghdâd itself; among other things, with proof that he knows details on three hundred and sixty Adams.

[41] Ivanow, *JBBRAS*, XIV (1938), 63–72. Tâmir 'Ârif, 'Sinân Râshid ad-Dîn aw Shaykh al-Jabal,' *al-Adîb*, May 1953, p. 43, presents this position.

[42] Outsiders, of course, looked on him as a trickster. Thus Defrémery reports the tale of a speaking head – a man whose head sticks out from the ground witnesses for Sinân's exalted rank; and then is killed lest he tell! Abû Firâs on the contrary has a story of how Sinân exposed a fire-walker by forcing him through fire without protective salves and clothes.

The types of Sinân's wonders.

There is a consistency in the type of anecdote which Abû Firâs reports of Sinân which suggests some basis in fact for his selections. They all paint Sinân the hero of his people, of course; but they are more precise. Among the common wonders of the age, Sinân's more distinctive wonders consist predominantly in cases of telepathy or clairvoyance, never in cases of healing or of production from nothing, rarely of cases of prowess (as, travel through the air would be) or of prescience.

The cases of prowess include two of moving or stopping great rocks. This is the kind of story that grows up readily around prominent precarious ones in any mountainous area, and will be attached to the most prominent figure available locally. Also, they include the occurrences at Saladin's siege, when Saladin's men cannot approach Sinân – being held immobile at a distance – but Sinân can readily reach Saladin in his tent, unseen and unhindered. (The latter incident is to be ascribed, *if* it is based on fact at all, to the visit of an agent of Sinân to the tent of the sleeping potentate, as in all other cases of knives by their heads.)

There are four predictions mentioned, all of the distant future (Abû Firâs' own time) and so presumably not reflecting contemporary impressions made by Sinân. Among stories less easily classifiable, there are three sudden deaths of animals – a monkey, a mare, a serpent – which Sinân then explains curiously; as well as the two tales of savants who presumed to dispute with him. Sinân does not predict the animals' deaths nor is he their author; but he seems to be their occasion. These and other stories all show a tendency to expect Sinân's presence to be marked with wonders, rather than any special ascription of powers to him. They are of the same sort with the appearance of a green bird at night, who talks with Sinân; with the unwonted weight of a sack carried by a young man whenever he thought ill of Sinân; with Sinân's lack of reflection in water.[43]

But the weight of the tales, as Abû Firâs emphasizes both in the beginning and the end, is on telepathy and to some extent on clairvoyance. Of these he has fourteen tales, almost as many as of all other types of wonder together. And of these tales, two describe a repeated action, not just one case: he knows what has befallen a fidâ'î so soon as it befalls him; and he

[43] That a body of light – as in some early Shî'a sources it was supposed holy bodies must be, light being the vehicle of spirit as darkness was of evil and matter – should cast no shadow, is easily confused with its casting no reflection, in a language where *shadow* and *reflection* can be designated by the same word. Anecdote III of Abû Firâs.

answers questions *thought* outside his window (but only by saying *yes* or *no*). It is clear that this must have impressed his contemporaries, and whether or not it was done with pigeons, as Guyard suggests on the basis of Sinân's concern for pigeon young in one story, it illustrates the bent of his character.[44]

SINÂN AND ALAMÛT: THE SYRIAN RESPONSE TO THE QIYÂMA

The Syrian Ismâʿîlîs, who had come to accept the leadership of Iṣfahân and Alamût rather than that of Cairo, were by that fact as Ismâʿîlîs rather isolated. They were cut off by a difference of sect from their fellow-Ismâʿîlîs in near-by Egypt, and from the Ismâʿîlîs of Îrân both by a difference of language and by a considerable distance. Moreover, though they undoubtedly shared with the other Nizârîs a sense of gradual disappointment of their early high hopes, they had not the compensating respite of relative immunity from embroilment in the world: they were in the midst of high tension politics. Under these difficult circumstances, the history of the Qiyâma is bound to have been different in Syria from what it was in Îrân.

Sinân as independent not in name but in effect.

Sinân came to power in Syria about the same time as Ḥasan II in Alamût: probably during his reign, and as representative of his Qiyâma policy. The gradual way in which he took power suggests that the Qiyâma was not readily introduced into Syria. However, Sinân overcame whatever difficulties there may have been, and at some time held the ceremony of breaking the fast of Ramaḍân, as had been done in Alamût; but possibly

[44] In fact there seems no reason to suppose that the whole story of telepathy was based on a cleverly concealed use of pigeon post. But Sinân's tendencies were at best exaggerated. When men stood outside his window with their problems in mind, awaiting his yes or no, the procedure reminds one of other equally arbitrary ways of reaching decision, in which much faith has been placed; as, opening a revered book at random. (It might be mentioned as a point of interest that one of the stories shows Sinân knowing in advance the location of a charm against snakes in the wall of Khawâbî; and this charm seems to have persisted, for it is mentioned again in some detail by Ibn ash-Shiḥna in his survey of the lands around Aleppo. *Ad-durr al-Muntakhab*, ed. Jos. Sarkîs (Beirut, 1909), p. 266.)

not simultaneously with the Alamûtîs.[45]

We find among the Guyard Fragments one in which Sinân is quoted, which seens to represent fairly closely the sort of Ṣûfism found in the Alamût Qiyâma – though without the emphasis on seeing God in the imâm, or on the three levels of viewpoint, which we have supposed to have been developed by Muḥammad II after the death of his father. It elaborates the idea that one must know God by Himself, through knowing oneself, on the ground that all selves are God – there being no other existence than He. Relative being is nonexistence. The Ṣûfî doctrine of *fanâ*, the ecstatic disappearance of the individual existence, is attacked on the ground that what has no separate existence cannot lose existence. There is in the fragment no reference to the Qiyâma as such; the impression is rather that now, as in all yesteryears, it is our everrecurring lusts which prevent our knowing the ultimate Unity. Nevertheless, one may suppose from his being quoted in it, that this piece harks back to the doctrine of Ḥasan II as taught by Sinân.

What we are to suppose the Qiyâma meant in Syria, however, depends on how much Sinân's hands were tied by Alamût. In fact, he seems to have had a great deal of leeway. Contemporaries in Syria gained the impression that Sinân was quite independent of Alamût. There are reports that Muḥammad tried to have him killed, as Mustanṣir was once forced to deal with an insubordinate dâʿî in Sind; but that Sinân discovered or won over all the would-be assassins. He is treated by Ibn Jubayr as a god, and Ibn Khallikân refers to his sect being called by his name.[46] It is pointed out, by those who believe that he set up quite on his own, that his sending a mission to Jerusalem offering conversion to Christianity (as reported by William of Tyre) was an act possible only to an independent chief of sect. It could be added as a trace of what might have been a parallel case, that the Ḥâfiẓiyya claimed Sinân for their own. Perhaps Sinân played with them, but that was surely all.[47]

[45] Defrémery, *JA*, ser. 5, V (1855), 7. Here it is done on the order of Kiyâ Muḥammad – I or II? That the sharîʿa was ended in Syria is confirmed by William of Tyre, à propos of the Ismâʿîlî suggestion of conversion; and by the fact that at the time of Ḥasan III's Islamization their conversion is described. It is clear from Abû Firâs that they had no mosques in the later years until they lost their independence. Sinân's first missive from Alamût (in Kamâl ad-Din) is pre-Qiyâma.

[46] Ibn Khallikân, *Biographical Dictionary*, III, 340, lists him as founder of the "Sinânî" sect. It must be noted, however, that he was as often linked with Alamût. Dimashqî (d. 1327), *Nukhbat ad-Dahr*, p. 208 says (confusing names a bit) that Râshid ad-Dîn Muḥammad was a student of ʿAlâ ad-Dîn ʿAlî, lord of Alamût, headquarters of the daʿwa.

[47] Qalqashandî, *Subḥ al-Aʿshâ*, XIII, 243. He calls the Ḥâfiẓiyya simply *Mustaʿ*-

Rashîd ad-Dîn, working from Alamût sources, does not mention Syria in this period, nor are any Syrians at the Qiyâma as described by Abû Isḥâq; though in both authors Quhistân is prominent, as well as Alamût. In general the Alamûtî tradition seems to make very little of Syria, and has no notice of Sinân. Abû Firâs has just as little to say of Alamût. But he implies allegiance to it on occasion. He refers once to the imâm of whom Sinân is *nâ'ib*, lieutenant (a title later at least common for the head of the Syrian Ismâ'îlîs);[48] but ascribes the glory of Sinân's achievement directly to God. He describes Sinân in terms which could be roughly appropriate to any recipient of ta'yîd, either an imâm or a ḥujja; making his soul the universal soul, his reason the universal reason. The moral which he draws is simply that *rijâlu-nâ* – our men – are worthy of unlimited respect.[49] (*Rijâl* appears also in Ṭûsî as a synonym of the *ḥudûd*.)[50] At most, the tie – though it existed – left only slight traces.

Soon after Sinân's death, nevertheless, the Syrian Ismâ'îlîs were in unquestioned obedience to Alamût. Though this could have been a renewal of old ties after the great personality was gone, my guess would be that without necessarily throwing off allegiance to an imâm too distant to do him much harm, Sinân in his practical work might have come in time to feel defiant of his friend Ḥasan's son, with his nicely developed theology. Sinan might have felt free to depend on his own ta'yîd to determine what the Qiyâma should mean in Syria, and to cooperate with any group that might suit his purposes.

The Fragment Nr. One: appearances of the Lord to men.

In any case, there is a distinguishable sort of attitude consistently associated with Sinân's name, which one can almost dub the Syrian version of the Qiyâma, and which is well illustrated in brief compass in Guyard's fragment number one, of which a translation from the Arabic follows here.[51]

lawiyya, but it is the Ḥâfiẓî line of imâms, not the Ṭayyibî that is given. If Sinân wanted to set up independently of Alamût, the unknown imâm of such of the Ḥâfiẓîs as persisted in the faith after Saladin's attempt to kill off their dynasty might be innocuous and convenient. It might then be the dâr ad-da'wa of the Ḥâfiẓîs which Abû Firâs refers to as erected – or protected – by Sinân. Lewis (*BSOAS*, XV, 242) notes Sinân's interest in the pro-Fâṭimid plot in 1174.

48 As is *mawlâ*, lord, a title also used of the imâm.

49 Tâmir 'Ârif, *al-Adîb*, May 1953, p. 45, quotes al-Amîr Mazyad al-Ḥillî in verse praising Râshid ad-Dîn in high terms; the same poet is quoted as praising the imâm in a different passage.

50 *Rawḍat at-Taslîm*, p. 96.

51 S. Guyard, *Notices et extraits*, XXII (1874), 193.

"In the name of God the merciful and compassionate:

"Faṣl of the noble words of the lord [*mawlâ*] Râshid ad-Dîn (upon him peace); it is most excellent as an explanation. My reverence is to my Lord [*rabb*], there is no god but He (the high [*al-ʿalî*], the great).

"Comrades [*rufaqâʾ*,] we have been absent from you by two absences, by that of potentiality [*tamkîn*] and by that of actuality [*takwîn*]; and we veiled ourselves from the earth of your knowledge [*maʿrifa*].[52] And the earth groaned and the heavens shook, and they said, O Creator of creatures, forgiving! And I appeared [*ẓahartu*] in Adam, and the daʿwa was Eve – we assembled the hearts of the believers [*muʾminîn*] the earth of whose hearts groaned in love for us; and we looked upon the heavens of their spirits in our mercy.[53] And the period [*dawr*] of Adam, and his daʿwa passed; and his ḥujja disappeared, through our mercy, among the people. Then we appeared in the period of Noah, and the people were drowned in my daʿwa; whoever trusted in my knowledge [*maʿrifa*] was saved by my mercy and grace, and whoever among the people denied my ḥujja perished. Then I appeared in the cycle of Abraham under the three titles of star, moon, and sun. And I destroyed the ship, I killed the boy, I built up the wall, the wall of the daʿwa;[54] whoever trusted in my daʿwa by my grace and my mercy was saved; and I talked with Moses openly [*ẓâhir*] not veiled; it is I that know the mysteries.[55] I was a door for the seeker, Aaron. Then I appeared [*ẓahartu*] in the master [*sayyid*], the Messiah, and I wiped [their] faults from my children with my generous hand;[56] the first pupil who stood before me was John the Baptist; outwardly [*bi-ẓ-ẓâhir*] I was Simon [Peter]. Then I appeared [*ẓahartu*] in the ʿAlî of the time, and I was concealed [*sutirtu*] in Mohammed [or: concealed him?];[57] and he who spoke of my knowledge [*maʿrifa*] was Salmân.[58] Then

[52] The relation of heaven and earth in Ismâʿîlî bâṭin can symbolize teacher and learner among ḥudûd. All these terms can also have Ṣûfî overtones.

[53] There is a pun here on the name of Eve with the word for assemble. The daʿwa is embodied, or perhaps better, symbolized in Eve.

[54] Noah's flood, the waters of which are taken for the daʿwa (water always equals knowledge, as, rain from sky to earth), here replaces Eve; only to be replaced by the wall which Khiḍr built in the Koranic story. No daʿwa is mentioned for Abraham, about whose search for God the Koran tells a story of his successive rejection of stars, moon, and sun as not good enough. (The last sentence refers to the actions of Khiḍr, by which he paradoxically showed himself to be more knowing than Moses; here they are taken symbolically.)

[55] *Wa-anâ ʿallâmu l-ghuyûb*. Guyard left this out of his text by an oversight.

[56] Again a pun between *Messiah* and the word for *wipe*. The talking with Moses refers to the events at the burning bush and on Sinai, taken again in an Ismâʿîlî sense.

[57] Possibly, but probably not, *satartu bi-hi Muḥammad* rather than *sutirtu bi-Muḥammad* as in the edition; the hand of Mss. A, which I have checked, is not smooth, but does suggest "I appeared in ʿAlî and concealed *Mohammed through him*".

arose Abû dh-Dharr the true [*ḥaqîqî*] among the children of the old [*qadîma*] daʿwa, as support of the Qâʾim of the Qiyâma, present, existent.[59] And religion [*dîn*] was not completed for you until I appeared to you in Râshid ad-Dîn; some recognized me and some denied me; the truth [*ḥaqq*] continues on and those who speak truth [*muḥiqqûn*] continue on, sure in every period and time.

"I am the master of what is [*ṣâḥib al-kawn*]; the dwelling is not empty of the ancient sprouts. I am the witness, the spectator, dispenser [*walî*] of mercy in the beginning and the end. Do not be misled by the changing of forms. You say, so-and-so passed, and so-and-so came; I tell you to consider the faces as all one face, as long as the master of existence [*ṣâḥib al-wujûd*] is in existence, present, existent.[60] Do not depart from the orders of him who received your engagement [*walî ʿahdi-kum*] whether Arab or Persian or Turk or Greek. I am the ruler, dispenser of orders and of will. Whoever knows me inwardly [*bâṭinan*] possesses the truth. Knowledge of me is not perfect unless I say, My slave, obey me and know me in true knowledge of me: I shall make you alive like me, you shall not die; and rich, you shall not be poor; and great, you shall not be abased; hear and pray, you will be advantaged. I am the one present and you are those present in my presence. I am the one near who does not depart. If I punish you, it is my justice; if I forgive you, it is my generosity and my excellence. I am the master of mercy [*ṣâḥib ar-raḥma*] and dispenser of forgiveness and of the clear truth.

"Praise to God, Lord of the worlds; this is a clear explanation."

[58] Here is the great trio for early Shîʿa extremists, Mohammed, ʿAlî, Salmân; their order of precedence and exact interrelations were much disputed. Here it cannot be clear whether ʿAlî or Mohammed is placed higher unless the implications of *satara*, as against *ẓahara*, are known. I have translated *bi-ʿalî az-zamân* as if the writer conceived of many ʿAlî's, as if every imâm were another ʿAlî; but it may be that some word like *ṣadr* or *imâm* has dropped out, and it should be simply, "in ʿAlî, the imâm of the time".

[59] Abû Dharr is another hero of the Shîʿa, like Salmân a companion of Mohammed. The verb *arose* here is *dharra*, an unusual word used among other things for the rising of the sun, and in connection with the great Resurrection. (The sentence runs, "*thumma dharra abû dh-dharri l-ḥaqîqî fî awlâdi d-daʿwati l-qadîma bi-qiyâmi qâʾimi l-qiyâma ḥâḍiran mawjûdan*." Guyard translates, "A ce moment s'est manifesté Abou Dharr qui, parmi les enfants de l'ancienne prédication, est le veritable Qâʾim (chef) de la résurrection, toujours présent, incarné." Apart from the fact that *thumma* elsewhere here marks a transition from one prophet to the next, not "à ce moment", both the order and the choice of words in this translation seem to be arbitrary. The sentence remains puzzling.) One must note that children, here as above with the Messiah, refer to pupils, disciples.

[60] This phrase, which recurs here, is found also in the incipit of one of the epistles read at the Festival of Qiyâma, *Kalâm-i Pîr*, p. 116: "*naḥnu l-ḥâḍirûna l-mawjûdûn*."

Sinân's version of the Qiyâma.

Guyard supposed that this was a writing of Râshid ad-Dîn Sinân himself; but as Guyard points out, this is not necessarily the case: for the introductory phrase about the *words* of Râshid ad-Dîn is also used to introduce the anecdotes of Abû Firâs, and may have been a standard phrase to refer to any piece bearing upon Sinân. Indeed it is conceivable that this is originally a statement from Ḥasan II himself, dressed up later when Sinân came to coalesce in the popular memory with the imâms. We cannot be certain that the apparent differences of approach would not disappear if we knew the Qiyâma better.

However, this may be actually a composition of Sinân's in which he takes upon himself the august role ascribed to him in the third person in the course of it. This would not yet make it clear just what role Sinân claimed. Guyard supposed that he claimed to be the Seventh Nâṭiq, and at the same time that he set up all nâṭiqs as incarnations of God.[61] Dussaud on the contrary supposed that Sinân here claimed to be the asâs of Abû Dharr, who would be the Seventh Nâṭiq; and that he made the asâs be God.[62]

Actually, the expression *ẓahartu bi* is used of the nâṭiq twice (Adam and Jesus); it is implied or used of the asâs (Aaron(?), Peter, ʿAlî) thrice. Some cases are even more ambiguous: in the case of Abraham the speaker appears not as Abraham, it would seem, but as the heavenly bodies he was tempted to worship – which stand in bâṭin for several upper degrees of the ḥudûd: including both nâṭiq and asâs ordinarily. In the case of Moses he may be both Aaron and Khiḍr, the mysterious outsider: an identification that recurs in Ṭûsî's modification of the Qiyâma series, the imâm-Qâ'im, as we have noted. In the case of Mohammed, he is apparently *hidden* in Mohammed, the nâṭiq, while being open in ʿAlî. And Salmân, John, and Abû Dharr are given roles that could easily imply they also were other "faces" of the speaker. The Qâ'im of the Qiyâma is mentioned without being named or explained. No one figure emerges as supreme;

[61] Accordingly he deliberately obscured in his translation the careful distinction made in the text between God, the Lord (*rabb*), and the lord (*mawlâ, walî, ṣâḥib*) who is speaking. That he claimed to be God, Guyard feels is shown by the idea of appearance in several persons at once – a feat presumed to be beyond the capacity of the mere Universal Reason or such. Guyard's translation of *mawjûd* as *incarné* seems to defy gratuitously the universal Muslim prejudice against the idea of incarnation, which makes them consistently avoid such words as *ḥulûl*, which actually do have such an implication.

[62] René Dussaud, 'Influence de la religion noṣairî sur la doctrine de Râchid ad-Dîn Sinân,' *JA*, 1900 (part II), p. 61.

rather all the great heroes – the "rijâl" – show forth God in one way or another.[63]

I should suppose that Sinân was able to make the abrogation of the sharîʿa, originating from Alamût, bear a distinct Syrian flavor – perhaps a first step in the popular divagations which mark the modern Syrian doctrines. Sinân perhaps went further than Muḥammed II in admitting to official favor the popular impressions available in Ismâʿîlism; after all, Syria would be even less well equipped with learned scholars than Alamût or the populous Quhistân.[64] Surely this fragment represents such a development, whether Sinân's or no.

The readers are not presented with a fixed hierarchy, but are enjoined to see in all and sundry manifestations the same being, and to be obedient to the current one; Sinân being only one of many. He says, religion was not complete *for you* until I appeared – this does not necessarily indicate that Sinân's appearance completed all religion, but only the religion to which they were obligated. Such flexible doctrines might not be strictly inconsistent with those of Alamût, but at the same time would simplify the problem of a rough and ready leadership far from the center. Any and all of the ḥudûd seem to reflect the divine, in various ways. The feeling in Abû Firâs as well as in this fragment seems to be that manifestation of divinity is a personal matter, repeated in imprecise degrees according to personal excellence in the heroes in contrast either to the graded *ta'yîd* of the formal doctrine, or to the special exaltation of the one imâm at Alamût. The imâm at Alamût was too far away; the knowledge of God might be arrived at not only through him, but through his aides.[65]

[63] A final blessing in Mss. A was omitted by Mss. B and Guyard, but serves to bring out this universalism. After conventional Shîʿite blessings on Mohammed and his pure family and also on *âli bayti-hi ajmaʿîna* (all the people of his house – including Salmân?), among praises of God it includes the phrase *wa-l-ḥamdu li-ahli l-ḥamd*, "praise to the men of praise".

[64] Sinân's own learning, however, should not be ignored. In his letter to Saladin cited by Ibn Khallikân (but under *Nûr ad-Dîn*), Sinân compares his opponent to an accident of which he himself is the substance. This could be simply a piece of ridicule, like comparing his opponent in the same letter to a pigeon, and himself to a hawk; yet it is also after all a good piece of Qiyâma doctrine, the non-existence of the people of opposition except as accidents to the man of union.

[65] Cf. Ibn ash-Shiḥna, *ad-durr al-muntakhab*, p. 265: on the basis of Ibn Faḍl Allâh 'Umarî he gives the typical impression that outsiders had, the chief doctrines are reincarnation, obedience, and maẓhar – the manifestation of God.

Flavor of the Syrian ḥaqîqa: unregimented hopefulness.

Sinân's people, in the anecdotes of Abû Firâs, appear simple-hearted, kindly, courageous, and on occasion rather thievish; but above all they had great expectations of what life could mean. In these times of Qiyâma this hopefulness blossomed all over. While Sinân, with the force of a personality that inspired unlimited confidence, was consolidating the political strength of the community, the imaginative life of the group was flourishing, sometimes beyond the point where Sinân would have been willing to lead it. Perhaps they interpreted the new dispensation as a general signal for the independent exploration of esoteric truth, rather than as a commitment to any particular synthesis thereof.

Sinân is probably himself responsible for the boldest move of all – the flirtation with Christianity recorded by William of Tyre. Shortly before the death of Nûr ad-Dîn, the Ismâʿîlîs sent an envoy to ask the King of Jerusalem for teachers to come and make them Christian; requiring only that their tribute to the Templars be given up. To the consternation of the king and his court, who had gladly accepted the proposition, the Templars murdered the envoy on his return, and the project came to nothing, though the king apologized profusely. Perhaps the Ismâʿîlîs had thought to become a special Christian order, like the Templars themselves. Considering that some Christian sentiments are frankly acknowledged in the writings of the Qiyâma, an inquiry whether they might not find themselves at least as close to the Christians as to the Muslims might be perfectly genuine. But had such a move come to fruition, it would almost certainly have strained any remaining tie with Alamût.[66]

A move toward Christianity on any deep basis was no light matter, it must be pointed out. The Ismâʿîlîs continued to be distinctly Muslim. Berchem on one occasion supposes that the usual Muslim blessing on the dead would in an Ismâʿîlî hand not necessarily imply that the man was not living, since the same word, *raḥama*, had for the Ismâʿîlîs a special meaning of inspiration as well as blessing.[67] Such special meanings, however, did not usually enter the *language*, but only the interpretation of it. Similarly, there is nothing odd in finding the Ismâʿîlîs quite genuinely using the all-Muslim invocation, "In the name of God", etc.; they used the Koran as did other Muslims.

[66] William of Tyre, *RHC Occ.*, Book XX, Chapter 29, p. 995. Walter of Map, *De Nugis Curialium* (Cymmrodorion Record Series, nr. IX), London, 1923, Ch. xxii, p. 37, writing in 1182, mentions the same event among his moralizing stories.
[67] *JA*, 1897, p. 462.

Sinân on the other hand is certainly not responsible for the most enthusiastic ventilation of popular expectations of the Qiyâma times. At the very time that Sinân was having his fight with Saladin, some of the Ismâʿîlîs – evidently of the Jazr, rather than within the Jabal Bahrâ fortresses themselves – went in for what is described as an orgy of licentiousness, on the basis of an antinomian program. They called themselves the "Pure", the *Ṣufât*; supposedly drawing their inspiration from Sinân's injunction to live together in purity, as befitted the new dispensation. Women are said to have worn men's clothes – that is, presumably, they went about freely in public. From this Muslims could deduce any amount of licence, whether practiced or not.[68]

Sinân was able to forestall Aleppine action, which was threatened – it was the time of the cooperation with the Aleppine lord – and to punish the leaders of the *Ṣufat* in the Jazr himself, on the grounds that their actions were not authorized by him. (Nor was there probably any direct authorization from Alamût; certainly the name does not suggest it.) Sinân was not able to intervene, however, in the case of the Ṣufât of Bâb, a little beyond Aleppo. There the nearby population, with the aid of Turkish tribes, rose against them; they fled to caverns, whence they were smoked out and slaughtered. The traveller Ibn Jubayr, telling of the incident later, rejoiced that now all the inhabitants of Bâb are true-believers.[69]

Popular Shîʿism.

Whether attributable to Sinân or not, in the Syrian ideas of the time we come across a number of popular Shîʿite motifs appearing which we find less clear trace of in the Alamût Qiyâma. As in the doctrine of Alamût, we

[68] Kamâl ad-Dîn, *Taʾrîkh Ḥalab*, transl. Blochet, p. 60.

[69] Tr. Schiapparelli, *Viaggio*, p. 240.

[70] Guyard doubts that this refers to Khiḍr. He supposes that the whole phrase, which in the Koran is ascribed to the figure elsewhere called by that name, is here ascribed to Abraham. The phrase comes immediately following his mention in the series. He supposes that the boat destroyed is taken for Noah's ark, thought of as symbol of Noah's teaching, superseded by Abraham (generally, however, the flood is his teaching, either sharîʿa, or as here daʿwa; and the ark is his bâṭin, which would not be repealed by Abraham); and the child killed is thought of as Ishmael the immolated (whom the Muslims suppose to have been offered to God, rather than Isaac); and the wall is taken for the Kaʿba which Abraham is said to have built. This is ingenious, but dubious. The grammar runs, *thumma ẓahartu fî dawri ibrâhîma . . . fa-kharaqtu s-safînata . . . wa-khâṭabtu mûsâ . . .* Both these "ands" are vague compared to the *thumma* which separates the prophets from each other at other points in this sequence; but since the Khiḍr incidents are generally associated with Moses, it seems reasonable to so associate them here also. There is no need to fear, as Guyard evidently did, that unless he be identified with Abraham, Khiḍr must become the eighth Nâṭiq in the series.

find Khiḍr, the deathless seer, among the heroes of the Fragment Nr. One.[70] Khiḍr had been popular among the Ismâʿîlîs as early as we come to know of their beliefs, though he does not figure in their learned tradition particularly.[71] Malik as-Salâm, on the contrary, who plays a greater role at Alamût, was less prominent among the Shîʿites, and is (perhaps of course only by chance) not found here.

Abû Dharr, an ascetically minded first-generation Muslim specially favored by Shîʿite legend, appears here very prominently. Here he is connected explicitly with the Qiyâma, in almost the only Syrian reference which seems to recall directly that of Alamût, although apparently he does not figure in Alamût sources at all. Abû Dharr may be referred to here as doing part of the work of the Qiyâma, for *dharra*, the verb used, is used of God in this connection. Did Abû Dharr resurrect the earlier believers, spiritually, as retroactive agent of Ḥasan II? Or is he here identified with Ḥasan-i Ṣabbâḥ in spiritual rank, who (as identified with Jesus) prepared the way for the Qiyâma?[72]

The most obvious case of the emergence of popular Shîʿite ideas would be that of reincarnation. Here Sinân is at least not without some complicity. The states of transmigration – which idea need not indeed presuppose a doctrine of human reincarnation – which Sinân recognized by grace in the stories of Abû Firâs may well have been special cases of punishment within a more ordinary routine. Such cases are not unknown within ordinary popular Muslim thought (cf. the *Thousand and One Nights*). It is possible also that Sinân could be consciously giving out a ẓâhir, of which the bâṭin is that mentioned by Ṭûsî (there are animal tendencies within men) or, more likely, that mentioned by the *Haft Bâb* (this is to scare people, like Hell). Those who had not reached the full state of Union in the Qiyâma could have been exposed even after that event to the ẓâhir, in the mind of Sinân. Although transmigration, then, does not yet amount to a regular endorsement of the idea that human life is repeatable till its purification from darkness is accomplished, the man of God being known and obeyed; yet surely the formal justification of that doctrine must have received impetus from Sinân's views. At any rate, it is found among the Syrian Ismâʿîlîs persistently thereafter.[73]

[71] Masʿûdî, *Tanbîh*, tr. Carra de Vaux, 1896, p. 269.

[72] If it is true that the early Nizârîs referred to the Fâṭimid Ismâʿîlîs as the *daʿwa qadîma*, then from the viewpoint of the Qiyâma the idea of *daʿwa qadîma* would merge with that of pre-Qiyâma; since Ḥasan-i Ṣabbâḥ, with his followers, is assimilated by anticipation to the Qiyâma. Abû Dharr, in the latter-day form of Ḥasan, could readily bridge the gap between the two dispensations on this basis, as he seems here to do.

[73] The *Masâlik al-Abṣâr*, tr. by Quatremère, in *Mines de l'Orient*, vol. IV, p. 368. The doctrine is set forth in Guyard's fragments XII, XVI, and XI.

Abû Firâs tells an ambiguous anecdote which intimates the assurance the Syrian Ismâʿîlîs had in themselves and in their leaders, ranged though they might be against all the world. At night on a mountain top Sinân was discovered conversing with a green bird, which glowed with light. He explained to his astonished followers that this was Mawlâ Ḥasan come to ask for help.[74] Now a green bird, in the Muslim mind, must be a martyr; though any Shîʿite hero might be thought of as an honorary martyr, no doubt this Mawlâ Ḥasan will have been Ḥasan ʿAlâ Dhikri-hi s-Salâm, the imâm murdered during Sinân's own lifetime. Ḥasan-i Ṣabbâḥ, if we consider other prominent Ismâʿîlî Ḥasan's, died in bed; and as to Ḥasan the son of ʿAlî, his alleged poisoning is surely not the most distinctive part of the usual tradition about him. Sinân's strength, then, is required to save the imâm at Alamût; nor is there wanting a distinct tone of self-reliance in the mawlâ to whom Mawlâ Ḥasan comes for help.

Sinân's legacy in Syria (1192–1210).

Sinân left the Ismâʿîlîs of Syria straddling a frontier between the Franks and the Muslims, and as such able to maintain some sort of detachment from both. After his death, in 1192, though they continued to pay tribute to Christians, exchanged embassies with them, and were nearly surrounded by them, they kept up relations with the Muslims also – relations which took on a marked importance during the Satr times after 1210. So far as concerned the Muslim world, they acted in concert with the Ismâʿîlîs of Alamût, presumably. It seems that in 1205 they assassinated in Damascus a friend of Khwârazm, the current enemy of Alamût: a man from Qazwîn.[75]

Ibn Taymiyya said much later that the heretical character of the Nuṣayrîs, in the same Jabal Bahrâ, was overlooked by the Muslims during the Frankish period, for the Nuṣayrîs were then too nearly isolated.[76] The heretical character of the Ismâʿîlîs was not overlooked, for they took too active a role in general affairs. After recounting one of Saladin's last conquests, Ibn al-Athîr noted that all the routes in the area were now in Muslim hands, save for such and such, which belonged to the Christians, and such, which belonged to the Ismâʿîlîs.[77]

Nevertheless, until the Crusaders were finally expelled, the Syrian

[74] Abû Firâs, *JA*, ser. 7, IX (1877), 482, Anecdote XIX.
[75] D'Ohsson, *Histoire des Mongols*, III, 172–3.
[76] S. Guyard, 'Fetwa d'Ibn Taimiyya', *JA*, VI: XVIII (1871), 165.
[77] Ibn al-Athîr, *Kâmil*, year 584.

Ismâʿîlîs (at least, those independent in the Jabal Bahrâ) seem to have had more to do with them than with the Muslims. The Crusader territories were much reduced after Saladin's victory, but they still held the coast firmly. Cahen believes that in the Thirteenth Century the Ismâʿîlîs not only paid tribute, but came to be allied, in a subordinate position, to the Hospitallers as their protectors; and that such Christians as they asassinated were enemies of the Hospitallers.[78] Probably indeed the fear of them was more widespread now among the Franks than before the murder of Conrad. It seems that Philippe Auguste of France sent an envoy to them, asking for assurance that they were not plotting against his life on behalf of Richard of England; when they said no, he believed them.[79] Alexius, Emperor at Byzantium, is said to have hired Ismâʿîlîs against the Muslim lord of Kûniya in Anatolia. It was believed that the Ismâʿîlîs even sent assassins once against St. Louis as a youth in France, but then countermanded the project.[80]

Their unwilling tributary position toward the military orders was later given a special explanation by Joinville, in view of the fact that their reputation as assassins was supposed to have gradually come to win them tribute from the kings of the earth. He suggests that the knights, having a head replaceable immediately on the basis of merit, rather than a hereditary one, were not vulnerable to assassination. Certainly the Hospitallers were singled out by the Crusaders as guardians against the Ismâʿîlîs; but it was probably their military prowess in general, at least as much as their form of organization, which made them successful.[81]

In the Ismâʿîlî relation to the Hospitallers we find the earmarks of a pattern which was already adumbrated in Sinân's time: one of accommodation to the more powerful rulers round about. From the beginning, and especially in Syria, the Ismâʿîlîs had been glad to accept the protection or favor of the local rulers. This type of dependence was shaken off when the Ismâʿîlî headquarters were moved to the mountains. Yet even at the

[78] He gives a few details in *Syrie du Nord*, ps. 344, 526, 620, 665 (the Pope forbids the Hospitallers to seek an Ismâʿîlî alliance).

[79] Gestes de Philippe-Auguste, Grand Chronique de Saint Denis, in *Recueil de l'Histoire des Gaules et des Français*, XVII (Paris, 1818), p. 377.

[80] G. Mariti, *Voyages dans l'isle de Chypre, la Syrie, et la Paléstine avec l'histoire générale du Levant*, tr. from the Italian, vol. II, Paris, 1791, gives many of the transactions of the Assassins with the West. P. 52: their envoys were received in Europe in 1232 along with those from Egypt; and the Council of Lyons decreed excommunication of whoever became their partisans, in 1245, with Frederic of Sicily especially in mind.

[81] Cartulaire générale de l'ordre des Hospitaliers, ed. Delaville de Roulx (Paris 1894–7), I, 682–3, nr. 1096: in 1199, the Count of Tripoli gives the Hospitallers forts in fear of the lord of the Assassins.

height of Ismâʿîlî power, under Sinân, we find a clear alliance with the son of Nûr ad-Dîn; then a similar relation appears to have been contemplated with the Frankish Jerusalem; and at the end the Ismâʿîlîs appear to have received the protection of Saladin.

Now, if they looked to the Hospitallers for protection against other powers, such as Antioch, this will have carried on a dependence which was at last made thoroughgoing and permanent by Baybars of Egypt, when he eliminated the Crusaders and reduced the Ismâʿîlîs to an autonomous obedience. It was from Egyptian hands that the Ottomans eventually received them into full fledged *millet* status in their empire: as a backward and dependent religio-social group, autonomously enclaved within the dominant community. Although there were cases of payment of tribute elsewhere among the Ismâʿîlîs, there were none of such an acceptance of protection; and when as a millet, after the fall of Alamût, the Syrian Ismâʿîlîs preserved at least an internal independence, even that was denied to the less accommodating Ismâʿîlîs of Îrân, who, scattered abroad, lost everything.

Sinân provided an answer for Syria, both in the social and in the imaginative sphere, to the failure of Ḥasan-i Ṣabbâḥ's grand endeavor. Though likewise building upon Ḥasan II's Qiyâma, the latter lacked grandeur perhaps, as compared with the answer being given in Alamût. With its exaltation of Sinân in his local hero's role, it lacked no doubt the wide sweep and the intense cosmic concentration we find Alamût exulting in. Yet even the personal character of Sinân's solution may have served to emphasize the local autonomy of his people, and to have given them a coherence quite as important as his sound ordering of their fortresses.

CHAPTER X

RAPPROCHEMENT WITH SUNNISM: THE SATR

If we may reckon a generation as roughly thirty years, till the children have on the average replaced their fathers in active participation in affairs, we have now carried our story of the Nizârîs through four generations. In the first part of the volume we watched the first two generations, caught up in the effort to destroy the Saljûq power. The generation of Ḥasan-i Ṣabbâḥ and Aḥmad ibn ʿAttâsh, in a huge social spasm, had carried the struggle from its fervent, hidden commencements before 1080 to its first great defeat in the fall of Shâhdiz in 1107. It was a new generation which bore the brunt of building and defending the territorial bastion of their hopes which remained, till the death of Buzurgʾummîd. In this second part, we have seen how their children in turn, in the generation of Ḥasan ʿAlâ Dhikri-hi s-Salâm, tired of the unimaginative regime of Buzurgʾummîd's son, and tried a new spiritual venture in the Qiyâma; and how still another generation sought to work out this new way of life, sharing the youthful elation of Muḥammad II, or walking by the sure guidance of Sinân. There remain two further, somewhat quieter, generations of hope and disappointment before Alamût falls, and our story is done.

ROMANCE AND REALITY AMONG THE SUNNÎ POWERS

Clouds over Muḥammad II's reign (1192–1210).

Muḥammad II outlived at Alamût by a comfortable margin his older contemporary of Syria; he outlived the successors of the Sulṭân Sanjar, and Saladin; and therewith outlived also the Resurrection quiet of his own long reign. In his later years, the Ismâʿîlîs began getting into trouble with power after power among the Sunnîs – but on an almost casual basis: the Sunnîs seem sometimes almost to have forgotten the presence of their old enemies, and to attack them only when reminded of them by the course of politics or by chance.

First of all, trouble stirred with the nearest neighbors. Since the death of Sanjar, the local territorial lords were relatively untroubled by the larger powers; they happily carried on their disputes among themselves. The Ismâ'îlîs supported a rebellion of the Istandar of Rûyân against his Mâzandarân overlord, it seems, and even received certain villages in reward. They were reckoned as very strong in the area now; and two assassinations followed – an 'Alid of Ṭabaristân, as well as a Bâwandid of the ruling family.[1]

Meanwhile, trouble also broke out with Sîstân, which played a role of inimical neighbor to the Quhistânî Ismâ'îlîs like that of Mâzandarân to those of Rûdbâr. To be sure, our record is very scanty, and the fighting recorded for the first time in more than sixty years, in the *Ta'rîkh-i Sîstân*, two years after Sinân's death, may not be so unusual as it there appears. But a few years later, the Sîstânîs were cooperating in their Quhistân campaign with a new great power from the north, Khwârazm, which was to upset all the political life of the Iranian lands in its meteoric career, and in the end usher in the Mongols.[2]

Khwârazmshâh and the Middle Eastern universal monarchy.

The last remnant of Saljûq power in Îrân disappeared in 1194, being replaced in its last strongholds by a sequence of more or less independent generals. The more recent Syrian Ghâzî tradition had taken refuge in Egypt, which is forever a centralized state, and from which Syria was now to be ruled so far as it had any political unity at all. But in this world of transient, personal Sunnî states – held together otherwise only by the inescapable sharî'a – there appeared two other political ideas of some interest.

The most spectacular power of the time was that of the Khwârazmshâh. Less solid than the Ayyûbid power of Egypt, the growth of this power which centered on the merchants and nobles of isolated Khwârazm far in the north of Transoxania was more rapid, and also more ambitious. Already as a rebellious vassal of Sanjar, the lord of Khwârazm had been building his power; at the end of the 12th Century the current Khwârazmshâh, having already inherited the general position once held by

[1] Ẓahîr ad-Dîn, *Ta'rîkh Ṭabaristân*, p. 264; Ibn Isfandiyâr, p. 256; cf. Rabino, *JA*, 1949, ps. 314–316. Years 590–606.

[2] *Ta'rîkh-i Sîstân*, yrs. 590, 596. Ibn al-Athîr, *Kâmil*, year 596.

Sanjar, was in the course of expanding his rule over as much as possible of the former Saljûq territory.

He was heir, accordingly, to the tradition of the Middle Eastern universal monarchy, as had been the Saljûqs; in a line which can be traced back through the whole Iranian, and finally Assyrian, Sumerian tradition. Especially in Muḥammad Khwârazmshâh's hands (d. 1220) the idea was distinct, however, from what it was with the Saljûqs, whose glory had been that of the tribe. With the Khwârazmshâh it would seem to have been a purely personal adventuring, erratic and finally disastrous in policy. Barthold points out that such administrative continuity as remained from of old was now given almost a death blow, in the course of the quarrels between Muḥammad and his mother.[3] The imperial idea itself had degenerated under warlord conditions to one almost on the level of the Alexander romance. It was scarcely to reappear save under the early Mongols – who were out to conquer the world from a different point of view – and Tîmûr; till it receded at last conventionally into a purely Persian nationalism.

Soon after the quarrels with Mâzandarân and Sîstân reopened, Alamût found itself at outs with the expanding Khwârazm. The latter had for the moment succeeded to the Saljûqs in ʿIrâq ʿAjamî, and brought thither its imperial zeal. It attacked Mâzandarân; and than about five years after Sinân's death, the Khwârazmian general, Miyâjiq, made a trick raid against Alamût. After a failure in Baghdâd, Miyâjiq asked their protection as if he were in trouble; they evacuated a village for his benefit; whereupon he betrayed them, killed some of their leaders, took spoils, and went off.[4]

Soon after, the Khwârazmian troops were formally attacking the Ismâʿîlîs from Qazwîn, spurred on by the traditional local enmity.[5] It seems that one night the Ismâʿîlîs seized a hill fort called Arslân Kushâd, very near Qazwîn, and by morning had so entrenched themselves as to be able to prevent passage along the road. The rulers in the vicinity were unable or unwilling to do anything; so a local shaykh with a wonder-working reputation, ʿAlî al-Yûnânî, wrote the Khwârazmshâh, revealing to him his (the Shâh's) secret thoughts, and warned him to come to the aid of Qazwîn. The Khwârazmians came, set siege, and took

[3] W. Barthold, *Turkestan Down to the Mongol Invasion* (2d ed., trans. H. A. R. Gibb; E. H. W. Gibb Memorial, n.s. V [London, 1928]), 379–80.

[4] Râwandî, *Râḥat aṣ-Ṣudûr*, ed. Iqbâl, p. 390.

[5] Râwandî, cf. E. G. Browne, summary, *JRAS*, 1902, p. 881. Ibn al-Athîr, *Kâmil*, yr. 602.

the place on terms. When the main body of the Khwârazmian troops had left, however, the Ismâʿîlîs re-entered by a secret passage, and did away with the Khwârazmian garrison stationed there. The shaykh sent for Khwârazmshâh again; and after a two months' siege, the Ismâʿîlîs were willing to surrender if their garrison were allowed to go free. They said they would come out in two parties; if the first party were molested, the second would not follow, but would stay in the fort and fight. The Khwârazmians agreed, and the first party came out, paid their respects to the Khwârazmshâh, and went off. The besiegers waited for some time before they realized that this first party had in fact been the whole garrison. ... This time the fort was razed.[6]

The lords of Ghûr, a family which supplanted that of Maḥmûd of Ghazna in the Afghan lands, were the most notable rivals of the Khwârazmshâhs for the honor of Iranian empire. They made much of their ancient family allegedly derived from the ancient heroes; and, while they seem not to have had the universal pretensions entertained at Khwârazm, did a good deal of conquering themselves. They also came across the Ismâʿîlîs – it is said of one of them that as he was marching through Quhistân it was brought to his notice that there was an Ismâʿîlî town nearby, so he turned aside to sack it. They made more than one campaign; and liked it so much, that when the Ismâʿîlîs had already offered obedience to Ghiyâth ad-Dîn, when he was conquering Khurâsân, his brother Shihâb ad-Dîn came along and attacked again, expelling a chief from his town. The Ismâʿîlîs had to ask Ghiyâth ad-Dîn to intervene, and allow the chief to be restored.[7]

Not many years after, Shihâb ad-Dîn was assassinated. He had many enemies, and as so often in these cases there has been much inconclusive debate as to who killed him. Since one source says that his killers were half of them circumcised and half uncircumcised, it has been suggested that the Ismâʿîlîs got together on the job with a certain Indian tribe which was also accused, having been recently subdued by him.[8] At any rate, the Ismâʿîlîs claimed the deed (saying it was done on behalf of

6 Qazwînî, *Âthâr al-Bilâd*, ed. Wüstenfeld (Göttingen, 1848), p. 194, year 595.

7 Ibn as-Sâʿî, *Jâmiʿ al-Mukhtaṣar*, ed. Mustafa Djawad and Anastase-Marie de St. Elie (Baghdâd, 1934), Vol. IX, p. 52; year 597. Ibn al-Athîr, *Kâmil*, yrs. 597, 600. Cf. Ibn Muyassar, year 597, evidently referring to the same defeat of the Ismâʿîlîs as prominent enough to be noted even in Egypt.

8 Cf. the discussion in Raverty, tr. Minhâj-i Sirâj, *Ṭabaqât-i Nâṣirî*, p. 485, n.; and in the more recent A. B. M. Habibullah, *Foundation of Muslim Rule in India* (Lahore, 1945), p. 79.

Khwârazm) according to Nasawî, who carried on negotiations with them not long after.[9]

The Caliph Nâṣir and the civil empire.

The Caliphate of Baghdâd now figured among the powers of the age. Especially from the time of the Caliph Qâdir (991–1003) it could count on a backlog of respect as ultimate center of propriety and honor; respect which a Caliph like Mustarshid was already trying to use in gaining his independence from the Saljûq tutelage. The Caliph Nâṣir (d. 1225) seems to have used the tradition of civil rule embodied in his office to cultivate a second political idea, rivalling that of Muḥammad Khwârazmshâh. The Caliphate had become primarily an accrediting agency for Muslim sovereigns, with practically no authority on its own. But its potential moral authority was enormous. Nâṣir, even though personally a Shîʿite, evidently tried to make of it a center for an imaginative reintegration of Islâm.

Nâṣir's predecessors had already acquired a minimum of power around Baghdâd, during the Saljûq decline; Nâṣir is chiefly known for his making the Caliphate again, briefly, an aggressive territorial power, carrying its force beyond the limits of ʿIrâq. Even so, the territorial claims which he pushed were limited. More universal within Islâm was his attempt to form a special sort of league of its chiefs under his leadership – putting into a more effective and possibly more fruitful form the accrediting function which he already had.

On the one hand Nâṣir drew many of the lords of the time into common bonds under his personal leadership in his *futuwwa* order. This has been compared, in its formal structure, to knighthood; for it set up, in the name of chivalrous ideals, a relation of honor between each initiate and the master who initiated him. The futuwwa had been developed among the artisan classes as a means of religious and social training and cohesion. It gave them a strength that proved turbulent, and it may be that when Nâṣir had himself initiated, and made himself head of the order, it was for the practical purpose of controlling these classes.[10] But Nâṣir extended it so as to bring in many of the rulers of the time; and here the idea

[9] Md. Nasawî, wr. 1245, *Histoire de Jalâl ad-Dîn Mankoubirti*, tr. O. Houdas, Paris, 1895, ps. 356–7.

[10] Cf. Salinger, *Proceedings of the American Philosophical Society*, XCIV, No. 5 (October, 1950), 481. He criticizes Taeschner's theory that the futuwwa was designed to restore the Caliphal power at large.

possessed possibilities of political discipline in Islâm on the basis of honor. At the same time, Nâṣir readily made alliances to bolster the Caliphal prestige: against Muḥammad Khwârazmshâh on the one hand, expanding as he was at the expense of lesser chiefs, and against the more glaring usurpers (as Minkulî in the Persian ʿIrâq) on the other.

These alliances, and the futuwwa itself, were no doubt designed to maintain the *status quo* – in which Nâṣir had given the Caliphate a large stake. But while Nâṣir's policy was politically conservative, the futuwwa ceremonial must have helped bring to the Muslim community at large some of the color and personalized loyalty which an atomized legal Sunnism could make no effort to provide, unless at Mecca once a year. Nâṣir's way of rejuvenating the Caliphal authority was not without promise.

On the contrary, the Ismâʿîlîs retained their reputation as subverters, assassins, and protectors of refugees. In spite of the fighting around Qazwîn, the Khwârazmshâh could be accused of inciting the Ismâʿîlîs at the same time to assassinate his vizier.[11] Some time in the reign of Muḥammad Khwârazmshâh, the lord of Zawzan in Khurâsân was accused of Ismâʿîlî tendencies, and had to flee to their Quhistân fortresses for protection. (He was lured back to Zawzan later by the Khwârazmian governor, betrayed, and killed.)[12] The horror of the Ismâʿîlî name was still so great, when it was brought to the attention, that we find recorded in Baṣra, as late as the opening of the Thirteenth Century, a massacre of such as were deemed Bâṭinites – whether actually Nizârîs or not, we cannot know.[13]

Yet as an all-Islamic political idea, Ismâʿîlism was by now at best latent. From the time of the Qiyâma a rather greater proportion even of those assassinations which were committed are to be associated with outsiders' squabbles, particularly in Syria. The Ismâʿîlîs were not yet of course an impotent millet: they continued to be a potential threat at all points in Islâm. Yet the scope of their activity was generally in fact local, and comparable to that of the warlords about them. In sharp contrast to the Sunnî caliphate, they seemed to reap the disadvantages without the benefits of their unyielding dissent.

Breach between Muḥmamad II and his heir.

Within the Ismâʿîlî community, moreover, the dispensation of the

[11] Ibn al-Athîr, *Kâmil*, yr. 596; cf. Râwandî, E. G. Browne, *JRAS*, 1902, p. 881.
[12] Nasawî, *Histoire de Jalâl ad-Dîn Mankoubirti*, tr. Houdas, p. 47.
[13] Ibn al-Athîr, *Kâmil*, year 600.

Qiyâma cannot have been too permanently satisfying in its pure form. The grand viewpoint, which alone would be set before the eyes as the ideal, would require too intensive a level of spiritual experience to suffice most. And though the pageantry of the Qiyâma dispensation, with its imâm-Qâ'im figure, might fill in the gap somewhat, the tension with the outside world, which the Qiyâma had exalted into a metaphysical absolute, must often have seemed at best a galling necessity. One suspects that as the great Saljûq campaigns died away, and the Ismâ'îlîs themselves became less aggressive, a generation would be arising which did not know the constant expectation of an interruption of all normal activities by outside attack. Not only in Quhistân, but even in the smaller, mountainous areas, there must have been an increasing expectation of peaceful agriculture and trade with the world at large; an expectation which we later find clearly expressed during the time of Satr. In such circumstances, the Qiyâma would be no longer an answer to a historic crisis, but rather at best a spiritual luxury.

Even while he was elaborating his doctrines of the infallible character of his own imâmate, Muḥammad II had to watch the very son to whom he had given the irrevocable naṣṣ in childhood become dissatisfied with his father's ways, and long to become part of the large, orthodox world which his father had so decisively turned away from.[14] The heir to infallibility was turning to the world just proclaimed nonexistent, and looking to it for hope of honor, and perhaps for profit material and spiritual. Rashîd ad-Dîn and Juwaynî eagerly record the breach between the manifestation of God's word and his pledged successor in the same role where none may call to account. They suggest that each was in fear for his life from the other; that in public assemblies they avoided each other, going armed; and that before his father's death, Ḥasan III had already prepared alliances among the Sunnî princes far and near, pending his accession.

Nevertheless, Muḥammad seems to have made no attempt to deny that the naṣṣ had been actually given to this son; nor did he use any actual violence; nor was there any contest of the succession when Muḥammad finally died. There were tales of poison as causes of his death. But this seems unlikely: poisoning is an easy charge, and Muḥammad had lived a life of average length. Ḥasan in his efforts to convince the world at large that he had rejected his ancestors' faith, though he cursed his father and grandfather, is not recorded to have claimed to have done away with the accursed.

[14] Juwaynî, *Ta'rîkh-i Jahân Gushâ*, pp. 241 ff.

It is not clear therefore how far the breach actually went; yet that it embittered the later years of Muḥammad II is surely likely. He could perhaps see in the situation the fact that he had, whatever level of spiritual growth he urged upon his followers, more authority as simple Shîʿa imâm than as Qâʾim; and his son after him would have the same authority by the same old-fashioned loyalty, again whatever was his theory in turn.[15]

The Khwârazmshâh's romanticism, and the Caliph's likewise, were due to be swept away, along with the lesser powers, in the Mongol holocaust and the associated confusion. They possessed for the moment, however, a charm and a specious grandeur which the old Ismâʿîlî hopes seemed to have forfeited. Into this futility, then, Ḥasan III led his Ismâʿîlîs, on his father's death; making himself a Sunnî amîr on the usual pattern, ruling a state among states. Taking advantage of the notoriety of his ancestors, Ḥasan moved from an anomalous position on the margin of Islamic society to an equally anomalous position in the spotlight. He became known far and wide, amid general acclamations, as Ḥasan *Naw-musulmân*, the new Muslim.

ḤASAN III's ISLAMIZATION (1210–1221)

Restoration of the sharîʿa.

The declarations he had already made before his father's death paved the way for Ḥasan's ready acceptance as an orthodox ruler by the Caliph, by Muḥammad Khwârazmshâh, and by the other lords to whom he sent his announcement of religious reform upon or soon after his accession in 1210. The sharîʿa was re-established in the Ismâʿîlî dominions after forty-seven years' abeyance, and the younger generation had to learn at least to seem able to fulfill the ritual duties of Sunnî Muslims. Ḥasan ordered the building of mosques; and he invited in from the neighboring parts of ʿIrâq ʿAjamî and Khurâsân Sunnî jurists to instruct his people in their use.

The Ismâʿîlîs of Syria chose the Shâfiʿite form of the law, among the four forms available to Sunnîs;[16] perhaps this was chosen elsewhere also. There was probably no question of restoring the old ẓâhir Shîʿite law;

[15] One wonders whether he may not have been waiting for a grandson to whom the naṣṣ might have properly continued, before finding some way to be rid of the embarrassment of an unbelieving imâm. The grandson did not come in Muḥammad's lifetime.

[16] Ibn Sâlim ibn Wâṣil al-Hamawî (d. 1298) *al-Mufarraj*, mss. of the Bibliothèque Nationale, Arabe 1702, fol. 169 r.

even had it been possible to set up again the former Ismâʿîlî sharîʿa, it would have been unacceptable to the Sunnî world, which had been moving toward the position that only four particular forms of the sharîʿa could be accepted. No longer was it possible, as in the days of Sanjar, to argue that so long as they follow the sharîʿa, even in a Shîʿite form, they must be immune to Muslim attacks. Nor will there have been any strong interest among the Ismâʿîlîs themselves in whether the law was Sunnî or Shîʿite: it was an outward imposition in any case – taqiyya, in the sense in which Ḥasan II had eliminated it at the Qiyâma; if its purpose were assimilation to the ẓâhir population, it may as well be as like theirs as possible.

Getting his Ismâʿîlîs accepted by the world had its difficult moments. He sent his mother – said to have been a pious Sunnî – on pilgrimage to Mecca. She gave great amounts in charity, had many wells dug (this was a standard charitable procedure for the wealthy when they pilgrimaged – the way led through deserts), and was treated with highest honors by the Caliph. But when the ʿIrâqî pilgrimage caravan reached Mecca, with the Alamût delegation in it, it came into confict with the Syrian caravan; which blamed it for harboring such heretics, and tried to prevent the ʿIrâqîs from performing the pilgrimage. At last four Ayyûbid princesses intervened insistently with the Meccan authorities in the ʿIrâqîs' favor, and all ended well.[17]

Ḥasan left no stone unturned to make clear his new orthodoxy. After he had received recognition at Baghdâd and Mecca, he still had to convince the incredulous Qazwînîs, his neighbors. To prove to them the truth of his Sunnî claims, he had some learned Sunnîs come from Qazwîn to go through the library at Alamût and burn all books deemed heretical. At the same time he solemnly cursed the imâms his predecessors, dissociating himself (and by implication, his people) in all possible ways from their tainted past.

Ḥasan's authority at home.

In this course he was accepted with relative alacrity by the Sunnî powers, in spite of some first doubts; even by the skeptical Qazwîn. Nor was he rejected by his own people. Quhistân and Syria, as well as Rûdbâr, obeyed him; and he was able to leave his capital in Daylamân,

[17] Ibn Wâṣil, *Mufarraj*, fol. 168 v.

visit and campaign in foreign lands for two years, and return with no difficulty.[18]

This acceptance of Ḥasan III's move seems impressively complete. It can be accounted for logically. The imâm was endowed with special grace from God, quite apart from any theological commitments; his commands might legitimately lead to anything – including the aid and the blessing of Sunnî princes; or even the denial of his own excellence. Whatever he might order was good for the soul; it was not to be questioned by lesser men. Ḥasan never denied his own right to rule; and the right to rule was a sufficient claim to make, in such a community, for only the divine ta'yîd, inspiration, could justify it.[19]

But it was probably not logic that gave Ḥasan his power. The people were more attached to the community, to its independence and the hereditary leadership with seemed inseparable from communities at that time, than to the theories which explained or supported that leadership. The community was ready for new experiments. The Qiyâma as such no doubt meant a great deal to some few, who left their mark in doctrine; but now they must go along with the bulk of the new generation, rationalizing the changes as they might, ready for the more fundamental and lasting allegiance to carry them to new things.

These new things amounted in fact to a rather grandiose attempt to make of the Ismâ'îlî mountain strongholds a first class state. Ḥasan ordered the building not only of mosques, but of baths in every village. This ought to convert each village into a well-ordered town: for the mark of a town is a mosque and a bath. By this one order he had turned his

[18] So it stands in Rashîd ad-Dîn. But there are suggestions of some resistance. In a curious passage of the *Rawḍat at-Taslîm*, which we shall examine, it is possible to suppose that Ḥasan is represented as killing the *Zabân-i 'Ilm*, the Speaker of the Truth. Nor is it clear that all the Syrian Ismâ'îlîs were persuaded to follow the new policy without the intervention of Aleppine power. Defrémery reports from Dhahabî that Ḥasan III sent at his accession a messenger to the ruler of Aleppo, not only announcing the new policy, but asking that ruler to kill the former representative of Alamût in Syria so as to make place for a new one. Presumably this refers in fact only to Ismâ'îlîs surviving in the Jazr and Aleppo itself, not to the Jabal Bahrâ forts, which nevertheless also accepted Ḥasan's innovations. *JA*, 1855, p. 39. But cf. Yâqût, who, in speaking of the Ismâ'îlîs, s.v. *Jabal Bahrâ*, says most of them are under Aleppine rule.

[19] Tâmir 'Ârif, in *al-Adîb*, May 1953, p. 45, quotes a letter said to be from Ḥasan III to the Ismâ'îlîs of Syria, in which he invites them to follow certain prescriptions of the sharî'a on the grounds of his own position as ḥujja of God and cause of day following night. If this be genuine, one would be tempted to place it in his first year, before his announcement of Sunnism; but it could easily have followed it, and served as a means of enforcing his commands. The letter includes an admonition to repair the bath at Kahf – supporting the Sunnî reports of his concern with baths and mosques.

mountain hamlets into a well-peopled kingdom; a fancy in keeping equally with the desperate grandeur of the Ismâʿîlî past and with the great and futile endeavors of the Sunnî present.

All this had a very practical side, however. The Quhistânî Ismâʿîlîs had already suffered much at the hands of the Ghûrid armies. The Syrians were also in danger: we read that in 1210 the King of Jerusalem (who was now reduced to Acre and the coast) was raiding their lands.[20] In the case of the Syrians, certainly, the new dispensation meant a precious respite. Perhaps as a result of betting on the wrong side in inter-Frank quarrels, the Ismâʿîlîs murdered the son of the lord of Antioch, and brought down against them, at the fortress Khawâbî, a formidable army, in 1214. Surely it was largely due to Ḥasan's new policy that the ruler of Aleppo now vigorously intervened, sending troops to their aid and forcing the Antiochians to retire, though not quite unavenged.[21]

Rather unexpectedly, in Quhistân the new policy turned to the practical benefit of the Sunnîs. We find that at the time of the Mongol catastrophe at the end of Ḥasan's reign the head of the Quhistân Ismâʿîlîs outdid himself in hospitality to Sunnî refugees, overwhelming them with gifts, and affording the nobility and learning of Khurâsân a shelter in his mountains from the storm.[22]

Military adventure abroad.

In his external affairs Ḥasan made perhaps the bigger splash. One gathers from Nasawî that he first was allied with Khwârazm, making the *khuṭba* in Muḥammad's name;[23] very soon he became allied with the Caliph. That the Caliph valued his friendship is shown by his treatment of his pilgrimaging mother; the special honor shown to her is said to have angered the Khwârazmshâh, slighted by comparison, so as to have precipitated his enmity to Nâṣir.[24] The Caliph also intervened to make possible his marrying noble wives from the Gîlân territorial nobility. Evidently these had some scruples about giving their daughters to the alleged "new-Muslim", which were set aside effectively by the Caliphal letters. Among the wives which he then took was the daughter of the amîr of

[20] Continuator of William of Tyre, *RHC Occid.*, II, 316.

[21] Abû Shâma, year 612, has the Franks take 300 prisoners from them. Cf. Defrémery, *JA*, 1855, ps. 40–41. According to the continuator of William, the Ismâʿîlîs continued their interference in Christian affairs, assassinating Adam, guardian of Little Armenia, in 1219: *RHC Occ.*, II, 347.

[22] Minhâj-i Sirâj, *Ṭabaqât-i Nâṣirî*, tr. Raverty, p. 1197.

[23] Nasawî, *Histoire*, tr. Houdas, p. 355.

[24] Nasawî, p. 21, also makes this point.

Kûtam, claiming ancient Iranian descent, who became the mother of the next imâm, Muḥammad III.[25]

This sort of alliance inaugurated incidentally a new kind of territorial aggression for the Nizârîs: the direct conquest of alien territory by formal armies without settlement or conversion. Villages had been taken before; but only as it were in a rectification of frontiers. Now they took towns frankly for the tribute from them.

Ḥasan seems to have gone into his chief military adventure more in the spirit of an excursion – an enormous hunting expedition – than of a campaign. It was evidently intended no risks should be taken. His great military project was made jointly with Muẓaffar ad-Dîn Ûzbag, lord of Âdharbâyjân to the west of Daylamân, and in alliance with the Caliph and the Caliph's allies; against Minkulî, who had been an Âdharbâyjânî general, but had made himself independent as lord of ʻIrâq ʻAjamî. First, overwhelming force was gathered for the alliance; Ûzbag paying most of the bills.[26] Not only did the Caliph send troops to aid the allied armies of Ḥasan and Ûzbag, but the prince of Irbil and others were summoned, and troops came even from Syria. After a year and a half of preparations (Ḥasan living evidently as Ûzbag's guest), all these descended upon the rebel lord, and killed him near Hamadân. (Even so, they scarcely deserved to, having entered mountainous defiles where, had he been clever, he could have harrassed them into destruction.)[27]

The loot was not evenly divided. Most of the area, Hamadân, Rayy, and Iṣfahân, the heart of modern Persia, went to Ighalmish, a slave of Ûzbag's brother.[28] But Ḥasan received more than did the Caliph and his allies, apparently: he received two towns, Abhar and Zanjân, and their environs. Abhar is the town which had successfully appealed to the Saljûqs against the Nizârî fortress in its vicinity long ago; now it was handed over with the blessing of the Caliph himself. Rashîd ad-Dîn notes that they stayed in Ḥasan's possession a number of years – thus implying they were lost near the end of his reign or soon after. After all

[25] Probably he had had at least a daughter by former connections. His daughter is said to have married a Bâwandid, Kînakhwâz, whose son not much later became the founder of a fresh line of Ispahbads of Mâzandarân. Such a marriage is likely to have taken place while Ḥasan was still ruling, and if so, the daughter will have been born before that.

[26] Ḥasan was evidently heavily subsidized by Ûzbag; but whether this means he used mercenaries in addition to his own mountaineers is not clear.

[27] Rashîd ad-Dîn has Ḥasan go to visit Ûzbag in 610, and places the defeat in 611. Ibn al-Athîr places it in 612.

[28] M. Qazwînî, in his notes to his edition of Juwaynî, *Ta'rîkh-i Jahân Gushâ*, pp. 407 ff., gives full data on the political events in ʻIrâq ʻAjamî in this period.

this, Ḥasan returned home as if for a rest. He did no more warring, it would seem, after these first two years, though he continued, by assassination or by embassy, to be a loyal ally of the Caliph. In his next chief action he returned to the method of sending assassins; who (disguised as pilgrims) got rid of that same Ighalmish whom he had helped to set up in power, but who had rebelled, turning for help to Khwârazm.[29]

After only ten years of his labors, Ḥasan died of dysentery. His vizier, into whose hands he had put the guidance of his son Muḥammad III, either believed – or in order to rid himself of the Sunnî element, feigned to believe – that Ḥasan's wives had poisoned him. (Rashîd ad-Dîn says the accusation was false.) He had a large part of Ḥasan's womenfolk executed. It does seem unlikely that these women, aliens dependent upon Ḥasan for their dignity, would have done such a thing; and since neither Rashîd ad-Dîn nor Juwaynî, in all their hostility, finds reason to suggest that any other grouping killed him, we may suppose that Ḥasan died naturally.[30]

Probability of Ḥasan's sincerity.

It is a question that raises curious side-issues, how sincere Ḥasan III was in his Sunnism. It is an interesting coincidence, noticed by Berchem already, that the Caliph Nâṣir and Ḥasan were both in an anomalous position. Ḥasan derived the power which he was putting at the service of orthodoxy from his position as a Shîʿite imâm; the Caliph in turn was using the power derived from his Sunnî eminence at the biddings of a Shîʿite heart. May not both have secretly agreed to be Shîʿite within while Sunnî without? Berchem cites the inscription on the Talisman-gate at Baghdâd, where Nâṣir used an innocuous-sounding formula to express his devotion: naming *ad-daʿwat al-hâdiya*, "the true-guiding summons", as his leading

[29] Nasawî, *Histoire*, tr. Houdas, p. 23: yr. 614. D'Ohsson, *Histoire des Mongols*, III 173–4, says, without a reference, that assassins were also sent, on behalf of the Caliph, against the ruling sharîf of Mecca – but they killed his brother by error instead.

[30] The *Dabistân*, vol. II, 447, has Ḥasan III kill his father, and then Muḥammad III avenge his grandfather, Muḥammad II, on those who had killed him. This interpretation, which rejects Ḥasan III entirely, contrary to usual Ismâʿîlî procedure, might suggest nevertheless that the womenfolk killed were held responsible for inciting Ḥasan III against his father – not for killing Ḥasan himself.

[31] M. van Berchem, 'Baghdad Talismantor,' *Archaeologische Reise im Euphrat- und Tigris-Gebiet*, ed. by F. Sarre and E. Herzfeld (Berlin, 1911), I, 34. There have been contrasting interpretations of the Talisman gate inscription and decorations. These show a human figure with his hands at the heads of two dragons. Berchem supposed this was Nâṣir victorious over the two great enemies: the Khwârazmshâh and the Nizârîs; it is more likely to be a simple astrological figure: a child between the two

principle. But this happens to be the standard Ismâʿîlî phrase for the Ismâʿîlî daʿwa.[31]

Nâṣir showed Ḥasan such very special favor that one could almost suppose the two to have been fellow-believers in secret: either Nâṣir was at heart not Twelver, as assumed, but Ismâʿîlî – which seems highly unlikely; or Ḥasan had been secretly converted not to Sunnism, but to the Twelver Shîʿa; which is possible. Nâṣir not only accorded Ḥasan's conversion recognition as a major event, seeing that legal decisions were everywhere registered giving the Ismâʿîlîs full rights as Muslims; this might have been expected in a Caliph, as the official beneficiary of the change. His intervention in Gîlân in favor of Ḥasan's marriages was surely service beyond the call of duty, as was the unusual honor shown to Ḥasan's mother on the pilgrimage in despite of both Khwârazmshâh and the Syrians; for after all, territorially Ḥasan was no very great prince. It is curious to note that apart from Ûzbag the other ruler who showed Ḥasan special favor at this time, perhaps at the Caliph's behest – the Ayyûbid of Aleppo – had adopted Shîʿism in that ever-Shîʿite town.[32]

In turn, Ḥasan was noticeably loyal to the Caliph. This is supposed to have gone so far that when the (pagan) Mongols invaded (Sunnî) Khwârazm territory,[33] allegedly at the invitation of the (secretly Shîʿite) Caliph, the Ismâʿîlîs claimed that Ḥasan sent them a friendly embassy even before the invasion. Juwaynî, who, unlike Rashîd ad-Dîn, doubts this claim,[34] admits that they were the first to make their submission after the Mongols crossed the river Oxus. Ḥasan's own people, certainly in the next generation, regarded all Ḥasan's Sunnism, and his other political manoevering, as sheer Shîʿite taqiyya.[35]

Nevertheless, it seems unlikely that Ḥasan was playing a triple game: using an Ismâʿîlî position for Twelver purposes in a Sunnî disguise. Ḥasan shows no signs of being either so adventurous or so deep: he was probably neither Ismâʿîlî nor Twelver, but just what he claimed to be.

nodes of the Dragon, i.e., the points at which sun and moon can pass and may be eclipsed. I owe this point to the kindness of W. Hartner.

[32] Gordlevski has found that the Shihâb ad-Dîn Suhrawardî who was sent by the Caliph as a revered man to browbeat Khwârazmshâh was accused of being an Ismâʿîlî! – along with that Suhrawardî Maqtûl also, of whom such an accusation is rather to be expected. Ivanow, *JBBRAS*, Vol. XXII (1946), ps. 68–70.

[33] Even though Khwârazmshâh went so far as to reject the ʿAbbâsid Caliphate, he did not adopt any Shîʿite *line* of imâms in place of the former ʿAbbâsids, and so could hardly be called Shîʿite in the contemporary sense.

[34] Juwaynî, writing under the Mongols, would regard it as an honor to have submitted to them early.

[35] Cf. the letter, quoted by Tâmir ʿÂrif, cited just above.

The Muslims he associated with personally seem to have been Sunnîs.

Ḥasan was not only in alliance with Nâṣir, but also at first with the Khwârazmshâh, and most especially with Ûzbag. This latter alliance was based, according to Rashîd ad-Dîn, upon real friendship, evidenced by the long visit at Ûzbag's capital at the beginning of Ḥasan's reign. Both the war against Minkulî and the assassination of his successor, which are ascribed to the stimulation of Nâṣir, were carried out against revolted *mamlûks* (slaves) of Ûzbag's. It seems most likely that Nâṣir's chief interest in Ḥasan - and also in Ûzbag – was in winning them against the Khwârazmshâh, who came to be Nâṣir's great opponent. Nâṣir did not succeed at once. For a while Ḥasan continued the *khuṭba* to Muḥammad Khwârazmshâh; but already in honoring Ḥasan's mother over the Khwârazmids Nâṣir had worked for a division between them; and finally the breach between Ḥasan and Khwârazm was shown to be complete when Ḥasan's men assassinated Ighalmish for becoming a Khwârazmian vassal.[36]

Ḥasan's concern to convince his Sunnî neighbors of Qazwîn of his orthodoxy even after all the important rulers were satisfied seems more than would be necessary if Sunnî approval was wanted only for a simple front. To have an inquisition in his libraries, a burning of books, and a public cursing of his father and grandfather is a great thing when recognition by all but a few burghers is already won, unless it satisfied a conscience.[37] More cogent demonstration of his Sunnism, perhaps, is what we can guess of Ḥasan's family circumstances. Rashîd ad-Dîn speaks of Ḥasan's mother, who went on pilgrimage, as not only a believer, but *zâhid*, ascetic: which implies more knowledge of her than simply that she professed Sunnî Islâm. Ḥasan chose four Sunnî wives; moreover at his death his sister, presumably the daughter of this Sunnî mother, was so closely associated with these Sunnî wives that she was accused with them

[36] Even the Ismâ'îlî alliance with the Mongols was not unalloyed, as witness the Quhistânî hospitality to refugees from them. There is a curious item, cited by Ivanow, *JRAS*, 1938: a prophecy written from Alamût to Khwârazmshâh (but recorded later) that there should come a king from east of the Oxus, setting up a Shî'ite Caliph that might come from the Daylamân mountains. This ought to have something to do with the Nâṣir-Khwârazm fight, if Khwârazmshâh at one time tried to set up an 'Alid in rivalry to Nâṣir.

[37] Von Hammer notes that there remained heretical works for Juwaynî to discover later, at the fall of Alamût; he therefore supposes that this proves Ḥasan's hypocrisy. This could do so only if one supposed that all the books later found had existed as unique copies at the time of Ḥasan III, none being in private Ismâ'îlî hands; which even the Qazwînîs must have realized was unlikely. Von Hammer, *History of the Assassins*, Engl. trans. p. 154. To be sure, he might be afraid lest Qazwînî propaganda reverse his good fortune.

of his death; it is easy to suppose that she, like his mother, was Sunnî.

Under such circumstances, it is easy to believe that Ḥasan's relations with his father were strained, as they are pictured. Muḥammad II had been accustomed to rule in unprecedented exaltation since he was eighteen, and was moreover strong-minded enough to have forged for himself a good part of the justification for his own majesty. It would be surprising if Ḥasan would not resent this father who expected of him an impossible role, cooped up withal in a religion as small as were its fortresses restricted. Freud quite aside, we might well expect him to embrace readily any viewpoint which would most fully liberate him from a predetermining paternal influence, and permit him to go out into the world. To do this he need only adopt his mother's faith as against his father's. He sought the friendship of another newly enthroned ruler (Ûzbag had also had family troubles before coming to power) who saw in him no unnatural claims; and even stayed away from Alamût itself for a long time – as a general, not as a god. Orthodoxy might bring him both the honor – even the respect, perhaps – of the world; and the freedom of his own soul.

THE AFTERMATH OF ḤASAN's CONVERSION: THE DOCTRINE OF THE SATR

The relaxation of Ḥasan's policy: transition into the reign of Muḥammad III.

Though Ḥasan was not the only man in Alamût to be chafing under the restrictions of an overly demanding Qiyâma, yet his attempt at a total break with the past was personal to himself, and not finally supported by the community. The Ismâ'îlîs were still proud of their tradition, still conscious that they had a mission above other peoples (though they might not be sure what it was); and, it must be said, they were attached to their own ways.[38] Perhaps already in Ḥasan's own time this last trait began to reassert itself, when assassination was substituted for an army

[38] The conscious continuity of the Nizârîs is shown, incidentally, in a Syrian inscription. Muḥammad III is mentioned as overlord at the time, and his genealogy traced back to Ḥasan II; but not beyond on either of the two lines possible, the one Ḥasan II himself used, to Buzurg'ummîd, nor the one leading to Mustanṣir of Egypt. The great Qâ'im of the Qiyâma is regarded as the proximate founder of the line. Berchem, *JA*, ser. 9, IX (1897), 482. Likewise Ḥasan III seems to have traced his own line primarily to Ḥasan II – whose ancestry is given summarily as "ibn Nizâr" – in the letter cited by Tâmir 'Ârif, *al-Adîb*, May, 1953, p. 45.

in implementing even the pro-Sunnî policy, and Ḥasan was content, after his great excursion, to sit at home.[39]

The policy of outward conformity with Sunnism continued officially under Muḥammad III at least for some years, nevertheless, even though in fact the sharîʿa ceased to be much enforced. We have the witness of Ṭûsî, who was certainly writing under Muḥammad III, that his was a time of satr – which in his thought meant the acceptance of the sharîʿa.[40] The Khwârazmian Mankûbirtî expected his envoy to persuade the Ismâʿîlîs under Muḥammad III to mention his name in the khuṭba, the Friday sermon; a ceremony carried out only under the sharîʿa.[41] The vizier appointed by Ḥasan III continued to rule for some time; and Juwaynî and Rashîd ad-Dîn, who speak as if all the work of Ḥasan III were undone in his son's reign, are unable to mark any specific moment of turnover. It seems indeed likely that Ḥasan's policy was never formally renounced. At the end, when Rukn ad-Din Khwurshâh came to the throne, he is said by Juwaynî to have ordered all his subjects to behave like Muslims.[42] Yet he was in no position to undertake great reversals in policy; Juwaynî reports that his people threatened to kill their youthful imâm if he left the fortress to surrender to the Mongols (they could afford to kill him, as he had a son already).[43] One must suppose that an ineffective taqiyya was simply being reactivated for the emergency.[44]

The policy suffered a gradual change in spirit, however. This Rashîd ad-Dîn and Juwaynî are inclined to attribute to Muḥammad III himself; but it seems to have begun while he was yet a boy. It is said that from the start those who continued to follow the sharîʿa were persecuted: no doubt there would be a reaction, after Ḥasan's personal insistence was gone, against those who took the Satr too seriously. We have the story

[39] Qazwînî, *Âthâr al-Bilâd*, s.v. Alamût, lists this assassination, ironically enough, among the famous ones undertaken by the heretics.

[40] *Rawḍat at-Taslîm*, p. 87. Berchem, *JA*, 1897, p. 489, reports that a Kahf inscription of 635, in Muḥammad III's reign, has Koranic verses in it "for the first time" in the Syrian inscriptions; but that it also refers to the imâms. This is at best ambiguous evidence.

[41] Nasawî, *Histoire*, tr. Houdas, p. 350.

[42] *Ta'rîkh-i Jahân Gushâ*, p. 259/60. According to Rashîd ad-Dîn, the head of Girdkûh at the end of Muḥammad III's reign held the title of *qâḍî*.

[43] Ed. Qazwînî, p. 129–30.

[44] But compare the continuator of Ibn Isfandiyâr, who says that Muḥammad III was called "*al-Qâ'im bi-amri-llâh*" – Qâ'im being a title specifically of the Qiyâma not of the Satr. However, this is not a very detailed witness. Ibn Isfandiyâr, *History of Ṭabaristân*, abr. trans. E. G. Browne (E. J. W. Gibb Memorial, II [Leyden, 1905]), 259. Ordinarily he is given, like his father but unlike Ḥasan II, a Sunnî type title in *ad-Dîn*. The *HBBS* says that the series of imâms following Ḥasan II are all to be called *Qâ'im*, and the *term* might occur as legitimately as the term *imâm*, and be misunderstood.

in detail from Minhâj-i Sirâj, how the Quhistânî Ismâʿîlîs complained of their learned chief, who was so generous to Muslim refugees from Khurâsân at the time of the Mongol invasions. They wrote to Alamût – evidently a year or so after Ḥasan's death – saying that he was spending all the Ismâʿîlî substance on outsiders; and Alamût summoned him home, replacing him with a military man, who was more community-minded – though even he took care that Sunnîs should not be molested in his territory.[45]

With Ḥasan III the dispensation of the Qiyâma had unmistakably come to an end. If the Ismâʿîlîs were not to become Sunnîs, they had to develop during the following years a new interpretation of their faith consistent with the actual course of events. We may call the doctrine which was adopted the doctrine of *Satr;* for it explained the policies of Ḥasan III and his son as a return to that *satr*, occultation, which had preceded the appearance of Ḥasan II in the Qiyâma. In the name of the Satr, the new doctrine toned down the Qiyâma system to the point where it could be lived with by ordinary people, in ordinary times. It meant further triumphs of popular notions, apparently, as against the learned tradition; nevertheless, the new system was fairly elaborate, if we may judge by the form it takes in the works ascribed to Ṭûsî, which alone seem datable to this period.[46] Pious Ismâʿîlîs were not at a loss to account in theological detail for what had happened.

Adjustment of the Qiyâma to history: a new mood shifts the meaning of old terms.

Even if Ḥasan had not introduced so notable a break with the past, the Qiyâma doctrine would sooner or later have needed revamping for men whose lives in one way or another continued subject to the gross vicissitudes of history. The Qiyâma was no private fulfillment of various individual lives, as it might have been among Ṣûfîs, but inescapably a cosmic event, with a before and after in history. When the "after" began accumulating its own sequence of significant events, it was high time to explain why the true faith still suffered the buffets of historical fortune, even in its quiet retreats.

The greatest of these buffets was the blow dealt it by Ḥasan III himself; and that very blow determined under what auspices the Qiyâma was to

45 *Ṭabaqât-i Nâṣirî*, tr. Raverty, p. 1198.

46 The same ideas reappear in later writers like Abû Isḥâq, but are then likely to be overlaid with still further strata.

be reinterpreted. With the brusque end of the Qiyâma, the official disciplining of the doctrine ceased for the time being; and its revamping was left to the popular imagination, which could interpret in its own terms the relation of the new state of affairs to the Qiyâma, unrestrained by the high demands of the learned imâms. In many minds, the most important thing about the Qiyâma seems not to have been that it made possible intercourse with God, but that it removed the veil of taqiyya – removed the ritual law; the sharîʿa and all the prosaic bars to imaginative richness that went with it. This was after all its clearest result in practice. From this time on, therefore, *qiyâma* and *haqîqa* tended to be identified with what was technically only one phase of them: the ending of taqiyya. Though the original mysticism was never really given up, the whole structure of Qiyâma thought and terminology underwent a seachange in sympathy.

The most obvious conclusion which popular feeling might have already come to, and which Ḥasan III's action simply confirmed, was that qiyâma and taqiyya depended freely on the will of the current imâm.[47] But the justification of such a conclusion required a change in the sense of the word *Qâ'im*. The Qâ'im was now to be distinguished from the ordinary imâm simply in that he chooses to appear for the moment with greater power.[48] Every imâm was potentially Qâ'im; and the Qiyâma was a perpetual condition, made apparent however only occasionally – not only at the culmination of all things, but from time to time as a grace to be withdrawn at pleasure. With Ḥasan III the grace had been withdrawn, and taqiyya reimposed; as Ṭûsî said, it was a time of *satr* – concealment of the imâm – during which the imâm cannot be known in his true sense, and the sharîʿa must again be obeyed.[49]

When the implications of one term – such as *Qâ'im* – were changed, related terms were liable to the same fate. All must answer to the same changed mood. So now with *satr*. If every imâm is in truth a Qâ'im, then every withdrawal from Qiyâma is a concealment of the true existence of the imâm. The word, therefore, which had been used for the absence of the imâm, as a person, from the world's sight now came to mean something quite different. The word *satr* was evidently given the same broad

[47] The need to accept as true what the *current* imâm decrees, in contrast to any other, is often stressed in the *Rawḍat at-Taslim*, e.g., p. 66. In this doctrine Ṭûsî could borrow arguments to the same effect from Ḥasan-i Ṣabbâḥ (e.g., that the teaching of former imâms is only fragmentarily known), but these arguments hardly suffice to interpret Ḥasan III as a regular imâm! Ṭûsî is forced to go much further.

[48] *Rawḍat at-Taslîm*, p. 94.

[49] *Ibid.*, p. 87.

implications as were recognized in *taqiyya* by Ḥasan II. Then, instead of meaning dissimulation of the bâṭin merely, it had come to imply, under popular influence, the positive display of all those parts of the faith which were not bâṭin, but external: the whole sharîʿa. Now *satr* came to imply not just the hiddenness of the imâm, but the suppression of all that the imâm in truth stands for. A renewed state of satr called, therefore, for an abandonment in appearance of the Ismâʿîlî truth far more complete than had been expected before – extending even to the acceptance of a Sunnî, not the old Ismâʿîlî ẓâhir. It was as if one deliberately chose the most false sort of ẓâhir available, once the truth was to be suppressed at all. The Ismâʿîlîs must have all of their faith, or nothing.[50]

Compared with earlier periods of satr, accordingly, the Satr following the advent of Ḥasan III was a new sort of thing. When Muḥammad ibn Ismâʿîl and his descendants were in satr, they were hidden from the world at large, but in theory not from their own followers. When Nizâr and his son were in satr, they were hidden from everyone: it is implied in the stories of Ḥasan II's birth that even Muḥammad ibn Buzurg'ummîd was unaware of who was the imâm. In the Satr following 1210, the person of the imâm was visible to all the world: it is his status that was hidden. The situation bears more resemblance, in fact, to the previous periods of *kashf* – unveiling or openness – than to those of satr. At the height of Fâṭimid glory, before the satr of Nizâr, the person of the imâm was visible to all as a worldly ruler, but the sharîʿa was in force (the Ismâʿîlî sharîʿa at that time), and the true status of the imâm was known only to the initiates. In the Qiyâma an Ismâʿîlî community, forced to express its universal claims only in its remote holdings, had proclaimed in the Qiyâma a super-kashf to outdo the historical Fâṭimid kashf. Any recurrence now to what had been mere kashf would be satr to these Ismâʿîlîs.

Satr and qiyâma as alternating periods.

Once the rough intervention of Ḥasan III had landed affairs in this state, Ismâʿîlî learned piety was quick to make the best of a bad situation. We have, now, an alternation of periods of sharîʿa and of ḥaqiqa; or, what amounts to the same in the new approach, of satr and of kashf, of taqiyya and of qiyâma. Something like this had been allowed for in the classical doctrine; this is now revived and reapplied. Ṭûsî assures us

[50] This practical merging of satr (tasattur) and taqiyya is illustrated in the *Rawḍat at-Taslîm*, p. 93.

THE PERIODS OF THE PROPHETS ÛLÛ L-‘AZM

(the great week of seven thousand years)

	date before or of Hijra	*Prophet*	*Waṣî*	*Imâm-Qâ’im*
I:	5000 b.H.–4000 b.H.	ADAM	Seth	Malik Shûlîm
II:	4000 b.H.–3000 b.H.	NOAH	Shem	Malik Yazdâq
III:	3000 b.H.–2000 b.H.	ABRAHAM	Ishmael	Malik as-Salâm
IV:	2000 b.H.–1000 b.H.	MOSES	Aaron (or Joshua)	Dhû l-Qarnayn
V:	1000 b.H. (in fact 600 b.H.)–Hijra	JESUS	Peter	Ma‘add
VI:	Hijra (that is, 622 C.E.)–1000 H.	MOHAMMED	– ‘Alî –	
	(500 H. – in fact, 483 and 559 – the two trumpet blows of the Qiyâma at Alamût)			
VII:	1000 H. (that is, 1592 C.E.)–2000 H.	THE QÂ’IM: the great sabbath (Qiyâma)		

calmly, "the period of each prophet of the ẓâhir of the sharîʿa is called the period of satr; and the period of each qâʾim, who possesses the ḥaqîqas of the sharîʿas of the prophets, is called qiyâma."[51] That is, Mohammed himself introduced the period of satr! The norm of this sequence in the old doctrine (where the contrast was between ẓâhir and bâṭin) was by millennia, six of "satr" (the six prophets "ûlû l-ʿazm" (and one of Qiyâma. It must now be explained therefore how it is that before the end of the current millenium, that of Mohammed the sixth of the prophets ûlû l-ʿazm, the periods should likewise alternate from imâm to imâm.

Ṭûsî speaks of the millennium following Mohammed as the beginning of the Qiyâma: "Mohammed ... was the seal of the periods of the sharîʿas, and the opening [*fâtiḥa*] of the period of Qiyâma"; or, "The period of Mohammed ... was the beginning of the period of Qiyâma, and the Qiyâma is special to the imâm (to his mention peace [li-dhikri-hi s-salâm]) who is Qâʾim of the Qiyâma."[52] Accordingly, later in the same chapter the Prophet can hope to be left in his grave not more than half a day – half a millennium – before the Qiyâma should arrive: technically, in the middle of the sixth millennium. One gathers that the completion of the Qiyâma is not expected until the end of a millennium after Mohammed, which would indeed be the beginning of the seventh millennium, the great Sabbath; but that the beginning of the Qiyâma occurs as a special honor to Mohammed within his period of sharîʿa.[53]

In his period not only is the Qiyâma itself temporarily initiated, but throughout it the imâm, due to be the lord of the following and last millennium, is in unusual evidence. Mohammed speaks more clearly of him than do the other prophets; and moreover he "at the same time entrusted his *nubuwwa* to his [ʿAlî's] imâm, and united the sharîʿa to the qiyâma."[54] Hence kashf or satr, haqîqa or sharîʿa during this period can vary freely according to the disciplinary needs of the believers.[55]

Restriction of the privilege of waḥda to the men of taʾyîd.

When it thought of the Qiyâma primarily in terms of getting rid of taqiyya, the popular imagination was presumably content to leave the

[51] Ṭûsî, *Rawḍat at-Taslîm*, p. 49.
[52] *Ibid.*, pp. 102, 104; the mention of the grave, reference to which follows, is p. 118.
[53] *Bayân-i Shinâkht-i Imâm*, fol. 13b.
[54] Ṭûsî, *Rawḍat at-Taslîm*, p. 104.
[55] In the very late pseudo-Abû Isḥâq we find an explanation of why the Qiyâma did not bring all things to an end, which might be consistent with this picture, and would

awesome rigors of a strict waḥda, spiritual Union, to the elite. Ḥasan III's action likewise encouraged such a relegation of the stage of waḥda to a few (if to any!); it was in such a sense then that the language of the Qiyâma about the three viewpoints was reconciled with the doctrine of total Satr. It was declared that the waḥda, the divine Union, was open only to a few: for all practical purposes, it would seem, to a newly emphasized ḥujja alone. Along with this went a rehabilitation of the stage of the people of Order, *tarattub;* which represented now again the limit to which ordinary men could aspire.

In the *Haft Bâb*, as we have noticed, it was expected that each human being should ascend through the condition of the people of Order to that of Union. But in the *Rawḍat-at-Taslîm* the people of Union are commonly identified with the people of ta'yîd – those who by their nature from birth are subject to the divine *fayḍ*, inspiration.[56] Thus Ṭûsî says at more than one point that the men of union, waḥda, never have fallen from necessary being.[57] He gives other indications that the men of waḥda are no longer to be thought of as potentially all mankind, but as only the ḥujja and perhaps others of a like rank.[58] Thus, even Salmân, who is here referred to as the type of the believer, rather than as the ḥujja, remains in the imperfect viewpoint of the *mubâyana* – while only ʿAlî is

precise it: that the Qiyâma at Alamût was only the day of Union; that the actual day of Judgment was to follow. *Kalâm-i Pîr*, trans. p. 61.

[56] Nâṣir-i Khusraw, in the *Shish Faṣl*, ed. Ivanow (Leiden, 1949), p. 53, typically restricts the ta'yîd to the nâṭiq, asâs, imâm, bâb, and ḥujja. Here the ḥujja has taken the place of the bâb, and the nâṭiq and asâs drop out as superfluous, leaving only the imâm and the ḥujja. But the imâm is obviously above all that.

[57] *Ibid.*, p. 60. "ahl-i waḥdat ba-ḥaqîqat az wujûb na ba-yuftâda and": the people of Union, in the ḥaqîqa, have not fallen from Necessary Being. Ivanow's translation, "those who profess the oneness of God . . . in reality cannot fall out of being by necessity" obscures deliberately the category being spoken of, which is not the professors of union, but the participators in it: after all, every Ismâʿîlî professed the oneness. Throughout Ivanow's treatment of these matters he seeks to replace the reference to mystical union (which he cannot understand: he even refuses to use the word *mystical* in any technical sense, equating it roughly with all nonsense and imposture) with a variety of alternates. With such an approach, it is not surprising that the simple past of the Persian becomes a "cannot fall" which Ivanow apparently finds necessary to satisfy common sense. Later on, p. 65, Ivanow translates almost the same phrase more accurately: "they have not really become separated (lit. they have not fallen) from the world of Unity"; here Ivanow feels a contrast to the other instances, and supposes that Ṭûsî is here speaking loosely, and means only the imâms! It seems to be only the substitution for *wujûb* of the more dating *ʿâlam-i waḥdat* which has prevented Ivanow from translating this passage as cavalierly as the other.

[58] *Rawḍat at-Taslîm*, pp. 65–67, 136.

[59] *Ibid.*, p. 116. It must be noted that *mubâyana* does not mean, "the element of rational attitude" introduced into "the imitative following of the prescriptions of the law", as Ivanow would translate *mushâbahat-i sharîʿa.* What Ṭûsî is discussing is not

associated with *waḥdâniyya*, unity, and ḥaqîqa.[59] This gives to the middle rank the dignity of Salmân himself, restoring the people of Order, tarattub, to grace. For in the *Haft Bâb* it was stressed that these must perish quite like the people of Opposition.

But the original outlook of the Qiyâma could not be gotten rid of altogether. The problem involved – the problem of those who felt themselves already resurrected, emancipated, and under no need to come back under the yoke of the Law – is illustrated in a story about Satan selected by Ṭûsî. In the Ṭayyibî literature we find Adam's fall interpreted as his letting out secrets of the daʿwa to the inquisitive Iblîs (Satan); thus the Fall of Adam is only another instance of the recurrent prescription of secrecy.[60] In Ṭûsî, rather, it is the duty of Adam to end the Qiyâma which had fulfilled the preceding seven thousand years, and institute instead the first of the new sharîʿas. He was persuaded by Iblîs, who as a notable teacher of the Qiyâma doctrine did not want to go back to the puerilities of the sharîʿa, to renew the Qiyâma teaching prematurely. Adam was then corrected, and forgiven, by the Qâʾim of the Qiyâma of the time.[61]

Ṭûsî admits that the special persons who have achieved waḥda, and can receive the pure wine of the taʾyîd, need not be bound by the taqiyya.[62] In the *Maṭlûb al-Muʾminîn* he allows for substituting an awareness of God for the sharîʿa; but only if one can truly and totally maintain that awareness. For whoever neglects the sharîʿa without achieving a very rigorous spiritual perfection is neither of the sharîʿa nor of the ḥaqîqa, but a mulḥid, a heretic, without religion at all.[63] Accordingly, we sometimes find mentioned a distinction between the *strong* and the *weak*, the strong being usually only the people of waḥda, however, in the *Rawḍat at-Taslîm*.[64]

In the *Bayân-i Shinâkht-i Imâm* much later there is what looks like a

an attempt by the Shîʿa to bring good sense to bear among the people who were slaves to custom; but a metaphysical division between those who see certain distinctions not evident to the senses (which *liken* the distinct things to each other) and those who confuse them. Here as always one must refer to the text and not to the translation.

[60] B. Lewis, *BSOS*, IX (1938), 691; cf. also Strothmann, *Gnosistexte* [sec.] A, [part] X, p. 34.

[61] *Rawḍat at-Taslîm*, pp. 49–50.

[62] Ṭûsî, *Rawḍat at-Taslîm*, p. 113.

[63] P. 54–5. One cannot help wondering at this point whether this is not a rather patent castigation of the ordinary Ismâʿîlîs of Ṭûsî's own time, who must have generally fallen into this category!

[64] P. 60. Occasionally there may be a passage in which the believer is urged to seek for this ḥaqîqa himself, becoming one of the strong after being weak; but generally the passages which seem in the translation to indicate this will be found upon examination of the text to be at most ambiguous in this respect.

resolution of the two points of view on who may be among the people of waḥda. There the author is quite direct in asserting that the people of waḥda are precisely the people of ta'yîd, which means simply the ḥujjas. But the strong, there, have a position expressly different from the people of waḥda. There both strong and weak are among the people of tarattub, Order; and some of these, the strong, can become a sort of secondary people of waḥda and ta'yîd, even while in the strictest sense only the ḥujjas can achieve either waḥda or ta'yîd. Apparently the Satr had imposed the idea that waḥda was no longer available to all; but from the Qiyâma was retained the idea that in some sense it must be available to all; and the result was a compromise. It is curious to note that among these imperfectly "strong" is ranked Mohammed himself.[65]

Restrictions on manifestation of the imâm: ḥujja as sole channel of access.

As sole exemplar of the waḥda, of the ḥaqîqa, the ḥujja takes on a new importance in the Satr. From the time of Ṭûsî forward, though Ḥasan-i Ṣabbâḥ continues to be the great ḥujja, the term more insistently refers to a figure who is the sole access to the imâm's truth at all times, and is a recurrent inspired (ta'yîdî) entity equally with him.[66]

For Ṭûsî this doctrine of the ḥujja can become quite complicated; probably reflecting past or present experience of the sect, which of course he does not cite. In recounting the ḥudûd he lists the muta'allim (learner), mu'allim (teacher), dâ'î, bâb-i bâṭin (gate of the bâṭin), the zabân-i 'ilm (tongue of knowledge), the ḥujjat-i a'ẓam (greatest ḥujja), and the dast-i qudrat (hand of power). He describes each, in the usual fashion; and notes that the zabân-i 'ilm can be regarded as the same as the ḥujja. He then describes the ḥujja in terms which would fit Ḥasan-i Ṣabbâḥ (he represents the imâm when he is hidden, defeats human reason with his proofs, and founds the ḥaqîqî da'wa of the imâm). Then he notes that ḥujjas, though they appear differently, are actually all one; and proceeds to describe the relations of the two new ḥudûd, the zabân-i 'ilm and the dast-i qudrat – as if these were both possible forms of the ḥujja. The latter is the ẓâhir ruler when the grace of the imâm is withdrawn, and the da'wa is not preached in words. The zabân-i 'ilm, whose business is to bring truth, must submit to his orders, or lose his ẓâhir

[65] *Bayân-i Shinâkht-i Imâm*, folio 5 and 8 v.

[66] One comes across a similar doctrine in Fâṭimid Ismâ'îlism sometimes, though it does not play so important a role. Cf. Zahr al-Ma'ânî, pp. 62, 65, in Ivanow, *Rise of the Fâṭimids* (London, 1942).

existence; likewise, the dast-i qudrat must submit to the truth of the zabân-i ʿilm, or lose his salvation. On occasions, the zabân-i ʿilm may be given the functions of the dast-i qudrat as well as his own.[67]

A few pages before, he had referred to two different forms of the manifestation of the imâm; and the occasion for the rule of the dast-i qudrat seems to be connected with the harsher of these two forms. The imâm is either "lord of slaves" or "lord of hearts", according to whether he is trying or rewarding the people; whether he is requiring of them a purely physical submission, or graciously allowing them to approach the inner truth. Consequently his daʿwa can sometimes be one of deeds and not of words at all, whereas at other times it is of both.[68] The former case is that singled out for the appearance of the dast-i qudrat.

Evidently Ḥasan III was the "lord of slaves", and he possibly had a figure associated with him who could be regarded as the dast-i qudrat; and who perhaps came into conflict with another figure, of ḥujja rank, who maintained the ḥaqîqa teaching. For at no other time in the history of Ismâʿîlism was the daʿwa of words totally suspended in favor of the imâm's appearance purely as a secular ruler.[69] Moreover, the Satr is freely interpreted as a time of wrath, such as would befit the dast-i qudrat – and, from the believer's viewpoint, Ḥasan III.[70] After Ḥasan's death, so complex a way of retaining the proof of God on earth could be dispensed with; but probably a ḥujja continued to be necessary in the form of a Zabân-i ʿilm.

There may have been some reading back of this situation into previous times of Satr. If not of the relation between Muḥammad ibn Buzurgʾ-ummîd and his son, where it would be a bit strained, at least one could

[67] *Rawḍat at-Taslîm*, pp. 97–98.

[68] Ṭûsî, *Rawḍat at-Taslîm*, pp. 94 ff. At this point Ivanow makes one of his most unfortunate slips in translation: where the text refers to a daʿwa of deeds not of words, "*daʿwat fiʿlî kunad na qawlî*", Ivanow inserts a "merely": "not merely of words". Ivanow then points out that this is the same in substance as the alternative, "of both deeds and words" – and supposes a corruption in the text! Here as so often Ivanow has presupposed an evolutionary development, as Ismâʿîlî doctrine, which would make sense by his naturalistic standards; and is thrown off by the reality, which is not truly evolutionary at all.

[69] Ivanow, who notes that nowhere else in Ismâʿîlî literature are the terms used, supposes that the *dast-i qudrat* would refer to Buzurgʾummîd and his son, as "dictators" when the imâm was absent; this has little to commend it, unless one suppose that Muḥammad Ibn Buzurgʾummîd (who refused to recognize Ḥasan II) is the dast-i qudrat referred to who may destroy a rebellious zabân-i ʿilm, but will be punished for doing so. *Rawḍat-i Taslîm*, pp. xlv, lxiv. It may be noted that some of the things said of the dast-i qudrat and the zabân-i ʿilm might apply to the vizier and the chief dâʿî of the Fâṭimids; perhaps the two terms were originally used in connection with them.

think of the relation of Badr al-Jamâlî, the generalissimo in Egypt, to Ḥasan-i Ṣabbâḥ; Badr had the power, and could persecute Ḥasan, who was ḥujja and could be well called the tongue of knowledge; and such a relation between the dast-i qudrat and the zabân-i ʿilm is precisely allowed for by Ṭûsî. It must be recalled that Ṭûsî also speaks of satr as having been introduced precisely under Mustanṣir.[71]

Of a wider import is the possibility that the dast-i qudrat idea may have been read back into the time of the first split between the Shîʿa and Sunnism. The later *Bayân-i Shinâkht-i Imâm* gives to the first (Sunnî) Caliph, the detested Abû Bakr, a rank among the four figures who initiate any prophetic period. He as *ḥakîm-i sharîʿa*, "lord of the sharîʿa", is revealed on the level of the sharîʿa only; the prophet on the level of sharîʿa and of bâtin; the imâm on the level of the ḥaqîqa as well as the other two levels; and the ḥujja on the higher levels but not on the level of the sharîʿa. Abû Bakr, as completer of Mohammed's outward revelation, spreading it over the earth, must appear on the same level only as the "people of Opposition", else they would not follow him – which is necessary, since they must be ruled by the sharîʿa. Even ʿAlî must obey Abû Bakr, so that the ignorant "people of Opposition" will be willing to do so also.[72]

Though without these special titles, much the same role is given the Sunnî Caliphs in the *Rawḍat at-Taslîm* itself.[73] The sharîʿa appears in these cases as the prerogative, a divinely sanctioned prerogative, of the Sunnî Islâm. Perhaps in fact the ḥâkim-i sharîʿa and the dast-i qudrat, who have very similar roles, are one; or at least result from the same

[70] *Kalâm-i Pîr*, p. 62/66; *Rawḍat at-Taslîm*, pp. 93–94. In the *Bayân-i Shinâkht-i Imâm*, fol. 3, the ẓuhûr-i maʿnawî (bâṭin appearance) of the ḥujja alternates with the ẓuhûr-i shaklî – the ẓâhir appearance – of the imâm: which latter is a punishment.

[71] *Rawḍat at-Taslîm*, p. 120. Mustanṣir would be the only imâm besides Ḥasan III who could be regarded as being at once in satr, since he allowed the truth about Nizâr to be suppressed, and at the same time possessing a worldly rule; unless ʿAlî himself be so considered – who indeed obsiously exercised taqiyya from the Ismâʿîlî point of view. It is not explained how the Fâṭimid kashf, here still implicitly admitted, is to be reconciled with the new indentification of sharîʿa, in force under the Fâṭimids, with satr; no doubt there were degrees of satr – if anyone troubled himself about this – and perhaps these new figures helped explain these somehow.

[72] Folios 13–14. This is surely the correct interpretation of the text, though Ivanow punctuates and interprets it quite differently, admitting his bafflement. He wants to identify the "completer", the *tamâm-kunanda*, with Mohammed (*Bayân*, transl., p. 45), but this is impossible. He excludes Abû Bakr apparently, because of a preconception that the hated Caliphs could never appear among the Shîʿite ḥudûd. (But compare the curious Ṭayyibî reference to the first three caliphs as messengers to the jinn, *Gnosis-texte*, A, I.)

[73] P. 116.

circumstances. In the Satr, Ḥasan chose Abû Bakr's Sunnî form of the sharîʿa to restore, not that of the Shîʿite imâms. It would seem probable that the idea that the true sharîʿa is the Sunnî one entered the Ismâʿîlî theology itself at this point. The persistent orientation of the Ismâʿîlîs to the larger Sunnî world – rather than to squabbles with other Shîʿite sects – makes for this curious twist, where the triumphant Sunnism is grudgingly given its due.

The outcome of Ḥasan's démarche.

In principle, the Satr – the introduction of which was the unexpected upshot of Ḥasan's moves – sets off the last two generations as distinctly as the Qiyâma sets off the two which preceded it. The imâms ruled not as God on earth, but officially as chiefs of a worldly community, with worldly titles in *ad-Dîn*.[74] And in fact, throughout the period a certain cordiality to non-Ismâʿîlî scholars and notables persisted; the Ismâʿîlîs never quite cut themselves off from the world again.

Nevertheless, as regards general tendencies, throughout the episode of Ḥasan III there was more continuity in the Ismâʿîlî tradition than interruption. Ḥasan's very orthodoxy was treated in the spirit of the Qiyâma, as a reimposition of taqiyya; and probably served chiefly to accentuate the popular influence in Qiyâma doctrine. Even his cultivation of the sharîʿa served to reinforce the old attitude that Sunnism, in its power, was the great opponent somehow to be dealt with: if it could not be destroyed, it could not really be ignored, and finally even entered into the ḥudûd. His grandioseness also – the ponderous expedition as the Caliph's ally, his elaborate certification with all the rulers of Islâm – together with his futility, marginal in Islamic thought and power as he continued to be, exhibit the Ismâʿîlî predicament: a people increasingly helpless at each new effort to assert its majesty.

Von Hammer no doubt perceived something of this, in a distorted way, when he charged Ḥasan III with hypocrisy.[75] In addition to his charge that the heretical library was not burned, he noticed that Ḥasan was willing to receive a refugee from the lord of Mâzandarân, Bîstûn of Rûyân, and refused to extradite him save in return for a village or so. Von Hammer considered his refusal to let his guest be killed as proof of

[74] Names in *ad-Dîn* – Splendor, Support, etc. "of the faith" – had become common among Muslims already, and were now adopted by all the notable Ismâʿîlîs. (They had not been quite unknown before, witness *Râshid ad-Dîn Sinân.*)
[75] *History of the Assassins*, Eng. trans., p. 154.

Ḥasan's dastardliness. I would be inclined to see in his willingness to sell him for a village an opportunism of the same kind that led him to seek glory as well as spiritual profit from the faith of the outer world.[76] But in either case it is a continuation of a role already played before, where the Ismâ'îlîs, seated at the margin of the world's game, received in quiet asylum the refugees now of one side and now of the other. Even Satr could make little difference; the role was played to the end.

[76] It is not in fact clear just what year the refugee arrived; it may have been a few years before Ḥasan's accession. Ẓahîr ad-Dîn, p. 79 ff. In the continual struggles between the local ruler of Rûyân, his nobles, and the Mâzandarânî suzerain, the weaker party – which was sometimes that of the nobles – several times allied itself with Alamût.

CHAPTER XI

THE LAST GENERATION OF FREEDOM

LEARNING AND LIFE UNDER THE SATR (1221–1256)

The generation which flourished in the reign of Muḥammad III was the last to maintain its independence. It was not a generation that could be called great. Though they continued in principle the Satr policy of their fathers, it was only halfhearted with them; and though they turned in practice to the Qiyâma faith of their grandfathers, it was an emasculated Qiyâma, which no longer sought exclusively the face of God, nor despised the world. The imperious zeal of their grandfathers' great-grandfathers was almost forgotten along with the Saljûq power itself which those had opposed. Yet though their life might bring forth no striking new departure, it remained distinctive, and to that extent great: holding fast to its assurances of special divine guidance, its own persistent social integration, its own traditions of dedication to a community which (even tucked away in its own mountains, now) could still face the rest of the world on equal terms.

The respect for learning: Naṣîr ad-Dîn Ṭûsî.

In all the chief Ismâʿîlî areas we find that community cultivating the learned disciplines. Juwaynî tells us he was eager to see the library at Alamût, it being famous for its scientific collection, apparantly. Presumably it was a collection of long standing; but it was only at this time that we find scholars of repute in the outside world making use of it. We know of a number of such scholars residing at the Ismâʿîlî courts – under constraint as they claimed. The most prominent of these was Naṣîr ad-Dîn Ṭûsî, perhaps the most important philosopher of his age in Islâm.

Ṭûsî was a decade older than Muḥammad III, having been born in 1201 – in the non-Ismâʿîlî town of Ṭûs. His father was an astronomer also.[1] For his first official position, however, he seems to have gone into Quhistân, lying south of his own city, to become astrologer to the chief of the Quhistânî Ismâʿîlîs. This was presumably in his young manhood, just after Ḥasan III's reign, when Ismâʿîlism as such was being kept out of sight, and not only Sunnîs, but Twelver Shîʿites, such as Ṭûsî was, were freely welcomed. Indeed, he may have been one of the refugees from the Mongol storm. He is associated, however, with the last Quhistân head, Nâṣir ad-Dîn, to whom he dedicated his great work on ethics.

It seems that Ṭûsî was eager to rise in the world, and negotiated with Baghdâd for a position at the Caliphal court. He was rebuffed; but, he claimed, the Ismâʿîlî ruler discovered his negotiations, and he was thereafter watched so that he could not leave if he did get an offer.[2] (This was, it might be noted, neither the first nor the last Muslim court which treated its decorative scholars as valuable property, which none should steal.) After some time, he was sent to Alamût, where he remained till his middle fifties, when it fell. Evidently he had become famous even while there; within a few years after its fall he was set by his new master, Hûlâgû the Mongol ruler, to building a great observatory at Marâgha in Âdharbâyjân.[3] He lived eighteen years after leaving Alamût, basking in Mongol favor for his astrological learning, and making use of this favor for the benefit of his Twelver co-religionists.

Ṭûsî seems to have been of a strong and original turn of mind. He is reported to have experimented, for instance, with the effect of sudden noise on soldiers, to discover what difference it made if they were warned in advance.[4] Such a mind gained him fame in the world in the fields of physics and astronomy and philosophy. But such a mind also was one not easily to be fitted into conventional categories. It is noted as highly exceptional, for the time, that although he was a loyal Twelver Shîʿite,

M. b. Shâkir al-Kutubî, *Fawât al-Wafâyât* (Bûlâq, 1283=1866), Vol. II, p. 186-9. Cf. *E. I.* article on him.

[2] Ṭûsî insisted on the involuntary nature of his connections with Ismâʿîlism. Ivanow suggests, in his introduction, that he may have been born an Ismâʿîlî, but educated in Twelver schools (which must have been better than the mountaineers could afford to maintain) on the basis of a practical taqiyya, pretense at being a Twelver. Then presumably Ṭûsî was actually converted, but dared not let the Ismâʿîlîs know this; and so passed among them for an Ismâʿîlî still while the Twelvers knew he was at heart a Twelver. This would account for his hearty acceptance in both groups.

[3] It is said that Hûlâgû's sovereign in Mongolia liked geometry and had therefore heard of Ṭûsî; and when he sent Hûlâgû on the expedition against the Ismâʿîlîs, he told him to send Ṭûsî to him in Mongolia. Rashîd ad-Dîn, ed. Quatremère, *Histoire des Mongols de la Perse* (Paris, 1836), Vol. I, p. 324.

[4] Donaldson, *The Shîʿite Religion*, p. 294.

he was also in correspondence with Sunnî Ṣûfîs, and presented a Ṣûfî position, in Shîʿite form, in an important treatise. It will not be readily settled, therefore, just what his inward relations with Ismâʿîlism were.

He admitted himself that the first draft of his great book on ethics was tinged with Ismâʿîlism, to please his Ismâʿîlî patron.[5] The Ismâʿîlîs have gone so far as to reckon him one of their great authorities. In India in the Seventeenth Century, the author of the *Dabistân* cited him on Ismâʿîlî questions;[6] in the Twentieth Century, Semenov found him to be considered a great authority by the Ismâʿîlîs of the upper Oxus.[7] We have already had occasion to cite two books ascribed to him, in which the doctrine of the Satr is developed. Whatever his own feelings, certainly he played a major role in the Ismâʿîlî thought of his time. The two works ascribed to him which we have cited are very likely genuine, as Ivanow shows in his preface to the *Rawḍat at-Taslîm*.[8] They reveal a scholar who at least passed in the community for an Ismâʿîlî, and who knew the faith thoroughly. One of them is an elementary treatise, setting forth a sophisticated doctrine in disarmingly simple terms; the other is an exposition designed to face all the philosophical problems of the Ismâʿîlî creed, and succeeding at least in avoiding naiveté. Perhaps the Satr doctrine was largely formed by him in these works; – and that doctrine is one of the chief Ismâʿîlî accomplishments of his generation.

Ṭûsî's Ismâʿîlî work.

If Ṭûsî did play so great a role in Ismâʿîlîsm, this did not give him opportunity to appear at his best. By his time, Ismâʿîlî doctrine was waiting upon events with painful obsequiousness. As Ṭûsî presents it, the doctrine of the Satr seems to echo at every point some peculiarity of the reign of either Ḥasan III or of his son. Several items seem to bear directly on the first proclamation of Satr (as Ismâʿîlîs would regard it) by

[5] It appears that even at the time of Khwurshâh's surrender to Hûlâgû, when Ṭûsî went over to the conqueror, he did not insult the Ismâʿîlî imâm. Quatremère's Rashîd ad-Dîn on Hûlâgû, p. 212, quotes dignified verses from him on the surrender: "When the year of the Arabs was [such and such a date] Khwurshâh king of the Ismâʿîlîs rose from his throne and stood before the throne of Hûlâgû."

[6] *Dabistân*, tr. Troyer and Shea, p. 417.

[7] One of their two lawbooks was a *Bayân-i Sharîʿa* by him. R. Majerczak, in *Revue du Monde Musulman*, Vol. 24 (1913), p. 218.

[8] He adduces the style, as vouched for by Persian scholars; the masterful manner, unusual in lesser men; the lack of any internal contradiction of the explicit ascription; and even a certain ambiguity in various phrases – some of the ones he cites, at least, suggest indeed the hand of a person hedging a bit on his allegiance, as might be expected of the Ṭûsî known to the world as an avid Twelver.

Ḥasan III. The story of Iblîs, who wanted to continue teaching the qiyâma doctrine, would be almost irrelevant under the laxity of Muḥammad III. It is also Ḥasan's reign in which the da'wa of the word was given up altogether, and the imâm clearly appeared simply as "lord of slaves". On the other hand, certain points would fit equally well the apostate imâm, or the reputedly mad one who was his son. It is insisted repeatedly that the believer must never try to judge the actions or the words of the imâm. The Ismâ'îlîs had all along insisted that actions of the imâm are unaccountable; the stress on his words' also being unaccountable is distinctive. The same double situation would account for the stress laid upon a ḥujja as unique channel to the imâm, though we find no one recorded in either reign who might be such a figure, and the traditional list of ḥujjas is not helpful in this respect. If under Ḥasan III a zabân-i 'ilm was required, an active ḥujja might be even more in order under Muḥammad III, who was certainly no theologian. At any rate, the associated principle that at the top levels, or at least at the level of ḥujja, the freedom of the Qiyâma still applied is to be linked to Muḥammad III rather than to his father, if Ḥasan III was, as we have supposed, sincere.

Nevertheless, the community evidently appreciated intellectual subtlety, and Ṭûsî handled the material with a cautious skill. The *Rawḍat at-Taslîm* is full of close reasoning; both on general philosophical points as they entered the Ismâ'îlî system, and on particular Ismâ'îlî terms. Nor is this done without reference to classical Ismâ'îlî doctrines.[9] The author must repeatedly recur, for instance, to the difficult – and no doubt initially rather popular – concept of *tashakhkhuṣ:* that Paradise, Hell, etc., are men; which involves the direct identification of two contrasting *substances.* He handles the problem with a smoothness which leaves us almost convinced that the phrases involved are very proper modes of expression; but doubtless we see very little, in Ṭûsî's elucidation, of the original impulses that created the phrases. Rather, we get a genteel and rather supererogatory set of lessons in certain philosophical doctrines that can be made to yield appropriate formulations.

In order to account in an orderly way for all the implications built into the notion of tashakhkhuṣ, he explains it in two forms, as is often

[9] Ivanow, *Rawḍat at-Taslîm,* p. xxvii, seems to think that Ṭûsî was ignorant of classical Ismâ'îlî writings, and used only the writings of the imâms of Alamût. This seems doubtful, even on general grounds. And in fact, the old Ismâ'îlî ideas recur repeatedly. One supposes, for instance, that Ṭûsî's deliberate confusion of the Qâ'im and the waṣî figures, which does not occur in the unlearned *HBBS*, stems not from Muḥammad II, but from a familiarity with older writings.

his practice: as a single total phenomenon (*jumal*), and as a phenomenon made up of an indefinite number of particular instances (*tafṣîl*). In the first form, his explanation accounts for the idea that certain individuals embody Hell or Paradise. In the upward gradation of being, as regards each stage, Paradise is the stage above, and Hell that below itself. Thus Paradise is for men that higher stage of angelic being where the limitations of body are quite sloughed off, and Hell is that lower condition of animality where life is lived exclusively within the limitations of body. But within each stage there is a gradation of individual cases, in which at the top and the bottom there is a marginal case – the highest man being, from the viewpoint of the human world, Heavenly; but from the viewpoint of Paradise, still worldly. And likewise, the lowest man is, from the viewpoint of the human world, Hellish. Such marginal persons can be singled out as representing Hell or Paradise to the rest of mankind.

But that Hell and Paradise are metaphysically persons is better explained in the second manner; that is, in terms which yield an indefinite number of instances of Hell and Paradise. In referring to any good or bad thought we must refer to the spiritual being which effects it in us; for all happenings are effected by such beings, and therefore do not exist independently, but merely as their traces. Now Hell and Paradise, in the spiritual sense, are a state of mind – good and bad thoughts; hence they also are such spiritual beings. But these beings, according to classical Ismâʿîlî doctrine, are what are called "angels" and "devils"; and angels and devils are referred to legitimately as persons; therefore Hell and Paradise may be referred to as persons.[10]

Ṭûsî's effect on Ismâʿîlism is hard to weigh, in the absence of knowledge of other Ismâʿîlî work of the time. The effect of Ismâʿîlism on Ṭûsî is more intriguing, but perhaps almost equally difficult to weigh in the absence of full studies of Ṭûsî. It is nevertheless not too much to point out that the combination of Ṣûfism with a reverence for Shîʿite imâms, which is noted as remarkable in Ṭûsî, is precisely the characteristic trait of the doctrine of Qiyâma; which Ṭûsî helped adapt to a situation where, as in the case of the Twelvers also, the imâm was in some way hidden. If Ṭûsî did not play quite the role in Twelver Shîʿism that Ghazzâlî did in Sunnism, nevertheless his position is not to be despised, nor is the influence on him of the faith he so long practiced to be discounted too much in advance.

[10] *Rawḍat at-Taslîm*, p. 43 ff. He touches the problem also elsewhere, e.g., p. 99, and with the same perspicacity. This longest passage, here summarized, is rather obscure, but I hope I have not misapplied it.

The Quhistânî sense of dignity.

We know of Quhistân during this last generation chiefly through the pen of a bigoted Sunnî, Minhâj-i Sirâj; yet even at his hands, the community retains its essential dignity. The men whom the "heretics" supported in the world can be painted in the worst of colors – something like this could also be said of Riḍwân of Aleppo, and of the Sulṭân Barkiyâruq, in earlier times; but the Ismâ'îlî chiefs themselves seem to evoke in him nothing but respect. The Ismâ'îlî dignity was expressed in very different ways by the two Quhistânî chiefs whom he knew. Both, just after the reign of Ḥasan III and the Mongol conquests, were able to maintain a very unbending independence of that Ghûr whose rulers troubled the Ismâ'îlîs so seriously shortly before. Yet as we have noticed, they were men of very different temperaments. Shihâb ad-Dîn was the man who was so very hospitable to the refugees pouring in from the Mongol invasion, and who was said to be very learned himself. His worthiness, however, conflicted with an equally respectable sturdiness on the part of his people. It was in a spirit of frank local independence that his people complained at Alamût about his lavish favoring of aliens, and obtained a governor more willing to keep the Ismâ'îlî funds at home. At this point, at least, the sovereignty of Alamût, whose appointee held the purse-strings, coincided nevertheless in its effect with the local community sentiment.[11]

If Shihâb ad-Dîn received praise as a scholar and a gentleman, his successor, Shams ad-Dîn Ḥasan-i Ikhtiyâr, was acknowledged a soldier in the best sense. It seems that the Quhistânî Ismâ'îlîs, loyal to Alamût as they were, nonetheless saw to their own interests through an agent at the Khwârazm court. At the fall of Khwârazm to the Mongols, this agent, a pious old Sunnî, fled to Quhistân and was very kindly received by Shihâb ad-Dîn. But Shams ad-Dîn, who succeeded him, was not so cordial, though evidently still correct; and the old man decided to avenge the recall of Shihâb ad-Dîn upon him. Shams carried a keen dagger always; and the old man, having obtained a private audience, contrived to get the dagger into his own hands as if in a gesture, and stabbed the governor with it. The old man's weak thrust was not fully effective, and

[11] Considering how independently the various fortresses tended to act at the final Mongol conquest, one may suppose that this sentiment was thoroughly local. Evidently neither in Syria nor in Quhistân was there a permanent central residence of the governor, though in Muḥammad III's time we find Maṣyâf as residence most of the time; in Quhistân Mu'minâbâd no longer appears as such, but both Tûn and Qâ'in do, as well as Sartakht. Even in Rûdbâr, the imâm lived now in one, now in another place.

at Shams' cry the attendants came and finished the old man off. But now the Ismâ'îlîs who heard of the attempt were aroused, and there was danger of a massacre of all non-Ismâ'îlîs in the town; only the governor's firmness prevented bloodshed. One man was killed, evidently a scholar, by a private enemy. The Ismâ'îlî who did it was impaled.[12]

Shams ad-Dîn arrived in Quhistân just as troubles with Sîstân were re-entering a relatively serious phase. It seems that the Sîstânî ruler Yamîn ad-Dîn Bahrâm Shâh had fought two long wars against them; and when his nephew had sold them a fortress not far from Nih, in Sîstân, Yamîn ad-Dîn had demanded it back, with threats. He had thereupon been assassinated in a bazaar on his way to the Friday prayer.[13]

There was now a succession dispute, in which Minhâj-i Sirâj says the "heretics" supported a reprobate son against his brother, raised to the Sîstânî throne by the more proper elements of the community; and were even able to have the reprobate enthroned for a short while. One would suppose these would be identical with the "heretics of Quhistân", the Ismâ'îlîs; but Minhâj-i Sirâj can use this notion very loosely. Nevertheless, we cannot be sure the Ismâ'îlîs were not now interfering in Sîstân affairs. When the Mongols had come and gone, and the Sîstânîs were setting up another of their old line as ruler, the "heretics" called in a Khwârazmian general, Bînaltigîn, operating around Kirmân, to set up still another candidate. It was at this point, when Shams ad-Dîn was ruling in Quhistân, that Bînaltigîn had a falling out, perhaps with the "heretics" who had invited him in, but certainly with the Ismâ'îlîs of Quhistân. He was defeated by them, and sent Minhâj-i Sirâj, a visiting scholar, to negotiate a peace. Minhâj made an accommodation with the Ismâ'îlîs before the walls of Nih; but Bînaltigîn refused to accept it, and wanted Minhâj to go back and declare war – which Minhâj refused to do, and was imprisoned for a time for his obstinacy.[14]

Minhâj-i Sirâj had occasion to visit the Quhistânî Ismâ'îlîs thrice; and his purposes there suggest the ambiguous status of the Ismâ'îlîs, at once within and outside of the Islamic life. The last time he went, to make peace for Bînaltigîn, he was asked to go because (or so he assures us) all

[12] *Ṭabaqât-i Nâṣirî*, trans., ps. 1212–14.

[13] Year 618. The fortress in question was called Shâhanshâhî. Minhâj-i Sirâj, 196.

[14] Minhâj-i Sirâj, *Ṭabaqât-i Nâṣirî*, pp. 199–201, 1203–1205. The *Ta'rîkh-i Sîstân* also mentions the war, year 622. One is inclined to suggest, in this connection, that in Quhistân (and perhaps even at times in Syria) Ismâ'îlî policy could sometimes be determined by an effort to incorporate more fully into the Ismâ'îlî *state* places where numbers of Ismâ'îlîs lived more or less under Sunnî rule.

the resident Sîstânîs were afraid to go, though in fact a scion of the royal family was sent with him. But he had already been through twice, once during Shams ad-Dîn's regime, to reopen trade routes by negotiations on behalf of the no longer truculent Ghûr authorities, after the Mongols left; as well as to do some personal shopping for fine clothes, which had elsewhere become rare after the Mongol devastation. Clearly Quhistân was economically integrated with the larger world – whence it came that Shihâb ad-Dîn was able to give appropriate gifts to the Sunnî scholars who fled there from the Mongols. A certain hostility with neighbors was common enough in Muslim lands, and might be overlooked if it were not for the great fear which accompanied these particular squabbles: for if you were at war with the Ismâʿîlîs you were at war with a people, not a transient lord. The Khwârazmian lord Ûrkhân, whose lieutenants raided Quhistân, not long after this paid with his life.[15]

Of the last chief, Nâṣir ad-Dîn, we know little, except that he was Ṭûsî's patron; and that he patronized at least one other scholar, as Ivanow reports.[16] Both that scholar, who translated an ethics classic into Persian, and Ṭûsî wrote on ethics for him; but one may suppose that his interests extended to other of the fields in which Ṭûsî was more noted.[17] As a very old man he gave himself up to the Mongols in their final attack, who then tried to use him as an agent in subduing his fellows; but he died.

The Syrian lieutenants: high expectations.

Although the community there was less powerful, the Syrian Ismâʿîlîs show many of the same traits as those of Quhistân. They were equally dependent upon Alamût. A Maṣyâf inscription from the beginning of Muḥammad III's reign gives us, along with Muḥammad's name, a Kamâl ad-Dîn as lord, mawlâ, in Syria; who is mentioned four years later by Nasawî at Alamût, as past Syrian governor. During the governorship a little later of Sirâj ad-Dîn al-Muẓaffar, whom Nasawî also knew of, an inscription on a bath at Kahf mentions not only the lords of

[15] Nasawî, *Histoire*, tr. Houdas, p. 220.

[16] Ivanow, *Rawḍat at-Taslîm*, p. xxiv.

[17] That the interest in ethics arose from the legal freedom after the Qiyâma, as Ivanow suggests, is doubtful. Dropping the sharîʿa meant primarily dropping the ritual; ethical standards of a more general character were not really covered by the sharîʿa anyway, and legal matters have always been as much a matter of local custom among Muslims as of the ritual law. The Syrian *moral* texts were probably typical.

Alamût and of Syria but also the local head of Kahf itself, who is called "the Persian, the Alamûtî". Sirâj ad-Dîn's successor, Tâj ad-Dîn, who rebuilt the wall of Maṣyâf, is also said to be a Persian from Alamût by his friend Ibn Wâṣil.[18] But, as also in Quhistân, these Syrian Ismâʿîlîs kept up their own initiative. Tâj ad-Dîn played the traditional Ismâʿîlî role of strong bystander. When the Qâḍî Badr ad-Dîn of Sinjâr got into trouble by betting on the wrong horse among the Ayyûbids, he took refuge with Tâj ad-Dîn in the Ismâʿîlî strongholds, till he could straighten his affairs out. Shortly before, Tâj ad-Dîn had gone so far as to intercede on behalf of a certain Ḥakîm Zayn ad-Dîn, who was then let free by the Sunnî rulers.[19]

However, when it served their turn the Syrians could appear very dependent upon Alamût. It seems that Frederick, on his Crusade, sent an embassy to the Syrian Ismâʿîlîs, who were very hospitable, but insisted that to get any results the embassy must go on to Alamût, which was represented as hazardously distant. In spite of this caution, the Franks raided them for having dealings with Frederick.[20]

The Syrians were not so modest in undertaking other diplomatic ventures. It was perhaps in Tâj ad-Dîn's time, in 1250, that an embassy was sent to King Louis, in Syria on his Crusade, asking that the tribute still paid to the Templars and to the Hospitallers be lifted. Joinville tells us the story, and reports a mission to the Ismâʿîlîs in return – thus providing us with a first-hand report on Syria in this generation, just as we have such already from envoys to the Quhistân Ismâʿîlîs and to Alamût. A friar, Yves the Breton, returned with the Ismâʿîlî ambassadors, and visited with the chief at Maṣyâf. Yves spoke Arabic, and discussed religion with him in his inner apartments. Joinville wrote fifty years after hearing Yves' account; when he reports from Yves that the chief traced back Peter's soul through Abraham, Moses, and Abel it is not clear just which Ismâʿîlî doctrine is being followed. But the amiable character of the man shines through. He had at his bedside what Yves took to be a

[18] Berchem, in the *JA*, 1897, p. 498, gives a summary of the data he collected on the Syrian Ismâʿîlî governors: Kamâl ad-Dîn Ḥasan, 620 (recalled before 624); Najm ad-Dîn, 624. Sirâj ad-Dîn Muẓaffar 625-or-6 and 635. Tâj ad-Dîn abû l-Futûḥ 637 and 646. Riḍâ ad-Dîn abû l-Maʿâlî 656 to the Mongol invasion.

[19] Zayn ad-Dîn b. ʿammî – a nephew of Ibn Wâṣil, who says he was on good terms with Tâj ad-Dîn? yr. 637. Ibn Sâlim ibn Wâṣil, fol. 328r. On Badr ad-Dîn, fol. 333v.

[20] Al-Ḥamawî abû l-Faḍl (fl. 1233), ed. M. Amari, ad. Appendix, *Biblioteca Arabo-Sicula*, Leipzig, 1887, p. 30, yr. 624. Ḥamawî has the Hospitallers raiding them, but Cahen, *Syrie du Nord*, p. 641, makes it Bohemond of Antioch, and indeed has Bohemond raid them precisely as allies of Bohemond's enemies the Hospitallers.

Christian book, and seems to have accepted patiently the friar's attempts to put his theology straight.[21]

His display before King Louis does not impress one as very subtle, however. He sent as threat to King Louis, landed at Acre, bearers of three daggers, and behind them the bearer of a shroud. The threat was evaded, and then rejected at a second audience, when the envoys were met with the frowns of the masters of the two orders from whose exactions they were trying to get free. They were told to return with appropriate gifts if they wished a royal audience. The Ismâ'îlî chief thereupon determined to make friends. His symbol of friendship was his shirt, the garment nearest his heart.[22]

The crystal ware which he sent as a gift was heavily decorated with amber, such as to perfume a room; but it was greatly admired by the Franks, as were some chess men also sent. If the report which Joinville has of his behavior when he rode abroad is true, his taste will be found distinctly provincial. Yves seems to have reported that as he rode a herald proclaimed before him that it was he who had the life of kings in his hands. One cannot imagine such an institution in the time of Râshid ad-Dîn Sinân.[23]

Surviving Syrian literature: the fragments.

Yves reported an Ismâ'îlî doctrine in Syria, that one would be favorably reincarnated if one died at one's lord's behest, which is to be roughly identified with that reported somewhat later in the *Masâlik al-Abṣâr*, which we have already mentioned as probably reflecting Syrian popular

[21] One wonders whether Joinville's report on the Shî'a generally, which sounds like a popular impression of it but is not at all unfavorable to it, could have come from this visit to Maṣyâf. He includes under the heading not only Ismâ'îlîs, but the bedouin (Bâṭinî?) of Egypt. It seems that it was 'Alî who had originally set Mohammed up, but Mohammed had rejected 'Alî, so the latter set up a new law on his own behalf. This included the principle of fatalism, and of favorable reincarnation if one is killed at one's lord's behest. (One suspects that Yves had access to some literary sources: it must have been from such sources that he had an incident which Joinville describes as actually witnessed in the Egyptian streets – a woman, evidently the famous old mystic Râbi'a, who was carrying water to Hell and fire to Paradise so as to ensure men's disinterestedness in serving God.) Joinville, *Histoire de Saint Louis*, ed. N. de Wailly (nouvelle édition; Paris, 1888), pp. 189–94, 105, 186.

[22] Such a detail appears also in the account of Frederick's embassy.

[23] Sinân's sobriety would be indicated by a point made by Wm. of Tyre, which reminds one of the Ra'îs Muẓaffar's boast (in Rashîd ad-Dîn) at Gird Kûh – that he had given up the world, to be addressed very simply among the Ismâ'îlîs. Wm. says not only that the Ismâ'îlî head was elective, but that they refused him any more fancy title than *shaykh*, "chief".

sentiment. No doubt by this time also the general tradition of the types of literary materials kept by the Syrian Ismâʿîlîs was established; and we will get some sense of a different side of the intellectual life of the time than that represented by Ṭûsî, if we consider briefly the surviving fragments of Syrian Ismâʿîlî literature – evidently dating from many periods of time, but all read side by side.[24] Such of this as has been published is mostly undatable; in those cases where it is ascribed to an author there is no way to be sure that it is justly so. Sinân figures importantly in it, but no other post-Fâṭimid figure. We find work ascribed to Muʿizz, among the Fâṭimid Caliphs; we find Jâbir Juʿfî and other early Shîʿite worthies cited. On the whole it is apparently a heritage from Fâṭimid Ismâʿîlism, and will be distinctive of Syrian life only to the degree that it is selective from the great range of available Fâṭimid materials.

There seem to be four types of thought represented in these documents. First there are the expressions of standard morality and devotion, whose Ismâʿîlî tinge is incidental, and whose main burden is to consider the other world and not be deceived by this: going chiefly to show that the devotionally moral tone of Islâm, going back beyond it already to the old East-Christian devotion, remained substantially constant in spite of esoterism or intellectualism. Examples of this are most of the "Suras" among the Guyard fragments.

Second is the classical Ismâʿîlî sectarian material, such as all the Salisbury fragments, and some of the Guyard items. These materials might have come from the end of the Fâṭimid reign, one would suppose: the full hierarchy of the ḥudûd is intact, the ta'wîl is used in its direct form, and the intellectual character is marked, over the emotional. We find variations corresponding to those of classical Ismâʿîlism. One tendency noteworthy is toward exaltation of the imâm. One of Salisbury's fragments, obviously classical (it looks to a future Qâ'im; and deplores the Ghuluww who would make the imâms be God) insists throughout its first part more particularly on the equality of Mohammed and ʿAlî, and of the *Sâbiq* and the *Tâlî* (Precedent and Follower). In another fragment the imâm is equated with the ʿaql, the first emanation.[25] Dussaud got the impression that the first three of the Guyard fragments all placed the asâs, ʿAlî, above the nâṭiq, the Prophet.

The third strain, tied up with the classical Ismâʿîlî theology, is the straight scholastic Philosophy cultivated under the Fâṭimids: disregarding

[24] Ivanow supposes these are all modern, but gives no reason. 'Ismailitica,' *Memoirs of the Asiatic Society of Bengal*, VIII (1922), 25 and 64.
[25] Guyard Fragments, p. 212/388.

the specially Ismâ'îlî ḥudûd, to concentrate on technical problems. Here we have among others an Ismâ'îlî favorite, the proof of the non-existence of nothing (i.e., deprivation has no positive existence). Finally, there are a certain number of pieces in the Guyard collection which reflect rather a Ṣûfî point of view; the chief among which we have already noted as reflecting the Syrian response to the Qiyâma. It was a people well-read, and glad to find the universe intelligible.

HOPES OF EXPANSION

These sturdy people, whatever limitations of taste or perspective they labored under, did not cease to have a world-wide outlook; indeed, during the Mongol times they seem even to have widened this outlook, as did others in the same astonishing age. We find a prophecy in the *Rawḍat at-Taslîm* of the course of conquest of the imâm after he arrived in Daylamân. It is an old prophecy, found also in the *Haft Bâb* of the time of Muḥammad II, where we learn that upon setting up his power in Daylamân the imâm will then move on to India. In the *Rawḍat at-Taslîm* we find it in a more detailed form. It is said that after taking Daylamân, the imâm would go into Mâzandarân, Gîlân, and Mûqân in the same sub-Caspian area; and then move on to the holy war in India, China, and Europe: that is, throughout the world.[26] Dare one suppose that it had entered someone's mind to build up an imperial base in the stimulating mountains and rich lowlands strategically placed at the foot of the Caspian Sea, and from thence set about the conquest of the Old World?

Fighting with the Khwârazm power (1221–1231).

At all events, in one way or another their activities reached fairly widely in that last generation. In the years following Ḥasan III's death, in the midst of the general confusion following the collapse of the

[26] Ṭûsî, *Rawḍat at-Taslîm*, p. 117. Ivanow has omitted all but India and China from the translation. (He noted the others, however, in his 1931 summary). The terms Hindûstân, Chîn, and Rûm are all vague, it might be noted; they can refer to merely the nearest portions of the larger territories. *Hind* can mean, essentially, the Punjab, and *Rûm* be restricted to Anatolia and the Balkans. But they are also extendable beyond to the whole of the three main civilizations sharing the Eurasian continent with Islâm. Ibn Jubayr (*Viaggi*, p. 4) applies the term *Rûmî* to Italian sailors, for instance.

Khwârazmian empire before the heathen Mongols, they seemed to have tried to make hay – perhaps in active alliance with the Mongols, and certainly not in hostility to them. About the time of Ḥasan III's death they seized Dâmghân, the town near Gird Kûh; and presumably at the same time other fortresses which we find mentioned at their fall.[27] Evidently they were also trying to seize Rayy, for we find that one of Muḥammad Khwârazmshâh's sons was killing their dâ'îs in that town about 1222.[28] Probably these seizures were not just an army occupation, as with Ḥasan III's conquests, but to some degree an echo of the old insurrectionary spirit of the days of Ḥasan-i Ṣabbâḥ. But this was not their chief basis of hope. Later, when the (false) news came of the death of the Khwârazmian refugee heir, Mankûbirtî, in defeat near Iṣfahân, the Syrian Ismâ'îlîs boasted to the ruler of Anatolia that their comrades of Alamût were about to take over the whole of 'Irâq 'Ajamî, which Mankûbirtî had held.[29] Evidently at a time when everyone else was routed, the Ismâ'îlîs expected the world to fall into their ready hands.

The Ismâ'îlîs inherited from Ḥasan's pro-Caliphal policy a quarrel with Khwârazm. This empire had been destroyed by 1221; but the debris of Khwârazmian power were gathered up by the dashing prince Mankûbirtî during a brief spell of meteoric and troubled power, in province after province of his father's empire, before the Mongols caught up with him. While he lasted, the Ismâ'îlî quarrel proceeded with him; and whatever vast hopes were gradually developed, this quarrel was the rather inglorious reality of the first decade of Alamût policy under Muḥammad III. Though Rashîd ad-Dîn does not bring us for this period any chronicle of such events from within, Mankûbirtî's secretary Nasawî, in telling the story of his master's life, gives the events from the Khwârazmian viewpoint; so that we have some idea of their tenor.

Ibn al-Athîr notes that a six-year aggressive spree on the part of the Ismâ'îlîs was brought to an end by Mankûbirtî, who forced the Ismâ'îlîs to pay tribute to him for Dâmghân a couple of years after he arrived in the area.[30] This agreement with the Ismâ'îlîs was made just after the assassination of Ûrkhân, who had despised Quhistânî protest against raids by his lieutenants. The three assassins, Nasawî says, ran crying the name of 'Alâ ad-Dîn Muḥammad III in the streets, till they were killed by

[27] Cf. especially the reference to Qûmis, in Rashîd ad-Dîn, ed. Quatremère, p. 213.
[28] Nasawî, *Histoire*, tr. M. Houdas, p. 119.
[29] Nasawî, p. 280. At the moment it happened that the heirs to both Âdharbâyjân and 'Irâq 'Ajamî were refugees at Alamût, which fact added point to the claim.
[30] *Kâmil*, year 624. Nasawî, *Histoire*, tr. Houdas, p. 221.

stones hurled at them from the houses. An envoy from Alamût, Badr ad-Din Aḥmad, was on his way to Mankûbirtî's court at the time; when he heard the news, he hesitated to proceed further, but was reassured by Mankûbirtî's vizier, Sharaf al-Mulk. The Khwârazm-Ismâ'îlî treaty was then agreed to. But one day when sharing a drink with Sharaf al-Mulk, Badr ad-Dîn boasted of Ismâ'îlîs posted in Sharaf al-Mulk's service, and summoned them to show themselves in proof. At this Sharaf al-Mulk debased himself completely; but Mankûbirtî made him burn the five men who had been pointed out; these called on Muḥammad III's name as they died. The Ismâ'îlîs then sent to demand ten thousand gold pieces in recompense for each Ismâ'îlî burned, and Sharaf al-Mulk agreed to pay it by remitting for five years ten thousand of the thirty thousand gold pieces required yearly for Dâmghân.[31]

Tortuous negotiations.

This treaty, however, did not last. By the next year, the Ismâ'îlîs were protecting two refugees from Mankûbirtî – the son of that Ûzbag who had been the friend of Ḥasan III, and had been displaced by Mankûbirtî; and Mankûbirtî's own brother Ghiyâth ad-Dîn, who had ruled in western Îrân before Mankûbirtî had arrived, and was dissatisfied with taking second place. The Caliph supplied Ghiyâth ad-Dîn with money, and Alamût protected him, though Mankûbirtî set up a blockade upon all the roads leading out of the Ismâ'îlî territory. Nasawî says that the Ismâ'îlîs offered, at this point, to put assassins at Mankûbirtî's disposal – an offer which Mankûbirtî refused for fear of disclosing his political secrets to them. He did, however, offer his pardon to Ghiyâth ad-Dîn at their intercession; but Ghiyâth ad-Dîn preferred not to trust him. Meanwhile the Ismâ'îlîs were angered at a high-handed action of Mankûbirtî's. Accordingly, they gave Ghiyâth ad-Dîn aid in making an escape. He fled to Kirmân, where a former agent of his was in control; but the agent had gone over to Mankûbirtî, and killed him.[32]

In spite of the treaty with Mankûbirtî, the Ismâ'îlîs were still on the side of the Caliph and also of the Mongols. Badr ad-Dîn was sent the next year after the treaty to the Mongol court across the Oxus. The same connection is suggested in Mankûbirtî's high-handed action just referred to. In order to catch a Mongol envoy known to be on the way to Anatolia,

[31] Nasawî, *Histoire*, pp. 220–23, yr. 624.
[32] Nasawî, pp. 237 ff.

Mankûbirtî ordered the stopping of all caravans in that direction; and at Sharaf al-Mulk's orders a seventy-man Ismâʿîlî caravan, with which the envoy was supposed to be travelling, was massacred. Mankûbirtî tried to pacify the Ismâʿîlî envoy who was sent in protest by blaming Sharaf al-Mulk, and promising amends; but the amends were not adequate.[33]

Upon the subsequent escape of Ghiyâth ad-Dîn, Mankûbirtî was enraged, and reopened the quarrel with the Ismâʿîlîs. He managed to capture an Ismâʿîlî vizier, and execute him.[34] When the Ismâʿîlîs eventually turned up with only part of the tribute for Dâmghân, he sent Nasawî to Alamût to demand full satisfaction with threats. Nasawî finally persuaded them to let him have an interview with the young Muḥammad III himself, which was not usually done. Nasawî stated his case – that in Ḥasan III's days Alamût had at first been submissive to Khwârazm, that now it not only withheld agreed tribute but was negotiating with the Mongols. The Ismâʿîlîs answered that they had done the Khwârazmians the service of ridding them of Shihâb ad-Dîn of Ghûr, whereas the Khwârazmians had plundered a large amount of money on its way from Quhistân to Alamût – admittedly, however, before the late treaty; and pleaded Sharaf al-Mulk's reduction of the tribute to explain the rest of the shortage of the tribute. Nasawî denied Sharaf al-Mulk's competence in the matter (he disapproved of Sharaf al-Mulk personally), and the Ismâʿîlîs, with great familiarity with Mankûbirtî's court, asserted it; and the final result was a compromise. Nasawî was very proud of the impression he made at Alamût through his bold presentation of his case. His companion, there to deal with local matters of dispute, was emboldened by his example; and the Ismâʿîlîs themselves loaded him with unusual presents, and made him a present of some sheep he had intended to buy there for a Ṣûfî monastery he wanted to found, and in which Muḥammad III said he wished a share of the blessing.[35]

Here again, as in Quhistân, we find the combination of involvement in the everyday world – evidently the neighboring rulers were accustomed to negotiations with Alamût and vice versa; with a specially awesome position a little apart from ordinary affairs. At Alamût itself, this ambiguous position was the springboard for high politics. Such was the familiarity with which an Ismâʿîlî envoy could be received abroad, that the man who was sent back with Nasawî as envoy from Alamût was a

[33] *Ibid.*, p. 262.
[34] *Ibid.*, p. 327.
[35] Nasawî, pp. 354 ff.

personal enemy of Sharaf al-Mulk, and was known to stir up the court against him. Sharaf al-Mulk found a pretext to destroy him after a while – that he was persuading the distant Mongols to come against Mankûbirtî; nor did such an idea seem improbable.[36]

World-wide outlook.

The Ismâ'îlîs had other irons in the fire than their quarrel with the Khwârazmians; and they continued to be a very local power in many of their preoccupations. At some time or another they acquired territory around Ṭârim, westward in Gîlân. No doubt the execution of the Gîlân princesses will have broken relations with some of the neighboring princes; and we do hear of rebels in Rûyân seeking Ismâ'îlî aid against Fakhr ad-Dîn Namâwar, quite in the old style.[37] But from the time of Ḥasan III forth, they never ceased being involved also in wider quarrels.

When Mankûbirtî was killed after only a half dozen years in the area, therefore, the Ismâ'îlîs no doubt fell to quarreling with the Mongols who succeeded to his place. Dâmghân was of course lost to them. At any rate, seven years after Mankûbirtî's death, in 1238, they are said to have sent an embassy to the farthest West to solicit a joint effort by Muslims and Christians against the Mongols.[38]

Since the Christians in turn were soon trying to persuade the Mongols to combine with them against all Muslims, this had little possibility of success. If the report of it can be trusted, however, it lends verisimilitude to the report that payments now came to the Ismâ'îlîs – at least those of Syria – from as far away as Germany, Aragon, and Yaman, as protection against their daggers.[39] The complete break with the Mongols, however,

[36] Ibn al-Athîr takes it up; *Kâmil*, year 628.

[37] Before 633. Ẓahîr ad-Dîn, p. 80.

[38] Perhaps such a formulation suggests they were still in some sort of entente with the Caliph. Matthew Paris, *English History*, tr. J. A. Giles (London, 1852), I, 131. If the story is true of the sending of assassins against young Saint Louis of France, which was countermanded the year before this, this may be regarded as marking a major change in policy.

[39] According to Zakariyâ Qazwînî, *Kitâb Âthâr al-Bilâd*, ed. F. Wüstenfeld, *Kosmographie*, part II (Göttingen, 1848), p. 201, it was in Yaman that one of their assassinations in this period was carried out. But it seems to have been a Zaydî imâm who was killed, and there were plenty of Ṭayyibî Ismâ'îlîs in Yaman quite ready to kill him if they could. The payments from distant monarchs are witnessed to by the not perfectly reliable 'Abdallâh Muḥyi ad-Dîn ibn 'Abd aẓ-Ẓâhir, who makes Sinân and Baybars contemporaries, it seems. See Maqrîzî, *Sulûk*, tr. Quatremère, *Histoire des Sultans Mamlouks de l'Egypte*, 1840, Vol. I, part 2, p. 24. No more sure are the implications we can draw from Joinville, Ibn Muyassar, etc.

seems to have come almost a decade later, when the Ismâʿîlî envoys to the great assembly in Mongolia were not accepted.[40]

Possibly at this time, when we find their representatives in Britain and in Mongolia, the Nizârîs were entering India also. The earliest of the legendary founders of Indian Nizârism, Nûr Satgûr, is placed (about 1179–1242) in Qiyâma or post-Qiyâma times, in one of the several datings assigned him, which range over centuries. He is also said to have come from Alamût.[41] Since there was active Nizârî propaganda the generation before in Ghûr, whence India was conquered during the life of Ḥasan III, it seems possible that Nizârism entered India with the Ghûrî conquest. Ṭayyibî Ismâʿîlism was already well-established there, of course. Muḥammad III seems to have had several Indians at his disposal (these could of course have been slaves conquered in war); one was sleeping at his side when he was killed; and another was among the five Ismâʿîlîs posted in the service of Sharaf al-Mulk, Mankûbirtî's vizier.[42]

The Ismâʿîlîs almost matched the Mongols in the length of their reach, and perhaps the breadth of their ambition; it is not surprising that they could not remain allies to the Mongols when it became clear that these intended to dominate the world on a permanent basis. Ḥasan III had, with a minimum of actual effort, and a maximum of allies, introduced the Ismâʿîlîs to the taste of expansion in the broader world. As the allies disappeared, the urge for expansion persisted under his son, till eventually the Ismâʿîlîs were left playing a lone hand. Yet at the same time the weakness of their mountain community, against which weakness Ḥasan III had been rebelling, persisted too. The Syrian Ismâʿîlîs, who had dealings with such distant monarchs, had to pay tribute to their knightly neighbors, and reaped only humiliation from an attempt to frighten the French king. Alamût, which expected to fill Khwârazmshâh's shoes, had to pay tribute meanwhile for Dâmghân, and was reduced to bargaining over a reduction in the sum. The Ismâʿîlîs were independent

40 Ibn al-ʿIbrî, p. 411.

41 Cf. John N. Hollister, *The Shîʿa of India*, unpublished thesis, 1946, Hartford Theological Seminary, pp. 575 ff., who has a good summary on the matter.

42 Nasawî, p. 222. Minhâj-i Sirâj has a certain Nûr Turk, teaching in Delhi in 634 in the time of Queen Raḍiyya, be an Ismâʿîlî (Qarmaṭian) heretic; he was suppressed in a riot. Minhâj says that Nûr Turk had gathered his numerous sectaries from all over Muslim India to seize power. *Ṭabaqât-i Nâṣirî*, p. 646. Minhâj describes him as speaking like a Shîʿite, though not necessarily either Ṭayyibî or Nizârî. But the great mystic of Delhi of the time, Niẓâm ad-Dîn Awliyâ', said that Minhâj had slandered Nûr Turk, whose words were all true, and who piously ended his days in Mecca. Amîr Ḥasan ʿAlâ'î Sanjarî, *Fawâ'id al-Fu'âd* ([Lucknow], 1302). I must thank Shaykh ʿAbd ar-Rashîd and Khalîq Niẓâmî of the University of Aligarh for pointing out the passage to me.

in the world, and inspired fears and even respect with their aloof dignity; they had a genuine strength against their enemies; but could not quite deal with them without humiliation.[43]

THE DEATH OF MUḤAMMAD III

Increasingly important in the fate of the Ismâʿîlî community, with all its hopes and its dangerous involvements, was the man who sat at its center in absolute command, as inspired representative of God. In the earlier years, during the negotiations with Khwârazm, the imâm Muḥammad III was still a youth; and apparently was not the moving spirit behind events – outsiders were sure an envoy would not be permitted even to see him. By the time the Ismâʿîlîs were coming to be admitted opponents to the world-conquering Mongols, he was full-grown, and his decisions could determine the course of events.

Muḥammad's character: the dynasty in degeneracy.

Muḥammad III came to the imâmate at the age of nine. At the age of fourteen or fifteen he is reported to have bled excessively, as a result of self-treatment, and to have contracted a permanent case of what the Medievals called *melancholia*. He is said to have been treated as a ruler with full powers, but to have been increasingly incapable of facing reality. But Rashîd ad-Dîn and Juwaynî give no real details to exemplify their reports on his condition, and it is hard to be sure what is meant.[44] Juwaynî called him worthy of chains; this is perhaps, however, as much a moral as a medical judgment, for he condemns strongly the ideas entertained about his divine infallibility.[45] Rashîd ad-Dîn tells how Muḥammad would be drunk three days at a time. It is said that he would get violent if any bad news were presented to him; that accordingly his

[43] Ibn Muyassar notes that, though all kings sent them protection money, since 620 or so the danger to Muslims from them was not so great as formerly. Ed. Massé, p. 68.

[44] The *Dabistân* has the Ismâʿîlî tradition admit some sort of disability, which they explained on the ground that every holy man must have some bodily defect – just as did Moses, who stammered. Vol. II, p. 447 (transl.)

[45] *Ta'rîkh-i Jahân Gushâ*, III, 251. We shall now again be following Rashîd ad-Dîn and Juwaynî closely in chronological order. Other portions of these works will be noted explicitly if cited.

courtiers learned to dissimulate, and not always let him know what was going on. Evidently he was not kept so much in the dark that he could not effectively rule, however, for it is said that Ḥasan Mâzandarânî, his favorite, became wealthy as intermediary between him and all the other courtiers. Muḥammad's wives and sisters are said to have supported him to the end, in his quarrel with his son. One will guess that, what ever medical symptoms he suffered from, he was not so much mad as perhaps brutalized – degenerate.

Nonetheless, Muḥammad took a keen interest in the outside world. He was surrounded by outsiders: Ḥasan Mâzandarânî is himself represented as a Sunnî; and when Muḥammad died he had a Turk on one side and a Hindu on the other. His chief amusement is represented, even in adulthood, as being that goatherding which was the childhood play of him and his friends; but that his herding expeditions were only occasional is indicated by the assertion that his son Khwurshâh made use of them as special opportunities to escape from his father's watchfulness. Muḥammad himself, according to Rashîd ad-Dîn, appears to have admired Ṭûsî; and his court boasted several non-Ismâʿîlî scholars, particularly physicians.[46]

The guide of his conscience is said to have been a shaykh of Qazwîn, Jamâl ad-Dîn. This man accepted money from him, as well as from another ruler; and justified his relation to Muḥammad on the ground that loot from the unbeliever is always licit. Muḥammad assured the Qazwînîs that if it were not for that shaykh he would destroy the town. When a messenger brought him an exhortation from the shaykh while he was drunken, he had the messenger beaten for not waiting till he had bathed and could receive it properly. Muḥammad still had some awe before that respectable world, which had converted his father, and in deference to which the Satr was still maintained in principle.[47]

Juwaynî tends to ascribe the aberrations of Muḥammad's times to his own perversity, and to imply that his madness and the flattery of the gullible Ismâʿîlîs were responsible for a fresh fall from the excellent example of Ḥasan III into an undifferentiated wickedness, with general disregard of law and morality, as well as of orthodox doctrine. He notes that the Ismâʿîlîs killed and stole and robbed highways – though it is mentioned that this was at least in part without Muḥammad's knowledge,

[46] Rashîd ad-Dîn, *Histoire des Mongols de la Perse*, ed. and trans. Quatremère (Paris, 1836), I, 184.

[47] The *Dabistân* reports that the Ismâʿîlîs believed the *shaykh* to be secretly an Ismâʿîlî.

since none dared tell him of it. One must balance this report with the report of items brought up in the negotiations carried on by Nasawî; among others are two attacks upon Ismâʿîlî caravans, which were considered unusual enough for both sides to discuss. No counter charges were brought up of the sort. Perhaps in later years conditions deteriorated; highlanders like the men of Rûdbâr have never shown much respect for the life or property of lowlanders, as we are reminded again in Freya Stark's story of her modern travels in the Alamût valleys.[48]

With Juwaynî, the world was waiting eager for the end. The short-lived welcome accorded to Ḥasan Naw-Musulmân had turned to detestation as the Ismâʿîlîs backslid. Juwaynî is delighted to be able to chronicle the more sordid details of a life cooped up, even though the imagination soared to Rûm and Hindûstân, in the Rûdbâr valleys. (Yet it was a life no more ugly than that of most dynasties of despots in their later days.) Ḥasan Mâzandarânî was a refugee from the Mongols, and had been sexually loved by Muḥammad III as a youth and even after his beard was grown; thence he came to be Muḥammad's favorite. Muḥammad gave him one of his own concubines for a wife, and Ḥasan became rich through his position. But there were sorry disadvantages to it. He could not leave, nor make use of his wealth at all, but must continue herding goats with his master; and at one time he was sadly mutilated by the moody imâm. Juwaynî says that Ḥasan, being a good Muslim, consulted with other Muslims captive there how to get rid of Muḥammad for the sake of the faith; but Rashîd ad-Dîn does not give him so pious a motive for his decision to kill his lord.

Meanwhile, Muḥammad's eldest son, Khwurshâh, who had early been given the naṣṣ as successor, became alienated from his father.[49] He was now in his early twenties, and when Muḥammad tried to change the naṣṣ, the community which had accepted even the Islamization of Ḥasan III would not accept that. Then when his people began obeying Khwurshâh as readily as his father, Muḥammad shut him up in the harem, from which he escaped for a drink only when his father was away.

War with the Mongols.

To these domestic problems facing the imâm were meanwhile being added external ones. Already the Mongols had turned away the Ismâʿîlî

[48] Nasawî, *Ta'rîkh-i Jalâl ad-Dîn Mankûbirtî*, p. 262. Freya Stark, *Valleys of the Assassins*, 1934, p. 205 ff.

[49] Rashîd ad-Dîn calls him *Ḥasan* – he would be the Fourth – but also *Khwurshâh*. Since *Khwurshâh* already functions as a personal name, *Ḥasan* would be redundant, and is nowhere else used.

delegation at one grand assembly. At the next, where Mangû was elected supreme Khân, it was decided to send major expeditions into China and the Middle East to complete the reduction of those sections of the world. Mangû's brother Hûlâgû was put in charge of the armies in the Middle East (which were also to attack India), and with majestic deliberateness he slowly prepared to proceed to his provinces.

If the expansive policy of Alamût could not directly set about overwhelming the Eurasian continent according to prediction, yet the master of that continent could find it worth his while to overwhelm Alamût. There were already two Mongol armies in Îrân, and the commander of one of them, Bâyjû, is said to have informed the court in Mongolia of the obduracy of two foes in particular, the Caliph and the Ismâʿîlîs.[50] He was told to attack Anatolia. But Mongol zeal against the Ismâʿîlîs was not allowed to slumber, surely, so long as there were inimical Muslims about. It is said that a supreme qâḍî, Shams ad-Dîn of Qazwîn, appeared one day before Mangû attired in a coat of mail and explained that he was forced to have such a coat on under his other clothes all the time, for fear of the Ismâʿîlîs. The Ismâʿîlîs had probably been bolder than most in resisting the Mongol tide, and Muslim hatred will have exascerbated the Mongol resentment. When Hûlâgû's expedition finally got under way, the destruction of the Ismâʿîlîs was made its first goal.[51]

After lengthy preparations, Hûlâgû started to march in 1252 and finally arrived at Samarqand in Transoxiana three years later, not entering Îrân itself until 1256. He seems as if uninterested in warfare, despite his official policy of blood and skulls. He was the last of the Mongols of horror here: and the first to be seriously defeated, by the only enemy which put up a real resistance, the Egyptian Mamlûks. The various Iranian rulers hastened to submit, eager to lend themselves to his magnificence; but one feels that he was riding on the reputation of a vivid past. With all the resources of these united powers at his disposal, the reduction of the little towns of Quhistân was a matter of years; Muḥammad at Alamût defied him.

It seems possible that some of the Rûdbâr fortresses might have held out indefinitely, long enough to persuade the Mongols to make a favorable accommodation. Rashîd ad-Dîn especially congratulates Hûlâgû's good fortune in being able to reduce the Ismâʿîlîs so quickly.[52] Rashîd ad-Dîn and Juwaynî, in their life of Khwurshâh, note that on the surrend-

[50] Perhaps still allies?!

[51] The account of the Mongol attack follows Rashîd ad-Dîn's history of Hûlâgû, edited by Quatremère, and Juwaynî's corresponding account in the Qazwînî edition.

[52] Quatremère, *Histoire*, p. 218.

er of Alamût the fortress was found to be so strongly built that the leisured efforts of the workmen designated to destroy it seemed almost futile. Water was provided through channels of solid rock, and stored in tanks hewn of solid rock. Provisions of weapons and food were enormous; the tanks of food are described with wonder, deep within the Rock; that the greater part of the food dating even to the time of Ḥasan-i Ṣabbâḥ was in good condition still in those subterranean hollows was attributed to the special blessing of that hero. The winding steps, the high plastered buildings, the large expanse which astonished Hûlâgû combined to give the impression of a self-sufficient and impregnable world.

We know that other fortresses were also well equipped. We have mentioned the rock well that the Ra'îs Muẓaffar had had dug at Gird Kûh. Even intellectually, with their libraries, and morally they were prepared to out-endure the Mongols. In each fortress was a garrison of men who knew how to take care of themselves, no one of whom is recorded as ever turning traitor. Presumably it was Muḥammad's plan that each fortress should hold out on the basis of its own resources, except in case of emergency, as at the time of an epidemic in Gird Kûh; receiving from each other rather moral support than a concerted military strength. Such a plan might have been feasible so far as we can see; but the crucial resource it depended upon was a supreme confidence – in themselves, and in the ultimate goal for which they resisted.

The Mongols for their part seem still to have retained something of the sense of great destinies which held them together to dominate the world. The Mongol activity did not entirely wait upon the presence of Hûlâgû. His general Kîtubûqâ went ahead at a more expeditious pace, and tried to conquer as much of the Ismâʿîlî territories as he could during the three years preceding Hûlâgû's personal advent.

Kîtubûqâ demonstrated that the Mongols were still a fighting force, though not overwhelming in so relatively small a detachment as he commanded. In the first year he raided most of the Iranian Ismâʿîlî areas, including Rûdbâr and the Ismâʿîlî lands nearby in Gîlân; he evidently took some places in Quhistân; but his lieutenant suffered a major defeat at Gird Kûh, which he was besieging. Kîtubûqâ had the siege of Gird Kûh renewed, but when disease decimated the Ismâʿîlî ranks there Muḥammad III was able to send decisive reinforcements which broke through the encircling lines with no casualties. Kîtubûqâ then concentrated on Quhistân, taking Tûn and some other towns. Evidently in the last year before Hûlâgû arrived the Ismâʿîlîs recuperated, retaking Tûn and no doubt other places, and preventing Kîtubûqâ from making any fresh advances. Nonetheless, the Mongols kept up a constant pressure, which was reinforced by the looming threat of the approach of Hûlâgû's ponderous hosts.

The Mongols possessed a terrifying past, which they were careful to keep fresh. Almost all men accepted the Mongols as men apart, and dared not resist them. Perhaps it was something of this temper that made for the recorded estrangement of Muḥammad III from his principal subjects at this time. Muḥammad was clearly insistent in defying the Mongols.[53] Evidently many of his grandees were not. Perhaps they thought Muḥammad's hopes madly delusive in the face of a power to which all the world submitted. Perhaps friction over their fainthearted-ness deepened Muḥammad's melancholia.[54] At any rate, it was said that Muḥammad's mental condition took a turn for the worse now, and that the chief men of Rûdbâr were beginning to fear for their lives. Khwurshâh also had now begun to suspect the worst from his jealous father. Toward 1255 all these diverse tensions, internal and external, converged against the unhappy imâm.

Crisis and Murder.

According to Rashîd ad-Dîn and Juwaynî, Khwurshâh considered flight to Syria or seizure of one of the fortresses in Rûdbâr as a refuge from his father. But instead he came to an agreement with his father's principal men for what would have amounted to an enforced regency. As opportunity arose, Muḥammad was to be set aside in such a manner that he should receive no personal harm; Khwurshâh was in effect to rule in his place; and was particularly to treat with the Mongols, so removing the external as well as the internal causes of anxiety.[55] But before the plan was put into operation, Ḥasan Mâzandarânî carried out

[53] In 1254 it was reported that Ismâʿîlîs had been sent to Mongolia to assassinate Mangû in reprisal for sending Hûlâgû against them. Wm. Rubruck, tr. W. W. Rockhill, 1900, p. 222.

[54] Perhaps the accusation of Muḥammad's increasing madness at this time was in part a politic self-justification of the Ismâʿîlîs later to the Mongols.

[55] Juwaynî seems to imply the agreement was to protect Khwurshâh from assault by Muḥammad's agents, but not by Muḥammad personally, while Khwurshâh treated with the Mongols. Rashîd ad-Dîn's wording makes more sense.

[56] Juwaynî says he was asleep drunk, *Ta'rîkh-i Jahân Gushâ*, III, 254; but Rashîd ad-Dîn does not retain this detail in his Ismâʿîlî history, at least in this mss.; though it appears in his earlier history of Hûlâgû along with a more assured accusation of Khwurshâh's complicity than later. Quatremère ed., p. 174.

his own private plan to slaughter Muḥammad with an axe while he was asleep in a goatherd's hut.[56]

Ḥamd Allâh writes that Ḥasan Mâzandarânî had consulted Khwurshâh beforehand, and interpreted his silence as consent.[57] Juwaynî, rejecting the idea that Khwurshâh himself did the killing, argues in favor of his complicity on the basis of his chary behavior toward Ḥasan after the fact, and of alleged accusations by his mother and sisters. But it seems doubtful that Khwurshâh was at all involved. At the first there was a miscellaneous slaughter of suspects, but when Ḥasan was betrayed by his wife (presumably Muḥammad's former concubine) the run of suspicions seems to have ended conclusively. Ḥasan and his family were killed and burned. Had Khwurshâh been consulted, this would be a strange sequence; perhaps even stranger would have been such a move by Ḥasan on the verge of his liberation by the enforced regency; but strangest of all would have been anyone's knowing of a conversation which must have been unusually private. Juwaynî supposes that Ḥasan, who was killed at Khwurshâh's orders while out tending goats, was deliberately being prevented from talking; perhaps so; or perhaps it was desired to duplicate appropriately the conditions of Ḥasan's own deed, in a place where no Sunnî alien in Alamût could rise to protect him.

Muḥammad's death was hailed by the Ismâʿîlîs' enemies, and with reason. We have verses from a scholar in exultation over the event: "When the Angel of Death met his soul at the time set for its seizing, he complained of the calamitous day, that they should interrupt his drunkenness. The cupbearers of Hell came to meet him, to shatter the gladness of prosperity in his breast."[58] Muḥammad's death left the whole burden of resolving the internal conflicts and of facing the Mongols in the hands of young Khwurshâh and his friends. The world-wide plans of the Ismâʿîlîs now seemed chimerical; rather, the little community was faced with a very real world situation, the ingrained hatred of Islâm, and a massed power bent on destroying them. The Mongols were already entrenched in parts of Quhistân, and were a present threat to Gird Kûh and to Rûdbâr. The Ismâʿîlî power was left in the hands of a little knot of very ordinary, and very frightened people.

[57] Ḥamd Allâh Mustawfî Qazwînî, *Ta'rîkh-i Guzîda* (E. J. W. Gibb Memorial, XIV, part 1, [Leyden, 1910]), 256.

[58] Ḥamd Allâh, *Ta'rîkh-i Guzîda*, p. 526. The *Dabistân*, on the other hand, includes laudatory verses upon him at this point, composed by an Ismâʿîlî.

CHAPTER XII

THE FAILURE OF THE NIZÂRÎ VENTURE

RETROSPECT

Juwaynî, and with him no doubt the Sunnîs and Twelvers generally, regarded the destruction of the Nizârî power which quickly followed as an unmixed blessing to a purified earth, where men could now walk without fear. Perhaps he consoled himself that way for having to behold at the same time the Islamic world reduced to one province in a heathen empire. Rashîd ad-Dîn saw in it a fitting retribution for Khwurshâh's suspected parricide, though he took pains to point out that every dynasty must fall some time. As to the Ismâʿîlîs, the loss of their homes and their power, to which was soon added a stupendous massacre, was a desperate blow; yet not yet, perhaps, a total calamity. They were used by now to supporting extravagant claims as the effective power of their venture dwindled; used to an ever greater involvement in the Sunnî society upon which they had centered their hatred; they might make a new adjustment. But it marked an end to their active role as a challenge to the whole of Islâm.

The Nizârî venture had been like running a race in a dream. The very air tugs at one's feet, and one scarcely moves – yet the race is very urgent, one presses on. The landscape about one gradually changes. The goal one viewed at first disappears, one's fellow-racers vanish. Yet the urgency to keep moving does not leave one.

The farflung Ismâʿîlî campaign against the Saljûq power looked very different, as Ḥasan-i Ṣabbâḥ quietly directed its ubiquitous might from out an unyielding Alamût, from the manly but unco-ordinated resistance of the Rûdbâr mountaineers. The stern doctrine of taʿlîm, which had challenged the urbane mind of Ghazzâlî, had been replaced by an eclectic mysticism or a local hero-worship. The far-flung partisans of an Islamic revolution had insensibly become a rustic people, jealously set apart from the world.

At every step of the transformation, however, the same themes had appeared, in varying forms. The imaginative splendor of the ancient bâṭin had persisted, though rebaptized *ḥaqîqa* by Muḥammad II; or transformed with a more personal touch by Sinân; or rewoven to suit a less immoderate age by Ṭûsî and his humbler fellows. The old demand for a universal ideal, given a spectacular turn by Ḥasan-i Ṣabbâḥ, laid upon every later generation the need to seek its own climactic vision. If Ḥasan II proclaimed the end of the world, and his son invited men to look on him and see God Himself, his more prosaic grandson dreamed of turning his villages into a mighty kingdom, and even the sullen Muḥammad III set his eyes on a visible conquest of mankind. Accordingly, to the end their love of esoteric imagery confronted uneasily the hope of a sterner universality; requiring each generation to reinterpret for its own needs the imâm that should guarantee its universal vision – the abstract history that should enshrine its truth – the sense of its intellectual mastery over the world.

Back of these recurrent themes of interpretation, had been recurring the same tendencies, the same problems, in the community life. From the beginning there had been a tension between the self-reliant sense of community power, and the challenge of the triumphant world – a tension which called for drastic short-cuts to fulfill those vast ideals; issuing in those desperate coups, those desperately held forts, in assassinations. At every stage persisted the keen community solidarity, to be broken neither by the attacks of Muḥammad Tapar, nor the retrenchments of Muḥammad b. Buzurg'ummîd, nor the innovations of the Qiyâma, nor the genius of Sinân, nor the conversion of the imâm himself. But at the same time persisted the appeal of a world that could not be ignored – though one should fight it, or deny its existence, or claim as right of conquest its gentle Ṣûfî splendor or its sophisticated admiration, which tugged at Muḥammad III perhaps no less than at his father.

Finally, from the beginning had persisted the fear and hatred shown by that same world. Here and there to be sure, scarcely appreciated by the Nizârîs or by the world either, were the unplanned-for impacts on that world: in the fertile ploughing of Ghazzâlî's soul, in the romantic portrait of Niẓâm al-Mulk, in the paradoxical career of Ṭûsî. More constantly, and this the Nizârîs could know and grimly value, appeared the horror tales, the weird figures of a fascinated imagination, the massacres.

The Nizârî venture had begun as an all-out assault upon the insolent power that was sweeping away the barely won hopes of the Shîʿa. They were beaten, but refused to acknowledge defeat. They retired to mountains to carry on the effort. In reduced circumstances, they attempted a new tack – hailing their independence of a perverse world. But the world remained to be struggled with. The Saljûq power had given way to a constellation of quixotic pretenders. The Nizârîs found themselves caught up in this new race; and then as the old Islamic world shrank into provinciality, they aimed to master a world wider than the Saljûqs had dreamed of. Their exhausted energies dribbled unnoticed from India to France. At last they were called on in their turn to meet the dread Mongol scourge, while a world once again strangely altered stood by unanimously gloating.

It is a temptation to show, when apparent cataclysms sweep away once great edifices, that after all they would soon have passed on in any case, with internal decay. Such an analysis can always be supported, for every new development of life presupposes an equally continuous decay of the old. But I suppose it is not always tenable. One is free to assume, then, that had it not been for the Mongols, other less grandiloquent powers might have allowed the Ismâʿîlîs to moulder on in their hills for an indefinite time. The Syrian branch, though it recovered from the Mongol attacks (to all appearances) completely, was within two decades subjugated definitively by Baybars of Egypt; yet this might be set aside as evidence, on the ground that it was the weakest grouping in the community and was now isolated. Yet one feels when one comes to the end of the third Muḥammad's ambitious, aggressive, yet almost impotent reign that now the community had tried everything; they had tried with spirit and with courage; but now it was time that they must give up and admit defeat. Had they persisted as a state it would have been an excess of indulgence on the part of the gods.

THE END OF THE NIZÂRÎ POWER

Khwurshâh's surrender (1256).

Before opening negotiations with the Mongols, Khwurshâh arranged affairs at home. He completed an expedition into Khalkhâl – to the west of Rûdbâr in Gîlân – which his father had set on foot; after the objective there was taken and the garrison put to the sword,[1] however, he wrote to the various neighboring rulers announcing his father's death and his own

[1] Ḥamd Allâh, *Ta'rîkh-i Guzîda*, facsimile p. 526.

accession. Evidently he wanted first to make his peace with the Muslims in his rear. No doubt to the same end, he wrote to all the Ismâ'îlîs that they should behave as good Muslims – presumably, that is, that they should hold to their taqiyya more closely than they had in his father's time. Then some months after his accession he wrote to Yasûr, the Mongol commander at Hamadhân in 'Irâq 'Ajamî, offering his submission.

Meanwhile, Kîtubûqâ had been sent on a campaign in Quhistân, in which in one week a large area was overrun. Soon Tûn was recaptured, and all the inhabitants killed except the artisans, as was a common Mongol custom. The aged Nâṣir ad-Dîn came to Hûlâgû to make his own submission, but explained that the rest of the Quhistânîs would not submit, for they were at Khwurshâh's orders, not his. Hûlâgû set the old man over the remains of Tûn, but Nâṣir ad-Dîn died the next year.[2] Evidently the greater number of Quhistânî strongholds continued to hold out.

When Khwurshâh now offered his submission to Yasûr, Yasûr answered that he must go in person to Hûlâgû. That monarch was proceeding by slow stages, interrupted by long and ostentatious drinking bouts, westward across Îrân. Khwurshâh sent his younger brother Shâhinshâh, who met Yasûr near Qazwîn, and was sent on to Hûlâgû's court of the moment in Khurâsân. Yasûr himself came into Rûdbâr and camped. The Ismâ'îlîs established themselves on a mountain above them, and when the Mongols tried to take that position from them there was a considerable battle, in which the Mongols were forced to retire. They set about destroying the crops and anything else they could instead. At this point messengers came from Hûlâgû, who had received Shâhinshâh, and expressed his willingness to consider Khwurshâh guiltless of all his father's crimes, provided he would destroy all his fortresses and come in person to submit. At the same time, Yasûr's army ceased its depredations and moved off.

Khwurshâh, however, was not quite ready to give up entirely yet. He began the work of dismantling several of the Rûdbâr fortresses, but begged that Alamût and Lammasar be excepted, for their venerability; and above all asked for a year's delay before coming himself, so that he could

[2] At this point I am following Rashîd ad-Dîn's history of Hûlâgû, p. 174, which is not very clear; perhaps deliberately so in order to make the Mongol campaigns seem universally successful. For most of the narrative I prefer to take as basis the history of Khwurshâh, in which Rashîd ad-Dîn and Juwaynî permit themselves more details about what the Ismâ'îlîs in Rûdbâr were doing.

complete the work of dismantling. Hûlâgû thereupon sent a Mongol to take charge while Khwurshâh was at court. Khwurshâh sent his vizier Shams ad-Dîn Gîlakî to plead again for more time; and also sent messengers to order the chiefs of Gird Kûh and Quhistân to go to Hûlâgû and submit. Hûlâgû sent Shams ad-Dîn on to Gird Kûh to secure its submission; and its head, the Qâḍî Tâj ad-Dîn, did come – but the fortress itself still held.[3] On the other hand, Hûlâgû assured Khwurshâh that if he could not himself come within five days, he should send his son on ahead. By this time, Hûlâgû was in the vicinity of Rayy. His general had already taken an Ismâʿîlî outpost in the vicinity, and he himself was coming closer all the time.

Khwurshâh chose to send his son. Evidently Hûlâgû privately suspected that this was not his real son – an opinion which Juwaynî adopted, writing in Hûlâgû's lifetime, in spite of unanimous Ismâʿîlî testimony; but which Rashîd ad-Dîn rejected. At any rate, Hûlâgû sent the boy back on the grounds of his tender age – he was about seven years old. He suggested that Khwurshâh send another brother to relieve Shâhinshâh, who had been away from home a number of months by now. Khwurshâh sent a large number of his grandees with his brother Shîrânshâh, who however found Hûlâgû only three days' march from Rûdbâr, and had to bring back an ultimatum couched in the classical Mongol form, that Khwurshâh must destroy Maymûndiz, the fortress in which he was living, and come himself; or God alone could tell what would happen. Soon thereafter he had many of the Ismâʿîlî grandees who were with him secretly slaughtered.[4] At the same time Hûlâgû's armies entered Rûdbâr – explaining that they had come for forage.

With little delay, however, Hûlâgû himself arrived, and frankly set siege to Maymûndiz, in which Khwurshâh still lingered. He arrived so suddenly, that but for the accident of rain that night he might have taken Khwurshâh at the foot of his fortress. There were some skirmishes; and it seems that Hûlâgû doubted the practicability of taking it yet that year, and considered coming back another time; but he sent Khwurshâh an ultimatum that he must be down within five days or expect war.

It seems that the non-Ismâʿîlî scholars, whom Muḥammad had gathered together, had long since determined to dissuade Khwurshâh from

[3] We do not know whether this is the same Tâj ad-Dîn who was earlier ruling in Syria. That one is Mardânshâh and the other Abû l-Futûḥ, does not tell us much. Khwurshâh's ḥujja in the traditional list is a Tâj ad-Dîn.

[4] This detail is from Juwaynî on Hûlâgû, Vol. III, p. 112.

holding out; expecting themselves (and justifiedly) to be received into still better positions in Hûlâgû's service. Khwurshâh now appears to have begun to rely more on their judgment. Supposedly Ṭûsî advised him to give in on the grounds that the stars were unfavorable.[5] For a few days he still temporized – first the garrison denied Khwurshâh was there at all; then Khwurshâh explained he had not before realized that Hûlâgû was there in person, and would now come, if he were not in fear of his life from some of his followers.[6] Nevertheless, he did send out some top men to negotiate a surrender with Hûlâgû; among them was Naṣîr ad-Dîn Ṭûsî, who was in league with the Sunnî scholars; and a few days later, when Khwurshâh himself came down, it was in his company and theirs, as well as with his vizier. Khwurshâh was received, and the Mongols immediately took care to receive also all his treasure; but it was not so great as expected. Khwurshâh's scholarly friends, including Ṭûsî, very quickly dissociated themselves from the Ismâʿîlîs, and were given high positions at the Mongol court for the rest of their comfortable lives.

Though most of the Ismâʿîlîs evidently followed Khwurshâh's lead in surrendering, they could not expect a happy fate in doing so; and many refused. The patriot souls who had been too few to prevent Khwurshâh's surrender with their threats at least stayed and gave their own lives rather than face ignominy. When the Mongol forces entered Maymûndiz, they were attacked by a devoted remnant, whom they had to exterminate before they could take possession.[7]

Khwurshâh among the Mongols.

Khwurshâh personally, for a while, was treated very well at Hûlâgû's court; but his chief job now was to persuade the remainder of the Ismâʿîlî fortresses to surrender. This was not necessarily an easy matter, even without reckoning in the "extremists" that resisted at Maymûndiz. Though he was imâm, and the bulk of the Ismâʿîlîs seem to have been willing to sacrifice their whole social existence at his bidding, yet it will have been hard for some to convince themselves that his summons to give up was not a new sort of taqiyya, to be disregarded in fact. Khwurshâh sent his orders; and evidently the great majority of fortresses in Rûdbâr, in Quhistân, and around Gird Kûh in Qûmis now surrendered,

[5] Ibn Isfandiyâr (Continuator), transl., p. 259.

[6] These details are taken from the victory bulletin, which Juwaynî cites from his own hand, ps. 125–30.

[7] Juwaynî, ed. p. 135.

to the number of about a hundred. The places were all evacuated and destroyed.

In Rûdbâr, Alamût and Lammasar refused to surrender, even at Khwurshâh's personal appeal. Hûlâgû stayed a few days before Alamût, then went to besiege Lammasar. While he was there the governor of Alamût changed his mind, and sent to ask Khwurshâh to intercede for them with Hûlâgû. The Alamût garrison was permitted three days after the surrender for carrying away their possessions; then the Mongols went in, and set about the very difficult task of demolishing the place. Alamût proved the marvel of the Mongols; Hûlâgû himself climbed up and wondered at it. Presumably this lent all the more charm to its destruction. Except for what the garrison had been permitted to take away, or certain books that Juwaynî salvaged, the Mongols managed with zeal and much hard labor to destroy all else that had been created in a hundred and sixty six years of vision and resourcefulness.

Lammasar held out still (and for a year more), so Hûlâgû left it to be besieged by a smaller army, and retired himself for celebrations at Qazwîn. From there Khwurshâh was made to send letters to the Syrian fortresses, bidding them surrender whenever the Mongols should appear. Gird Kûh also was not yet in Mongol hands. But by and large Hûlâgû seemed to be satisfied with Khwurshâh's work, and treated him indulgently. Khwurshâh fell in love with a Mongol girl, and was given her in marriage.[8] Khwurshâh liked to see camel-fighting, so Hûlâgû made him a present of a hundred male camels for the purpose. Khwurshâh's baggage was allotted storage space in Qazwîn (no doubt to the disgust of the Qazwînîs), while Khwurshâh himself was to follow Hûlâgû in his next march – toward Baghdâd.

Khwurshâh's personal fate seems almost a side issue in the general debacle. The Ismâʿîlîs were no doubt even from the start less concerned for him than that his son (and heir) be spirited out of sight – as the later sectarians claimed was done. Khwurshâh, for his part, seems to have been relieved to escape from the series of intolerable situations he was born to; it was a bad dream with a happy ending. He clearly enjoyed Mongol hospitality – treated like a great prince, he behaved like a freed prisoner. He himself, we are told, asked to be sent to Mongolia to visit the great Khân. On the way, he tried in vain to persuade Gird Kûh to surrender. Juwaynî accuses him of sending it at the same time secret orders not to. Whether Khwurshâh actually took the trouble to indulge in duplicity at this point is almost irrelevant. Ismâʿîlî garrisons were

[8] Juwaynî says it was the daughter of a low-class Turk; I follow Rashîd ad-Dîn.

capable of holding out on their own; and as far as Ismâʿîlî leadership was concerned, no doubt Khwurshâh's little son was effective imâm from the moment his father set off for anticipated glories in Mongolia. But Mangû Khân finally is said to have rejected him, on the grounds that Gird Kûh and Lammasar were not yet surrendered. There were many accounts of his end at the time, but we may assume that he was murdered by his guards on the trip in 1257; and that whoever gave the immediate orders, the murder was ultimately the effect of Sunnî intrigue.

The revenge of Islâm.

While Khwurshâh was on his fatal voyage in distant Transoxania, his community was tasting the accumulated hatred of generations of orthodox Muslims. After the strongholds had been razed, the surrendered garrisons had been parcelled out among the Mongol commanders and evidently interspersed honorably among their troops. But very soon the order came to destroy all Ismâʿîlîs upon whom hands could be laid; and especially the family of Khwurshâh even to the babies. The Mongol commander in Quhistân, Ûtâkûjînâ, is said to have rounded up eighty thousand on the pretext of a general meeting (presumably for counsel – the hardy spirit of men who expected to be consulted en masse, even by Mongols!)[9] and massacred them. When finally the two resistant fortresses were taken, their garrisons were of course obliterated. Juwaynî assures himself that every Ismâʿîlî was killed; yet even if all the members of garrisons were in fact killed, a great many others will have escaped. But, as Ibn Isfandiyâr says, Khurâsân especially was flooded with the captive women and children, sold as slaves.

The bigotry of Islâm was not quite satisfied with blood and misery. At Alamût it expressed itself through the learned hands of Juwaynî himself. The famous, dangerous library was taken in hand. Korans and other safe items were exempted. Then the mass of sectarian material, archives and expositions, hardly duplicable no doubt, was picked over with a smug curiosity. Juwaynî selected what facts about the fallen folk he found edifying or curious enough for posterity to be informed of; and committed the rest to the flames.

Two years later Baghdâd itself followed Alamût to destruction. The Mongols, with a commendably impartial lust to subdue or destroy, summoned the Caliph as they had summoned the Imâm, and easily

[9] D'Ohsson, however, suggests the pretext was counting them with regard to military service. *Histoire des Mongols*, III, 202.

defeated the armies he could send against them. There are suggestions that the Caliph was betrayed by Twelver Shîʿite intellectuals in his service. At any rate, he held out until the military decision was practically final. Then he surrendered himself, but won pity neither for his city nor for himself. Baghdâd has recovered only in our own time.

Our Ṭûsî, who had himself been so tortuously gripped in the deceit and violence of his time, is sometimes given credit for persuading Khwurshâh to surrender the Ismâʿîlî power; and likewise, for assuring Hûlâgû that nothing out of the ordinary would happen if he should attack the Caliph. A Twelver at heart, he could rejoice in the fall of both the great opponents of his faith one after another. In the general ruin he was able to protect, at least, many of the centers of his own religion. It is doubtful if he wished either the Imâm or the Caliph personally any harm; we hear of the trickery he used with the gullible Hûlâgû to save the Sunnî Juwaynî's life when it was threatened by the Mongol's whim. But Ṭûsî had learned how to pursue his own interests in science and no doubt also in devotion through whatever pretence or outward humiliation might be necessary to humor and make use of such men as might be in power. Whatever happened to his generation, he had emerged unscathed.

For a while it seemed as if all Islâm, all the Middle East, were in the dust before the heathen Mongols; and that it scarcely mattered any longer which sort of Islâm, Sunnî or Shîʿa either, might have claimed an edge over the other. In fact, the Mongols proved impotent before the two great Muslim powers of Cairo and of Delhi; and even in Îrân were themselves converted after a few decades to Islâm. Yet in another sense, as to the outcome of their long rivalry, what happened to Baghdâd or to Alamût no longer mattered indeed; for the outcome had been long since decided. The Ismâʿîlî alternative had been defeated already; even the Fâṭimids had lost their opportunity; and if the Nizârîs had once been an active challenge, the fall of Alamût now made little difference. The fall of Baghdâd made little difference either; the Sunnî cause, the fully developed official faith, had already won. Sunnî Islâm could cast off what remained of the ancient pre-Islamic imperial shell, and merge in right of its own universal sharîʿa law, which required neither hierarchy nor outward unity to administer. So long as there were men who took it on themselves to know the law, the vast community could proceed in perfect confidence. Despite Twelver or Christian or indeed Ismâʿîlî rivalry, it had little trouble in converting its Mongol conquerors, and setting off upon its modern career, long unhindered by serious rivals.

AFTERGLOW

As for the Ismâʿîlîs, they did not know for some time that it was all over. In Îrân for a number of years there were strenuous, sometimes partly successful efforts made to regain their fortresses and their power. In Syria the fall of Alamût seemed somewhat remote. The Mongols appear in Abû Firâs only as an astounding interlude. Those who held out in their fortresses at the time the armies came were enraged and disgusted at the four garrisons which had submitted. One leader, in prison for having helped surrender his fortress, is recorded to have vowed to build a shrine to Râshid ad-Dîn if he were saved alive. It must have seemed, when he and others (but not the four commanders) were in fact released, as if the most permanent result of the Mongol conquest would be that shrine.[10]

The Mamlûk triumph in Syria.

Yet the Ismâʿîlîs had fought vigorously against the Mongols, evidently in some collaboration with the Syrian Muslims. Immediately after the fall of Alamût Riḍâ ad-Dîn, who the next year was to become head of the Syrian Ismâʿîlîs (frankly by local selection, now, the imâm being presumably not in a position to appoint), went on a mission to the Egyptian ruler. When the Mongols did finally arrive in Syria in 1260, and occupy among other places certain of the Ismâʿîlî fortresses, it was the great Baybars, hurriedly replacing as ruler the Ayyûbids of Egypt, who chased the Mongols away. The Ismâʿîlîs themselves, however, then helped the lord of Ṣaḥyûn against a Mongol and Armenian army; and two or three years later chased another Christian-Mongol combination from Sarmîn, in that Jazr area where no doubt Ismâʿîlîs still lived.

Meanwhile, the Ismâʿîlîs were becoming ever more involved with the Egyptian government. Already in 1261 Baybars is reported to have granted to the prince of Ḥamâh rights to the (nearby) Ismâʿîlî territories in return for his support. That same year the Ismâʿîlîs demanded, and received, the concession of all privileges they had held under the Ayyûbids, including a subsidy. Yet at the same moment Baybars attempted to divide the Ismâʿîlîs by appointing the envoy, whom they had sent him, to be their lord: not without some success, for on the current lord's death he attempted, fruitlessly, to take his place. There were repeated

[10] Guyard, *JA*, ser. 7, IX (1877), 470. Cf. Ibn Muyassar, p. 68.

embassies from the Ismâʿîlîs to Baybars, increasingly humbler in tone till the end; which arrived, by duplicity and force, very quickly.

In 1265 Baybars found himself strong enough to tax the presents from foreign powers passing through Egypt, and sent a threat to the Ismâʿîlîs. They answered by asking that they be included, as Baybars' subjects, in any treaty with the Franks (who still held certain positions along the Syrian coast). In 1266 he demanded their allegiance, claiming that his current campaigns against the knightly orders were to the Ismâʿîlîs' benefit, after they had so long paid (along with most Syrian towns) the hated tribute to these orders. When as a result of the campaign the tribute was lifted from them all, the definitive change in Ismâʿîlî circumstances had arrived. The Ismâʿîlîs were now no longer on the frontier; they were henceforth an enclave within Muslim territory. Baybars demanded that now the same amount be paid to himself as had been paid to the orders – and it was.

By 1270 the Ismâʿîlîs were begging for a reduction in the terms; Baybars countered with another attempt to install the envoy as their ruler, and in addition asked for the stronghold of Maṣyâf for himself. The envoy, instead of trying to force his own rule generally, tried to hold Maṣyâf in Baybars' name but for his own benefit; Baybars thereupon ousted him, and gave his support to the regular ruler – at the price of keeping his son hostage at Cairo. A plot of the Ismâʿîlîs to gain help from Tripoli was of no use. By the next year Baybars was taking the Ismâʿîlî fortresses one by one militarily; though not without the use, as far as possible, of concessions and bribes to the chiefs. The last attempts by the various – evidently now isolated – garrisons to resist him failed; including a couple of attempts at assassination. In 1273 Baybars had his own lieutenant in each of the Ismâʿîlî strongholds.[11]

One suspects an element of confusion and of loss of morale behind so facile a manipulation of the Ismâʿîlî allegiance on Baybars' part, especially since the Ismâʿîlîs failed to act in unison even in their resistance. Indeed, Ivanow reports that within two generations after Khwurshâh there was a split among the Nizârîs, the Syrians accepting a different line of imâms from the Iranians.[12] One gets the impression, indeed, that the Sulṭâns of Egypt were finally accepted as their rightful lords, at least on one level.[13]

[11] Defrémery, *JA*, ser. 5, V (1855), 48–65, summarizes these details at length.

[12] W. Ivanow, 'A Forgotten Branch of the Ismailis,' *JRAS*, 1938, pp. 57–79.

[13] Cf. Qalqashandî, *Subḥ al-Aʿshâ*, XIII (Cairo, 1918), 245, who says that the Ismâʿîlîs regarded any ruler of Egypt as entitled to their obedience; also cf. Defrémery's notations, *JA*, ser. 5, V (1855), 70–74.

Under Egyptian rule.

From the Egyptian point of view, the Ismâʿîlîs now lived autonomously under their own chief, serving as assassins at the Sulṭân's disposal whenever needed, for a fixed price.[14] (However, one sulṭân is said to have been deposed on the grounds of having used these assassins too freely.) Already before Baybars had reduced all the fortresses, he is said to have sent one of the Ismâʿîlîs against an enemy prince.[15] So much did the Ismâʿîlîs become the special hirelings fo the sulṭâns that the payment for protection which the Armenians were wont to make to the Ismâʿîlîs was diverted to the Sulṭân in about 1283. In that year and two years later the Ismâʿîlîs were included in the Sulṭân's treaty with the Franks – the second time, in the proviso that the Sulṭân reserved the right to send them against the Franks if he chose. Even more than against the Franks, the Sulṭâns used them against the Mongols. We hear of many Ismâʿîlî lives sacrificed in such attempts; even the attempt on Juwaynî, in 1271, though he could be regarded as a special enemy of the Ismâʿîlîs, may have been initiated in Egypt; for he was governor of Baghdâd, a high Mongol official.

No doubt from the Ismâʿîlî point of view the Egyptian connection was a secondary one, ordered for their spiritual good by their true rulers. Abû Firâs says that after Baybars took over there were mosques built; but no doubt they were little used: no more than in the Nineteenth Century, according to travellers' reports.[16] The truer bent of Ismâʿîlî piety then and henceforth will be found in the triumph of popular sentiment as illustrated in the shrine built to Sinân. Such a shrine, a *mashhad*, is a puzzle to the logically-minded historian; if Sinân embodied a cosmic principle, then they should logically turn to his successor; or if there is a spiritual worship without outward forms, what is the use of a shrine? But the shrine was nevertheless more than a pious memento where the faithful could be reminded of how God-led their leaders had been and would always be. Sinân had appeared in a dream to support the project and, as throughout Islâm, this meant that Sinân himself was there, and would give his blessing to the worshipper. Seeking the blessings of Khiḍr,

[14] So the situation appears in the *Masâlik al-Abṣâr*, whose author interviewed the chief of the time (*Mines de l'Orient*, IV, Quatremère).

[15] Two assassinations of Franks mentioned in the *Gestes des Chyprois*: *RHC Arméniens*, pp. 775, 779 for 1270, and for 1272 (the attempt on Edward of England) may not be ascribable to the Ismâʿîlîs at all; or if to them, then not necessarily to Baybars, though the first is blamed on him. Nowell thinks the word "assassin" was by then used in its general sense: he cites a usage in Dante. *Speculum*, 1947, p. 155.

[16] Fred Walpole, *The Ansayrii* (1850), III, 299.

of Sinân, and of all the imâms, the Syrian Ismâʿîlîs have lived isolated in their mountains to this day.

The Iranian Ismâʿîlîs attempt a comeback.

The Iranian Ismâʿîlîs were unable to preserve even so much of a shadow independence as the Syrian; but their spirit was more nearly indomitable; and it is from among them that the great future of Nizârî Ismâʿîlism sprouted again. It is said that the child imâm was carried into Âdharbâyjân, where the imâms lived for some time. But the Ismâʿîlîs were not content to retire just yet into full obscurity. Alamût had been rebuilt as a Mongol stronghold, and they recaptured it in 1275 after the death of the Mongol monarch Arghûn, in a coalition with a descendant of the Khwârazmshâhs. The next year, however, the new monarch Abâqâ was able to put them out again.[17] They were not able to repeat this success.

Nevertheless, both Quhistân and Rûdbâr continued for a long time to harbor large Ismâʿîlî populations. Von Hammer has given us extracts from a booklet by one Jalâlî of Qâ'in, who reports that in the time of his grandfather in the first part of the Fourteenth Century the land was so thoroughly Ismâʿîlî that Sunnî missionaries arriving to remedy matters had to begin almost from scratch. Jalâlî reports, however, that in his own time early in the Fifteenth Century the bulk of the population was orthodox; though he was assured there were still some Ismâʿîlîs around.[18]

We learn that for a long time the grave of Ḥasan-i Ṣabbâḥ at Alamût continued to be visited from both Rûdbâr and Quhistân.[19] Dimashqî also seems to suggest that the Rûdbâr area continued to resist Sunnism, in the early Fourteenth Century, in a strange notice about men in Gîlân who believe God appears in human form, and expect him to appear on a gray ass.[20] Only gradually did the old centers of Ismâʿîlî power become assimilated to the rest of the land about them; there are evidently a few Ismâʿîlîs left in Quhistân even now, though with numerous shifts in population the remnants of Persian Ismâʿîlism are now scattered about.[21]

[17] Ḥamd Allâh Mustawfî, *Ta'rîkh-i Guzîda*, trans. Browne, 1913, p. 583.

[18] Von Hammer, *History of the Assassins*, Engl. transl., ps. 205 and 209.

[19] Ḥamd Allâh, in *JA*, 1849, pp. 49 ff.

[20] Dimashqî, *Manuel de la Cosmographie du Moyen Age*, tr. M. A. F. Mehren (Copenhagen, 1874), p. 315.

[21] Ivanow, *Kalâm-i Pîr*, p. lxi.

It is even possible that the Ismâʿîlîs attempted a comeback in the west – in Âdharbâyjân or in Anatolia; we find that one of the Saljûq princes of Anatolia, reigning immediately after the fall of Alamût, was accused of Ismâʿîlism – apparently on the grounds that he was curious about religious questions in general.[22] There is a strange association of Shams-i Tabrîz, the mystical dedicatee of the great Anatolian poet Jalâl ad-Dîn Rûmî, with Ismâʿîlism: Dawlatshâh makes him son of Ḥasan III, while later Ismâʿîlîs have made him one of their imâms.[23] Somewhere the Ismâʿîlî and Rûmî traditions must have rubbed shoulders.

Deprived of the responsibility of a state power, the Ismâʿîlîs rapidly began to lose sight of the finesses of religious doctrine. The popular sentiment often triumphed unrestrained. We find often the idea that all the imâms had been in satr since Ismâʿîl son of Jaʿfar aṣ-Ṣâdiq;[24] and such crudities as that those who criticize the imâm will be, at the day of Resurrection, hung by the heels and tormented.[25] The Iranians, however, seem to have kept alive a more distinctively Nizârî tradition, continuously developed from Alamût times, than did the Syrians; perhaps because of the great developments that later occurred among them, and which led to the powerful sect of modern times.

The Nizârî heritage.

Within Îrân the Ismâʿîlî heritage entered into the general current of Persian mystical and esoteric thought. On the one hand, the Ismâʿîlîs could appear to the world as a particular group of Ṣûfîs, following their own hereditary shaykh as did other Ṣûfîs also. On the other hand, as Îrân gradually became Shîʿite (but Twelver), their doctrines apparently entered into the extremer Persian Ṣûfism, now adapted to a Shîʿite public, as one resource to be drawn upon among others. Ivanow claims that dervishes in Twentieth Century Persia still had to learn by heart the list of Ismâʿîlî imâms, though they held no allegiance to the sect.[26] It seems probable that the several Persian sects which have made much of number analogies and the like, such as in modern times the Bâbîs and Bahâ'îs,

[22] Ivanow, reviewing Gordlevsky in *JBBRAS*, XXIII (new series) (1947). My reader could not find any serious substantiation there. Rukn ad-Dîn Kilij Arslân, 1257–65.

[23] Tâmir ʿÂrif, 'Sinân Râshid ad-Dîn,' *al-Adîb* (May, 1953), p. 45.

[24] *Dabistân*, p. 399.

[25] *Kalâm-i Pîr*, p. 46, evidently in an Abû Isḥâq section, that is, not taken so directly from Twelver doctrine as other parts of the *Kalâm-i Pîr*.

[26] *Dîwân of Khâkî Khurâsânî*, ed. Ivanow (Bombay, 1933), Introduction, pp. 8–9. Here and elsewhere he has much to say about the Ismâʿîlî role in Persian esotericism.

have made use of this strain in Persian esoteric tradition. Having already joined Ṣûfism and Shîʿism in itself, the Ismâʿîli strain will have given a great impulse by its sheer existence to the accommodation of Ṣûfî experience to Shîʿite loyalty which the extremer Shîʿite speculation commonly seems to express. This will be so even apart from the possible personal intervention of a Ṭûsî, or later of an imâm himself, posing as a Ṣûfî pîr.

The Ismâʿîlîs nevertheless never allowed themselves to be submerged in the general esoteric medley. Their form of Shîʿite Ṣûfism remained distinctive, even when most Ṣûfic: they read the standard Ṣûfî literature gladly, but commented it according to their own doctrines.[27] Nor did popular notions ever quite submerge the Ismâʿîlî learned tradition (as they threatened to do in the late *Kalâm-i Pîr*, which adopted Twelver popular ideas wholesale); the very survival of earlier and purer texts, together with that of strictly Ismâʿîlî doctrine in the later texts, shows the persistence of the tradition; though the doctrine continued to be modified from time to time. The sense of a war against the world was gone, to say nothing of the still earlier hope of creating a pattern for Islâm at large; but loyalty to the imâms and to the chosen fraternity which followed them remained, and prepared the sect a great future.

Ivanow believes that the modern Nizârî Ismâʿîlî expansion can be dated back to the "Anjudân revival" of the late Fifteenth Century – just before Twelver Shîʿism came to its definitive triumph in Îrân – when one of the lines tracing back to the imâms of Alamût presumably took advantage of the Shîʿite trends in the air to revive and extend its own form of Shîʿism.[28] They seem not only to have reunited the Nizârîs of Syria and the various parts of Îrân; but to have won also the Ismâʿîlis of the upper Oxus, isolated since Fâṭimid times in their unquenchable loyalty to Nâṣir-i Khusraw – who were outside the Saljûq empire, and evidently took no part in the whole drama which we have portrayed. Moreover, they held the allegiance of the Nizârîs of India – perhaps already then the most numerous of all Nizârî groups.

When in the last century the Âghâ Khân, heir to that line of imâms, had to flee from Îrân to India for political reasons, he found a large community awaiting him, pious and loyal, but almost Hindu in their faith. ʿAlî – who was found again in the imâms his descendants – had been reinterpreted as the expected tenth Avatar, divine epiphany, of

[27] Ivanow tells of an Ismâʿîlî commentary to the *Gulshan-i Râz*, popular Ṣûfî text. *JBBRAS*, 1932, p. 69.

[28] Ivanow, *Rawḍat at-Taslîm*, p. xxviii, and elsewhere.

Hindu thought. Indeed, most of the ideas and practices of the community seem to have reflected more the ancient traditions of the castes which had been converted to Ismâʿîlism than they did Islâm. These Indian Ismâʿîlîs went, and go now, by the ethnic name of *Khojas*. They were, however, at heart always true to their adopted faith, and the difference between their practices and those of his Iranian and Syrian followers did not daunt the Âghâ Khân, who surely knew where the heart of religion lies. He and his descendants have nourished their Indian community until it has not only become an important section of Islâm, but one of the more alert and active commercial communities of the world. The Âghâ Khân continues to receive the allegiance of the greater part of the scattered Ismâʿîlîs of Syria, Îrân, and the Oxus, in their thousands; but to the world, at least, he now appears principally as honored head of the Khoja community of India, whose people are now numbered in the hundreds of thousands, and spread in remote places wherever western Indians have migrated, particularly in East Africa. In India, Nizârî Ismâʿîlism received a vital reincarnation, which has made it a great power in our modern world.

APPENDIX I

THE POPULAR APPEAL OF THE QIYÂMA

TRANSLATION OF THE *HAFT BÂB-I BÂBÂ SAYYID-NÂ* AND COMMENTARY THEREON

It will help in understanding the appeal which the daʿwa of the Qiyâma had to the Ismâʿîlîs to consider in detail what sorts of traditions the doctrine brought together, and the impact of their deployment before the popular mind. For this purpose we shall use a direct, but commented, translation of the major document which we possess from that period, which was designed precisely to expound the excellence of the doctrine for a relatively unsophisticated audience. The *Haft Bâb* is almost certainly from the reign of Muḥammad II – that is, it represents the full blown Qiyâma doctrine, as developed under the son of ʿAlâ Dhikri-hi s-Salâm, and unchanged as yet by the grandson's policies of Satr. This is indicated not only by the date given in the treatise itself (about 1200), and by the fact that it names Muḥammad II but no later imâm; but also by the way in which the stark purity of its Qiyâma teaching fits into what Rashîd ad-Dîn hints of regarding the doctrine of the time, and moreover makes the *Rawḍat at-Taslîm* intelligible as a document of the succeeding period.

I have used the 1933 edition by Ivanow.[1] In the translation I have followed the following principles: 1) I have tried to be as literal as possible while still writing English; not because this will preserve all the elusive flavors, but because literalness is relatively less dangerous here than an attempted smoothness. Where extra help is needed, I have tried to give it within brackets or in notes. 2) Often an Arabic phrase is given in the

[1] One may regard the edition by Ivanow as probably trustworthy, since the arbitrary elements he sometimes introduces into his translations never seem to infect the corresponding portions of his editions. It is apparently impossible to have a look at the manuscripts. In any case they are recent; and like Ivanow (who gives no variants), I have had to make the best of an inadequate text. (When there are obvious errors in Ivanow's *lithograph* – as, words repeated overleaf – I have ignored them.)

text along with its Persian translation. (The Arabic phrases are Ivanow's reconstructions for the most part, he says, as the text itself was badly corrupt in those foreign portions; but the Arabic was taken mostly from standard works, and readily identifiable.) In my translation, I have rendered both Arabic and Persian, so as to indicate any points at which the Persian idiom varied in feeling from the Arabic; the Arabic portion I have then set off in single quotes. 3) In some instances, where both an Arabic and an equivalent Persian term were used in the text, I have translated the Persian, and merely transliterated the Arabic – e.g., the Persian *Khudâ* is rendered "God", but the Arabic *Allâh* is let stand. 4) I have followed Ivanow's paragraphing only where it did not seem to hinder clarity. 5) Although this is a Persian text, I have kept to the transliteration principles mentioned in the Preface; that is, I have rendered the sounds as if they were Arabic, with only the slight modifications for Persian there suggested.

PREFACE AND TABLE OF CONTENTS

Translation:

The seven chapters of Bâbâ Sayyid-nâ ["Father our Master", i.e. Ḥasan-i Ṣabbâḥ]

In the name of God, the merciful, the compassionate. To proceed: These few words have been written on the purpose which was intended in the compostition of this blessed dîvân [collection of poems] of praise and eulogy to Mawlâ-nâ [our lord] (may his power be glorified). But what business has this least of slaves in saying these few words of prose? The purpose is this, that readers be informed by these seven chapters, and not lose the advantage in them, if God Almighty will.

This is the list of the seven chapters: First Chapter: on the subject: people [MS p. 2] hold their own conceptions and ideas as God. Second Chapter: on the subject: The Great and Exalted [God] has a manifestation in this world in His own special form; by which form He has made a man noble.[2] Third Chapter: on the subject: in our time who is this blessed person? where does he reside? what is his name? Fourth Chapter: on the description of the physical world and its nature. Fifth Chapter: on the description of the spiritual world [rûḥânî], and the attributes [p. 5] of the people of Opposition [taḍâdd], of the people of Order [tarattub], and of the people of Union [waḥda]. Sixth Chapter: on the composition of this dîvân; and praise and eulogy to the lord [Khudâwand] (at his mention prostration and glorification) is his whole purpose [?] in this

[2] Or, *in which noble form He has made a man.*

chapter. Seventh Chapter: on dating, and the nature of its conditions. And God knows.

Commentary:

The simplicity of this little preface, as Ivanow has pointed out for the work as a whole,[3] suggests a relatively uneducated author, popularizing the faith on his own crude level for the humbler members of the sect.[4] Accordingly, we ought to have here, uncomplicated by intellectual refinements, the appeal of its ideas to the common sectarian. That we do not possess the dîvân referred to is apparently unimportant, for our unnamed author is commenting only in gross upon it, giving a summary of the whole faith as much for our general profit as for our assistance in the particular poems.

THE FOLLIES OF NON-ISMA'ÎLÎS

Translation:

First Chapter: On the subject: people hold their own conceptions and fancies and ideas as God.

In all the face of the earth, except for the men of the Qâ'im [Qâ'imîyân], who are the men of ḥaqîqa [muḥaqqiqân] of the age, [as to the] knowledge of God, which is the root of religion, they have taken their own conceptions as their model, and hold to it. They have made an exemplar for themselves, and argue about it; and they develop rancor and partisanship. [MS p. 3] Thus some ascribe privation to Him, and say, God has no head, and has no ears and eyes, and has no tongue, and has no hands and feet, and so forth. They reckon of each one of these that He does not have such a thing, even deliberately does not have [it], and is exempt from all this. Those who would know God this way will be among the erring [mubṭilân]. Some others give [Him] attributes resembling [something], and say He is on the heavens, or on a throne or on a couch, or is thus and so. They will be among the Mutashabbihân [comparers – anthropomorphists].

3 W. Ivanow, 'Introduction,' *HBBS*, p. 2.

4 Nevertheless, the Persian is more highly Arabicized than some earlier Persian Ismâ'îlî texts. In contrast to Sijistânî's *Kashf al-Maḥjûb*, technical terms like *Qâ'im al-Qiyâma* are usually left in Arabic. (But cf. *khudâ'î* for *rubûbiyya*.) The blessings and other such phrases are generally Arabic.

Now we must inquire into that first group; for a Daylamite man had an argument in Iṣfahân with one of them, and his opponent was depriving God of attributes [taʿṭîl] in his doctrine, and said, God deliberately lacks such a thing. That Daylamite man says [p. 6] in answer to the Iṣfahânî, addressing him, That which you are speaking of would be a cucumber seed, or a watermelon, it would not be God; one must see something excellent in a lord [khudâwand].

But both groups affirm that the reasoning and conception and fancy and thought and consideration and imagining of the creatures themselves – whatever is born of the creature – cannot know God [p. 4 MS] and does not arrive at God; yet they consider that there is no other guide than the conceiving and the imagining of the creatures themselves. Now He says in the Koran (exalted be His word): 'The evildoers talk very high';[5] but by their own word they are ignorant of God. But to all the children of Adam it is evident that the ignorant of God is a kâfir [infidel] and the place of the kâfir is in Hell. Hence by these premises, with the exception of this rightful community [jamâʿat-i muḥiqqa], the rest are kâfir and are things of Hell [dûzakhî].

And now: – one day I came to have a dispute with a man in Qazwîn; and near by was a person who had come into touch with the upright community [jamâʿat-i qâʾima], and words passed about the gate of Paradise, and the soul, and the lord. I began to converse with that sound man, saying, This Paradise and soul which you speak of are your own conception, and a conception would be nothing. He was an enlightened man, comprehended quickly, and answered, So it is. Then I said, The soul which is not in Paradise is not near God. That man, when he heard these words, looked at me in wonder for a moment; then [p. 7] his eyes became tearful, and he went without saying a word. He came back after a week, and at the hand of the Mawlâ-nâ [our lord] he became one of the men of the Qâʾim through me; and he said, If this religion were not true, I would not have uttered those words when you were at hand.

[P. 5 MS] In the worship of God they set their face toward a physical body, such as toward the heavens, or the sun, moon, and stars, or toward the fire temples among the buildings of the world, as is well-known and famous.[6] They make that an intermediary between themselves and God,

[5] Koran XVII, 43. "His word" is always God's word in the Koran.

[6] This passage seems chiefly directed against the Sunnî Muslims, and the Twelvers who also held to the sharîʿa, with the Kaʿba in Mecca as their qibla to which they turned in prayer; the other things, as qiblas, are brought in to show up the Kaʿba as just another idol, it being a building on the order of the fire temples of the Zoroastrians, which Muslims considered idolatrous.

and so they suppose that through that qibla they will arrive at God. On this point He states, 'Those are like sheep, or even further astray'.[7] In this situation the wise ought to devote some thought and meditation to this matter.

In the knowledge of God, which is the root of religion, a person will lose his way [with] conceiving and thinking. And in the worship of God, which is the fruit [far'] of religion, they likewise make of a stone or a house or a tree and so forth a qibla as an intermediary. When will they arrive at the lord, or how can they know God? His holiness Mawlâ-nâ keep [this error] far from all his servants by his favor and the generosity of his existence. As to this saved community, who are the men of the Qâ'im and the men of ḥaqîqa of the time, they have placed their hands on the skirt of the lord of their own time, so that [by] the Qâ'im of the Qiyâma (upon his mention prostration and glorification) they are saved eternally. And now in the second chapter that favor which the Great and Exalted gives will be spoken of in part, if God Most High will. [p. 8]

Commentary: appeal to personal intellectual adventure.

We have here a circumstantial picture of the appeal which Ismâ'îlism generally, and not least in the time of the Qiyâma, made to the personal quest for immediate experience as against a smug propriety. Tears came to the Qazwînî when someone offered him not sober words but a divine presence; and it was a ridicule of the proud words of the theologians which stopped the ratiocination of the Iṣfahânî.

The characterization here of the scholastic theology is, of course, unfair. Yet it has some justification; the crudity of an imprecise approach to it can indicate weaknesses it will have whenever inadequately developed – as perhaps would be the case with the common people to whom the Ismâ'îlîs appealed. At any rate, the various schools within the more orthodox Islâm had all charged each other endlessly with *ta'ṭîl* and *tashbîh*, purifying God quite away on the one hand, and anthropomorphizing Him on the other; the Ismâ'îlîs themselves had been charged with ta'ṭîl. The *Haft Bab* now claims to get beyond the dilemma altogether by rising to a level higher than verbal formulations.[8]

The appeal against the scholastic theology is actually directed against a popular misunderstanding of it; still more the attack on the outward rites of Islâm, the turning toward the Ka'ba at Mecca, is an appeal to

[7] Koran VII, 179; combined with XXV, 44, suggests Ivanow.

[8] The Ismâ'îlîs had always berated their rivals with these accusations, like everyone else. Probably it is Mu'tazilites that are here accused of ta'ṭîl.

people who have no feeling for the higher implications of ritual Islâm; or rather to those people who have wakened to a need for something more elevating than the ways they learned mechanically as children. It is to such persons – generally self-educated no doubt, and lacking in the rounded vision that can come from mature guidance – that not only a deprecation of the ritual would appeal, but also a sense of adventure in personally working through to an ultimate truth, a religion of experience; for they would be the least equipped to fulfill such a drive within the formal range of Twelver Shîʿism or of Sunnism, if for some reason they were disappointed with the discipline of the Ṣûfîs. The sense of belonging to the specially, even unaccountably, saved elect remnant – of being chosen out by the direct intervention of God – is a compelling one: "if your religion were not true I'd not [have been led to] say those words," and so to have been overwhelmed with your faith. We out of all the world have been graced with salvation, while the seventy-two other sects go under: used by Ismâʿîlîs, this conventional proportion has an awesome ring which is quite missing when it is used by the Sunnîs with their comfortable majority.

EXISTENCE OF A MAN WHO SHOWS FORTH GOD

Translation:

Second Chapter: Discussing and demonstrating that the Great and Exalted has a manifestation in His own form [p. 6 MS] for all eternity in this world; that He has made a man noble with that form,[9] and all the nabîs [prophets] and walîs [friends of God] have indicated a man who should be the Great and Exalted among people in the form of a man.[10] This is his special form; as He states in the Word, 'Lo, God chose out Adam and Noah';[11] and 'He created Adam in His form'; and has stated in another place, 'Lo, God created Adam in the form of the Merciful'.[12]

Another proof is this, that those who speak truth [muḥiqqân] call the Great and Exalted *Mawlâ-nâ* [our lord], indicating a man; and they

[9] Or, *has made a man in that noble form.*

[10] First he shows that man and God can have one form; in the next paragraph, that God is called "Mawlâ-nâ", our lord (a title of the imâm); then that God is even called imâm.

[11] Koran III, 33.

[12] These latter two phrases are not in the Koran, though our author implies that they are. Such a confusion seems distressingly common in later Ismâʿîlî work; perhaps it arises from the practice of tracing many ḥadîth back to God himself as "ḥadîth qudsî". The last ḥadîth implies the same as the second, for *the Merciful, ar-Raḥmân,* is one of the commonest names of God.

consider this name the greatest name of God. Just as the text of the Koran witnesses to the correctness of these words, by the blessed tongue of Ḥaḍrat[13] Rasûl [the Prophet] (bless him) already come, who stated 'Our Lord [rabba-nâ], do not make us bear what we are not able to, be easy on us, forgive us, be merciful to us; you are our Lord [mawlâ-nâ], so help us against the infidel people';[14] and has stated in another place, 'Say, nothing will come upon us except what God has written for us, He is our Lord [mawlâ-nâ]';[15] in another place he stated, 'That is because God is the Lord [mawlâ] of those who believe, and because the infidels have no Lord [mawlâ].[16] [P. 7 MS] The verses in the Koran in which is the name *mawlâ-nâ* are many, and one must [p. 9] seek them out. [There are] a thousand and one names of lordship [khudâwandî], and ninety-nine names are familiar; and it is well-known that the name of Ḥaḍrat Mawlâ-nâ is the name of the Lord most blessed and most high. *Mawlâ-nâ* means *our lord* [khudâwand-i mâ].

And further, Mawlâ-nâ has been called *Imâm.* In the Koran he states 'On a day when we call all men with their imâm';[17] and has stated further, 'We have reckoned all things in a clear imâm [guidance].'[18] And the name *imâm*[19] also is often in the Koran, which is a proof that the name *imâm* is also a name of God. And in ḥadîth, also, Ḥaḍrat Rasûl [the Prophet] states, 'If the world were without an imâm for a moment, it would be convulsed with its people'; and has stated in another place, 'Whoever dies without knowing the imâm of his time has died the death of the heathen [jâhiliyya], and the heathen is in the Fire [of Hell].' That is, if there were no imâm of the time, for a moment, assuredly the world and the people of the world would have no existence. And in another ḥadîth he has stated, Whoever dies without having known the imâm of his time, his death will be the death of the heathen [jâhilân], and the place of the heathen is in the fire of Hell. If the name *imâm* were not a name of the Lord [p. 8 MS] Most High, why would all who died without knowing the imâm of their time go to Hell? One time when a person asked of Mawlâ-nâ Zayn al-'Âbidîn,[20] What is the knowledge [ma'rifa] of the

[13] A title of honor, used with prophets.
[14] Koran II, 286.
[15] Koran IX, 51.
[16] Koran XLVII, 11.
[17] Koran XVII, 71.
[18] The word *imâm* is arbitrarily captured wherever it appears in the Koran. Here, XXXVI, 12. This is an all-Shî'a practice.
[19] Or, *the name of the imâm*, and so subsequently.
[20] Son of Ḥusayn and so great-grandson of the Prophet, Zayn al-'Âbidîn was in life the genealogical link between Ḥusayn, who claimed the Caliphate, and Bâqir and his

Lord Most High [khudâwand ta'âlâ]? he replied (the word of the imâm, peace to him), 'The knowledge of God is in the knowledge of the imâm of their time, who must be obeyed.' And it is well-known even among people at large that [p. 10] *imâm* is the name of the Lord [khudâwand], for among a thousand and one names of God, one must know ninety-nine names of the Great and Exalted; and *Mu'min* [faithful], *Mûqin* [certain], *Muhaymin* [watcher] are also names of the Lord Most High, as is very well known, and there is no need of explanation.[21]

It is transmitted among the people at large that the Prophet [payghambar] (peace be on him) stated, I saw God in 'Arafât[22] seated on a camel, with a white velvet cloak thrown over his head. And the rest have all referred to a man and given good news of him, as did Adam; his people are called *Ṣâbi'a*,[23] and say, Malik Shûlîm will come at the Qiyâma, will judge, and will make clear the divine secrets which the nabîs [prophets] [p. 9 MS] had kept hidden in the cycle [dawr] fo the sharî'a. And in the time and cycle of Adam they call Mawlâ-nâ *Malik Shûlîm;* and he said all that. The affair of Iblîs was in the cycle of Malik Shûlîm.[24]

In the time of Ḥaḍrat Noah they called his blessed name *Malik Yazdâq*, and his people are called *Barâhîma*[25] [Brahmans]; and those affairs of the Flood and of Noah's request that his people be drowned[26] happened with Malik Yazdâq; as He stated, 'My lord [rabbi], do not leave any houses of the kâfirs [infidels] upon the earth.'[27] When he answered the prayer of Noah, he ordered that he should manifest a cycle of sharî'a, till he had drowned them all in that [p. 11] external sharî'a; and those who were blind were drowned, except for what God willed.[28] Then among the

son Ja'far aṣ-Ṣâdiq, who claimed the imâmate. He is a favorite imâm to quote for moralistic (and no doubt spurious) passages among the Shî'a.

21 Epithets like *Mu'min* – commonly used for the true believer – would seem to refer to a man: perhaps this is why they are taken as proofs that the name *imâm*, a man's title, can be a name of God.

22 'Arafât is a hill near Mecca, associated with the pilgrimage ceremonies.

23 The Ṣâbi'ans are mentioned in the Koran as possessors of a prophetic revelation, like the Christians and Jews; and the name came to be applied eventually to all gnostic Pagans – who claimed that their teaching went back to the first sages of mankind. (Each of the traditional Prophets (ûlû l-'azm) is here assigned a people, beginning with Adam.)

24 Iblîs is Satan, who tempted Adam and Eve in the Garden.

25 The long *î* is original; Ivanow notes also a persistent long *î* in *Kalîma.*

26 In the Koran, Noah is a typical rejected Prophet.

27 Koran LXXI, 26.

28 It is understood that "drown" and "blind" are taken metaphorically; it is an old ta'wîl among Ismâ'îlîs that Noah's flood is the outer law which hides the inner truth from the "blind" who cannot see it, and so are lost.

people of sharî'a and of qiyâma[29] none remained with Noah in that saving boat. Thus today the people of Noah say, Malik Yazdâq will come back at the Qiyâma, and he will give the judgment of the Qiyâma, and will send the people of Hell to Hell, and the people of Paradise to Paradise.

In the time of Ḥaḍrat Abraham (peace upon him), they called Mawlâ-nâ *Malik as-Salâm*, and those affairs of Ḥaḍrat Abraham and the catapult and his passing through the fire happened with Malik as-Salâm.[30]

In the period of Ḥaḍrat Moses (peace upon him), they called Mawlâ-nâ *Dhû l-Qarnayn* [p. 10 MS]; and that light which Ḥaḍrat Moses saw that night in that tree[31] – the ta'wîl of the darkness of that night is the externality [ẓâhir] of the sharî'a, and the inward meaning [bâṭin] of the ṭarîqa [saving way]; and the ta'wîl of the tree is the person of a man, and the light is the mercy of Union and of oneness of Mawlâ-nâ. And there is a tradition that the affair of Ḥaḍrat Moses that night had to do with Mawlâ-nâ Dhû l-Qarnayn, and that he saw Mawlâ-nâ. And the affairs of Mount Sinai and of Khiḍr and of the water of life and all those affairs had to do with Mawlâ-nâ Dhû l-Qarnayn. The people of Moses are called Jews, and his dajjâl [anti-prophet] is called *Pharaoh*. And they called Moses[32] *Mawlâ-nâ Sabbath* [shanba]; and they call the judgment of the Qiyâma *Sabbath*. The heavens and [p. 12] the earth will be moved, but the judgment of the Qiyâma will not be moved. That is, the sharî'a and its judgment, which the giver of the sharî'a has made, will be moved, but the Qâ'im of the Qiyâma and his judgment will not be moved.[33] Moses and his people also call Mawlâ-nâ *Messiah*, and say, Messiah will come at the Qiyâma, and separate right [ḥaqq] from wrong [bâṭil], and will raise all the people, and give [p. 11 MS] righteous judgment, and cause everyone to enter into his own deserts [ḥaqq].[34]

In the period of Jesus ['Îsâ] they called Mawlâ-nâ *Ma'add*. Bâbâ Sayyid-nâ [Ḥasan-i Ṣabbâḥ] (may his tomb be hallowed) stated, Ḥaḍrat

29 Possibly this means that all the people, even those who had been privileged with the truth of Qiyâma, but had rejected it, were lost; but probably the reference to Qiyâma is corrupt.

30 This refers to the sufferings of Abraham for his faith. (Perhaps ultimately adapted from the Book of Daniel.)

31 The burning bush.

32 In the *Kalâm-i Pîr*, the Qâ'im. The whole passage is unsure, but perhaps exemplifies the tendency to make all things personal, even the cosmic sabbath that follows the six laborious laws of sharî'a.

33 This evidently refers to the tradition that the Sabbath will outlast heaven and earth, interpreted rather confusedly in the Ismâ'îlî manner. Cf. also Mark 13 : 31.

34 Messiah (*Masîḥ*, or *Masîḥâ*) is a common Muslim name of Jesus. Here it is being used in the older Jewish sense; its insertion into this imagined series of names is a concession to reality.

Jesus wanted to see Mawlâ-nâ Maʿadd; they did not permit it – on this account his people are called *Tarsâ* [fearful].[35] And in the time of Ḥaḍrat Jesus there were many dajjâls who did not obey his order and command.[36] Ḥaḍrat Jesus says, I am the only son of God. If it is so, then certainly his father would be a man.[37] And he says, I shall come back at the Qiyâma and manifest the work of my father; and he says, In the Qiyâma what works shall I do? That is, I shall show Mawlâ-nâ Qâʾim of the Qiyâma to the people. And his people [qawm], that is, his people [umma], are called *Tarsâ;* and they say, What Ḥaḍrat Jesus did in part in the period of sharîʿa, that is, make the dead alive, when he comes in the period of Qiyâma he will do fully, that is, he will restore all the people to life, and will cause the judgment of the Qiyâma to be completely fulfilled; and be an aid to his father. And the Muslims also affirm this their hope, saying [p. 13], Ḥaḍrat Jesus will appear in the period of his Qiyâma and reign forty years and judge righteously among the people, so that the wolf and the ram will drink water together.[38] That is, he will make truth and error, ẓâhir and bâṭin, all one.

And Ḥaḍrat Mohammed Muṣṭafâ (God bless him and his family and give them peace) says, My peoples after my death will become seventy-three, seventy-two perishing and for Hell, but one saved and right-doing. Among all these the Sunnî says, Our great men say, We have chosen among the people four thousand men; and of the four thousand, four hundred; and of the four hundred, forty; and of the forty, four; and of

[35] Maʿadd – eponymic ancestor of all "northern" Arabs (Ishmaelites) – is listed along with ʿAdnân as *mustaqarr* imâm, in the *Gnosistexte* ed. R. Strothmann, *Abh. d. Ak. d. Wiss. in Göttingen, phil.-hist. Kl.*, 3d. series, nr. 28 (1943), being an ancestor of ʿAlî; whereas Jesus appears in an Israelite *mustawḍaʿ* (temporary) line. The Ḥasan-i Ṣabbâḥ story is on the contrary not of Arabic but of Persian origin, for it is in Persian that *tarsâ* means both *fearful* and *Christian.* Could it echo some tale of Jesus' desire to go into the wilderness to pray (which to Ismâʿîlîs would mean as a matter of course, to see the imâm – in the Arabian desert), and his disciples' protests? (Cf. Luke 4 : 42, with perhaps an echo of Mark 8 : 32 ff.)

[36] *Dajjâl,* ordinarily Antichrist or an anti-prophet, seems here to refer to the evil spirits exorcised by Jesus (for disobedience?) unless it refers to the generally untriumphant cast of his life.

[37] The argument seems to be: if Jesus was son of anyone, it must have been of a man; he says he was son of God; *ergo,* God must be a man: all of which would seem to prove that God can appear in the form of a man, that is, the imâm-Qâʾim. Note that this is based on *Christian* sources, not on Muslim: for in the Koran Jesus has no father at all – neither God nor man, though indeed it is a manly angel that appears to Mary. (The "Chapter of Mary.") But it is a *Muslim* mind which takes it for granted that Jesus can not have been the son of God as such, but only of a man who might bear the name of God. Jesus' father is then the Qâʾim.

[38] This is, of course, a fair report of actual Muslim expectations.

the four, one. And he says, This one is the *Quṭb* [axle – spiritually pivotal saint]; and this world subsists on account of him, for the world will not be for a moment without him, and the world would have no existence remaining without him. And the Shî'a call Mawlâ-nâ *Qâ'im of the Qiyâma;* some hold to the name *Malik as-Salâm;* and some say also *Muḥammad* the *Mahdî;* and some say Muḥammad ibn Ḥasan 'Askarî will come out of a cave; and some are sure it is Muḥammad ibn al-Ḥanafiyya; and some say he is still in his mother's womb.[39] Everyone is saying something from his own reasoning and deduction. But the men of the Qâ'im, who are the truthful of the age, call Mawlâ-nâ *Qâ'im of the Qiyâma;* and call Mawlâ-nâ Malik as-Salâm the permanent [mustaqarr] imâm [p. 14; p. 13 MS] and the lord of the time. One person is intended.[40]

And the men of Hindustân who are called *Hindus* [Hunûd] and make idols call one by the name of *Nârin,* and one they call *Sâ'în.*[41]

As to the men of ḥaqîqa of the age, they have become certain, and say, So and so is the one. Because human turbidity and creaturely weakness exist [even] among the truthful community of the age, they have referred to one man, saying, this is the promised man; but some say he is hidden and away. It is for this reason that there is enmity between these two parties [ṭâ'ifa].[42] By the might and power[43] of Mawlâ-nâ (upon his mention prostration and glorification), that which finds favor on this subject will be said in the third chapter if God Most High wills.

Commentary: the various lines of tradition.

Many chords already alive in the public imagination (always eclectic) were struck by the Ismâ'îlî appeal: in this one chapter the number of

[39] The Quṭb, chief of the "four thousand" saints, is the Ṣûfî equivalent, among the Sunnîs, of the Shî'a imâm: he is the unknown perfected saint who in each generation represents God on earth. The other names are of Shî'a imâms whose return is or was expected by various sects. I do not identify Malik as-Salâm in this connection; Muḥammad is quite generally expected to be the name of the Mahdî who is to come at the end of the world and restore justice; Muḥammad ibn Ḥasan 'Askarî is the particular Mahdî of the Twelvers, the last of their imâms, now for several centuries somewhere in hiding; Muḥammad ibn al-Ḥanafiyya, son of 'Alî by a lesser woman (not Fâṭima, Mohammed's daughter) was held by an early sect to be the imâm.

[40] This special identification of Malik as-Salâm with the current Qâ'im of the Qiyâma is not here explained. Presumably he is not the imâm to whom Ḥasan II was "Caliph".

[41] Presumably these should likewise be messianic figures. (The Brahmans and the Hindus are commonly treated separately in Muslim surveys of religions.)

[42] This may refer to a party which rejected the imâmate of Ḥasan II – persisting in the older Nizârî position that the imâm himself was not now visible. It would be odd that this should be the only reference to so important a party. The text is unclear.

[43] *Ḥawl wa-quwwat*, a phrase generally used of God.

lines of traditional lore represented is striking. At its head, and indeed presupposed in every Ismâʿîlî work, is the philosophic *tanzîh*, the unwillingness to ascribe any characteristics to God which might conceivably be had in common with creatures, even to the point of avoiding a noun in referring to God, and substituting the associated conventional "the Great and Exalted". The effect to be sure is not so extreme as it would appear in modern ears, unused to expecting a set phrase with every name, a phrase which can also on other occasions replace the name itself; yet it is consistent enough to be noticeable.

It is this remoteness of God which makes needful as well as less obnoxious the almost unlimited exaltation of lesser figures – no matter how far exalted, so long as they are named and defined, they are infinitely nearer than God Himself. Nevertheless, in practice the exalted imâm and the ineffable God seem confused to a greater extent even than their technical identity of name (to the degree that God has a name, it is the imâm's) ought to permit. It is not always easy to draw the line between *Khudâ* and *Khudâwand taʿâlâ* – the *Lord Most High* – on the one hand, which should both mean *God;* and on the other hand the simple *Khudâwand* or *Mawlâ-nâ, our lord*, which should refer to the *imâm*. The confusion is less defensible in theory than the corresponding Christian one between the *Lord* God and the *Lord* Jesus, who are after all one Substance.

Although the remoteness of tanzîh, springing from the Philosophical tradition, makes a doctrine such as that of the names and proofs of Divinity seem especially needful, it is evidently the old Semitic tradition which actually supplies this element. Underlying the idea that if knowledge of the imâm is so important it is because his is the name of God, is the old idea that the name, if taken properly, determines the thing and so controls it. The Greatest Name of God is the secret clue to universal knowledge and power, and one is often disappointed, on being led to the verge of learning this great name, to be left there frustrated.[44] In the Qiyâma one is not frustrated, for one need know nothing further than the imâm: but one's rewards in knowledge and power, of course, lie only in the spiritual realm of ḥaqîqa, reality. A less popular conception, related to this although it does not enter this particular chapter, is that of the tangible *proof* of the intangible spirit, the person or object which serves to manifest its presence and authority, the *ḥujja:* the imâm is the

[44] Cf. for instance, even within Ismâʿîlism, *Umm al-Kitâb*, p. 393 (*Der Islam*, XXIII [1936], 22). But in the *Rawḍat at-Taslîm*, pp. 88/129, 98/145, this greatest name is the imâm himself.

ḥujja of God. All of this sort of thought, however, is to be found in the Twelver Shîʿa as well as the Ismâʿîlî; it was familiar to the audience, and only capitalized on here.

The more strictly regular Shîʿa strands are also not absent, of course. The sense of reverent loyalty to some particular individual who will in his generation be the hereditary inherent central authority in religion clings so strongly to the Shîʿa that even the relatively cosmopolitan Bahâʾîs have accepted it.[45]

But more striking, or perhaps more elaborately developed than the Philosophic, the old-Semitic, and the Shîʿa strains are those traceable to other older Middle Eastern sources. The accumulated resources of the Middle East formed together a great store upon which Islâm could draw through the centuries. The author seems to include here as many prophecies of a future advent as he has heard of, or more. One is not surprised at the inclusion of Christians, Jews, and Muslims, nor even at that of Zoroastrians (the people of Abraham,[46] they were often accounted); all which faiths were officially recognized in Islâm. The Brahmans, the Hindus, and for that matter the Gnostic Pagans are not generally accounted so highly; and in another work in the same tradition even the Manichaeans are included in the list, a sect which the Muslims, like the dominant faiths before Islâm, persecuted with special zeal.[47]

With the prophecies of the coming is combined most closely another tradition, the Gnostic one of the Perfect Man, which as Schaeder has pointed out is itself a compound figure.[48] The Perfect Man is at once the origin – and model – of mankind, and the teleological pivot of mankind in all ages. He is the first man, made in the image of God, whom all the angels must worship; and he is the microcosm, perfect condensed counterpart of the universe, about which the universe at large is built. As such he is technically the final cause of the universe, without which the universe, being not fully caused, could not exist. These conceptions of origin and ideal had already been combined, even within Islâm. We find *here* that the prophecies of the last Advent also apply to this *Urmensch* continuingly present. Thus past, present, and future are all brought into the one figure. The Adam of the first Paradise, the quṭb of every age, and the *Mahdî*-

[45] Among the strands of tradition should not be omitted the old-Arabic, which has contributed at least the name *Maʿadd.*

[46] For an explicit identification of the people of Abraham with the Zoroastrians, see *Kalâm-i Pîr*, p. 69/64.

[47] *Kalâm-i Pîr*, p. 44/51.

[48] H. H. Schaeder, 'Die islamische Lehre vom Volkommenen Menschen, ihre Herkunft und ihre dichterische Gestaltung,' *ZDMG*, LXXIX (1925), 192.

Messiah are but one, the object of Shîʿa loyalty, and the embodied greatest name of God.

The towering simplicity of the conception is worked out subsequently with the aid of Philosophic exegesis and of Ṣûfî devotional sense; but already here appears the appeal of such an organic but timeless unity, in which all the sacred lore the reader is likely to be aware of is made to center upon the single imâm: in Shîʿa feeling the object at once of allegiance and love, of awe and assured hope, as himself the knowability of the unknowable God, the one means of grace, and goal of perfection for all God's creation.

The Melchizedec figure as tying together the various traditions.

It is the new series of imâm-Qâʾims which is the principal expression of this new figure. This new series is in turn a combination of the timeless and ageless man of more than one tradition. Dhû l-Qarnayn-Khiḍr as we know goes back even in the name to the Sumerian: *Khiḍr* is derived from an alternative name of the ever-living Utnapishtim himself. Likewise the three names going back to Melchizedec are derived from the Biblical passage directly: *Malik as-Salâm* is the translation of the title – *King of Salem* (peace); *Malik Shûlîm* is a transliteration of the title, from the Syriac; *Malik Yazdâq* is one variant of a transliteration (given more exactly in Juwaynî) of the name *Melchizedec*, itself. Khiḍr and Malik as-Salâm seem to be equally vital here; but whereas Khiḍr, as the unfailing source of abundance to whom lone and pious saints can turn, is generally familiar among Muslims, Malik as-Salâm, whom more than once the Nizârîs are said to revere, and who enters even into the birth story of Ḥasan II, is otherwise obscure.[49]

In the new series is reflected in other ways the new attitude to the Imâmate. The shift from the system of the bâṭin to one in which the knowledge of God in the imâm is sum and substance is illustrated in the handling of the Prophetic figures here. For instance, not the sharîʿa itself, but Malik Yazdâq as the lord to whom Noah turned is central to the story of the flood here. The old Ismâʿîlî taʾwîl that the flood is the sharîʿa in which men drown spiritually is only a peg upon which to hang this more important moral: it was Malik Yazdâq who ordered the sharîʿa, and to whom the "my Lord" in the Koranic passage was addressed.

[49] This has been taken up in the text. The treatment of *Melchizedec*, of course, I still owe to Vajda, *JA* (1943–5). Once three forms of the name are separately mentioned in Fâṭimid literature, of course, Daylamân can easily take them for three separate figures.

Here may be seen a tendency to veer away from the sheerly analytical mythology of the classical Ismâ'îlîs toward a narrative mythology more commonly found among the Twelvers, but perhaps always present on the popular level. For Malik Yazdâq and Dhû l-Qarnayn are certainly still types, yet the sense of a particular personality accomplishing particular wonders illustrated in the stories – clearly almost thought of literally now – is surely stronger than any remaining sense of schematized ta'wîl which finds the principles of the bâṭin recurring monotonously behind any incident of the past. The sense of history of Qiyâma times, at the very point of reducing all time and nature to a single point, is already reintroducing anecdotes of a truly historical substance. We are not far removed from that focusing upon the folk heroes, in which the small sect could ultimately find its own living history.

There is a mystery about the new series, which fits not only the central uncertainty of Ḥasan II's birth and position but the atmosphere of cosmic secrets which is an undeniable aspect of the Qiyâma doctrine even at the point when all is supposed to be finally revealed. In contrast to the rigors of the earlier Nizârism, where cosmic secrets were almost contemned – the holding to the immediate authority was enough; and to the urbane mood of the Fâṭimid scholars, who sought step by step to unravel all secrets rationally; here where all life is revealed, it is revealed essentially as a mystery, and a paradox. (God both is and is not known.) Such a mystery is perfectly at home in a document like this, and the figure of the bright light solely visible in the general darkness is very well chosen for the primeval imâm-Qâ'im figure. The sophisticated Ṭûsî rationalizes this (the Qâ'im figure is one with the waṣî) and in straightening things out flattens them (whether God is known or not depends on the point of view – and in a higher point of view, neither is the case).

'ALÎ IS THE MAN

Translation:

Third Chapter [first part]: On the subject: in this period who is that person, where does he live, and what is his name?

It is known among people at large and among the élite[50] that the Prophet indicated Mawlâ-nâ 'Alî ibn Abî Ṭâlib (bless him) as the Qâ'im of the Qiyâma. When Ḥaḍrat Rasûl [Prophet] (bless him) was asked, Who will be the Qâ'im of the Qiyâma, he stated, 'Will it be [any but?] 'Alî (bless him) ibn Abî Ṭâlib?' When he was asked another time also,

50 *'Âmm* and *khâṣṣ* – for a Shî'ite this often meant "Sunnîs and Shî'ites".

he stated, 'The one I threw a pebble at, mending the sandal.' [?] When they looked back, then Ḥaḍrat Mawlâ-nâ (blessings of God upon him) had gotten his sandals out of repair, and was setting them right. [p. 15] Also, the summons of the Prophet on the day of Ghadîr Khumm, when he revealed the verses of the Koran [p. 14 MS] on his rights, which had arrived.[51] It is well-known that one day Sukkad (curse him), that is, that cursed dog, had seized the blessed collar of Mawlâ-nâ 'Alî and was dragging him to the first allegiance oath; and Salmân (bless him) said, addressing him, who is it upon whose rights you are transgressing [ghuluww], and whom are you now dragging in this mean manner?[52] And Salmân had no strength left, and said, This person whom you are dragging in this mean manner, if he wished to throw this upon that, and that upon this, he could. He pointed to earth and sky. And at that moment Ḥaḍrat Mawlâ-nâ looked at him, and stated, One does not say all one knows.

And another point, 'Abd Allâh-i Saba''s crying "Labbayka"[53] at the divinity of Mawlâ-nâ 'Alî (bless him): It is well known that Mawlâ-nâ 'Alî ordered fire brought, and ordered them, Stop saying this or I shall have you all burned. They said, What would be more desirable than that, for you are our whole essence. This duality which is a veil between us will become one; for you have been all, and you will be. Have [us] burned. Then he ordered that fire be rubbed in their faces, till relatively to the eyes of the people they burned; then on another day they were seen in the bazaar of Baṣra buying bread. [p. 15 MS] They underwent this affair in the service of Mawlâ-nâ.[54] [p. 16] Mawlâ-nâ states in a blessed faṣl [epistle], [Of] those who act in this way, there will be many who will expend their own blood; and whoever expends his own blood

[51] All the Shî'a maintain that on the way back from a pilgrimage to Mecca Mohammed was warned by an otherwise innocent-looking verse in the Koran to declare publicly 'Alî as his successor; which he proceeded to do at the Ghadîr Khumm, a watering place, making all his followers acknowledge 'Alî's rights. Accordingly, when the Muslims after Mohammed's death proceeded to choose an older man than 'Alî as their chief, the Shî'a consider this a clear case of disobedience to the command of God. (The Sunnîs also admit some such incident, but with a different interpretation.)

[52] Sukkad is a pet name of the Shî'a for their favorite enemy, 'Umar, who was the mainstay of the early Caliphal power when 'Alî was excluded. *Sukkad* is written *SKD*, and *dog* in Persian is written *SK*, or was; the dog is, of course, particularly despised by Muslims. 'Umar is here represented as a violent tyrant forcing 'Alî to accept the usurping Abû Bakr; Salmân is, of course, the loyal Persian follower of 'Alî.

[53] A cry of pilgrims offering themselves to God.

[54] The story of Ibn Saba', who is supposed to have called 'Alî divine and to have been burned for it by 'Alî himself, is indeed well known among Sunnîs, who may have invented it to discredit the exalters of 'Alî. Extremer Shî'a have used it in more than one way – for instance, to show that 'Alî punished as God punishes, with fire.

will share in the cursedness of that person.[55]

And further: ʿAbd Allâh ibn ʿAbbâs reports the tradition that, The depth of a man is like ʿAlî ibn Abî Ṭâlib, who says, I am the face of God, and I am the side of God; I raised the heavens, and I spread the earths. And there are many phrases of this sort. And who says, I am the hand of God, and I put my hand in the Fire, and bring my own servants out of the Fire, and I pass my enemies into the Fire. Then I say to the Fire: these for me, and those for you. Ḥaḍrat the Prophet (peace to him) states, Who is he 'who separates Hellfire from Paradise'? They say, It is ʿAlî (bless him) ibn Abî Ṭâlib. And in another place he stated, The meaning of it is that on the day of the Qiyâma all angels and jinn and men will come together and will want to lift the banner of the Qiyâma; but will be unable to. At that time ʿAlî (bless him) ibn Abî Ṭâlib will come and lift the standard of the Qiyâma. And there are many proofs of this sort that Mawlâ-nâ will be Qâ'im of the Qiyâma. [p. 17]

Above all imâms [?] is Mawlâ-nâ ʿAlî (bless him); and it is he who has no source nor returning [mabda' wa maʿâd], and has no end nor beginning. But relatively to the people he appears now as a son, now as a grandson, and now aged, and now young, now in a mother's womb, now as a boy, now as a king, now as a beggar, now rich, now poor, now propertied, now a pauper, and now oppressed, now forgiving, now merciful; he appears all this to the eyes of the people; he appears in the form of the imâm of the time, today, and tomorrow. Before this for a thousand years there has been [such] a man – and now also there ought to be; and there is, and shall be. And he appears as all these in the order of time; and in regard to space [he appears] now in the east, now in the west, now in the south, now in the north, now in this city, now in that city – this is all one man whom the people see.[56]

Now Mawlâ-nâ ʿAlî states in a sermon, I shall set up a pulpit in Miṣr [at Cairo] and shall take Damascus and make it small – that is, I shall strike off the necks of the rebels; and after that I shall go to the holy war of the district of Daylam. When I arrive in that vicinity I shall make the mountains low and pull the trees up by their roots; and the intention of the Great and Exalted was this: that is, I will appear in that district and make it Muslim, and bring the men of that vicinity to my own obedience

[55] This last sentence may be a tardy rejection of Ibn Saba''s breach of taqiyya; but "that person" may refer not to Ibn Saba' but to a persecutor who might kill one of the Shîʿa for speaking freely. In such a case, the man who had broken taqiyya would share his persecutor's guilt. (The quotation is fragmentary.)

[56] This is to say, all the imâms, in their various accidents of life, are really one – ʿAlî, their chief.

and servitude. And from there I shall go to the holy war of the district of Hindûstân. [p. 18, p. 17 MS] And he states in the blessed faṣl, A man asked Mawlâ-nâ, Will you come back to do these things? Since that man was not a pupil [zabândân] of Mawlâ-nâ, that is, he was ignorant, Mawlâ-nâ directed his speech to him, and became angry there; and Mawlâ-nâ said to him, I shan't come, but one of my sons will come and do these things, and so it will be that I shall have done it.[57]

Hence Mawlâ-nâ Mahdî [d. 934] (to his mention peace) appeared from the western parts and came to Miṣr and set up a pulpit, and took Damascus and broke the necks of the rebels.[58] And Mawlâ-nâ Muṣṭafâ Nizâr (on his mention prostration and glorification) with his sons appeared in rule and monarchy in Miṣr [Egypt]; just as the Great and Exalted had stated in the sermon which the Prophet speaks: On the day of the Qiyâma the sunrise will first come up in the west and arrive at midheaven, and from there go back and set in the west; and come up in the east. Wherever the sun of the Qiyâma is mentioned this phrase is there. It was that Mawlâ-nâ appeared from the west, and took every place up to Ḥulwân of Baghdâd, which is in the center of the world, bringing them under his own control; and after that because of the urgency of the time, again became hidden in the west.[59]

Before this chapter [it has] come out that all the imâms are ʿAlî (bless him) himself, and will be; and in all the blessed faṣls there is [discussion] of the meaning [maʿânî] of what has been mentioned. [p. 19] In a sermon he states, Our likeness is [repeated] in the imâms. [As to] the first ten: one refers to *waṣî*s so that from Mawlâ-nâ ʿAlî to Taqî Aḥmad the imâms are called *waṣî;* for this reason the imâm Muḥammad Bâqir

[57] ʿAlî is angry at an outsider's having deduced what only an insider should know: in the outsider it is irreligion to give a mere man so high a privilege as returning in person. We have here curious manipulations of ta'wîl. The making the mountains low is interpreted less wondrously, in the good Ismâʿîlî fashion. But on the contrary, the relation of ʿAlî to his descendants is reversed. The less wondrous explanation – that his sons will do these things – is treated as ẓâhir, knowable to the public, and to be explained by the more wondrous bâṭin, that it is in fact ʿAlî.

[58] This "prediction" refers, of course, to the Fâṭimid restoration to power of the family of ʿAlî. Damascus was the capital of the chief opponent of ʿAlî in his lifetime; but it was also a notoriously Sunnî stronghold at the time when the prediction must have been written.

[59] That is, Nizâr's line retired into hiding. Nizâr, in fact, never did effectively rule in Egypt, still less his sons. As to Baghdâd: though Mecca is the theoretical center for Muslims, Baghdâd was more prominent, between the Iranian and the Arabic halves of Islâm, and between the north and the south among the Climes; and being the seat of the Sunnî Caliphate. At the high point of Fâṭimid expansion in the Eleventh Century it was held for a few months.

(peace upon him) stated to Jâbir Juʿfî, They are waṣîs from the time of the Waṣî.[60] [As to] the second ten: one refers to *imâms*, so they call the person of unity [the imâm] from the eleventh to the twentieth *imâm;* from Mawlâ-nâ Mahdî, who was the eleventh imâm, to Mawlâ-nâ Nizâr, who was the nineteenth or twentieth imâm.[61] And [as to] the last ten: one refers to *Qâ'ims*, and from the twenty-first to lord Mawlâ-nâ Upon his mention prostration and glorification, up to thirty imâms, the person of unity will also be called *imâm.*[62]

Commentary: the exaltation of ʿAlî:

After the variety of strands of tradition noted in the last chapter, here we center onto the potent heritage of the Shîʿa in particular; especially the emotional exaltation of ʿAlî. In principle, it would be as correct to say – if this can be said at all – that all the imâms are *any* one of them, as that they are all ʿAlî. One form is presumably as real as another. It is the intense Shîʿa attachment to the figure of ʿAlî which gives him eminence among his surrogates: an attachment corresponding to the inexpressible hatred of ʿUmar which makes our author unsatisfied simply to mention him with a curse – he must come back clumsily to try to despise him more adequately, with a pun. Neither the Prophet nor the Devil receive such homage of love and hate as here go to ʿAlî and ʿUmar.

The proofs of the supremacy of ʿAlî take the form of a variety of excellent things said about him by excellent men (excellent among the Shîʿa). First, to be sure, are listed some of the sayings attributed to Mohammed, for Mohammed, traditionally, had a special authority with

[60] ʿAlî in the Fâṭimid system was *waṣî*, executor of the Prophet, not merely imâm; but ʿAlî combined with that rank any lower one, such as imâm, of course; and also, says our text, the higher one of Qâ'im. The imâms as a whole repeat among themselves the ranks which ʿAlî had within himself, each sequence of ten being named for a different aspect of ʿAlî.

[61] Nizâr was 19th if ʿAlî is included in the numbering but not Ḥasan; 20th if both are included.

[62] It is hard to say throughout here what is original inexactitude and confusion, what is subsequent corruption: certainly there is much of both. One would suppose this last word would be *Qâ'im*, on the basis of the parallel structuring which is inescapable in these texts; but this may be simply a casual reference to the fact that though Ḥasan II and his sons are Qâ'ims, they are still called *imâms.* (Similarly as to titles and honorifics: it seems impossible to deduce much from them certainly. Ivanow tries to show something of Ṭûsî's habits, in the introduction to the *Rawḍat at-Taslîm*, on the basis of "to" or "upon," *li* or *ʿalâ*, in his blessings; but these seem to be indiscriminately mixed in this text, as is also the use of *guftan* ("say") or the more formal *farmûdan* ("state") with the words of the same authorities.)

all. But the author soon runs on from the relative sobriety ascribed to the Prophet, to the fervid witness of Salmân, who is made to insist that ʿAlî had unlimited power over the creation. It is in these traditions of the extremists that our author's heart is. Salmân is still a popular figure among more moderate Shîʿa circles too; but the next figure, Ibn Saba', is the alleged founder of the generally despised Ghuluww (extremist exaggeration of ʿAlî's prerogatives). Now he cites miscellaneous phrases, all with Ghuluww implications, before a last short tale alleged to be from Mohammed himself, and so correspondingly sober: that ʿAlî alone can raise the standard (presumably of the bands of the righteous) on the last day – a thought well-suited to the Qiyâma at Alamût, where the saved and the lost were finally separated by him who raised the fateful banner.[63]

Our author is primarily interested in such imposing testimony; yet his eagerness to tell the tales involved in each piece of testimony reminds us that it is in such tales that lies the more colorful and perhaps the more profound imaginative heritage of the Ismâʿîlîs. Hence it is perhaps significant that the martyrdom of Ibn Saba' is included, but not the martyrdom of ʿAlî's son Ḥusayn, which has become the pivotal event for the Twelver Shîʿa. We have here a positive choice between traditions; in order to exalt the one great figure most colorfully, the less historical tradition is chosen – for Ḥusayn was really killed, but Ibn Saba''s death is probably an invention. Nor is the Ghuluww tradition, as here developed, purely colorful. In the story about duality and oneness is expressed a central Ṣûfî concern, and only the comment about later buying bread, which throws a docetic cast over the incident, is insistently of the Ghuluww; for whatever physical miracles the Ṣûfîs claimed, they looked to no such physical proof of spiritual unity.[64]

Apocalyptic theory of history:

The various Ghuluww groups, before Ismâʿîlî days, had little political success; yet their active attitude to political matters, carried into Ismâʿîlism, brought an apocalyptic attitude into its historical consciousness: every struggle of the imâm was a fulfillment of the world destiny. This attitude was variously expressed, according to circumstances. Ivanow suggests, on the authority of the Fâṭimid Qâḍî Nuʿmân, that among the

[63] The Qiyâma is to be initiated by a man, ʿAlî, just as it was in fact at Alamût.
[64] Ḥallâj's death was given a docetic interpretation by his followers – that only an ass had been killed when the government tried to kill him – but while he may be reckoned a Ṣûfî, his followers are ranked commonly among the Ghuluww.

Fâṭimids the function of the Mahdî – reforming the world – was assigned to the whole dynasty in sequence.[65] The external course of the dynasty could be seen as presenting the vicissitudes in the life of one individual, which vicissitudes could be passed over in view of the final triumph.

In the daʿwa of the Qiyâma the whole of history becomes even more directly the biography of ʿAlî and his friends and enemies.[66] The story begun in Madîna and Ṣiffîn, where ʿAlî struggled unsuccessfully with his opponents, is continued, via a detour to Egypt, to the hated Damascus itself; and from thence (the whole of Islâm having now been covered) to the infidel lands – Daylam (which in the early days was a Zoroastrian stronghold), India, and (Ṭûsî adds) China and Europe.[67] Externally it is a holy war; but now its internal course is even more important, for internally it is the grand unfolding of the inner and permanent meaning of the outer law, and hence of the destiny of the universe; and the Fâṭimid "imâms" are only one stage in this revelation. The revelation which began when ʿAlî took over from Mohammed culminated only in due time, after the various events of the Day of the Qiyâma and its western sunrise embodied in Fâṭimid history, in the final Qiyâma proclaimed at Alamût, and the liberation of all to their true destiny.

Here we have a justification of the fall of Nizâr from power; it is an incident foretold of the great day – and plays at least the role of fulfillment and sign, laying the groundwork for what must happen in time. Nizâr and his sons must retire "into the west", before the true rising of the sun in the east, in Daylam, can take place: the aspect of ʿAlî as waṣî, and then as imâm, must be displayed before he can be seen as Qâ'im. Thus a sense of history returns at the very point where philosophically it seemed most transcended.

ḤASAN II IS THE MAN OF QIYÂMA

Translation:

[Chapter Three, second part]:

One must examine the wording of the blessed sermon. Now when

[65] Ivanow, *Rise of the Fâṭimids*, p. 101 ff.

[66] One is reminded of the apocalyptic approach to history of the Jehovah's Witnesses, who also maintain that the end of the world has arrived. All events since 1914 are to them the earthly, almost symbolical reflections of the actual events in Heaven, where a single and in fact brief event is in the course of unrolling itself, I understand.

[67] Daylam was in earlier times a famous center of the holy war – hence the ḥadîth, noted by Yâqût, s.v. "Qazwîn", that Qazwîn was a gate of Paradise (because those who died fighting there went to Paradise), later noted in the *HBBS*. Daylam figures already in the prophecies of the imâm's conquests collected by Qâḍî Nuʿmân. *Rise of the Fâṭimids*, p. 117 ff.

Mawlâ-nâ ʿAlî (bless him) states, I shall set up a pulpit in Miṣr, he set it up; and, I shall take Damascus, he took it; and, After that I shall go to Daylamân, he went. But one must have an eye which does not see itself, and can look at him.[68] The words of the Great and Exalted are not contradictory.[69] Further, when the trumpet of Qiyâma is blown twice it will be blown from Daylamân; and the daʿwa of the Qiyâma, which is the sun of its period, will also shine from there; and the source of the sun – for how could it be in another place? – will also be there.

The light will not have become hidden from any town. It will be that someone says, The source of the sun of heaven is in the earth, and cut off from its own sphere [?]. These words are absurd, no wise man would accept them. [p. 20] If in the external sense it is absurd for the light to be cut off and separate from the sun of heaven which is a body among bodies; also in the sense of the Qiyâma [i.e., ḥaqîqa, reality] it is absurd for the light to be cut off and separate from the sun which is the blessed daʿwa. No, these are absurdities among other absurdities: the former is an allegorical absurdity, in a partial [view]; the latter is an absurdity in the whole, in reality.[70]

Further, the judgment of the sharîʿa is shared between God and the people, but the judgment of Qiyâma is special to God, Great and Resplendent. The people do not come to have a share in Godhood from the realm of Qiyâma [kawn-i qiyâmat]; nor do they even have, from that realm, any sign or existence for themselves. Then it would be absurd

[68] Reference to an eye which can see all save itself is common enough among mystics; here it is used to stress the importance of the level of viewpoint in the recognition of the true role of the imâm, which cannot be understood by the ordinary self-centered mind, which sees things in a false focus.

[69] Here again the phrase *ʿazza wa ʿalâ*, which should refer to God in the most absolute sense, seems to apply to the imâm, ʿAlî. This is part of the confusion noted above.

[70] The allegorical sun, as among the Ṣûfîs, is of course the physical one, which is only a transient representation of the enduring spiritual Sun. The absurdity in the one case, therefore, is a physical one, looked at from the viewpoint of giving various parts of the universe a separate existence. In the other case, the absurdity is on the level of Real existence, looked at from the viewpoint of the whole universe as in the Qiyâma. The point of the whole passage seems to be: to say that the source of the resurrection is in the locality of Alamût cannot imply that the Resurrection is merely a local matter, and does not concern the whole earth. This may be a defense against the dissenting group to which he refers at the end of the second chapter.

[71] The sharîʿa, as a matter of ritual and law, is a partly human matter; but in the Qiyâma the truth is purely divine, and the people of Union are not even aware of themselves apart from God – yet, of course, they are not God. This seems to justify the apparent obscurity of Ḥasan II as compared with the Fâṭimid Caliphs, but the text is unclear; the imâms of the Qiyâma, who do not administer the sharîʿa, will be even less well-known among the masses than former imâms who did administer it.

that [?] in the period of sharî'a, most of the time, he should be concealed; and in the period of Qiyâma be openly judging among the first and the last.[71]

Further, the Prophet (peace to him) stated, 'Qazwîn is the gate of Paradise,' that is, Qazwîn is one of the gates of Paradise.[72] Since Qazwîn is the gateway to Daylamân, [p. 20 MS] then necessarily Daylamân is Paradise. All the people of the world hope [and?] are assured that the Lord Most High will bear the good to Paradise and throw the bad into Hell. Then it would be absurd that Ḥaḍrat Mawlâ-nâ should have the good go to Paradise, and go among the bad in Hell and become hidden in a corner. 'My God, save us from the trials of this world and the punishments of the other.' Moreover, they themselves have said that those of Paradise will see God in Paradise [p. 21] and those of Hell in Hell.[73]

And another proof: the period of Qiyâma which was before Adam has persisted to this moment in which we are. Even though the Qiyâma is eternal, yet in relation to the sharî'a it is renewed [in time]. All good men have indicated the greatest ḥujja [ḥujjat akbar] and given good news, saying, The ḥujja and Qâ'im will be in that place which walîs [saints, or those in the position of 'Alî] and waṣîs [as, 'Alî] and nabîs [prophets] and ûlû l-'azm [the six great prophets] have testified of to all the believers.[74]

Ḥadrat Bâbâ Sayyid-nâ Ḥasan-i Ṣabbâḥ (may his grave be hallowed and may we be blessed in him) was the greatest ḥujja of the Qâ'im of the Qiyâma, and the Jesus of the period of Qiyâma who makes clear the work of his father.[75] Sayyid-nâ (may his grave be hallowed) states, When the Qâ'im appears, he will sacrifice a camel, and bring forth a red standard. Then Mawlâ-nâ will lay castles waste [p. 21 MS] and lift the curtain of taqiyya which is the door of the sharî'a; and his term will not be, in the world of being and not-being. And he will kill in regard to externals all the people of the Qâ'im [? – wa hama aṣḥâb-i qâ'im-ash ba-ḥukm-i

[72] We have noted above that this referred to the fighting in the unconverted territory just north of Qazwîn. Many Islamic cities treasured such alleged Prophetic distinctions.
[73] This last implies ordinarily that those in Hell will see God from that place, presumably in an angry aspect. The whole seems designed to prove that God must be revealed in Alamût, friendly to those there, inimical to those outside. (The outside world, as Hell, would be an unworthy "corner", not Alamût).
[74] That is, this is the Qiyâma which has been looked for since the days of Adam; it is no lesser qiyâma?
[75] That is, of the imâm-qâ'im, as shown above.

ẓâhir bi-kushad].[76] I have seen all this good news in the lord Upon his mention prostration and glorification: that Sayyid-nâ Ḥasan sent Ḥamîd as messenger to Upon his mention peace [ʿAlâ dhikri-hi s-Salâm][77] in service and submission, and asked forgiveness of him.[78] Moreover, one must read the Faṣl of Dih-Khudâwand to Ḥusayn ibn ʿAbd al-Malik so that this circumstance can become known. [p. 22]

And even the seal of taqiyya, which Ḥaḍrat Mawlâ-nâ had put on the hearts of people from the period of Qiyâma: – for whatever people had the boldness and friendship [?] for that, he broke the divine seal and removed the judgment of the sharîʿa.[79] And if [someone] else wanted to do that, one must consider that he is removing this [seal] from before the Koran itself. It is difficult unless Mawlâ-nâ Great and Exalted comes and removes it. He came, and removed the judgment of taqiyya which he himself had made, and the judgment of sharîʿa which he himself had laid down. And does not the lord also state, I had said and had promised I would remove the curtain of taqiyya with authority from the face of affairs; and I have fulfilled my promise.

Does not lord ʿAlâ Dhikri-hi s-Salâm in the end of the faṣl of Qâḍi Masʿûd reckon up [p. 22 MS] the ḥudûd of religion, and state, I am not this one or that one? In answer they say, If you are a prophet, show a miracle [muʿjiza]. He stated, God forbid, (and he did not do it), for it would become a cause of punishment of the people. They said again, If you are a ḥujja of God show a proof [ḥujja]. He says, God forbid (and indeed he did not do it); I am the ḥujja of God, and cause of the non-existence of the people. Among all the ḥudûd he reckoned, I am not this one nor that one; but he did not say, I am not the Qâ'im of the Qiyâma, and lord of all existences and beings.[80]

And further, the faṣl to Amîr Ḥaydar Masʿûd: – he states, *Ḥadîth-i*

[76] That is, they will become dead to the world, and alive in Him? – the truth-concealing veil of the ritual law being torn away.

[77] This is the phrase which is so regularly used with the name of Ḥasan II as to become a substitute for it.

[78] This message from Ḥasan-i Ṣabbâḥ (commonly called *Sayyid-nâ*) to Ḥasan II must be conceived of in the manner of the traditional greeting of the Prophet to his great-great-grandson, the imâm: he asked one of his younger companions to greet the child when it should be born.

[79] Cf. the Pauline "condemnation of the law". (The central part of this sentence is not clear in the text.)

[80] This rejection of all ḥudûd (limits) save the unlimited rank of Qâ'im may reflect such a note as that in the *Wajh-i Dîn*, p. 152, that on the day of Qiyâma there will be no glory save that of the Qâ'im himself. As to the demanded miracle: that unbelievers would still not believe, but would be punished still more heavily if a miracle were granted, is a good Muslim answer.

farzand ... [talk of a child ... ?][81] – and just such a way of thinking ought he have who is a lieutenant and Qâḍî of my religion; [p. 23] and this is a secret which does not appear [openly]. The pure birth of lord Ḥasan (his names be hallowed) happened, according to the externals, after so much time, so many years. In the Arabic faṣl which lord Dhikri-hi s-Salâm recited, in 'I encompass the world of time and space,' he proclaimed in part [juz'î] the secret of his own condition. After that [was] lord Muḥammad (his names be hallowed) – after lord Ḥasan (his glory shine); he stated at the end of the *Explanation of Lord Ḥasan-i Kabîr* [*the great*] *From the Beginning to the End:* the beginning and the end are in him.[82] On this point one must do some thinking. [p. 23 MS]

Our lordship [Ḥaḍrat-i mâ] (be he hallowed) states: Finally, what did Sayyid-nâ make da'wa for among the people? Did he not finally make da'wa for Mawlâ-nâ Dhikri-hi s-Salâm? Mawlâ-nâ was of that face [of] which he said, 'All things perish save His face.' He was that hand of God [of] which he stated, 'The hand of God above their hands' is myself and my hand.[83] And in another place he stated, 'the side of God'[84] is my nature, and my side. And all that day he spoke in Arabic, and in this faṣl he stated in Persian, If a created existence lays claim to divinity [p. 24] and causes other people to arrive at divinity – also, if [he makes claims] on behalf of a person who himself does not have this rank and makes the claim without inner truth [ma'nî], saying, I am the ḥujja of the Qâ'im – I should say to him, Your claim is not by right. It is the right of him who is always existent, and is the possessor of both worlds.[85]

He speaks relatively to all sorts [of men] to the effect that he is the cause of that realm [the realm of each sort]; for instance, with the people of Opposition [taḍâdd] he says, he is the cause of the existence of that realm; with the people of Order [tarattub] he likewise says he is the cause of the existence of that realm; with the people of Union [waḥda] he likewise says he is the cause of the existence of that realm; he releases people from turbidity, and causes the people of union to arrive at his own oneness.

81 There is apparently a fragmentary quotation.

82 Evidently here Ḥasan II and Muḥammad II are being listed in sequence, and to each is ascribed a statement on Ḥasan's legitimacy as imâm; but the statements are not themselves given. I should guess that Ḥasan-i Kabîr was here the imâm, Ḥasan II.

83 Koran XXVIII, 88; and XLVIII, 10. Apparently Ḥasan II is being quoted as in turn quoting the Koran.

84 Koran XXXIX, 57.

85 Here Ḥasan II seems to be discounting the claims of any other who might claim to be either Qâ'im or ḥujja. Evidently the references are to statements at the festival of Qiyâma.

Mawlâ-nâ Dhikri-hi s-Salâm states, 'I am one of the slaves of God, and brother of the Prophet [Rasûl],' that is, I am one of the slaves of the Lord, and I am brother of that Ḥaḍrat the Rasûl of God. And again he stated, If the lord [khudâwand] is known in this way, no other kufr [infidelity] is higher than it.[86] Mawlâ-nâ ought to be called the orphan pearl [i.e., incomparable], for he has produced faṣls on the limitations of the Reason. Altogether, there are a great many proofs of this sort of the lordship [khudâwandî] of Mawlâ-nâ ʿAlâ Dhikri-hi s-Salâm, but this amount is sufficient for the wise; or it would not end for length. After this there are four chapters more, and everywhere subtleties enter those chapters. [p. 25] In this chapter one must find the proof. And one must read the poetry with ta'wîl; so that the merciful look of the Lord of the world will grant his grace [tawfîq] and his favor and his bounty; and our Lord suffices us; and peace.

Commentary: links in establishing Ḥasan's Qiyâma.

Having surveyed summarily the evidence for the Shîʿa position in general, and in particular for the claims of the Fâṭimids, he must now prove that the Alamût regime is the legitimate fulfillment of these. But the work of Ḥasan II has a special character beyond them. It claims more, and so requires more justification than did even the appearance of Mahdî in 909; for it claims not just to herald the final order, but to be the ultimate transcendent Resurrection itself, the End of the World. It is not surprising that at this point the author feels constrained to warn us that accepting the prophecies in general is not enough. One must see them from the proper viewpoint: from a viewpoint which, disregarding the individuality of the viewer, can see all things in relation to the eternal order rather than to himself.

All this is a rather large order; and our author finds it necessary to expect his readers themselves to supply the required viewpoint, and perhaps a good deal more. He has a series of proofs which are meant to start a spatter of thought rather than to guide the thought in a clear line through to completion. As he likes to say, "One must think about this". His argument often takes the form of counterarguments to strictly implicit objections of his adversaries. The form his thought takes, therefore, is

[86] Possibly this means there is no infidelity greater than to know the imâm as *merely* a brother of the Prophet, i.e., a prophet himself: all prophets being considered brothers. (ʿAlî is called brother of the Prophet, among the Shîʿites, and therefore every imâm will be that.)

impressionistic rather than logical. But the notions he was working in terms of were current enough that each had its own aura of validity; the problem was not to demonstrate that validity, but to attach it to one claimant, and detach it from another. Hence an impressionistic way of writing need not be ineffective – particularly among those who were already committed.

In this allusive manner he first establishes that the Qiyâma can occur in one single place, and yet no place be deprived of it. Though God, or rather the imâm, be more easily visible in the time of the sharîʿa, when he is known everywhere indirectly as an inescapable mighty ruler; yet he is more truly visible in the Qiyâma, being then seen, if seen at all, through himself. With the legitimacy of localization established, he shows that Daylamân must be the locale, and that the Lord Himself must be seen there. He then refers to the general prediction of the Qâ'im by all the prophets and more particularly to the predictions by Ḥasan-i Ṣabbâḥ. All of these are fulfilled in Ḥasan II, for all his words and acts conform to the required pattern: he abolishes the outer law; he summons, as a Qâ'im should, to himself alone; and does not reject the high claims made for him, admitting his transcendence of all lesser ranks.[87]

The transcendence of Ḥasan II.

At each of these latter points we have an insistence upon the possibility of reaching the limitless in a concrete form. Ḥasan is limited by no ranking (ḥadd), as are all other believers – and unbelievers too, in the bottom rank – he must then be that further figure uncapturable within any system. In his unmediated daʿwa, Ḥasan brings men to the unlimited reality beyond ta'wîl. In the Ismâʿîlî atmosphere every statement of fact, once accepted and revered, is likely to be subject to a further ta'wîl. But Ḥasan at last summons to no statements, to no actions, but to himself as wordless and timeless,[88] at once concretely personal and yet possessed of infinite implications.

Naturally, it is especially when one is already inclined to accept Ḥasan in at least some one way – as ruler, as spiritual guide, as dâʿî – that this presentation will seem cogent for accepting him to the full extent of the claim. Yet if one has been led to expect that such a transcendent figure must exist, one will be inclined to accept anyone who uniquely

87 Some of these points will have had their fullest effect among those who accepted Ḥasan II, but doubted whether he claimed the dignity which his son was claiming for him – and for himself.

88 Cf. Ṭûsî, *Rawḍat at-Taslîm*, p. 100/148: Ḥasan "says nothing".

makes the claims appropriate to the figure. To a person whose seeking has been formed by the various traditions here appearing, the claims of Ḥasan may come as the inevitable and yet impressive fulfillment of a beautiful hope.

The first three chapters complete the polemical part of the book, for the most part, in which the author hopes to have proved the Ismâʿîlism of the Qiyâma correct as against any position taken by its opponents. In sum it runs like this: the Grand Tradition points to a Person of Union (*shakhṣ-i waḥdat* as it says in the *Kalâm-i Pîr*)[89] – a total figure in which all purposes and all authority meet. The Shîʿa insist that ʿAlî is the supreme man of history. The Qiyâma of Ḥasan II suits perfectly the requirements of both demands, and more – so that in it the seeker can find the culmination of all that is significant in life. In religion, a demonstration of possibility plus a demonstration of desirability is commonly taken for a demonstration of actuality. Accordingly, it is possible to say without fear of contradiction: to be in our community is to be in Paradise.

Commentary to the Fourth Chapter: truth of viewpoint as applied to the cosmos:

The author now turns to a presentation in Ismâʿîlî terms of the whole natural and religious cosmos. He includes just enough in this fourth chapter to give a sense of the logical completeness, of the all-inclusiveness which is part of the charm of an esoteric system. Nothing is left to common-sense or to an outside authority in such systems; every controverted point in life has its suitable nook.

The author makes his points in terms of a rational system, in the Medieval sense of manipulating elements of common experience as summed up in the Classical categories.[90] Each idea has some sort of logical relation with each other. The single effective potency in all things, which differ only in form, may not justly answer to the Greek *hylê*, but it represents an attempt at the same type of analysis of nature. The elements displayed in the universe are those of the Classical physicists; they are all to be found again in the human being, arranged organically to bring out their full potentialities. The single being from zenith to nadir answers perhaps to Stoic notions.

89 *Kalâm-i Pîr*, p. 108/112.

90 Our author is not really expounding any system for its own sake, as Ṭûsî does in the *Rawḍat at-Taslîm*.

The analysis leads up to the more central points of Qiyâma doctrine through its emphasis upon proper viewpoint in recognizing the roles – rather than the functions! – of various cosmic things. Whether man is regarded as subordinate to nature, or nature to man, depends upon what level one is regarding the universe from; but within each viewpoint the universe makes a logical whole. From the natural point of view, man is made up of parts; and the whole universe is the macrocosm of which man is only a remarkable compendium. From the point of view of Reality (ḥaqîqa), when we no longer see things from the point of view of the actor enmeshed in the contingencies that govern his acts, but from the point of view of the Creator who sees all things as timeless, the true macrocosm is man, for there the world is fulfilled; and the world at large merely reproduces fragmentarily the elements which take on in man their full excellence.

RATIONAL UNITY OF THE COSMOS

Translation:

Fourth Chapter: On the explanation of the physical world and its nature.

Thus, this world from the core of the earth to the zenith of the heaven of heavens is one body [shakhṣ], and is established through one power [or faculty – quwwa] of the divine light; but according to the form it is varied, and so appears. For instance, the same power which makes motion in the heavens is also in the earth the power which appears at rest.[91] In relation to the form which is fixed for the ordering of the heavens, and in the creation of the heavens, it has the form of motion; but the earth is at rest.[92] And the same power which appears in the sun and moon and stars, that power is in a black stone,[93] and in darkness. But it is necessary to see [this]. And one must treat all opposites analogously.

Then it is said that thus the divine light first shines from the heavens by means of the stars upon the earth; and [also] rises from the core of the earth. The [Ptolemaic] heavens are called "fathers", and the four natures [hot, cold, dry, wet] are called "mothers", and minerals and plants and animals are called "offspring". They [are] nine fathers [. . .] Within

[91] Already the analysis foreshadows on a physical level the spiritual doctrine of waḥda.

[92] Curiously, the ẓâhir takes on a cosmic role as *form* – but hardly as *formal cause*!

[93] Perhaps alluding to the stone at the Kaʿba?

the earth and upon the earth, since animals from the tiny ant to man [p. 26] form three types of animal.[94] Then that power [the quwwa, potentiality] of divine light causes whatever is subtly alive in the fathers and mothers and offspring to become gathered into the body of man, and in this special form to arrive at Godhood.

Then regarded relatively, man is the world of dispersion; but the physical world and the spiritual world [rûḥânî] regarded in ḥaqîqa are both the world of dispersion; and it is man that gathers together.[95] It is from this cause that the world is called a great man [insân-i kabîr, macrocosm], and man is called the small man [insân-i ṣaghîr]; but from the viewpoint of ḥaqîqa the world has been called the small man, and man, the great man. Then it is the world which is the sum of the excellencies of man; and it is man who is the excellency[96] of the summation of the world. When the dispersed world is gathered together, it is called the life of man; and when living men die and become dispersed, then this is called the dispersed world.[97] God is truth, and God is blessed, Lord of the worlds.

In the Fifth Chapter I shall follow the attributes of the spiritual world through to the end; and the physical will be finished in this place. But spirit and body are complete and perfect through each other. Separate from each other they do not exist; they are intimately joined. Mawlâ-nâ give grace; and bring [the work] well to completion; and He suffices us, God and Mawlâ-nâ.

Commentary to the Fifth Chapter: sense of spiritual maturity, and the pageantry of its symbolism:

The first three chapters gave us occasion to bring out the appeal which, based on traditional expectations and an esoteric vision, could attract

[94] Evidently some words have been lost.

[95] The spiritual world here is of course the world of the ḥudûd of the pre-Qiyâma faith – which from the point of view of the full revelation of unity in the Qiyâma is still a realm of dispersion, of plurality. Man is seen as a creature of dispersion in that he is the final product of the differentiation of the original power into elements and forms and organisms. Even from the point of view of the bâṭin hierarchy, the individual man is still at the bottom of the ladder, farthest removed from the one truth at the top. But from the waḥda viewpoint of the Qiyâma, a man sees only the imâm, and not himself as such; here all outward things are merely elements integrated in the Man who includes all truth in himself.

[96] *Tafḍîl* – one wonders if *tafṣil,* "detailing", might not have been the original in contrast here as elsewhere to *jam*ʿ, "sum".

[97] Cf. *Gnosistexte* A, I, where the Qâ'im, as "perfect man", has his "haykal", spiritual form, made up of those of all the believers.

men to the sect by proving the validity of its claims. In the fourth chapter we could suggest the continuing appeal it may have had for those already convinced, in its including and rounding out all knowledge. More pivotally appealing is the sense of spiritual maturity, to which we now come: a sense that the stage of development of the individual can justify a devotion demanding adult powers and responsibility – passing beyond concern with oneself or with physical routines.

At least two sides of this sense of maturity are reflected here. On the one hand is the assurance that the person who has realized in himself these truths possesses both worlds; he not only knows about things; in some way he is master of them, no longer hemmed in by unaccountable events like a child. On the other hand, and complementary to this, is that sense of a truly objective and universally valid viewpoint upon life as a whole – the achieving of which is indeed the occasion for his mastery over particular events.

The process of maturing is to a degree a process of gaining and enlarging one's viewpoint upon events. One becomes at once less fearful, in that a trivial disturbance can be set in perspective; but also more concerned, in that more of experience has relevance to continuing purposes. The viewpoint aimed at in the Qiyâma implies to a degree this double attitude. As it is put by a modern Quaker writer, "Nothing matters; [for all is in His hands; therefore] everything matters."[98] Accordingly, by the same doctrine which disposes of all external rules and purposes as accidental, every breathing moment of the individual becomes a moment of worship; and every item of nature fits into the scheme.

But the Qiyâma doctrine – more than that of the modern Quaker or of most Ṣûfîs – is wrapped up in systematic symbolism. The Ismâʿîlîs were not content to let words suggest the spiritual experience; the words must carry an elaborate symbolic system which will strike us as artificial. Thus the exact opposite of their intended meaning is often given to passages from scripture, no longer on the basis of the old arbitrary ta'wîl, but on the basis of seeing in the phrase itself an implication missed by the superficial. The familiar saying that whoever recites the monotheistic formula, the *shahâda*, will be saved, was designed to secure the acceptance of all professing Muslims without further questioning. Here the formula

[98] Thomas Kelly, *Testament of Devotion* (New York, 1941), p. 68. This collection of his essays is particularly full of thoughts which recall the Qiyâma doctrine. Compare p. 36 on the different realms we can live in; cf. p. 83, for a reference to living in Paradise while on the earth.

is interpreted not with the aid of the number-value of its letters, nor of an arbitrary symbolism, but rather somewhat after the Ṣûfî manner. Its "utterance" is expected to include a full consciousness of its implications; and the saying about the formula can thereby be held to require not as traditionally supposed a mere lip-service; but the deepest possible commitment. Likewise, a statement whereby Mohammed meant to insist on the physical resurrection is taken casually for proof of its opposite, the spiritual survival.

Symbolic treatment of problems: imâmate and death.

The artificial character of the doctrine strikes us especially in the elaboration of the doctrine of *tashakhkhuṣ* – personification or embodiment. But precisely here we can see something of the thrill achieved at the price of this artificiality. All creation becomes humanized for the truly mature. Combining the ideas of ḥudûd as representing cosmic principles, and of the microcosmic man representing the world, the doctrine proceeded in an all-consuming symbolical anthropocentrism.[99] Using the monism implied in Chapter Four, and stressing again the nobility of the human form, the author insists that all things must pass through that form before their final perfection can be reached (*final* in the Aristotelian sense). Often using symbolism inherited from earlier Shî'ite times – that angels or devils or fairies are simply certain kinds of men, for instance – all things of importance are given a place in the pageantry.[100] What before was words, talked of in theology books, in the Qiyâma becomes living men, or at least the relationships of such men. (For from the conception that only human beings possess final reality it is only a step to insist that the role of such human beings in this reality is a matter primarily of human attitudes rather than of anything external.) And when men are the fulfillment of the universe so concretely, it is only natural that the imâm can be held as in himself the fulfillment of the doctrine itself; almost the substance of the doctrine: not worship, not

[99] Even though its implications regarding sharî'a are rejected, the old position that the ẓâhir is necessary to the bâṭin (i.e., now, the ḥaqîqa, in psychological fact) is retained.

[100] It is no doubt the keenly intense sense of the role of *human* beings and attitudes that prevents the acceptance at this point of a transmigration which would have given all other living things an even more obvious link with man. Transmigration is already categorized here as the ẓâhir, pragmatic teaching of the prophets! a revealing comment on the *Haft Bâb*'s audience, for of course no Muslim-approved prophet ever taught it.

knowledge is what he calls to, but himself.[101] All formulations in word can be held as transient as compared with his figure.

But though much of the system – and even finally the role of the imâm himself – may seem to have purchased its maturity of outlook too artificially, yet the genuineness of the spiritual feeling of the chapter nevertheless shines through its narrowness. When death is dealt with, a fairly noble doctrine survives from earlier Ismâ'îlî times, which is clear enough. Those who have had the viewpoint of the ḥaqîqa take the role at death sometimes assigned in Philosophy to those who have achieved a rational level of existence, and so survive in the immortality of the Reason of which they have partaken. For only those who have achieved the ḥaqîqa are true men (capacity for the revealed truth of ḥaqîqa, as Ṭûsî tells us, being the specific character of man)[102] and so can have any permanent existence. To bring in physical death here seems almost embarrassing, after the Qiyâma has relegated further death to meaninglessness, and has turned the attention to spiritual life and death only. But in fact it serves not only to complete the picture at what is indeed an important point; it also emphasizes the inescapably final results of what viewpoint is chosen: it is a matter of life and death whether one sees oneself or the imâm. Any physically living are only a momentary foil to the imâm so far as they do not recognize him – they witness to truth, as it were, by demonstrating what untruth is. When they cease to perform this external function, i.e., when they die, they are totally extinct. Whoever does not accept the Qâ'im at the Qiyâma has only this negative role; he cannot become truly human, and so can never truly exist. Only the imâm and those who recognize him have a permanent being, in God Himself.

It is true that this philosophic immortality comes off in this tract rather confusedly; as if the author were trying to express a more sophisticated sense of life than he really had grown up to. He is at home again in what is perhaps yet more convincing as showing his sense of growing out of a naive childhood: his mocking of the gullibility of the masses who look for rewards and punishments in the after-life of like nature with this life's delights and terrors. But he is careful not to end on so common a note; he ends with an insistent call to see the liberating Unity just behind all words and all physical views.

101 Cf. Ṭûsî, *Rawḍat at-Taslîm*, p. 100 (Ar. pag.) – not the translation, which is as usual distorted.
102 Ṭûsî, *Rawḍat at-Taslîm*, p. 33.

THE THREE REALMS OF BEING

Translation:

Chapter Five: On explaining the spiritual world, and the attributes [p. 27] of the people of Opposition and of the people of Order and of the people of Union.

One must know that the physical world and the spiritual world are perfect together and are not separate from each other. For Mawlâ-nâ states, Body and soul together are body; and soul and body together are soul: and the reasoned and the sensed together are reasoned; and the sensed and the reasoned together are sensed.[103] But ḥaqîqa is [coupled only] with ḥaqîqa.[104] For instance, if you see the soul with a relative eye, it is body;[105] if you see a body with the eye of ḥaqîqa, it is soul. If one sees the man of Union with the lord with a relative eye, one will have seen a multitude of creatures; but if one sees the multitude of creatures with the eye of ḥaqîqa, he will have seen the Unity of the lord.

And of all opposites one must know similarly that whoever holds to the ḥaqîqa in place of himself becomes free of the conceptions and fancies of this world, and rests from the great distress. As Bâbâ Sayyid-nâ (God hallow his spirit) states, Whoever is attached to both these worlds must rest from all distress. And Mawlâ-nâ ʿAlâ Dhikri-hi s-Salâm states, Whoever is a man of ḥaqîqa [p. 27 MS] possesses both these worlds. And in a blessed faṣl he states, When God is fixed [muʿayyan] and embodied [mushakhkhaṣ] in the Qiyâma and when the sharîʿa of God is made conception and fancy, then what will remain that is not conception and fancy?

Now in the realm of sharîʿa its people [p. 28] are imagining God conjecturally.[106] But in the whole spiritual world it is said that the world is a man; for this reason it is said (the word of Him Most High), 'The last

[103] Such dichotomies mark aspects of single wholes, and are a matter of viewpoint. This refusal to admit a real distinction between body and soul, or among the faculties typically separated by body and soul, makes possible an insistence that what would strike us as being only the "soul" side of things actually includes the whole of reality, seen from a true point of view.

[104] Ḥaqîqa properly transcends both soul and body. But very soon ḥaqîqa is again confused with the *rûḥ*, soul, level. (This is one of the instances where the threefold division so prominent in the *Rawḍat at-Taslîm* appears in the *HBBS* extended beyond the three classes of person.)

[105] We might refer to seeing a person as "merely so much protoplasm".

[106] Here Qiyâma and sharîʿa are contrasted as two realms, but also as two periods, during which different viewpoints prevail.

world is life [or a living being] if they only knew.'[107] That is, The last dwelling place is alive [or, life]. And in another place he stated, 'Every stone and clod will speak.' That is, every stone and clod of that world will utter words, except for men, who will not be able to speak.[108] Then in that world there can be nothing except men.[109]

Now one must know that this same form of man is the special form of the Lord (His splendor shine); for it is in this form that He has manifested himself [p. 28 MS] – nothing else remains. [?] For in the spiritual world He is also in this form. For Ḥaḍrat Rasûl states, 'Lo God created Adam in the form of the Merciful,' that is, God Most High created Adam in His own form. Now it will be seen that God Most High manifested Himself in the form of Adam. But when some say, The Lord has manifested Himself in the form of a created being among created beings – they are said to be rather [?] babbling; for how shall God Most High be in the form of a created being? But the Lord has made man great and ennobled; [p. 29] regarded relatively, he has brought Himself into this special form; so that in regard to ḥaqîqa He may cause [him] to arrive at His own essence.[110]

The divine aim of the whole [is that] man, of [all] creation, should arrive there. In a blessed faṣl he states, God Most High created all things for the sake of men; and He created some men for His own sake. And from the core of the earth to the heaven of heavens all physical and spiritual things must arrive at their place of return [maʿâd]; and it is by way of mankind that anything can arrive at the place of return.[111]

Altogether the man who is good, and makes no break in his service of the Lord of the time and is near to the men of Union, is called an *angel*, just as in the Word it has come down (the saying of Him Most High): 'And if we had made [an angel] a messenger, we would have made him a

[107] Koran XXIX, 64. The "last world" is our "other world".

[108] At the resurrection the stones will accuse men of their sins, and men will be too overawed to say a word.

[109] The general sense of the paragraph is that what is real under the sharîʿa is here merely verbal symbols – as, ritual laws which stand for spiritual truths; and what is merely verbal talk and fancy under the sharîʿa – as, God – is here real; all this because the purpose of man has come into its own, where before it was only a promise.

[110] It is not that God becomes man – which would be at best a "relative" view – but that man becomes the revelation of God. All Muslim sects had to guard most especially against the accusation of "*ḥulûl*", incarnation: the tenet that the Creator could be included within one of His creations.

[111] To fulfill their purpose all things must pass through the organism which sums up all their potentialities, man the microcosm – at least in the sense of being subsumed under the proper human viewpoint?

man, and surely would have made him confusing to them to the extent of their [present] confusion.[112] [P. 29 MS] Verse:

> Happy Farîdûn was no angel;
> he was not compounded of musk and amber;
> he found this goodness through justice and liberality –
> if you do justice and are liberal you will be Farîdûn.[113]

The man who turns his face away from the lord of the time and has come to face himself, and leads another astray, is called *Satan* or *Ghûl* [ogre] or *Dîv* [demon]. And the man who has not arrived in goodness to the degree of angels [p. 30], but in badness is not yet like the dîvs, is called a *parî* [fairy or jinn]. A group which speak more than that in bâṭin [?], in ẓâhir are also called *parî*. Children and youths who are pure men of fair face are also called *parî;* and also the poets call *parî* their beloveds of fair face and fair temper.[114] Bâbâ Sayyid-nâ (God hallow his soul) says, These Turks are not Adam's descendants. Some call the Turks *Jinnî*, that is, call them *Parî;* before Ḥaḍrat Adam, Parîs, that is, Turks, held this world.[115]

And among the people there is talk about Paradise and Hell; [p. 30 MS] but Mawlâ-nâ 'Alâ Dhikri-hi s-Salâm states thus: Whoever wishes to see the person of righteousness and the person of eternal paradise must look at the man who calls the people to God, and knows God, and does not covet in religion.[116] On this subject, Ḥaḍrat Rasûl (peace upon him) states in a ḥadîth, 'As-Salmân is one of the gates of Paradise.' If the gate of Paradise is a man, then its court will also be a man. And in another ḥadîth Ḥaḍrat Prophet (bless him) said, Salmân is the life of Paradise. If the life of Paradise is a man [p. 31] certainly the person [shakhṣ] of Paradise will also be a man, as shown in these two ḥadîths which he stated. In another place and in the blessed faṣls he states, The person of punishment is also in Hell. Since he is the second, it is necessary

[112] In the Koran this serves to explain why a man, and not an angel, was sent to announce God's will to men: an angel would have had to look like a man in any case, and those who now refuse to believe would still refuse.

[113] Firdawsî, *Shâhnâma* (Ṭihrân, 1934), I, 61. It is perhaps the moral spirit of this verse from Firdawsî, and the idea that whoever is in Farîdûn's shoes is Farîdûn, that occasion this insertion, rather than any appositeness of the doctrine.

[114] Evidently the idea is to show that even in ẓâhir – among non-Ismâ'îlîs – excellent persons generally are called by the term *parî*: this makes it less odd that in bâṭin *parî* should refer to human persons, not to preternatural beings.

[115] The attractive facial features of the Turks were celebrated by the Persian poets.

[116] That is, there is nothing further for him to attain in religion?

that the first be Hell itself, by rational proof.[117] Sayyid-nâ states, When they punish the black stone they will make it second so that it stand opposite to the lord, and then they will punish it. And they will give a reward to the white stone when they make it the person of Salmân, so that it be the chosen of its lord.[118]

Now, when you see clearly that the black stone and white stone alike will be men in that world, and all, the tablet, the pen, [p. 31 MS], the throne, the seat, the faithful spirit, the holy spirit, and all that you choose to see and say in the world will also be men; also God, in that world, will be in this form.[119] What reported [thing] will there be which is not in this form? This world of reports will be fixed and embodied; now one must lift up the heart from creations and fancies, one must, till it escape from darkness and misleading and come to the light of the world of *dîn* [religion]. It will be obedience and worship of that which men call God.[120]

But in the realm of Opposition this knowledge is not achieved, and it is impossible that it be achieved, because the realm of Opposition is kufr [infidelity], and in kufr the matter is not accomplished. [p. 32]

Now I shall talk of the realm of Order.[121] In the realm of Order, also, that knowledge is not feasible, since the realm of Order is also a realm of shirk [of association of others with God – polytheism]. When they arrive at the world of Union, which is the world special to Him, they know themselves and their lord, and know all beings and all existences. There they can know everyone in his own place. The people of Opposition and the people of Order and the people of Union, [p. 32 MS] all three groups come within the view of their lord. To be explicit, a group which does not see and will not see the Great and Exalted, these see themselves; and are content with fears and fancies. This group is the people of Opposition.

117 He is second, one supposes, because of the following passage; the proof, possibly, lies in analogy to the preceding case.

118 The context of this, as of many other points here, is lost; but this reminds one of the Black Stone of the Ka'ba in Mecca, which was once white before contact with the sins of mankind.

119 All these are supernatural objects or angels mentioned in the Koran and taking a lively part in ḥadîth and speculation.

120 All this goes to show again that what is merely verbal information or conception in the world at large must become real – i.e., human – in the Resurrection, as it was at Alamût.

121 The realm of Order seems to include all Ismâ'îlîs before the time of Qiyâma as well as those not yet perfected in the time of Qiyâma. This would condemn the earlier generations to a harsh fate, except that any consideration of their case presumably would be mitigated by the old attitude that the doctrine and truth of the generation of one imâm has no application necessarily to any other.

A group which sees the Great and Exalted but also sees itself, and desires itself – this group will be the people of Order.

And a group which see Him and desire Him and call Him, and do not see themselves at all, nor know or desire themselves at all – they are called the people of Union. Now the believer must persevere and strive till he emerges from the realm of Opposition which is the realm of Kufr and arrives at the realm of Order; and he must strive till he emerges from the realm of Order also, which is the realm of shirk[122] and nifâq [hypocrisy in religion], and has arrived at the realm of Union, which is the realm of ḥaqîqa and is the oneness of Mawlâ-nâ. Then he will be saved and free.[123] [p. 33]

I shall recur to the first subject, that the believers may come to favor [fayḍ]. When physical death comes to the people of Opposition and of Order, and they leave the dwelling of this world, they perish, that is, they fall from God [khudâ] and lordship [khudâwandî] and arrive at their own eternal non-existence, which is Hell. But the people of Union are saved in the ḥaqîqa, that is, they come to God and His lordship, which is eternal Paradise. In proof is the word of Ḥaḍrat Rasûl (upon him peace), who stated, [p. 33 MS] 'what is after this world, the dwelling of Paradise and a Fire.' And Mawlâ-nâ ʿAlâ Dhikri-hi s-Salâm states, In the Qiyâma whoever arrives at God arrives for eternity, and whoever falls from the lord falls for eternity. Since all is godhood, then if someone falls from all, what is left? When you leave this world, there is just God or eternal nonexistence [ʿadm].[124] Blessed whoever possesses God and godhood; and blessed also whoever must have eternal nonexistence [nîstî]. For Ḥaḍrat the Prophet states, 'Woe to him who awakens after death.' That is, if someone does not awaken before the physical death, after death what would be the use? or in what way shall he awaken from nothingness [ʿadm]?

The truthful[125] show to the people what [is] a hard punishment in this

[122] The realm of Order involves *shirk* insofar as it still involves a *plurality* of ranks and beings – and particularly, no doubt, a plurality of bearers of value, besides God; since one's process of rising from rank to rank implies regarding *oneself* as having purpose and value.

[123] First one must join the Ismâʿîlî sect, then one must try to become spiritually mature within it on the lines of the Qiyâma. Clearly all three stages are open, in this conception, to any individual potentially.

[124] This and what follows is designed to show that Hell is simply nonexistence, not a state of torments.

[125] The truthful, *muḥiqqân*, will refer primarily to the prophets, *nâṭiqân*, here; but theoretically the imâms would be included if it were their job to touch on matters of the sharîʿa such as this.

world; but it will be missing in the last world. For instance, they have said, If you do wrong, God Most High will put you [p. 34] in Hell, and angels with sticks of iron and of fire will shrink your head and brain and turn them to ashes. And they will revive them and will always be distressing you. Snakes and scorpions will be biting you. They frighten the people with these things that they may do less wrong, and not be bold enough to do wrong; and not destroy each other; so that [p. 34 MS] the elegance of the physical world still persists, and one can arrive at the spiritual world and the realm of ḥaqîqa. And correspondingly [people] will become happy and cheerful on account of the same things as they enjoy in this world; and they are made hopeful, so that they strive to obey. For instance, they say, Paradise is a vineyard and a garden and running waters and golden trees and sweet smelling fruits and ḥûrîs [maidens of Paradise] and parîs; and sitting and rising with them in castles with bricks alternately of gold and of silver, and thrones ornamented and bejewelled; and to eat always fried birds and bread and sweets. And Sayyid Shâh Nâṣir-i Khusraw states, (verse) [p. 35]

> People would not have the name of the highest Paradise
> [on their tongues
> if there were no portion of birds and breads and
> [quails and sweets. [p. 35]

They say, They will drink pure wine. The Lord Most High will make a cupbearer for you there (His word Most High): 'And their lord will give them pure wine to drink.'[126] In this way they make [people] hopeful that if they try they may arrive at God.

And some of the truthful have said, If you do wrong and perish [?] you will turn around the earth, taking fifty thousand years; as He has stated in the Word: 'The angels and the spirit rise to him in a day whose measure is fifty thousand years.'[127] Or, in seventy thousand years. They have also said, They will make you a mouse and an ass and a pig; surely that time in these forms will not seem good to the ones possessing them. The [p. 35 MS] in respect to these forms, they frighten them; but they also make them hopeful, [saying:] Then also if you are obedient you will come under the protection of the mercy of God Most High. But if you are not obedient you will stay in Darak [a stage of Hell] fifty thousand years and will lament, 'Would I were dust.'[128] And there none will come to your cries.

[126] Koran LXXVI, 21.
[127] Koran LXX, 4.
[128] Koran LXXVIII, 40.

But the worship of God is what ʿAzîzî has said, (verse):

It is no more than two steps to the door of the friend;
you are stopping with the first step. [p. 36]

And the lord of the Qiyâma states, Righteousness is nearness to God; when you are nothing, He is all – do not desire a closer nearness than this. Further, the Great and Exalted states, I make daʿwa for God and Godhood, not for the knowledge of God nor the worship of God. Then in all the ḥaqîqa, the blessed faṣls affirm this idea [maʿnî]: that the people must see their own nothingness in this world, so that they may arrive at God and Godhood according to the ḥaqîqa, and escape from the realm of kufr and Opposition, and Order; for to this purpose Ḥaḍrat the noblest Rasûl states, 'Whoever says, There is no god but God, will enter Paradise.'[129]

Bâbâ Sayyid-nâ (his grave be hallowed) states, Do not weaken the believing brothers with that [specious] hope which you are conceiving of God.[130] Regarded in the ḥaqîqa the words of the truthful are one, just as their essence is one; but regarded relatively, their expressions are separated and scattered, just as their persons appear apart and scattered.[131] But the people of Union are all believers and certain, and knowing [ʿârif]. Mawlâ-nâ give generously his favor; He suffices us, and He is sufficient.

TRANSIENCY OF ALL EFFORT APART FROM GOD

Translation:

Sixth Chapter: Explaining the meaning of composing this dîvân; and praise and eulogy of Mawlâ-nâ (his mention be hallowed and his word be exalted).

It is written because the praise of the Great and Exalted in verses and prose is a need of the slaves [worshippers, human beings]. [p. 37] The Great and Exalted is the possessor of both these worlds; what need has He of the words or deeds of the slaves? It is [not?] written that His

[129] That is, there is no reality – nothing worthy of attention – save God. This is, of course, the usual Muslim shahâda, and for all except some Ṣûfîs means just the reverse: not that one must be wholly given to God, but that the slightest acceptance of the creed with the lips is enough.

[130] Having shown what true proximity to God is, he returns to castigate those who paint false pictures of an earth-like paradise; and to sum up his explanation of why the apparent meaning of prophets' words on such matters differs from the reality.

[131] – and therefore give a false impression of variation in different historical circumstances.

remembrance may continue, in the manner of the good poets who have called Ḥaḍrat Mohammed Muṣṭafâ their life [?] – so that their own names will survive on the face of the earth.[132] For His state is not like the state of the people; for His essence (His splendor shine) continues forever; and He has no first and no last, and no external and no internal, and it is He who – 'He has power and knowledge over all things.' What is the place where His name and remembrance are not on the tongue of the people? He is, in ḥaqîqa, whether [remembrance of Him?] remains continuously or not. Then the Great and Exalted is exempt from all things, nor has He need of anyone [p. 37 MS], but all have need of Him, as He has stated, 'Whence do the evildoers talk so very high'?[133]

And these verses and prose which the least of His slaves has written (His glory shine) he has not written so that something [new] may be known thereby.[134] The slave knows his inadequate measure by His excellence and mercy without end – if he did not know this, he could not write. And he has also [not?] written so that his own name may continue; whoever has temporal anxiety has fallen away from God and godhood. It is said that Ḥaḍrat Salmân reached God, and whoever reaches God will be the Salmân of the age. In general one must be with Salmân [p. 38] or with Sukkad ['Umar]. Ḥaḍrat the Prophet stated for this reason: 'After this world, the dwelling of Paradise, or a Fire.'

Again we go to our own words. He has also [not?] written to this [end?], that he be given the ennoblement of the ḥaqîqa [ḥaqîqî].[135] To whomever the lord Dhikri-hi s-Salâm grants to give this ennoblement of the ḥaqîqa, if that person lowers his head to this world and the other, he turns a desirous eye toward the world of spirits and bodies, and – let him tear his eyes from his head, let him tear his head from his body and let him throw them before the wolf and the hyena and the dog.[136] 'Azîzî has stated: (verse)

"Who lowers his head like a vulture to carrion, [p. 38 MS]
how can he like the parrot have the taste of sugar?"

[132] Throughout this chapter the statement of motives for writing is confusing as it stands. I have gathered his points to be as follows: he does not write to help God, nor for his own fame, nor to give new information, nor to achieve ḥaqîqa (has he already?), but to give encouragement to the weaker brethren. But the text, as may be seen, seems contradictory.

[133] Koran XVII, 43.

[134] Or: "Has he not written it . . . ?"

[135] Perhaps: "he has written . . . that he be given *true* ennoblement" – in contrast to the false fame referred to in the next paragraph.

[136] If one once turns back in the slightest from the ḥaqîqa he is utterly lost, such is the greatness and the honor of the ḥaqîqa? (Cf. "If thine eye offend thee . . . ".)

And elsewhere he has stated: (stanza)

> "The bird who knows of no limpid water
> has its beak the whole year at bitter water;
> If they bring the water of life before him
> he will drink of that water he has drunk all year."[137]

Further, it is not written[138] so that a remembrance [of the slave] will remain constantly among the people, because [it is] the Great and Exalted who causes the slave to remain and to continue for ever and ever constant and firm in the constancy of Him Great and Exalted. Then if the remembrance of the slave remained constant and firm [p. 39] or if it did not, what advantage would the slave [have] from it, or what damage (God save us) would make the slave accursed? Their own existence does not remain to the slaves in the two worlds, and they fall into eternal nothingness. Will the remembrance of the slave continue there or not? And then, again, what advantage or what harm will the slave [have] from [the remembrance among people]? No slave who is in nothingness will know of anything, neither of Godhood, which does exist, nor of created beings, which do not.

Whoever falls into nothingness will be as in the state of Sukkad. Someone asked Mawlâ-nâ ʿAlâ Dhikri-hi s-Salâm: Mawlâ-nâ, you are the fount of mercy and excellence and generosity and graciousness; bring back Sukkad both body and soul, and have mercy upon him. Ḥaḍrat Mawlâ-nâ stated in answer: Even if Mawlâ-nâ has mercy, yet he has become nothing; whence would he come back? or where are the outlines of an encampment which has quite vanished?[139] In general, whatever is seen in regard to all the false-speakers [mubṭilân] will belong to Sukkad; and whatever is spoken in regard to all the truth-speakers [muḥiqqân] [p. 39 MS] will belong to Salmân.[140] For instance, a slave falls from God and godhood.[141]

If someone speaks, whereto will he speak? To believing brothers who are weaker like ourselves.[142] Hence they say that the words of verse

[137] The sugar which the parrot loves is often compared to the ecstasy of the beloved's lips – or of the divine grace, in Ṣûfî poetry. The soul is often compared to a bird.
[138] Or, "is it not written...."
[139] Here again a conventional poetic theme is brought in, the vanishing of the traces of a camp in the desert.
[140] Hence no personal credit can come of anything expounded?
[141] Something may have fallen out here, unless this sentence is to set the scene for the missionary work now to be discussed.
[142] Having rejected writing for fame, apparently, he now shows how writing can be of use to others.

mingle more with the mind of a man and cling more to the heart than do the words of prose, because one likes the verse better. [p. 40] [Some] believers will have remained in the world of Opposition on account of weakness; if they are informed of this idea [ma'nî] they will make an effort and strive to arrive from the realm of Opposition to the realm of Order. And if he has remained in the realm of Order, he will make great effort to arrive in the realm of Union, for there is no end to the realm of Union, because His holy attributes have no beginnings nor a commencement nor an end, nor first nor last. In particular, knowledge is power; and grace and mercy and benevolence and all that is related to the Great and Exalted has no end.

Then there is a book which has reached the realm of Union;[143] and today, which is Qiyâma, one must make an effort, for whatever good you do you will find greater good from God. It has been said, If any comes one step towards Him, the Lord Most High comes two paces to meet him. Lord 'Alâ Dhikri-hi s-Salâm states: Take care, you who pilgrimage to the house of ḥaqîqa of God, strive today which is the day of Qiyâma. May Mawlâ-nâ (shine his splendor) grant favor to all, in his excellence and generosity; He suffices us.

DATE OF THE WORK

Translation:

Seventh Chapter: [p. 40 MS] On eras and on the date of the completion of this book.

From the hijra of Mohammed Muṣṭafâ (God bless him and his family and give them peace) [p. 41] thus many years . . . ; [144] agreeably to this, secondly [har dû], the era of Alexander Rûmî [the Greek], year . . . ; [145] and also agreeably to this, thirdly [har si], dating from Ṣadr Kawnayn [chief of the two realms of being] 'Umar Khayyâm Nîshâpûrî[146] and Abû l-Fatḥ Bisṭâmî and Muẓaffar Isfarâ'inî in the time of Malik Shâh Saljûqî in the land of 'Irâq thus many years: 121. This [is] the era which astrono-

[143] Is the book mentioned, *this* book?

[144] Two dates were already lacking in the manuscripts on the basis of which the edition was made.

[145] This is the Seleucid era, a solar era used by many Christians in the Middle East, which complemented the lunar era of the hijra of the Muslims. The Jalâlî solar era, which follows, was established under Niẓâm al-Mulk, and was probably currently in use for civil as well as astrological purposes – where the religious lunar calendar would be confusing.

[146] Omar Khayyam was claimed, among other notables, to have been an Ismâ'îlî – probably in a ready acceptance of what started as calumny. See B. Lewis, *Origins of Ismailism*, where he cites the *Falak ad-Dawwâr* of 'Abd Allâh al-Murtaḍâ.

mers write in the calendars. From the era of the planets, to the end of the period of Mercury[147]; and from the era of the fixed stars, and the position of the stars upon the chief of prophecy [Mohammed] there is one degree; thirdly [har si], the whole of the heavens return [to place] in thirty-six thousand years, and on this day the moon was auspicious and full in Cancer, and ʿAyûq [Capella?!] was in Gemini, and the ascendant of the sun was also in Gemini.[148]

Further, one must also reckon it from the era of the prophets ûlû l-ʿazm [the major nâṭiqs], to the end of the period of Adam of Sarandîb [Ceylon];[149] and from the era of the permanent [mustaqarr] imâms (blessings of God upon them).[150] He states that the Qâ'im of the Qiyâma (at his mention prostration and glorification) appears every seven thousand years; and when he appears seven times, the seventh time is called the Qiyâma of the Qiyâmas. In this period of ours they say Qâ'im of the Qiyâma. In the fourth clime, which is the clime of the sun,[151] in the land of Babel [Babylon] among the lands of the ʿAjam [Persians], in the midst of Jabal, that is, the mountains of Daylamân, at the castle of Alamût, he was Mawlâ-nâ;[152] and from the first of this blessed appearance to the time of the completion [p. 42] of this dîvân was forty solar years more or less.[153] This writing is finished; my God, in the truth of Mawlâ-nâ, o Mawlâ-nâ; the book ends with the help of the Munificent King. The end.

[147] Other types of eras are now listed, and it is not clear whether he attempts to date his writing in terms of each of them. If so, then he implies that a period of Mercury was just completed; such planetary periods ran from one special conjunction to a recurrence of it.

[148] The text is, as no doubt elsewhere also, clearly corrupt. Perhaps for *ʿAyûq* should stand the vaguely similar ʿuqdatî? (Dr. Willy Hartner). The idea that all things return full cycle in a certain calculable space of time can be traced back to fascinating mathematical speculations of earlier times. Thirty-six thousand is a decimal simplification.

[149] This is Adam, who was supposed to have landed in Ceylon when he literally *fell* from Paradise; he is the first of the ûlû l-ʿazm; but his period can be said to extend not only to the advent of Noah, but also till the end of his race – i.e., till the time of Qiyâma.

[150] This would be the same as the era of the prophets, who pointed to the imâms of each time. The author goes on to show just how long a time has elapsed since Adam to the writing of this book.

[151] The northern hemisphere was divided into seven parallel zones, "climes"; these were linked astrologically to the seven planets; the central zone in each case is the post of honor, and among the planets it is, of course, the sphere of the sun.

[152] Babel would be the ancient name for what was then called "the two ʿIrâqs", specified in a general way as in the Iranian lands – i.e., east of the Arabian desert. The ʿIrâqs – the southern Mesopotamian basin taken together with the central western part of Irân – have been mentioned as considered central in an east-west way; Daylamân is here treated as part of the Jabal, or ʿIrâq ʿAjamî. The mathematical term "clime", and the archaic terms *Bâbil* and *Jabal*, serve to lend dignity to the localization.

Commentary: cosmic vistas.

Even platitudes, as which Ivanow characterizes the sixth chapter, can have a distinctive appeal. The contrast between men's stark helplessness and the total divinity available to everyone is made sufficiently appalling. Bridging the gap is the fellowship in inner growth – to further which is evidently the object of this book – a fellowship symbolized in the sympathetic figure of Salmân, with whom each can identify.[154]

But the most persistent note here, as throughout, is the struggle for a response beyond the ordinary. The total condemnation of him who looks to either plural world of body or of spirit; the sublime expectations from Mawlâ-nâ ʿAlâ Dhikri-hi s-Salâm; the definitive demands of this day of Qiyâma are unquestionably serious. The Ismâʿîlîs had undertaken to mould the vision of Islâm; had set about destroying mighty empires; whatever their fate, no narrow vision could satisfy them.

The cosmic vistas sought by the author are epitomized nicely in the final chapter. He is not satisfied with dating from the hijra, which served the orthodox Muslim as so secure a limes (to bolster his sense of the universal cave, Spengler would say). Muslims often did use more than one era for securing precision in dating; but rarely for so incidental a purpose or with so large a range. Here we have three eras dependent on human history; and three eras more absolute, based on the metaphysical rounds of nature – in whose unending and recurrent patterns human affairs also move: the time of Mohammed is linked to a configuration of the stars, which will recur. Finally he moves to an era yet more fundamental, that of the prophets and imâms, and of the Qiyâma which they have foretold; here we have but one date, given with the full sense of cosmic splendor: set in the sequence from the unimaginably vast clime, (a segment of that earth round which men may wander for fifty thousand years); down to the particular castle and the man within it – and then linked with the present act of writing.

Here, as throughout, there is a sense, expressed in more than one

[153] That the festival of the Qiyâma introduced a new *dawr*, recurrent period, for the Ismâʿîlîs is clear. It has been thought that this meant the use of a new era instead of that of the hijra; but the imprecision of this "forty years more of less" shows that such an alternative era was at best not in common use. A prominent lunar day (17th Ramaḍân) was picked for the festival of the Qiyâma to be commemorated each year: this implies also the lunar hijra calendar. Cf. Defrémery, *JA*, 1849, in his translation of Mustawfî, on the era of the ʿîd al-qiyâm.

[154] This is the Ismâʿîlî version, I suppose, of the sense of spiritual fellowship shared among the disciples of a Ṣûfî pîr. Moreover, in the *Haft Bâb*, we already find the Ṣûfî type of poetry being used – and not for taqiyya, but out of frank preference.

direction to be sure, of a higher purpose than is to be found conventionally around one. No ancient tradition is ignored, nor any esoteric possibility despised, to augment the grandeur and perfection of the simple figure who sums up in himself all wonder and all hope. The whole universe is made rational and familiar; so that no helplessness is felt before the most awesome attempt at orientation; men are to be grown up, and at home beyond all horizons. To be an Ismâʿîlî is to be of the elite of the universe.

APPENDIX II

ḤASAN-I ṢABBÂḤ'S DOCTRINE

Al-milal wa-n-niḥal, ash-Shahrastânî d. 1153, ed. A. Fahmî Muḥammad, Cairo, 1948: vol. I p. 339: section on Nizâris:[1]

Then the partisans of the new daʿwa deviated from this way, when al-Ḥasan ibn aṣ-Ṣabbâḥ proclaimed his daʿwa. His words failed to be compelling, but he got the help of men and fortified himself in strongholds. He first went up into the fortress of Alamût in Shaʿbân of the year 483. That was after he had gone away to the land of his imâm, and had come to know from him how the daʿwa should be preached to his contemporaries. He then returned, and summoned the people first of all to single out a trustworthy imâm arising in every age, and to distinguish the saving sect from the other sects by this point: which was that they had an imâm, and others did not have an imâm. After the repetitions in what he says about it, the substance of his discourse reduces, ending up where he started from, in Arabic or in Persian, to just this. We will report in Arabic what he wrote in Persian, and no blame attaches to a reporter. He is well-aided who follows the truth and avoids error; and God is the giver of aid and assistance.

We shall begin with the four chapters [fuṣûl] with which he began his daʿwa. He wrote them in Persian, and I have turned them into Arabic. He said, He who delivers opinions on the subject of the Creator Most High must say one of two things: either he must say, I know the Creator Most High through reason and speculation alone without need of the teaching [taʿlîm] of a teacher; or he must say, there is no way to knowledge [maʿrifa] even with reason and speculation except with the teaching of a trustworthy teacher [muʿallimin ṣâdiq]. [Ḥasan] said, If one asserts the first he cannot deny the reason and speculation of anyone else; for when he denies, he thereby teaches; so denying is teaching, and an indication that the one denied needs someone else. [Ḥasan] said, The

[1] I have compared my translation with two former ones, those of Salisbury, *JAOS*, 1851, and of Haarbrücker.

twofold [dilemma] is necessary, for when a man delivers an opinion or makes a statement, either he is speaking on his own, or from someone else. Likewise, when he accepts a doctrine either he accepts it on his own or from someone else. This is the first chapter, which refutes the partisans of reflection and reason.

He notes in the second chapter: if the need for a teacher is established, is absolutely every teacher acceptable, or is a trustworthy teacher required? [Ḥasan] said, If one says that every teacher is acceptable, he has no right to deny the teacher opposing him; if he denies, he thereby admits that a dependable, trustworthy teacher is required. This is said to refute the partisans of ḥadîth [Sunnîs].

He notes in the third chapter: if the need for a trustworthy teacher is established, is knowledge of the teacher required or not? – assuring oneself of him and then learning from him? Or is learning permissible from every teacher without singling out his person and demonstrating his trustworthiness? The second [alternative] is a reduction to the first [proposition]. He for whom it is not possible to follow the way without a leader and a companion, let him "[choose] first the companion, then the way". This refutes the Shî'a.

He notes in the fourth chapter: Mankind forms two parties. A party which says, For the knowledge of the Creator Most High, a trustworthy teacher is needed; who must be singled out and distinguished first, then learned from; and a party which accepts in every field of knowledge some who are and some who are not teachers. It has been made clear in the portions that have preceded that truth is with the first party. Hence their head must be the head of the truthful. And since it has been made clear that the second party is in error, their heads must be the heads of the erring. [Ḥasan] said, This is the way which causes us to know the Truthful through the truth, in a summary knowledge; then after that we know the truth through the Truthful, in detailed knowledge; so that a circular argument is not necessary.[2] Here he means by "the truth" only the *need*, and by "the Truthful" the *one who is needed*. He said, By our need we know the imâm, and by the imâm we know the measures of our need. Just as by *possibility* we know *necessity*, that is, the necessarily existent [God], and by it we know the measures of possibility in possible things. [Ḥasan] said, The way to tawḥîd [declaration of God's unity] is that way, feather [of an arrow] balanced against feather.

Then he went on to chapters establishing his doctrine, either supporting or refuting [other] doctrines. Most of them were refutation and disproof;

[2] Following Cureton's *dawrân* rather than A. Fahmî's *dûn*.

demonstrating error by variety of opinion, and truth by agreement. Among them was the chapter of truth and error, and the small and the great. He notes that there is truth and error in the world. Then he notes that the sign of truth is unity, and the sign of error is multiplicity; and that unity comes with taʿlîm, and multiplicity with reflection. Taʿlîm is with the community, and the community with the imâm. But reflection is with the various sects, and they are with their heads.

He put truth and error and the similarity between them on the one hand, and the distinction between them on the other hand – opposition on both sides, and order on one of the two sides [?] – as a balance to weigh all that he uttered on the matter. He said, This balance is simply derived from the formula of shahâda [no god but God], which is compounded of negation and affirmation, or of negation and exception thereto. He said, It does not claim the negation is erroneous, nor does it claim the affirmation is true. He weighed therewith good and evil, truth and falsehood, and the other opposites. But his point was that he came back, in every doctrine and every discourse, to affirming the teacher. And tawḥîd was tawḥîd and prophethood, together, if it was tawḥîd at all; and prophethood was prophethood and imâmate together, if it was prophethood at all. This was the end of his discourse.

Moreover he prevented ordinary persons from delving into knowledge; and likewise the elite from investigating former books, except those who knew the circumstances of each book and the rank of the authors in every field. With his partisans, in theology he did not go beyond saying, Our god is the god of Mohammed. He said, Here we stand [?]; but you say, Our god is the god of our reasons, whatever the reason of every rational man leads to. If one of them was asked, What do you say of the Creator Most High, does He exist? is He one or many? knowing and powerful, or not? he answered only to this extent: My god is the god of Mohammed; He is the one who sent His messenger with guidance; and the messenger is the one who guides to Him.

However much I argued with the people over the premises just related, they did not go further than to say, Are we in need of you, or should we hear this from you, or learn from you? And however much I acquiesced in the need, and asked, Where is the one needed, and what does he determine for me in theology, and what does he prescribe in rational questions? – for a teacher does not have meaning in himself, but only in his teaching; you have shut up the door of knowledge and opened the door of submission and taqlîd [blind acceptance of authority], but a rational man cannot willingly accept a doctrine without understanding, or follow a way without proof – the beginning of the discussion was arbitrariness [taḥkîm], and what it led to was submission. "And by your Lord, they are not at all faithful till they make you [Mohammed] arbiter of what divides them, and then find no fault, in their hearts, with what you decide, but submit fully."[3]

[3] Koran IV 65.

APPENDIX III

BIBLIOGRAPHICAL NOTES

A – *Vladimir Ivanow's Work.*

From the point of the Qiyâma on, and especially in the eighth chapter, which analyzes its doctrine, we shall be largely dependent upon materials which Ivanow has published or translated. His translations, though a bit free, are commonly fairly satisfactory. We may list, however, types of passages in which one must be specially wary of using them. Examples from the *Rawḍat at-Taslîm:* he is astonishingly free with what he admits to be technical terms – e.g., putting *ḥaqîqa* in parenthetical or adverbial roles, ps. 61 ff; cf. p. 170. He refuses to regard the word *taʿlîm* as a technical term at all (p. lxii), though it appears frankly in contrast to *taʾyîd* in the Thirteenth Taṣawwur, for instance; perhaps this is because of its association with Ḥasan-i Ṣabbâḥ, whose role in Ismâʿîlism he deprecates. With a similar disregard for the structural feeling of the original, he almost consistently fails to bring out the schematic parallelism which is a major feature of the original: for instance, p. 54/40, where he distorts the meaning, apparently to soften the reference to Paradise. ... In his attempts to make the text give a sense of which he can approve, he often interpolates tendencious words, which sometimes land him in self-contradictions; for instance, p. 81 at the bottom; p. 138/94 – in these cases he feels it necessary to suppose a fault in the text. Finally, his translations are sometimes questionable, apart from any tendency; thus p. 66/48, "The people who first were ... ", for "wa-mardum-e awwal dar ân ʿâlam-e awwal ... ;" and especially p. 60/44, where a Qurʾânic verse is given an odd rendering that does not seem necessary to Ivanow's interpretation, or to the author's argument. The text commonly avoids the identifiable freedoms with which the translation is handled – thus, even though an interpolation in the translation may, after some repetitions, cease to be bracketed, the text continues pure. Ivanow has, however, made it impossible to compare the original manuscripts in most cases.

Ivanow's published work bearing on the Nizârîs is as follows:

1. 'Ismâʿîlî Manuscripts in the Asiatic Museum of the Russian Academy of Science,' *Bulletin of the Russian Academy of Science*, ser. 6, XI (1917), 365. Comments in Russian on a number of Mss. (Persian) whose *incipit*, etc., he gives. Cf. E. D. Ross, review in *Journal of the Royal Asiatic Society* (1919), p. 429.

2. 'Ismailitica,' *Memoirs of the Asiatic Society of Bengal*, VIII (1922), 1–76. Edition, translation, and notes on certain manuscripts and on the Ismâʿîlîs in Kirmân; Ivanow points out that the article is now obsolete, in his view.

3. 'An Ismailitic Pedigree,' *Journal of the Asiatic Society of Bengal*, new series 18 (1922), pp. 403–6. Also obsolete, he says.

4. 'Imam Ismail,' *JASB*, new series 19 (1923), pp. 305–310. Also obsolete, he says.

5. 'Alamut,' *Geographical Journal*, LXXVII (1931), pp. 38–45. A discussion of the site; "obsolete".

6. 'An Ismailitic Work by Nasiru'd-din Tusi,' *JRAS*, 1931, pp. 527–564. Analysis, superseded by the edition as regards the text (*Taṣawwurât*).

7. 'Ismaili Interpretation of the Gulshani Raz,' *Journal of the Bombay Branch of the Royal Asiatic Society*, VIII (new series) (1932), 69–78. Analysis of a commentary on the Ṣûfî work in terms of Ismâʿîlî ta'wîl.

8. 'Notes sur l'Ummu'l-kitab,' *Revue des Etudes Islamiques*, VI (1932), 419–481. Analysis of the text, and its language.

9. *Guide to Ismâʿîlî Literature*. Royal Asiatic Society Prize Publication Fund Series, Vol. XIII. London, 1933. The list of known Ismâʿîlî writings at that time, both Ṭayyibî and Nizârî, extant or not.

10. *Diwan of Khaki Khorasani*. Islamic Research Association Series, Vol. I. Bombay, 1933. Edition with an introduction about the author and his doctrine.

11. *Two Early Ismaili Treatises*. Islamic Research Association Series, Vol. II. Bombay, 1933. Texts of *Haft Bâb-i Bâbâ Sayyid-nâ* and *Maṭlûb al-Muʾminîn*, with brief summary of contents.

12. *True Meaning of Religion*. Islamic Research Association Series, Vol. III. Bombay, 1933. Text and translation of *Risâlat dar Ḥaqîqat-i Dîn*, by Shihâb ad-Dîn Shâh (d. 1885), heir to the Agha Khan.

13. *Kalâm-i Pîr*. Islamic Research Association Series, Vol. IV. Bombay, 1935. Text and translation. An introduction summarizes the Nizârî doctrine. The volume contains also – indicated in an appendix – most of an older book, *Haft Bâb-i Abû Isḥâq*.

14. Articles in the *Encyclopedia of Islam:* 'Râshid al-Dîn Sinân', 'Bohora', 'Khoja', and in the *Supplement*, 'Ismâʿîlîya'. Reflect Ivanow's special point of view.

15. 'Umm al-Kitâb,' *Der Islam*, XXIII (1936), 1–132. The text.

16. 'Sect of Imâm-Shâh in Gujrat,' *JBBRAS*, XIV (new series) (1938), 19–70. One some post-Alamût Nizârîs in India.

17. 'A Forgotten Branch of the Ismâʿîlîs' *JRAS*, 1938, pp. 57–79. On a post-Alamût split, the Muḥammad-Shâhî.

18. 'Tombs of Some Persian Ismaili Imams,' *JBBRAS*, XIV (new series) (1938), 49–62. Few results.

19. 'An Ismaili Ode in Praise of Fidawis,' *JBBRAS*, XIV (new series) (1938), 63–72. Interpreted; from the Alamût period.

20. 'Some Ismaili Strongholds in Persia (Alamut and Girdkuh),' *Islamic Culture*, XII (1938), 383–396. Few results.

21. *True Meaning of Religion.* Ismaili Society Series B. Vols. I and II. Bombay, 1947. Nr. 12, text and translation, in a different form.

22. *On the Recognition of the Imam.* Ismaili Society Series B. Vols. III and IV. Bombay, 1947. Text and translation of the *Faṣl dar Bayân-i Shinâkht-i Imâm*, revised from nr. 2.

23. 'Some War-time Russian Oriental Publications,' *JBBRAS*, XXIII (new series) (1947), 77. Reviews Gordlevsky, suggesting he found much on Ismâʿîlîs in Anatolia.

24. 'Satpanth,' in *Collectanea*, Ismaili Society Series A. Vol. II, ps. 1–54. Leiden, 1948. Discussion of Indian Nizârism.

25. 'Noms bibliques dans la mythologie ismaélienne,' *Journal Asiatique*, CCXXXVII (1949), 249. Adds little to what Vajda has to say on Melchizedec.

26. *Taṣawwurât.* Leiden, 1950. Ṭûsî's *Rawḍat at-Taslîm*, text and translation, with an introduction where he comments thoroughly in his own way on the doctrine.

27. *Brief Survey of the Evolution of Ismailism.* Ismaili Society Series B. Vol. VII. Leiden, 1952. His few pages on the Nizârîs add little to what he has already said.

Ivanow has also published, starting from 1936, at least ten items dealing with pre-Nizârî Ismâʿîlîs – texts, translations, and essays.

B – *Nizârî Texts Extant.*

I. Nizârî-preserved pre-Nizârî materials.

1. '*Umm al-Kitâb*' ed. W. Ivanow, *Der Islam*, XXIII (1936), 1–132. A Persian adaptation or translation (probably) of an early Arabic text – perhaps eighth century, probably later. The reasons Ivanow gives for reversing his earlier dating in the tenth century C. E. approximately, in favor of the eighth, seem inadequate: a reference to the third letter of the alphabet as the camel (such a memory could last two centuries longer); omission of any reference to Baghdâd (even a sectarian might avoid that anachronism, considering the fame of Baghdâd as an ʿAbbâsid foundation, if he was working from earlier materials). Its tradition is to be associated with Abû 'l-Khaṭṭâb, of the Ghulât of the time of Ismâʿîl ibn Jaʿfar; pictorially mythological, remote from usual Ismâʿîlî doctrine, but less so from ideas ascribed by their enemies to later Syrian Nizârîs; preserved among Nizârîs of the upper Oxus area. Smacks of Manicheanism.

2. The Guyard Fragments. Ed. S. Guyard, 'Fragments relatifs à la

doctrine des Ismaéliens,' *Notices et extraits des manuscrits de la bibliothèque nationale et autres bibliothèques*, XXII (1874), 177–428. These, together with some items indubitably later, include much that may be old. E.g., lines ascribed to the Fâṭimid Muʿizz. Preserved among Syrian Nizârîs; largely moral exhortation. Ivanow calls these and the following indiscriminately modern, giving no reason: 'Ismailitica,' *Memoirs of the Asiatic Society of Bengal*, XII (1922), 25 and 64.

3. The Salisbury Fragments. Trans. E. E. Salisbury, 'Translation of Two Unpublished Arabic Documents Relating to the Doctrines of the Ismâʿîlîs and other Bâṭinian Sects,' *Journal of the American Oriental Society*, II (1851), 257–324; and 'Translation of an Unpublished Arabic Risâleh by Khâlid ibn Zeid el-Juʿfy,' *JAOS*, III (1852: 1), 165–193. These are also undated, from Syria. Massignon seems to think one item, ascribed to a Juʿfî, goes back to Abû Shâkir Maymûn, father of the Ibn Maymûn al-Qaddâḥ of legend (*Esquisse d'une bibliographie qarmate*). Systematic expositions of doctrine.

4. The *ʿIrfân* fragments, in the Shîʿite magazine *ʿIrfân*, Bayrût. Fragments from the Syrian Nizârîs (cited by Bernard Lewis in a letter 16 II 1951).

5. Nâṣir-i Khusraw Corpus. References to these are in the *Encyclopedia of Islâm* article. Add: *Shish Faṣl*, ed. W. Ivanow, Bombay and Cairo, 1949; *Kitâb Gushâ'ish wa-Rahâ'ish*, ed. Saʿîd Nafîsî, Leiden, 1950; *Khân-i Ikhwân*, ed. Yaḥyâ al-Khachab, Cairo, 1940. Cf. also Ivanow's *Guide to Ismaili Literature*, p. 89 ff. These writings represent a particular viewpoint within the regular Fâṭimid doctrine, but in Persian (or more than one: cf. S. Pines, footnotes in 'Nathanael ben al-Fayyûmî et la Théologie ismaélienne,' *Revue de l'histoire des juives en Egypte*, I [1947], 5–22). Preserved and imitated in the upper Oxus area, except for such works as circulated among the public at large.

II. Nizârî texts of the Alumût period.

6. Ḥasan-i Ṣabbâḥ, d. 1124: part of the 'Fuṣûl Arbaʿa', trans. in Shahrastânî and paraphrased in Rashîd ad-Dîn and Juwaynî; also, in Rashîd ad-Dîn and Juwaynî, are his memoirs, to his arrival at the city of the imâm. These passages, though reported by hostile authors, appear genuine; Ivanow offers only suppositions against them. The doctrine as reported by Shahrastânî puts admirably the position which Ghazzâlî labors so recurrently to overthrow; the life, while of an all-Ismâʿîlî pattern, is distinctive and illuminating.

Massignon has suggested that the portion of Shahrastânî on the Ṣâbi'a is copied from Ḥasan-i Ṣabbâḥ's 'Fuṣûl Arbaʿa' (article on Ḳarmaṭians in *EI;* 'Esquisse d'une bibliographie qarmaṭe,' Browne Volume, p. 332; *Lexique technique de la mystique musulmane*, p. 58; *al-Ḥallâj*, p. 607–8). His reference, apparently to what P. Kraus published later, Fakhr ad-Dîn Râzî's *al-mas'alat al-ʿâshira*, in *Bulletin de l'institut d'Egypte*, XIX, p. 187ff, and the next year in *Islamic Culture*, 1938, p. 130 ff., is not adequate. In a letter from him of the 3d December, 1949, he regretted not being able to clarify the matter, indicating that Kraus could have done so had he been alive. In the cited article, Kraus seems to do no more than suggest that the item Shahrastânî himself called the "Fuṣûl Arbaʿa" – not the long discussion of the Ṣâbiʾa – is indeed Ḥasan's. But the point raised is interesting. From what we know of Ḥasan-i Ṣabbâḥ, it seems reasonable that he might have written the dialogue between the Ḥunafâʾ and the Ṣâbiʾa in Shahrastânî. It is unusually unlike the rest of Shahrastânî's relatively dry listing of tenets – seeming like the reflection of an eager but restrained personality whose doctrine would not be inconsistent with the Ismâʿîlî. It is striking that a very similar treatment of the idolaters – not only in the same spirit, but to some degree in the same dialog form – is to be found in *Rawḍat at-Taslîm*, Taṣawwur XXVII; and that this follows immediately upon (at the end of Taṣawwur XXVI) a description of Ḥasan-i Ṣabbâḥ and the reasoning of the "Fuṣûl Arbaʿa", with no logical break. I would be inclined to guess that here Massignon has hit by his famous intuition upon a fact, and that this interesting passage in Shahrastânî is indeed lifted from Ḥasan-i Ṣabbâḥ, whom Shahrastânî admits having read; but without more exact evidence the matter must be allowed to rest.

7. Rashîd ad-Dîn and Juwaynî excerpts. The "Sargudhasht-i Sayyid-nâ" and other records of Alamût life are quoted evidently fairly faithfully. The first seems to be a continuation of the memoirs of Ḥasan-i Ṣabbâḥ, is largely legendary, and breathes magnificently of the imaginative, as against the more strictly doctrinal, life of Alamût. The other excerpts are simply chronicles. All are clearly from the Alamût period.

8. Ḥasan II, d. 1166. In the *Haft Bâb-i Bâbâ Sayyid-nâ*, and in Abû Isḥâq, as well as in Rashîd ad-Dîn, are quoted declarations on the Qiyâma. His *fuṣûl* are likewise quoted in the later Nizârî texts – as are items from Ḥasan-i Ṣabbâḥ also.

9. Raʾîs Ḥasan, 12th Century. Some verses, in W. Ivanow, 'Ismailitica,' *Memoirs of the Asiatic Society of Bengal*, VIII (1922), 13–24 passim; and 'An Ismaili Ode in Praise of Fidawis,' *JBBRAS*, new series XIV (1938), 63–72; some are still in mss. These are inspirational rather than expository, and hence should throw unplanned side-lights on Nizârî thinking; but what we have are limited.

10. *Haft Bâb-i Bâbâ Sayyid-nâ*, ca. 1200. ed. W. Ivanow, *Two Early Ismaili Treatises*, Bombay, 1933, p. 4–42. An anonymous, unlearned exposition of the Qiyâma doctrine, evidently by an eye-witness of the event, and before the doctrine was modified after Ḥasan III (d. 1220). Translated in Appendix I.

11. Naṣîr ad-Dîn Ṭûsî, d. 1276: *Maṭlûb al-Muʾminîn*, ed. W. Ivanow, *Two Early Ismaili Treatises*, p. 43–55. A very clear, simple treatise on post-Qiyâma doctrine, apparently as modified after Ḥasan III. Ascribed to a man who claimed to have been held unwilling prisoner among the Nizârîs, who urged their surrender to the Mongols, and who thereupon appeared as a prominent *Twelver* Shîʿite minister of the Mongol regime.

12. Naṣîr ad-Dîn Ṭûsî, *Rawḍat at-Taslîm*, or, *Taṣawwurât*, ed. and trans.

W. Ivanow, Ismaili Society Series A Nr. 4, Leiden, 1950. Attributed (probably correctly) to the same as nr. 11. A detailed exposition of Nizârî doctrine, after the Qiyâma, again apparently as modified after Ḥasan III.

Cf. the Ṭûsî corpus generally (see the *Encyclopedia of Islam* and Brockelmann's *GAL*); most of these items are rather Twelver if anything, not Nizârî; but the *Akhlâq-i Nâṣirî* was originally dedicated to a Nizârî chief in whose protection Ṭûsî was living. The Nizârî work, *Mir'ât al-Muḥaqqiqîn* (lith. Munîr b. M. Qâsim Badakhshânî, in *Khayr-Khwâh*, Bombay, ca. 1333 H.) is ascribed to Ṭûsî, but is probably much later. Cf. W. Ivanow, *Guide to Ismaili Literature* (London, 1933).

13. Ḥasan III: fragments published by Tâmir ʿÂrif, 'Sinân Râshid ad-Dîn aw Shaykh al-Jabal,' *Al-Adîb*, XXIII (1953), May, p. 45.

III. Published Persian and Arabic post-Alamût texts from before the nineteenth century.

14. Nizârî Quhistânî, d. ca. 1320. According to Ivanow: ed. and trans. (Russian), E. Bertels, 'Dastûr Nâma,' in *Vostochniy Sbornik*, Leningrad, 1926. Verses whose Ismâʿîlî doctrine is well concealed, of the first generation after the fall; cf. the *Guide*, nr. cxxv, for other verses unpublished.

15. Abû Firâs: anecdotes of Sinân, written 1324. Ed. and trans. S. Guyard, 'Un grand maître des Assassins,' *JA*, ser. 7, IX (1877), 324. A Syrian Ismâʿîlî lovingly collected these anedcotes from the oral tradition of the community more than a century after Sinân's death; touches on some developments of the author's own time. (It seems the manuscript was at one time lost after its publication.)

16. Abû Isḥâq, ca. 1500: *Haft Bâb*. Ed. and trans. W. Ivanow, *Kalâm-i Pîr*, Bombay, 1935. An exposition of the Qiyâma doctrine two centuries after the fall of Alamût; also, reworked later to include much Twelver Shîʿa and other material, as the *Kalâm-i Pîr* ascribed to Nâṣir-i Khusraw.

17. Khâkî Khurâsânî, ca. 1600: *Dîwân*. Ed. W. Ivanow, Bombay, 1933. Verses in the Ṣûfî manner.

18. *Faṣl dar Bayân-i Shinâkht-i Imâm*, ed., trans. W. Ivanow, *On the Recognition of the Imâm*, Bombay, 1947. An exposition of doctrine, late, with emphasis on the Ḥujja; quotes Ra'îs Ḥasan, etc. (Also in *MASB*, VIII, 1922.)

19. *Qaṣîda Dhurriyya*, ed. and trans. W. Ivanow, 'Ismailitica,' *MASB*, VIII, (1922), 73 – in part. Ed. Semenow, 1928, according to Ivanow's *Guide*. Verses on the personages in the line of ʿAlî.

20. *Ḥaqq Mawlâ-nâ ʿAlî*, ed. and trans. W. Ivanow, 'Ismailitica,' *MASB*, VIII (1922), 58. List of the imâms and ḥujjas.

Cf. Ivanow's *Guide to Ismaili Literature* for nineteenth and twentieth century Persian Nizârî texts published. Ivanow himself apparently has access to further texts which he plans to publish; meanwhile he reserves them to himself. Tâmir ʿÂrif is currently publishing Syrian materials.

INDEX*

Aaron, 161, 170, 172, 200, 202, 230
al-Aʿazz ad-Dahistânî, 95n
Abâqâ, 275
ʿAbbâs b. ʿAbd al-Muṭṭalib, 80
ʿAbbâs, gov. of Rayy, 145f
ʿAbbâsî, honorary title, 117
ʿAbbâsid, 6, 8f, 11, 37, 117, 223n, 331
ʿAbd Allâh, 170
ʿAbd Allâh al-Murtaḍâ, *Falak ad-Dawwâr*, 321n
ʿAbd Allâh b. ʿAbbâs, 295
ʿAbd Allâh-i Saba', 294f, 298
ʿAbd Allâh Muḥyî d-Dîn b. ʿAbd aẓ-Ẓâhir, 245n
ʿAbd al-Malik Fashandî, 102n
ʿAbd al-Malik b. ʿAṭṭâsh, 45f; his character, 51f; 64, 143
ʿAbd ar-Razzâq b. Bahrâm, 43n
Abel, 247
Abhar, 74, 76, 221
Abraham, 4, 20n; relation to Ishmael, 161; 170f, 200, 202, 205n, 230, 247, 287, 291
Abû ʿAlî Ardistânî, 75, 118
Abû ʿAlî Sîmjûr, 44
Abû Bakr, in Sunnî thought, 53; as ḥakîm-i sharîʿa, 236f; 294
Abû Dharr, 201f, 206
Abû Firâs, on assassination, 113; 185f; on Sinân's relation to Saladin, 188f; 191; quotations from, 193-5; on Sinân's wonders, 196; 199, 202f, 334(b)
Abû Ḥamza, 76
Abû Ḥarb, 93
Abû Ḥasan, qâḍî, 77n
Abû Hâshim, Zaydî imâm, 103
Abû Isḥâq, *Haft Bâb-i* 149, 152n, 169, 227n, 334(b)
Abû Jaʿfar, Bâwandid, 100n
Abû Jaʿfar, Kiyâ, 119
Abû l-Faraj, Ibn al-ʿIbrî, *Chronography*, 106n(b)
Abû l-Fatḥ, receives Qadamûs, 106
Abû l-Fatḥ, nephew of Ḥasan-i Ṣabbâḥ, 51n
Abû l-Fatḥ Bisṭâmî, 321
Abû l-Fatḥ Sarmînî, 92, 106n
Abû l-Khaṭṭâb, 9n, 331
Abû l-Maʿâlî, heresiographer, 64f
Abû l-Maḥâsin Rûyânî, 123
Abû l-Qâsim, 49
Abû Manṣûr, name of Nizâr, 46
Abû Muḥammad, dâʿî, 93, 105n, 118, 186
Abû Muḥammad al-ʿIrâqî, *Firaq*, 52n(b), 66; condemns Ismâʿîlîs, 131
Abû Muslim, gov. of Rayy, 48
Abû Najm Sarrâj, 45
Abû Saʿd al-Harawî, 103n
Abû Shâkir Maymûn, 332
Abû Shâma, *Rawḍatayn*, 82n(b)
Abû Ṭâhir, 91f, 94, 106
Acre, 220, 248
Adam, 161n; creation of, 164; 170; Sinân knows of many, 195; 200, 202; fall of, 233; 284, 286, 291, 301, 313f, 322
Adam of Little Armenia, 220
ad-Dîn, titles in, 42, 237
Âdharbâyjân, 45f, 71, 114; Ḥasan III in, 221; 240, 251; post-Alamût imâms in, 275f

* The index includes proper names and technical terms, except common names like Islâm, Ismâʿîlî, Syria, Arabic; all authors cited (only once, unless discussed — **b** means bibliographical data); and some other items of interest. **f** — following page; **n** — only in notes.

Ṣabbâḥ on Ṣâbi'a, 332f
Shahriyârkûh, 48
shakhṣ-i waḥdat, 306
shakl, 173; ẓuhûr-i shaklî, 236n
Shamâlî, 192
Shams ad-Dîn, of Qazwîn, 259
Shams ad-Dîn, of Quhistân, 245f
Shams ad-Dîn Gîlakî, 267
Shams ad-Dîn Ḥasan-i Ikhtiyâr, 244
Shams al-Mulûk, 90
Shams-i Tabrîz, 276
Sharaf ad-Dîn Munshî, 101n
Sharaf al-Mulk, 252f, 255
sharî'a, basis of Sunnî community, 6f; guaranteed by Shî'ite imâm, 8; 10, 18; Sunnî, substitute for Caliphate, 39–41; Ismâ'îlî, maintained by Nizârîs, 60; question of sufficiency for legal acceptance, 96; 118; abolished, 150f; end of, as central to Qiyâma, 155f; Ḥasan II's attitude to, 158; 159, 172f, 177f, 198n, 203, 205n, 211; restored by Ḥasan III, 217f; 219n; under Muḥammad III, 226; 228f, 231, 233; Sunnî, enters Ismâ'îlî doctrine, 236f; 246n, 271, 282n, 286–8, 292, 300–2, 305, 310n, 312f, 316
sharîf of Mecca, 222n
shaykh, Ṣûfî, 21, 41, 81, 166; of Qazwîn, friend of Khwârazmshâh, 212f; Ismâ'îlî title in Syria, 248n; of Qazwîn, friend of Muḥammad III, 257
Shaykh 'Abd ar-Rashîd of Aligarh, 255n
Shayzar, 94, 107, 187
Shem, 161n, 170, 230
Shî'a, origin and dramatic piety, 7–9; Ismâ'îlî form, 9–12; disapproves of Ṣûfism, 21; politically dominant, 37; on succession to Mohammed, 52–3; refuted by Ḥasan-i Ṣabbâḥ, 54; accused of Ismâ'îlism, 64; inter-Shî'ite mobility, 71; of Aleppo, 71n; in Daylamân, 74; early, and assassination, 82; majority in Aleppo, 91; devotion in Qiyâma, contrasted to Ṣûfî, 165; early heroes of, 201n; motifs in Syrian Qiyâma, 205f; question of under Ḥasan III, 218; combined with Ṣûfism, in Ṭûsî, 243; in later Shî'a, 277; positions, in *Haft Bâb*, 289; strands, in *Haft Bâb*, 291, 297f; refuted by Ḥasan-i Ṣabbâḥ, 326; and passim
Shihâb ad-Dîn, of Quhistân, 244, 246
Shihâb ad-Dîn Ghûrî, 213, 253f
Shihâb ad-Dîn Suhrawardî, 223n
Shîrânshâh, b. Muḥammad III, 267
Shîrgîr, 97-99, 101, 112
shirk, 315f
Shughnân, 178
Sibṭ ibn al-Jawzî, 97n
Sicily, 12
Ṣiffîn, 299
Sijistânî, *Kashf*, 83(b), 191n
Sîmjûrid, 44, 74
Simon-Peter, *see* Peter
Sinai, 200n, 287
Sinân, 30, 71n, 82n, 93, 107; his life, 185f; political policy, 187–9; and defense, 190f; and Nuṣayrîs, 191; his personality, 193–5; and telepathy, 196f; tie to Alamût, 199; in Fragment Nr. One, 200–2; as divinely-hedged hero, 203; move toward Christianity, 204; and the Ṣufât, 205; and popular Shî'ism, 206; death and after, 207; 208-12, 237n, 248f, 264, 272; shrine to, 274f; 334
Sinânî sect, 198
Sind, 12, 38n, 69, 198
Sinjâr, 247
Sîra Ḥâkim, 134
Sirâj ad-Dîn al-Muẓaffar, 246f
Sîrat Mu'ayyad fî-d-Dîn, 69n(b)
Sîstân, 74f, 77, 80, 102, 211f, 245f
Siyâsat Nâma, 64(b)
Sogdian, 2
Spain, 24, 181
Spengler, 323
Spirituals, Franciscan, 177
Stark, F., *Valleys*, 27n(b), 258
Stephen, Armenian, 187n
Stern, S. M., *Epistle of Âmir*, 47n(b); *Succession to Âmir*, 109n(b)
Stoic, 305
Stranglers (Khunnâq), 82, 126n
Strauss, L., *Persecution*, 15n(b)
strong (qawî), 233f
Strothmann, *Nâṣir*, 74n(b); *Ismailitische Schriften*, 109n(b); *Gnosistexte*, 288n(b)
Ṣufât, 139, 205
Ṣûfism, Ṣûfî mysticism, as personal piety, 7; 19; disapproved by Shî'a, 21; 24, 29f; in Ivanow's usage, 31f; 38f; enters Sunnî synthesis, 40f; 70n; assassins dressed as Ṣûfîs, 75, 90; 121, 126; in Ghazzâlî's thought, 129, 131; studied by Ḥasan II, 147, 153; 155f; contrasted with Qiyâma, 165–8; 171, 174; influence in Qiyâma,